Teaching English for International Business

R.J. Goddard

Visit us online at www.authorsonline.co.uk

An Authors OnLine Book

Copyright © R.J.Goddard 2007

Cover design by Robert and Tina Goddard and James Fitt ©

All rights reserved. No part of this publication may be reproduced, stored in a retrieval system, or transmitted in any form or by any means, electronic, mechanical, photocopy, recording or otherwise, without prior written permission of the copyright owner. Nor can it be circulated in any form of binding or cover other than that in which it is published and without similar condition including this condition being imposed on a subsequent purchaser.

ISBN 978-0-755202-92-8

Authors OnLine Ltd
19 The Cinques
Gamlingay, Sandy
Bedfordshire SG19 3NU
England

This book is also available in e-book format, details of which are available at
www.authorsonline.co.uk

Note on the Author

Robert Goddard has considerable experience in teaching English for International Business in both the public and private sector. He lived and worked for thirteen years in Italy, two years in Portugal, one year in Jordan and three years in Germany. He has also travelled widely. In the UK he has worked in various educational institutions in Manchester and most recently was Senior Lecturer specialising in Business English at the University of Portsmouth. He is the author of many published journalistic articles, and twenty of his short stories have been published and/or read on BBC Radio. He has also written two novels. These are "The Schönbuch Forest" and "The Poor Singer of an Empty Day" and both are currently available on amazon.co.uk

Acknowledgements

My thanks go to all those people to whom I have taught EIB at home and abroad. I would also like to thank Chris Barwood from the University of Central Lancashire. He started it all by inviting me to write some of this material for his online training course in EIB. My thanks are also due to the University of Portsmouth. Some of the material for this book was developed while I was lecturing in the School of Languages between 2003 and 2007.

Contents

Introduction...1

Unit 1
The Environment and Scope of EIB

Chapter 1: EFL, ESP and EIB - 1............................7
Classification of TESOL, EFL, ESP and EIB. Characteristics of ESP. Corpora. Teaching ESP. Factors that influence ESP teaching methodology. The roles of the ESP teacher, i.e.: ESP teacher as teacher, course designer and materials provider, researcher and evaluator.

Chapter 2: EFL, ESP and EIB - 2..........................21
Characteristics of EIB. EGBP and ESBP. English as a World Language. Company culture. National culture. Professional

characteristics of the EIB teacher. What business people expect of the EIB teacher. What EIB teachers need to know.

Chapter 3: The EIB Environment..................................30
EIB and the global business environment. Appropriate methodology in the global world. Collectionist or integrationist academic cultures. Interpersonal skills for the EIB teacher in the corporate world. Marketing yourself as the EIB professional. EIB in the academic world.

Chapter 4: The Intercultural Scope - 1..........................45
Definitions of culture. Values, attitudes and beliefs. Cultural relativism. Why do business people need to be sensitive to the values of other cultures? Why do EIB teachers need to develop intercultural sensitivity? UK educational values and Chinese educational values. Single dimension models of national culture. High- and low-context cultures. Monochronic and polychronic time. Fukuyama's analysis of trust. Culture and power relationships.

Chapter 5: The Intercultural Scope - 2..........................60
Kluckhohn and Strodtbeck's six basic orientations. Hofstede's dimensions of culture. Trompenaars' analysis of culture. Lessem and Neubauer's analysis of culture. Southeast Asian management.

Chapter 6: Culture and the Classroom - 1.....................72
EIB teachers as cross-cultural performers. Hofstede's cultural dimensions and their possible relationship with educational values. Adapting material for other cultures.

Chapter 7: Culture and the Classroom - 2.....................80
Designing intercultural training programmes – general considerations. The qualities the trainer needs. Approaches to

culture training. Frameworks for culture training. The acquisition of intercultural communication skills. Classroom icebreakers. Presenting models of national culture. Developing skills. Role-play and critical incidents.

Chapter 8: Management of Programmes......................103
The nature and peculiarities of the EIB product. Goods and services. Differences and similarities between educational management and business management. Differences and similarities between business organisations and educational organisations. Theories of organisations.

Chapter 9: Marketing the EIB Product....................................118
What is marketing? What is marketing in the ELT/EIB industry? Internal marketing. Managing tangible evidence. Customisation of service. The importance of learning style and cultural background.

Chapter 10: Language, Communication and Culture.........125
What is the relationship between culture and communication? Sociolinguistic competence, strategic competence and illocutionary competence. Substantive and relational components of communication. Factors which influence behaviour in intercultural communication. High- and low-context cultures. Power, certainty and communication style.

Bibliography..141

Unit 2
Needs, Materials and Course Design

Chapter 1: Course Design – 1..................................157
Terminology and key concepts. The factors to consider when designing a course. The elements of course design – needs analysis, syllabus design, learning theory and methodology. What is a syllabus? Language descriptions. Theories of learning.

Chapter 2: Course Design – 2: Needs Analysis..............169
What is a needs analysis? Target situation analysis, learning situation analysis and present situation analysis. Getting information about target needs. Getting information about the present situation and learning needs. Where does the information come from?

Chapter 3: Course Design – 3: Putting it all together...........178
Approaches to course design – the language-centred approach, the skills-centred approach, the learning-centred approach. Selection of material. Course evaluation – how do we evaluate a course? Where do we get information for evaluation purposes?

Chapter 4: Materials for EIB..................................189
What are materials? Advantages and disadvantages of coursebooks. Carrier content and real content. Why use materials? Should EIB teachers always prepare materials from scratch? Available materials – evaluation and selection. Adapting available material. Adding, deleting, modifying and simplifying material. Supplementing materials – teacher-generated material and learner-generated material.

Bibliography..216

Unit 3
Methodology and Classroom Practice

Chapter 1: What is Appropriate Methodology?..............221
Examination of terms – approaches, methods, procedures, techniques and models. Cultural implications of methods and approaches. Challenges facing newly certificated teachers. Western methodologies and non-Western learners.

Chapter 2: Method, Postmethod or Pragmatism?...........238
Harmer and pragmatic eclecticism. Prabhu's theory of plausibility. Teacher development – action research. Kumaravadivelu's theory of postmethod pedagogy – particularity, practicality and possibility. Implications of postmethod pedagogy for teachers and learners. Native and non-native teachers (NESTS and non-NESTS) and the strengths and weaknesses of each.

Chapter 3: Teaching by Principles............................248
Is there a "best" teaching method? Douglas Brown's 12-principle approach to language teaching – automacity, meaningful learning, anticipation of reward, intrinsic motivation, strategic investment, language ego, self-confidence, taking risks, the connection between language and culture, the influence of the native language, interlanguage and communicative competence.

Chapter 4: Balancing Techniques and Teacher Roles.......258
Fluency versus accuracy. From controlled practice to free practice activities. Student groupings. Basic procedure for setting up pairwork and groupwork. The roles teachers play – TTT and STT.

Chapter 5: Lesson Planning..........269
Factors to consider before planning. Lesson aims. The plan – main steps. Variety, pace and timing. Planning a sequence of lessons – factors to consider. Lesson planning – practice.

Chapter 6: Using Simulations and Case Studies..........276
Defining terms – case study, role-play, simulation and game. Advantages and disadvantages. What language should learners produce in these activities? Setting up and running the exercise. The roles of the teacher. Examples and sources.

Chapter 7: Business Communication Skills..........301
Distinctions between EIB and general ELT. Introduction to business communication skills. Language skills and communication skills. What skills should the teacher focus on? The value of teaching content. Identifying real language. Specific communication skills, i.e. presentation skills, meeting skills and negotiation skills.

Chapter 8: Teaching One-to-One..........314
Advantages and disadvantages of teaching one-to-one for both teachers and learners. Specific techniques. Dealing with relationships. The variety of reasons learners may have for doing a one-to-one programme. Dealing with these varieties.

Chapter 9: Learning and Learning Styles..........324
Learning theories – behavioural theory, the cognitive theory, experiential, discovery and co-operative learning. Application of the theory to the EIB classroom. Variable characteristics of learners. Learner autonomy and learner independence. Self-access activities for the individual learner. Difference between learning strategies and learning styles. What is learning style and what different styles are there?

Chapter 10: Evaluation and Assessment..................342
Terminology and key concepts. Purpose of tests. Desirable characteristics of tests. Classroom assessment and classroom tests. Public examinations – the UCLES Business English Certificate (BEC).

Bibliography..361

Unit 4
Language, Communication and Culture

Chapter 1: Language Analysis - Introduction..............375
Discourse, genre, and conversational analysis – clarification of terms.

Chapter 2: Language Analysis - Discourse.................380
The findings of discourse analysis and the teacher of EIB. Levels of discoursal features and communication. Cohesion and coherence. Conversational principles. Coherence and knowledge structures.

Chapter 3: Language Analysis - Conversation.............392
What is conversation? Turn-taking. Pausing and length of pause. Basic format of face-to-face conversation. Communication filter. Ineffective speaking and ineffective listening. The differences between face-to-face conversation and telephone conversation, and between interviews and discussions. Questioning techniques.

Chapter 4: Language Analysis - Genre..........................404

Characteristics of genre. Genre analysis and the work of Swales. Business English genre and the work of Bhatia. The importance of communicative purpose. Cross-cultural factors in genre analysis. Discourse communities.

Chapter 5: Culture and Business Communication - 1..........413

Working in groups – formal and informal groups. Characteristics of informal groups. What is a meeting? What makes an effective meeting? Chairing style. The role of participants. The problem-solving process. Meetings in conflict. Culture and the problem-solving process. Culture, chairing and participating. Success in multicultural meetings. How can training help multicultural meetings be more effective?

Chapter 6: Culture and Business Communication - 2........433

Definitions of negotiation. Characteristics of negotiations. The stages of a negotiation. The influence of culture on the stages of a negotiation. The influence of company culture and individual personality on the negotiation process.

Chapter 7: Culture and Business Communication - 3..........449

Presentation skills. The presenter – who do you choose to present in other cultures? Content – what do you include in your presentation so that it is relevant for the audience and their values? Presentation style – techniques for making the presentation formal or informal.

Chapter 8: Non-verbal Communication (NVC)............457

The elements of non-verbal communication. Three variables that impact on NVC – gender, culture and personal characteristics. Kinesics, oculesics and vocalics. Space and communication – proxemics. Time orientation and communication.

Chapter 9: Culture and Relationships........................474
Terms and concepts. Culture and relationships. High- and low-context cultures. Relationships and communication style. Negotiations and relationships. Reasons for relationship breakdown. Dealing constructively with relationship breakdown and conflict.

Chapter 10: Communication in a Virtual World..........491
What is virtual communication? Communication in virtual teams. Virtual teams and culture. Virtual team development and relationships.

Bibliography...500

Introduction

It may be that you are currently standing in a bookshop, flicking through the pages of this book and wondering whether it could be useful for you. Most books are written with a typical reader in mind, and this book is no exception. Maybe you will recognise yourself in the description of the reader I had in mind when I started this book.

You are a teacher or lecturer wanting to develop your career in ELT by specialising in the teaching of English for International Business. Perhaps you are considering taking a course in Business English and wondering what you might be letting yourself in for. It may be that you are interested in doing an MA and you want to do your dissertation in the area of Business English. Of course the answer might simply be that your Director of Studies has landed you with a group of business people and you don't quite know what to expect or what to do.

I would suggest that to get the most from this book you should also:

➢ have a first degree or equivalent
➢ be a native speaker or have IELTS 6.5 if you are not a native speaker
➢ have an initial qualification in TEFL, e.g. Trinity Cert
➢ have at least 6 months full-time teaching experience
➢ have access to a library
➢ have access to a computer with internet access.

If you do take the plunge, fork out the money to buy this book and read it, you should get a number of benefits. Generally, you will be able to take a fuller and more active part in the global environment of teaching EIB. In particular, you will:

- be aware of the characteristics and range of teaching/training in English for International Business, and develop a critical and practical awareness of the main issues influencing global business
- be able to refer to and benefit from a range of approaches to teaching and learning in English for International Business in order to develop your practical expertise as a professional in the world of EIB
- develop a critical awareness of the various models of cultural differences and how these differences may influence both global business and your own teaching style
- better understand key areas of language analysis. This means: discourse, genre, and conversation analysis. You should be able to apply this understanding to the teaching of English for International Business.

The book is divided into four units.

1. **The Environment and Scope of EIB**. This unit focuses on the following.

- The relationship between English as a Foreign Language (EFL), English for Specific Purposes (ESP), and English for International Business (EIB).
- The characteristics of EIB.
- Teaching EIB in its various environments.
- The nature of the EIB teacher.
- The intercultural environment – including the teaching environment.
- Management and marketing of courses.

2. **Needs, Materials and Course Design**. This unit focuses on the following.

- Needs analysis and EIB.
- Syllabus design.
- Materials - selection criteria.
- Materials and EIB.
- Adapting published materials.

3. **Methodology and Classroom Practice**. This unit focuses on the following.

- Method and post-method pedagogy and EIB.
- Principled eclecticism and appropriate methodology.
- Lesson planning – theory and practice.
- Business communication skills.
- Balancing techniques, and the role of the teacher.
- Using simulations and case studies.
- Group teaching and teaching one-to-one.
- Approaches to evaluation and assessment.

4. **Language, Communication and Culture**. This unit focuses on the following.

- Discourse analysis and EIB.
- Genre and EIB.
- Conversation analysis and EIB.
- Culture and relationships.
- Intercultural meetings.
- Intercultural negotiations.
- Intercultural presentations.
- Non-verbal communication.
- Virtual communication.

In order to get the most out of the chapters in the book I suggest this procedure.

- Read and think about the issues contained in the text. How could you incorporate the ideas into your own classroom practice?
- Answer the questions to which sample answers are provided at the end of each chapter. These questions are designed to help you see whether or not you are on the right track.
- Think about the issues in the dotted boxes (pause for thought). Which of these issues do you want to follow up? There is an extensive bibliography for you to refer to at the end of each unit.

Finally, although we touch on virtual communication, this book is primarily concerned with classroom teaching. For those of you who are interested in the use of technology in the classroom, you might look at Sharma and Barrett (2007).

If you are still unsure about anything, or if you wish to discuss any of the issues in the book with me, or you would like to comment on the book, I would be delighted to hear from you. Please feel free to use my email: r.j.goddard@ukonline.co.uk

Southsea. Spring 2007

UNIT 1
The Environment and Scope of EIB

Unit 1: The Environment and Scope of EIB

CHAPTER 1

EFL, ESP and EIB - 1

1.1: Introduction
1.2: Objectives
1.3: Classification of TESOL, EFL, ESP and EIB
1.4: Characteristics of ESP
1.5: Teaching ESP
1.6: Answers to Questions.

1.1: Introduction

The first two chapters of this unit give you an overview of EFL (English as a Foreign Language), ESP (English for Specific Purposes) and EIB (English for International Business) and examine the relationship between them. We also consider whether or not teaching EIB is different from teaching ESP or General EFL. Both chapters also attempt to stimulate your interest in some of the more recent developments in EIB, notably: genre analysis, communication skills training and intercultural communication skills training.

In many ways the chapters are introductory, and much of their content will be developed in other chapters and units. We recommend that you follow up those areas in which you are interested by referring to the reading provided in the bibliography at the end of the unit.

Unit 1: The Environment and Scope of EIB

1.2: Objectives

The main aims of this chapter are to:

- consider the differences between EFL and ESP
- establish criteria that can distinguish EFL from ESP
- identify the defining characteristics of ESP.

Pre-reading task

Before you begin, consider the questions in the shaded box below. These are designed to stimulate your thinking and to focus your mind on the main points in the chapter.

> 1. *Is there such thing as "General EFL" teaching, or are all EFL courses specific in that they do focus on the specific needs of the learners?*
> 2. *Is ESP simply a matter of teaching specialised varieties of English? For example, do teachers teach science words and grammar to scientists and hotel words and grammar to hotel staff?*

1.3: Classification of TESOL, EFL, ESP and EIB

Pause for thought

> *You have probably discovered already that the world of EFL teaching is full of acronyms. Before you read further, write down as many of these acronyms as you can think of. How would you categorise them?*

The acronym TESOL stands for Teaching English to Speakers of Other Languages. It is a blanket term and refers to situations where English is taught both as a second language and as a foreign language. The acronym EFL (English as a Foreign Language) is adopted in places where English is not generally used as the language of communication or instruction. Such places would include Italy, Argentina and Russia.

In the 1970s, the development of communicative methodology

Unit 1: The Environment and Scope of EIB

focused attention on English as a tool for communication rather than on English as a system to be studied. Course content was chosen to match the communicative needs of the learner. This shift resulted in the emergence of needs-based courses, which were designed to meet the specific requirements of course participants. Such courses are known as ESP (English for Specific Purposes) courses. Within ESP, many other abbreviations are often used. Although these abbreviations may seem confusing, they will help you classify ESP and to understand how it relates to the term EFL.

Traditionally, ESP has been divided into EAP (English for Academic Purposes) and EOP (English for Occupational Purposes). Both EAP and EOP can be further divided according to discipline or professional area.

EAP may include: EST (English for Academic Science and Technology), EMP (English for Academic Medical Purposes), ELP (English for Academic Legal Purposes) and English for Management, Finance and Economics (no acronym) which is often taught to non-native speakers on, for example, MBA (Master of Business Administration) courses. A distinction can be made between common core English for General Academic Purposes (EGAP) and English for Specific Academic Purposes (ESAP). EGAP examines the skills and language associated with the study of all academic disciplines, for example: listening to lectures and reading textbooks. ESAP integrates the skills of EGAP with the features that distinguish one discipline from another.

EOP refers to courses that are not for academic purposes. EOP includes: English for professional purposes in administration, law, medicine, business, and vocational courses. A distinction is therefore made between English for Academic Medical, Legal or Scientific Purposes, and English for practising doctors, lawyers and scientists. EOP is therefore divided into English for Professional Purposes and English for Vocational Purposes. English for Professional Purposes can include: EMP (English for Medical Purposes) and EBP (English for Business Purposes). English for Vocational Purposes can be divided into Pre-vocational and Vocational English. Pre-vocational English is concerned with, for example, finding a job and interview skills. Vocational English is concerned with the language of specific trades or occupations. A distinction should also be made between English for General Business Purposes (EGBP) and English for Specific Business Purposes (ESBP). We suggest that EIB is a category within EOP and therefore one of a range of courses that can be taught under the umbrella term ESP.

So what exactly are the differences between General EFL and ESP? It could be argued that all learners of English have their own specific purposes and that, as a consequence, all English courses are ESP courses. For example, if English is on the school curriculum, the learners' purpose may be to pass exams. Other people may want to study English because they think it will help them in their professional lives. Thus, their specific purpose may be to get a better job.

Furthermore, EFL teachers will always restrict the content of their programmes. For beginners, teachers restrict the language to be taught. Teachers may also wish to restrict the choice of topics and activities based on the kind of students they are going to teach. For science students doing postgraduate work, teachers may also want to focus almost exclusively on reading. On General English courses, restrictions on the four skills are unlikely to be imposed. However, General EFL programmes tend to begin with lists, for example: a list of functions, a list of themes and topics, a list of vocabulary and a list of tasks and activities.

It is here that we can see the difference between EFL and ESP. If General EFL programmes begin with the language, ESP courses start with the learner and the situation. The key defining feature of ESP is that its teaching and its materials spring from the outcome of a needs analysis. The first questions to ask when preparing materials for a course in ESP are almost always: *What do the learners want to do with English? Which skills do they need? Which genres do they need to look at?* Specific needs can be identified by examining the learning or occupational situation in which English is used, and the written and spoken texts associated with those situations.

A second key feature of ESP is, therefore, concerned with looking at how spoken and written texts work, and how they are used within a particular community. If needs analysis and specific situational texts are two key features of ESP, they are not the only defining characteristics. It is to these characteristics that we now turn.

1.4: Characteristics of ESP

Hutchinson and Waters (1987) define ESP as an approach. They suggest that ESP does not concern a particular language, teaching

Unit 1: The Environment and Scope of EIB

methodology or material. The key to understanding ESP, in their view, is to find out exactly why a person needs to learn a foreign language. Needs can vary from study purposes to work purposes. These purposes may be negotiating contracts or writing monthly reports for head office. However, it is the definition of needs that is the starting point for decisions which determine the language to be taught.

Strevens (1988) makes a distinction between absolute characteristics and variable characteristics of ESP. The absolute characteristics are that ESP courses are:

- designed to meet the specific needs of the learner
- related in content to particular disciplines or occupations
- centred on language specific to those disciplines or occupations
- in contrast to General English.

The variable characteristics are that courses may:

- be restricted in the skills to be learned
- not be taught according to a particular methodology.

Robinson (1991) suggests two absolute criteria for defining ESP courses. The first is that ESP programmes are normally goal-oriented. The second is that they derive from a needs analysis. The needs analysis will state as accurately as possible what it is that learners will have to do when speaking the language. Other characteristics are that ESP courses are generally limited to a certain time period, and that they are taught to adults in classes that are homogeneous in terms of the work or study that participants are doing.

Dudley-Evans and St John (1998) suggest that any definition of ESP should include the fact that much ESP teaching makes use of methodology that will differ from General English teaching, especially when the course is specifically linked to a particular profession or discipline.

Pause for thought

> *Consider this last point. Do you agree with it? If the answer is yes, how relevant are TEFL teacher-training courses for the ESP practitioner?*

Unit 1: The Environment and Scope of EIB

Dudley-Evans and St John (1998) go on to suggest that ESP teaching must reflect the methodology of the disciplines or professions that it serves, and that interaction between the teacher and the learner may be very different from that in a General English class.

Pause for thought

> *Consider this last point. What do you understand by it in the context of EIB? In what ways may the interaction and relationship between the teacher of EIB and the participants be different from that of teacher of General English and participants?*

In their definition of ESP, Dudley-Evans and St John (1998) identify three absolute and four variable characteristics. The three absolute characteristics are as follows.

- ESP is designed to meet the specific needs of the learner.
- ESP utilises the methodology and activities of the discipline it serves.
- ESP teaching reflects the grammar, lexis, register, skills, discourse and genres of these activities.

The variable characteristics are listed below.

- ESP may be related to, or designed for, specific disciplines.
- ESP may use a different methodology from that of General English.
- ESP will probably be designed for adult learners.
- ESP is generally designed for learners at an intermediate or advanced level although ESP can be taught to beginners.

Computer-based corpora

We argue that the development of computer-based corpora of specific texts relevant to EAP and EOP also constitutes a characteristic of ESP. Corpora provide a valuable research, teaching and learning aid. For example, Wordsmith (http://www.oup.com/elt/global/isbn/6890/) claims the following.

Unit 1: The Environment and Scope of EIB

- The package enables you to find out how words are used in your own texts, or those of others.
- The Wordlist tool generates word lists in alphabetical and frequency order enabling you to compare texts lexically. It also provides statistics such as total number of words, length of words, number of sentences etc.
- The Concord tool creates concordances (lists of words in context), finds collocates of the word, identifies common phrases, and displays a graphical map showing where the word occurs in the corpus.
- The Keywords tool identifies key words in a given text. Key words are those whose frequency is unusually high in comparison with other more general texts. This enables you to characterise a text or genre. It displays a graphical map showing where each word occurs in the corpus.

You might want to examine the University Vocabulary Trainer (UVT) of the Hong Kong University of Science and Technology. (http://uvt.ust.hk/about.html#n4).

The UVT is a web-based, multi-media tool for the learning of key academic vocabulary. It is designed to help learners understand and use these key words so they can read and write more effectively at university. The UVT contains key academic words that have been taken from university textbooks in four main fields: business, engineering, humanities and social science, and science.

The field of business has been sub-divided into: accounting, economics, finance and marketing. Extracts from university textbooks in these sub-fields are taken and put together to form a corpus.

You are encouraged to browse the web for other Business English corpora. Useful sites are given in the bibliography at the end of this unit. Classroom use of corpora, as opposed to research use of corpora, tends to have two main objectives. First, using searches for function words as a way of helping learners discover grammatical rules. Second, searching for pairs of near synonyms in order to give learners some of the evidence needed for distinguishing their use.

Dudley-Evans and St John (1998) suggest that corpora provide an opportunity to examine the context in which a lexical item occurs, its collocation. For ESP teaching, corpora are an excellent resource for learners who need to check whether they have used the correct collocation in their writing.

Unit 1: The Environment and Scope of EIB

The crucial question for ESP teachers is how useful these programmes are for teaching or self-directed learning. Dudley-Evans and St John (1998) suggest that the programmes provide challenging and empowering activities for learners who wish to discover more about how vocabulary and grammar work. On the other hand, such activities may take much longer than traditional teacher-centred presentations. There is also the disadvantage that not everyone likes working with computers.

Question 1

In the light of what you have read in sections 1.3 and 1.4, consider the six teaching scenarios below. How would you characterise them according to your current understanding of EFL and ESP? Make a note of your responses and check with ours in the Answers to Questions section at the end of this chapter.
1. *A course for business people that focuses on grammar. Each part of the course is based on a grammatical weakness identified by tests.*
2. *A course intended to teach Social English to a group of European business people. The level of the students is intermediate.*
3. *A course designed to teach listening skills to a group of postgraduate students. The students are not studying the same subjects so the texts used are general in terms of their academic content.*
4. *A course designed for students studying for the Cambridge FCE (First Certificate in English) exam. The content of the course is based on an analysis of the students' needs.*
5. *A course that teaches presentation skills to a group of business people from the same company and the same department, who need to give sales presentations across Europe.*
6. *A course designed to teach students of law to write reports.*

To summarise, we are suggesting that there are four absolute defining characteristics of ESP. These characteristics make ESP a distinct and separate activity within English Language Teaching.

Unit 1: The Environment and Scope of EIB

1. **Needs analysis** (see unit 2, chapter 2). The approach to needs analysis will depend on the situation and context. For example, some years ago, the author worked with colleagues in the Italian state electricity company (ENEL) in Venice. We immediately began to establish a target profile of the language skills and activities that learners carried out in their jobs (target situation analysis). Then, we evaluated the personal abilities of the participants' proficiency in these skills and activities (language audit). We then were able to approach the management with the suggested number of hours (and cost) that would bridge the gap between the actual and target situations.
2. **Language**. Specific requirements arising from the needs analysis relate to activities that learners do. These activities generate and depend on registers, genres and associated language that learners need in order to operate within a specified discourse community. ESP teachers must consider the written and spoken texts learners have to deal with, identify the key features of these texts and design materials that will help learners use the texts effectively.
3. **Methodology**. The nature of the interaction between ESP teacher and learner can be very different from that in General EFL classes. Furthermore, all ESP teaching reflects the methodology of the discipline it serves. For example, a course in EIB may include case studies because these are widely used in business training.
4. **The use of computer-based corpora**. Technology has widened the choices in ESP teaching and has given learners more opportunities to study on their own. However, we would agree with Dudley-Evans and St John (1998), who suggest that any technological tool is probably most successful when it is integrated with a classroom course. In other words, technology supports teachers. It does not replace them.

So, what exactly does the ESP teacher do and what are his/her roles? In section 1.5, we examine the factors that may influence ESP teaching methodology, and the various roles of the ESP teacher. Having looked at these influencing factors and these roles, chapter 2 will consider the characteristics and teaching of EIB. We will then be in a better position to decide whether or not EIB is a separate discipline or simply one of a range of activities that are included in the term ESP.

Unit 1: The Environment and Scope of EIB

1.5: Teaching ESP

Factors that influence ESP methodology

The main factors that can distinguish ESP teaching methodology from EFL teaching methodology are:

- learners' knowledge
- methodological approaches
- integrating methodologies from other disciplines
- class size.

Let's look at each of these factors in turn.

ESP learners often bring to their language learning a knowledge which the teacher may not have. For example, doctors bring knowledge of medicine and of illnesses, and business people bring a knowledge of how businesses are run and managed. This can seem threatening unless the teacher realises that business people do not expect teachers to know how to run businesses, and doctors do not expect teachers to know how to cure illnesses.

Question 2

> *What do business people, doctors and lawyers expect from the ESP teacher? How much should the teacher know about the professions of the learners?*

In the same way that learners can bring specialist knowledge into the classroom, they can also bring approaches to communication and learning that reflect their professional world. For intermediate-plus learners, a deep-end methodological strategy is often more appropriate than the PPP (presentation, practice, production) approach. PPP may work well for beginners to intermediates, or when the language and the situation are new to learners. However, the deep-end strategy enables learners to use skills with which they are familiar (e.g. problem-solving, decision-making, making presentations) and try them out in English. The input stage of the lesson will probably come after the task is completed. This input will come from feedback from the teacher and other course participants. The focus of the feedback, i.e. language and/or skills, will depend on the requirements of the particular group.

Unit 1: The Environment and Scope of EIB

One of the strengths of ESP is its ability to integrate the methodologies of other disciplines. Management training courses may sit comfortably with the principles of ESP. For example, while working in-company in Germany, we were invited to observe courses for management and report whether such courses could be held in English. The question was whether or not the courses held in German could be adapted for English training. The objective was to "kill two birds with one stone" and focus on both language and skills. Almost all the courses we observed were subsequently adapted (minimally) for use within the company. These courses included team-building, leadership, group decision-making and problem-solving, and communication skills in a business context (e.g. dealing with conflict, telephoning, handling difficult clients).

The programmes that were developed used authentic materials and involved learners in group and individual work. There was challenge, participation and the use of immediate professional knowledge. Most of the programmes were multi-skilled, and the principal focus could be directed on language or skill.

With regard to class size, ESP classes may vary no less than those of General EFL classes. However, ESP in its purest form may involve just one learner. The needs of this one learner will entirely determine the learning and the content of the sessions.

Question 3

> *What can you do in one-to-one teaching situations that you can not do in group teaching situations?*

The roles of the ESP teacher

Dudley-Evans and St John (1998) identify five key roles for the ESP teacher.

1) ESP teacher as teacher.
2) ESP teacher as course designer and materials provider.
3) ESP teacher as collaborator.
4) ESP teacher as researcher.
5) ESP teacher as evaluator.

Let's examine these five roles in more detail.

Unit 1: The Environment and Scope of EIB

With the common core EGAP or EGBP programmes mentioned in section 1.3, the methodology of ESP may not be so very different from the methodology of General EFL courses. However, as courses become more specific, the teacher may no longer be the expert with regard to content. In some cases, the teacher may know far less about the content than the participants.

Pause for thought

> *This last point suggests that the teacher-student relationship is turned on its head. Before you read on, make a list of the things you can do to retain your professional standing. How will your role change?*

Here is an example from our own experience. We currently run courses in a German car manufacturer for employees who are engaged in negotiations with their suppliers. The suppliers, who are scattered around the globe, supply everything from leather for seats, electronic components, bumpers, paint and so on. Not only are we ignorant about the peculiarities of these particular items, participants are vague about the exact nature of the desired relationship with their suppliers. Furthermore, we are not business people and we have never engaged in negotiating contracts with suppliers. However, what we do have is an understanding of business principles, language and communication, and how business people communicate in their specific jobs.

In these circumstances, we adopt the position of consultants. We offer our expertise on communication practices and cultural differences but we need to help learners adapt these practices to the specific objectives and situations that they have. In other words, our relationship with them is one of partnership. ESP teachers will need to be flexible, to listen to learners, and take an interest in their professional activities.

ESP teachers may often find that, not only will they have to plan the course they are to teach, they will also have to provide the materials for it. Many programmes for highly specific purposes have no textbook at all. This means that teachers will have to find other suitable published material if it is available, and perhaps adapt it for the particular course. It may mean that teachers will have to write all the materials if nothing exists at all (see unit 2, chapter 4).

For example, we recently taught an in-company course that dealt

Unit 1: The Environment and Scope of EIB

with presentation skills for a sales force which has a truly global reach. There are published materials that deal with presentation skills and published materials that deal with intercultural communication. We found none that dealt satisfactorily with adapting presentations to suit the culture of the audience.

If an ESP course is closely subject-specific, it may be that the course is best approached in collaboration with a specialist in the subject. This may involve co-operation, in which the teacher finds out about the subject in an academic context or learns about the activities the participants have to carry out in their jobs. It may be that closer collaboration is needed. For example, it can mean that the teacher prepares learners for the language of a specific lecture/presentation or meeting some days before the event.

Alternatively, it may mean that a subject specialist checks and comments on the materials that the ESP teacher has prepared. The fullest collaboration would be team-teaching, in which the language teacher and the subject expert teach together. For example, the language teacher and the business trainer might work together to teach both the skills and the language that relate to chairing meetings.

If practicable, we suggest that ESP teachers go beyond the stage of needs analysis and target situation analysis. Teachers have to observe, wherever possible, the situations in which learners use the identified skill and the identified texts. In other words, ESP teachers should be prepared to undertake research in order to understand the discourse of the texts used. For example, we think that attending international meetings as observers is an invaluable experience for EIB teachers and may help them prepare materials that are meaningful for students.

ESP teachers may often be involved with the testing of their students (see unit 3, chapter 10). Teachers may be asked to assess whether students have the required language level for a particular academic course or profession. Similarly, at the end of a course of study, teachers need to devise achievement tests to assess how much has been learned.

Evaluating course design and materials should be done during and after the course. Evaluation can often be carried out during informal discussions at the end of the day so that content can be adapted for the remainder of the course (see also unit 2, chapter 3).

Unit 1: The Environment and Scope of EIB

Pause for thought

> Which of the five roles outlined have you already experienced? How many (if any) of these roles can extend to General EFL teaching?

1.6: Answers to Questions

Question 1
1) Not an ESP course. The main concern here is with the language system rather than language for an occupational purpose.
2) Not ESP although it has some features of ESP. The range of linguistic features is too broad for an ESP course.
3) An ESP course. The specific need is a skill - listening.
4) Not ESP. There is a specific purpose but the purpose is related to General English.
5) ESP. A specific need - the presentation skill with specific focus - the sales presentation.
6) ESP. The course is based on the specific need of report-writing.

Question 2
ESP teachers are not expected to be experts in the field of the learner. Learners will expect teachers to understand the interface between their profession and language. ESP teachers should at least show some interest in the jobs of the learner. They should also know something about the fundamental concepts of the jobs and be willing to learn more.

Question 3
The teacher can:
- go at the pace of the learner
- focus completely on the learner
- record and transcribe spoken material where necessary
- respond and not control
- let the learner direct the lesson and its content
- design material for the needs of the individual
- easily change the focus of activity
- respond to the learner's learning style.

Unit 1: The Environment and Scope of EIB

Chapter 2

EFL, ESP and EIB - 2

2.1: Introduction
2.2: Objectives
2.3: Characteristics of EIB
2.4: Teaching EIB
2.5: Conclusion
2.6: Answers to Questions.

2.1: Introduction

In this chapter we continue our exploration of EFL (English as a Foreign Language), ESP (English for Specific Purposes) and EIB (English for International Business). The main focus of the chapter is EIB, its characteristics and key issues. We also examine aspects of EIB that suggest its inclusion under the ESP umbrella may be problematic.

2.2: Objectives

The main aims of this chapter are to:

➢ consider the differences (if any) between ESP and EIB

Unit 1: The Environment and Scope of EIB

➢ examine the factors that influence the teaching of EIB.

Pre-reading task

Before you begin, consider the questions in the shaded box below. These are designed to stimulate your thinking.

> *1) Is teaching English for International Business (EIB) simply one of a range of courses included in ESP, or is EIB a separate discipline?*
> *2) Does the teacher of EIB need experience of business?*

2.3: Characteristics of EIB

English for International Business is very difficult to define in linguistic terms. Choice of language may be influenced by the purpose of an interaction, the professional relationship between the interlocutors, and the topic under discussion. Indeed some business communication may be no different from the English used by the general public. There are, however, a number of identifiable characteristics of EIB. Before discussing these, we need to revisit the distinction between EGBP (English for General Business Purposes) and ESBP (English for Specific Business Purposes).

EGBP and ESBP

Dudley-Evans and St John (1998) suggest that EGBP (English for General Business Purposes) courses are often for either pre-experience learners or for learners at an early stage in their careers. There is a similarity here between General EFL courses and courses in EGBP in that the latter are often extensive courses, with groups formed on the basis of language level, and with most material containing work on the four skills, vocabulary and grammar, but set in a business context. This context is simply used as carrier content. For example, financial statements could be used as the carrier content for teaching the specific language that is introduced at a certain stage. A profit and loss account could, for example, generate the present perfect (Distribution costs have increased this year). Hollett (1991) and Badger and Menzies (1993) are examples of courses in EGBP.

Unit 1: The Environment and Scope of EIB

We would suggest that these courses, which teach a range of English through business settings, can not accurately be described as ESP courses. The language activities tend to be core EFL activities and are not designed to meet particular needs. Nor do EGBP programmes match the other defining characteristics of ESP mentioned in chapter 1.

In contrast, ESBP (English for Specific Business Purposes) courses are often run for experienced business people with specific reasons for taking the time off work for study. These courses are often tailor-made with a focus on specific communication skills, for example: presentation skills, chairing skills or report-writing. The programmes are usually intensive, of short duration and with small groups. Furthermore, participants on ESBP programmes may be at different levels of language proficiency, and courses often adopt a deep-end strategy rather than the presentation, practice, production of more traditional approaches. The focus of the courses is often on fluency rather than on accuracy.

Question 1

For the teacher, what would be the principal differences between teaching an EGBP course and teaching an ESBP course?

Who speaks EIB?

Almost all of the courses in Business English we have done over the past ten years have been in global companies. By global, we mean that customers, colleagues, team-members and sometimes managers can be located in almost any part of the world. It is quite possible, for example, to find team-members scattered across Europe with a remote manager based in the US. All communication between them is English, and the English they use is English as World Language (EWL) or English as a Lingua Franca (ELF) rather than the native speaker (NS) English of such countries as the US or the UK. For more on ELF see Jenkins (2007) and Seidlhofer and Jenkins (2003).

ELF is a phenomenon that characterises EIB and therefore deserves a brief mention here. One of the consequences of ELF is that non-native speakers may be able to understand each other more easily when speaking English together than they can understand a native speaker (NS). One global company with which we are very familiar decided to open a call centre in the UK and staff it with local native speakers of

Unit 1: The Environment and Scope of EIB

English. The company was soon inundated with complaints from non-native speaker (NNS) employees who claimed they were unable to understand their colleagues in the UK. The call centre was subsequently relocated to Holland and staffed with non-native speakers of English.

International English is about effective communication, and our experiences suggest that although non-native speakers want to communicate effectively, they do not necessarily want to use native-speaker communication style. Equally, native speakers need to be able to use International English. Aspects of native-speaker English are not very helpful when communicating with non-native speakers. For example, idiomatic expressions which have their roots in British culture (e.g. "He's on a sticky wicket," or, "In for a penny in for a pound.") are unlikely to be understood by non-native speakers. Furthermore, non-native-speaker English is littered with first language interferences which, although technically incorrect, do not necessarily hinder communication. For example, it is very common to hear, for example, an Italian or a German using expressions like: "I am born in 1952," or "I work in Shanghai since two months."

Company culture

The fact of English as a World Language can be complicated by the use of English that is specific to one company and its culture. Apart from the use of acronyms, which are often unintelligible to outsiders, there can be many examples of lexis that are used only in the company but which non-native speakers often consider to be standard forms. Within Hewlett-Packard GmbH for example, employees would certainly understand the words and expressions: Hoshins, the rules of the garage, and the HP Way. However, it is unlikely that anyone outside the company would know the full meanings of these words and expressions.

National culture

Cultural differences will be dealt with fully in chapters 4 and 5 of this unit. However, this is another area that characterises EIB and therefore deserves to be noted here.

Sensitivity to cultural issues and an understanding of our own and others' cultural values are vital if effective communication is to take place in international business. Language reflects culture and culture has a profound influence on the way language is used. As White points out:

> In the transnational business world, the ability to communicate interculturally in a shared language, such as English, has become an essential skill. It is clear that linguistic skill alone will not equip Business English students for such transnational and transcultural interaction, and that developing cultural awareness and adaptability is necessary. The provision of such intercultural training within the Business English programme is a way of filling the gap. (White 1997)

Our experiences of teaching students from around the world strongly suggest White (1997) is correct and that a clear understanding of cultural values is necessary for efficient and effective communication. For example, Germans tend to prefer a direct and unambiguous communication style which can often seem rude or aggressive to UK business people. On the other hand, Germans often see English politeness strategies as an inability to communicate clearly. The irritation that this can cause may often effectively block communication before it has really started.

Communication style is not restricted to the example above. Consider presentation skills. What constitutes a "good" presentation can often depend on the cultural values of the person or persons who are learning to present. For example, we would suggest that a "good" presentation in the UK and the US would be focused on the listener, be humorous and start with a joke. In contrast, we suggest that a "good" presentation in Germany would be focused on content, be serious and start with a straight introduction (see also unit 1, chapter 7, section 4).

The guidelines above should be used with caution. There are many other factors that can influence presentation style, for example: industry sector, company culture and the personality of the presenter. However, the main point here is that language and cultural values can not be separated, and that an appreciation of this is crucial for the Business English teacher. The Chinese and French, for example, may use English to present, to chair meetings or to negotiate a deal, but there is no reason why they should adopt a British or American cultural attitude while they are doing it.

Unit 1: The Environment and Scope of EIB

Question 2

> *Try and access the two articles by White (1997). White seems to be suggesting that radical changes should take place within the context of EBP. What are these changes?*

2.4: Teaching EIB

Pause for thought

> *In your opinion what are the professional characteristics of the teacher of Business English? How might the teacher of EIB be different from the teacher of EFL? Think about behaviour, knowledge, skills and the teacher-learner relationship.*

Teachers of EIB need experience, knowledge, and a genuine interest in business matters. Furthermore, there may be a good deal to learn. Most teachers of EIB have not experienced the world of business at first hand. This is in contrast to teachers of EAP, who have almost certainly experienced the academic system. They would, therefore, be familiar with lectures, note-taking and essay-writing, for example.

With regard to in-company programmes, our experience suggests there is an increasing emphasis on courses which focus on both language and skills. Such courses would include meeting skills, team-building and presentation skills. In addition, intercultural issues are becoming increasingly recognised as important, both inside and outside the classroom. For example, one manager, who had responsibility for a European team, asked us to explain to him why the company policy of bottom-up feedback (where employees discuss their boss while the boss himself sits behind a screen and listens only) was more or less accepted in Germany but completely unsuccessful in Italy. We referred him to Hofstede's (1991) dimension of high and low power distance (see unit 1, chapters 4 and 5) and explained that in high power distance cultures like Italy, overt criticism of the boss is difficult for both boss and subordinates. As a result of this consultation, the company feedback mechanism was changed to accommodate these cultural differences.

EIB teachers also need to be sensitive to the expectations that business people may have. For example, our experience suggests that they expect groups of between about 6 to 8 people or to have one-to-one tuition. Furthermore, they tend to expect value for money and effective use of time. This may mean short, intensive courses with clearly defined objectives. Business people tend to expect high standards both of the teacher and of the learning environment. Flipcharts, beamers, carpeted floors and comfortable chairs are seen as the norm. Furthermore, handouts should be of the highest standard, and copies of any slides are usually expected. Although business people do not expect the teacher to be an expert in business matters, they will expect some knowledge of business practices and an interest in their world. What they will certainly expect is an understanding of how language works in a business environment. For this reason, EIB teachers should keep abreast of research findings into language and communication in their field.

This means that EIB teachers need to keep up to date with research into discourse communities and how they operate. Individuals may belong to many discourse communities, and the communities themselves may be so large that they are best perceived as "virtual" communities. However, writers or speakers should be fully aware of the expectations and requirements of the particular community, even if that community is imaginary.

Secondly, teachers of EIB need to be aware of the research into Business English genres and the attempts to identify the linguistic features that differentiate one genre from another (e.g. Unger, 2006). For example, are presentations and lectures examples of the same genre? If the answer is no, then how can we differentiate between the two? Furthermore, how can we differentiate between meetings and negotiations? For more on genre and genre analysis you might want to look now at unit 4, chapters 1 and 4.

Thirdly, teachers of EIB need to know how language works in the key communicative events of business. These may be identified as: telephoning, socialising, making presentations, taking part in meetings and negotiations, writing reports and corresponding. It is advisable for teachers of EIB to attend "real" business events in order to hear how language is used in these key activities. This research is especially important when the interaction is between non-native speakers using ELF.

EIB teachers also need to be familiar with management training courses which focus on business communication skills in the learners' native language. Attending such a course would reveal that in many communicative events, language and skills can not be separated. For example, Mehrabian (1971) suggests that face-to-face communication has three components: the verbal, the vocal and the visual. Words play only an 8% part in the impact of the message. 37% of the impact comes from how the words are spoken, and 55% comes from visual aspects, e.g. facial expression and gestures. For many EIB courses, these basic aspects of communication skills can not be ignored. How good is a presenter who mumbles his perfect English towards the floor, with his arms folded and with his shoulders turned to the audience? For more on language training versus skills training you might want to look now at unit 3, chapter 7.

2.5: Conclusions

While the principles of ESP can usually be applied to the teaching of EIB, there are some significant differences. The fundamental concern of most business people is not language learning for its own sake, but how language learning will impact on the company's bottom line and/or their salaries. The expectations of learners may, therefore, differ from the expectations of participants on an EAP programme. Furthermore, the teacher of EIB is working in a world where most communication is between NNSs, and the language of communication is EWL. Moreover, there is no reason why NNSs should adapt to both English language and English/American culture.

The growth of EIB will increase the need for awareness of cross-cultural issues. It may well be that EIB teachers become consultant and advise on the effectiveness of intercultural communication in global companies.

Another area of importance for the EIB teacher is the study of discourse communities and the role of text within those communities. This may involve the use of specific corpora to look at what is said and how it is said in particular genres. An increasing number of courses combine language and communication skills training, and more and more teachers will find that it is not experience of running a business that they need, but a thorough knowledge of management training principles. For many business people, with little time, a combined approach can be very powerful.

Unit 1: The Environment and Scope of EIB

2.6: Answers to Questions

Question 1
When teaching EGBP the teacher will probably have more time to get to know the learners because the course will almost certainly be an extensive course. Furthermore, teachers will be able to familiarise themselves with the coursebook, and there will be a predictable pattern to the lessons.

Teaching ESBP will probably mean that instant relationships will have to be formed because the duration of the course is likely to be short. There will probably be no pattern to courses and different materials will be used for each session. It is also likely that teachers will have to write or adapt materials to suit the needs of the learner or learners.

Question 2
In short, White is suggesting that the English language is no longer owned by NSs. He suggests that intercultural sensitivity and communication are more important than integrating learners into native English-speaking cultures. Communicative competence will revolve around the issue of intercultural competence and awareness.

Chapter 3

The EIB Environment

3.1: Introduction
3.2: Objectives
3.3: The Global Revolution and the Business Environment
3.4: Appropriate Methodology in the Global World
3.5: Interpersonal Skills - the EIB Teaching Professional
3.6: Marketing Yourself as the EIB Professional
3.7: TEIB in the Academic World
3.8: Conclusions
3.9: Answers to Questions.

3.1: Introduction

Teachers of EIB are working within a dynamic and insecure environment. Technology, institutions and values are changing, and the way society operates is being overturned. The international corporate world is also going through enormous changes. In order to work within this global environment, around 100,000 people graduate each year with MBAs (Ridderstråle and Nordström 2000). These people, and others, need EIB in order to successfully operate in their chosen careers. However, it is not yet clear how English, the lingua franca of this world, will develop. Nor do we know how it will be used. Graddol

Unit 1: The Environment and Scope of EIB

(2006) suggests that the idea of English as a Foreign Language may well be in its death throes, and the notion of English as a basic skill is developing in its place.

The corporate environment is one in which you might work. Alternatively, you may choose to work in an academic institution or a private language school. Perhaps, like the author, you will work in all three at different points in your career.

3.2: Objectives

At the end of this chapter you will have a better understanding of:

➢ the variety and nature of the environments where EIB is taught
➢ the qualities and skills required of the EIB teacher
➢ how the EIB teacher can adapt to the different environments.

Pre-reading task

Before you begin, consider the questions in the shaded box below. These are designed to stimulate your thinking and to focus your mind on the main ideas in the chapter.

> *Make a list of all the places you can think of where EIB is usually taught.*
> 1. *What are the differences between these various environments? Consider the learners, their expectations and the language they need.*
> 2. *Consider these environments again. How does/should the environment influence the EIB teacher? Consider the skills and knowledge required, and teacher behaviour.*
> 3. *Why does the EIB teacher need to be sensitive to cultural differences?*
> 4. *How can teachers of EIB market themselves in the corporate environment?*

3.3: The Global Revolution and the Business Environment

> Like it or not, change can not be turned on and off. At the moment it is flowing uncontrollably. Put your hand over it and the water will spread in all directions. Sit back and you will drown. Welcome to the real revolution, Fidel. (Ridderstråle and Nordström 2000)

The quotation above suggests that enormous changes are going on in our societies; and the English language, and the way it is used, is also changing. Teachers of EIB will need to be ready to cope with this.

Internationalisation is, perhaps, a fact of life. There are no borders for terrorist activities, changes in climate or for the movement of capital. During the last forty years, international trade has increased by 1500% (Time, 1998). Average tariffs have also decreased from 50% to less than 5% (Knoke, 1996). We have global television channels, international magazines, global popular music and global films. Any language at the centre of such changes in international activity would have gained prominence, but English was in the right place at the right time. This is the world in which the teacher of EIB must operate.

English is the language of global business - and that business is based on capitalist theories of economics. Everywhere capitalism seems to be developing strongly. Eastern Europe and the former Soviet Union belong to one area of the world that wants Western affluence, but China and India are fast developing into the new economic superpowers. This means that around 3000 million people are now within reach of a capitalist life-style. (Ridderstråle and Nordström 2000).

The economic realities suggest that everyone competes with everyone else. Individuals are in global competition for jobs. Companies are in global competition, and the new competitive battlefield, perhaps, is not products but people. How people are managed and led, and how operations are organised will determine whether or not a company succeeds.

If leadership and management are more important than ever, then communication with people across borders is more important than before. The most important resource is the human resource, and the management of this resource is critical. How you attract, retain, and motivate people, and how you treat customers and suppliers is, perhaps, more important than technology (Ridderstråle and Nordström 2000).

Unit 1: The Environment and Scope of EIB

New skills are also needed - skills like networking for example, and all of this done in English across national boundaries. For example, in May 2007 the author travelled to Glasgow to run a course on intercultural meetings. Course participants came from England, Scotland, Poland, Rumania, Russia, Germany, Belgium, Spain and France.

Pause for thought

> *We have mentioned networking as a skill which needs to be developed, and the need for English to help develop that skill. How many other skills and functions do global managers need to carry out in English? Make a list.*

In order to communicate internationally, we need more than language. We also need cultural understanding; after all, language shapes culture and culture shapes language. Teachers and learners of EIB must be aware of the issues at stake so that they may avoid the misunderstandings that can arise from culturally insensitive use of language.

Pause for thought

> *In this changing environment, what personal qualities and skills do EIB teachers need?*

3.4: Appropriate Methodology in a Global World

If business is global, then teachers of EIB are working in a global context and they need to examine their teaching methodologies in the light of the professional, academic cultures in which they are working. If teachers teach without taking into account the differing interests and values of different cultural groups, they may teach in a way that may be bewildering, ineffective and possibly offensive to some learners. Unit 3 deals with appropriate methodology in detail. However, we feel that we need to introduce it here and give a brief overview of the issues.

Teacher-groups may form professional/academic cultures and these often receive much of their status and tradition from the subjects they

Unit 1: The Environment and Scope of EIB

teach. Bernstein (1971) identifies two types of academic culture. These are described as collectionist and integrationist, and an understanding of them is vital if teachers of EIB are to perform successfully in their global environment. The following are characteristics of the collectionist code.

- Separate subjects.
- Strong subject-boundaries.
- Didactic content-based methodology.
- Rigid timetabling.
- Staff identities oriented towards knowledge of subject.
- Classroom practice invisible to most staff.
- Oligarchic control of institution.

The following are characteristics of the integrationist code.

- Inter-disciplinary.
- Blurred subject-boundaries.
- Skills-based discovery-oriented methodology.
- Flexible timetabling.
- Staff identities oriented towards classroom skills.
- Classroom practice is open to observation.
- Democratic control of institutions.

Holliday (1994a) argues that the professional academic culture of the public sector, non-Western ELT situation in Tertiary, Secondary and Primary education (TESEP), is essentially collectionist. Consequently, teachers in this group are tied to the disciplines of literature or linguistics and much of their status comes from knowledge of grammar and the literature of the language. Moreover, Bernstein (1971) suggests that there is a tendency for collectionist cultures to prescribe knowledge/content and to have a transmission view of education.

Holiday (1994a) argues that students in the TESEP situation are often taught by expatriate teachers who have been trained in the integrationist British, Australasian and North American (BANA) model of ELT. For Holliday (1994a), BANA methodology and TESEP realities are often mismatched. He suggests that BANA-produced methodology is culture bound, and teachers should question its appropriacy for TESEP situations (see also unit 1, chapter 6 and unit 3, chapter 1).

Unit 1: The Environment and Scope of EIB

3.5: Interpersonal Skills - the EIB Teaching Professional

Question 1

> *Consider the expectations that corporate learners of EIB and learners of EFL might have. Think about the following and make a list before checking with our suggested answers in the Answers to Questions section at the end of the chapter.*
> - *Group sizes.*
> - *Hours.*
> - *Materials and handouts.*
> - *Course length.*
> - *Classroom layout and appearance.*
> - *Assessment procedure.*
> - *Appearance/dress of teachers.*

> Personality, knowledge and experience are important to a Business English teacher. In...EAP classes there may be a few opportunities for personal contact; on a one-to-one or small intensive course, personal contact is a key factor and trainers need to be outgoing, tactful and genuinely interested in business issues. Successful Business English teachers will have the flexibility and adaptability of any ESP teacher; they will like people and be good at handling them. (Dudley-Evans and St John, 1998)

We would agree with this statement, but we would add to it. Increasingly, EIB teachers work in-company or on company-specific courses, and many of these courses include language, skills and an intercultural element. All this places great demands upon the teacher of EIB.

Question 2

> *1. Make a list of courses that contain a language element and a skills element.*
> *2. How can the EIB teacher learn these skills?*

Unit 1: The Environment and Scope of EIB

The EIB teacher as consultant

Many EIB teachers who work in companies are obliged to behave as much like consultants as they do teachers. In order to organise seminars, the teacher may be required to work with staff at many levels. The final teaching day(s) will simply be the tip of the iceberg. For example, in order to do a needs analysis and make decisions regarding course content, teachers will need information. That information will be obtained from face-to-face contact, phone contact and e-mail contact. In order to operate in this environment, EIB teachers need highly developed interpersonal skills.

In several management events I have helped organise in-company, I have been just one team member. The others have included the people responsible for logistics, those responsible for managing the event (often external sub-contractors who deal with, for example: lighting, sound, the provision of lap-top computers for presentations) and HR people ultimately responsible for course content and its success or failure.

This means that teachers will need to be good team members. What does this mean in practical terms? First, it means swapping your jeans and shirt for a suit and tie. EIB trainers can not expect to be treated like professionals unless they look like professionals. Second, teachers will need to develop good teamworking skills. Teamwork depends on the ability to get on with colleagues and requires collaborative skills. This means that you must be able to support your fellow team members, to take criticism and handle conflict constructively so that decision-making with regard to your course is more efficient. Destructive conflict-handling may mean that discussions become contests that result in poor decisions, lasting damage to working relationships and no repeat business.

We can not overstate the importance of this last point. While working as a freelance EIB trainer in Germany, all of my business came through personal recommendations from satisfied customers. Not one of my successful business contacts was made through a glossy brochure or any other type of personal advertising.

We recommend that teachers who are considering working in a corporate environment take some time to think about how they may develop their interpersonal skills (e.g. Nelson-Jones, 2006). There are many work-based situations in which "normal" life gives us little practice, for example: giving feedback, negotiating, taking part in formal meetings and making group decisions.

Guirdham (1990) suggests that there are five critical interpersonal skills. These are: understanding other people's behaviour, managing impressions, communicating, persuading and using power. Let's look at them in turn.

Understanding other people's behaviour

Understanding others refers to interpreting their speech and actions. This means looking beyond the surface content and listening actively. Active listening implies listening to those things that are not explicit. For example, emotions, motives and attitudes may not be stated, but the listener should be sensitive to them. Important aids in the active listening process include:

- being quiet and letting the other person finish
- showing attention, for example: eye contact, facing position, smiling and nodding
- verbal agreements, and encouraging words and sounds
- observing non-verbal behaviour
- asking useful questions
- repeating answers
- summarising the gist of a statement correctly.

Active listening is just one technique that can help us understand other people. We also need to practise empathy and to postpone judgement. By using these techniques we may be able to better work with colleagues and to understand what motivates them, how they see the world and how they feel about things.

Managing impressions

Essentially, managing impressions means presenting yourself in the best possible light to other people. We have already mentioned the importance of a suit in the corporate environment. Other aspects of your personal presentation and behaviour are also important. Unless you take time to consider these, people may get a false impression of your attitudes and motives. You, in turn, may often express yourself in a way which is misleading. In particular, this may involve your gestures, body movements and voice. By increasing your knowledge

Unit 1: The Environment and Scope of EIB

and control over non-verbal behaviour, you can avoid conveying an impression which is contrary to the one you intend.

Body language consists of gestures, expression, eye contact, posture and movement. It can substitute for, accompany, reinforce or moderate spoken language. When the body language does not match the spoken message, listeners tend to react more strongly to the body language. Communication is not only a question of what someone says, it is also a matter of how, when and why s/he says it. We can learn a lot about the speaker when we see him/her speak. The speaker's bearing, expression, gestures and voice tell us something about his/her self-confidence, friendliness, calmness, dominance, openness and so on.

Body language may also indicate how verbal statements should be interpreted. A serious statement can be accompanied by a wink, or a suggestion can be emphasised, played down or turned on its head by a gesture of the hand. Non-verbal signals can also regulate what happens. A glance, a raised hand or an open mouth can determine who should speak and who should fall silent.

Using body language effectively is just one way of increasing your control over the impression you give to others (for more on non-verbal communication, see unit 4, chapter 8). Many of us can improve impression management by learning to act assertively. This is a middle-way position between submissiveness and aggression. There are specific techniques for behaving assertively. These involve what you say and your body language, and both may be improved through practice.

Teachers of EIB will need special skills in managing impressions. Think of what you will have to do if you work in a company. Introducing yourself, presenting and working as a team member are just three examples where you will need to control the impressions you make, and all this before you enter the classroom.

Communicating

Communication is the transmission of meaning. If person X sends a message to person Y, and the message is comprehended in exactly the same way as it was intended, then communication has taken place. Communication may be verbal or non-verbal, face-to-face or indirect, formal or informal.

Unit 1: The Environment and Scope of EIB

Question 3

> *Think about our definition above.*
> 1. *Do you think that perfect communication can take place?*
> 2. *What means do we use to communicate on a face-to-face basis?*

To communicate well, we need to remember that communication is a two-way process. We should allow for the fact that receivers take in, understand and remember about 8% of what they hear. Listeners are usually distracted, and what they hear they often distort or interpret in a way that was not intended. Ineffectiveness on the part of speakers can include that they:

- do not structure their thoughts
- do not speak in a language that the listener understands
- express themselves too loosely
- speak too long
- try to put as many ideas as possible into one statement
- do not deal with the statement of the partner
- speak too quickly or without clarity.

Ineffectiveness on the part of listeners can include that they:

- are inattentive
- think about their answer while the other person is speaking
- only hear certain details and overlook the essential meaning
- react to charged words
- pay more attention to how something is said rather than what is said
- interrupt the speaker because they think they know what is coming next
- show no sign that they have understood what has been said.

For a thorough analysis of research, theory and practice in the key skill areas of communication, we suggest you look at Hargie (2006).

Persuading

Persuasion is an activity directed at influencing other people. Influence here means changing people's behaviour. There are no infallible ways of doing this, and persuasion does not depend on authority or power. Applications of persuasive methods can be seen in selling, that is: selling yourself, selling your ideas or selling your product.

Pause for thought

> *Imagine you are working as a freelance teacher of EIB. You are working in-company. What might you have to sell to the HR department? How would you do this?*

Using power

Guirdham (1990) describes power as the influencing of others to do your will despite their resistance. Power thus depends on others believing that they need to carry out your demands, requests or wishes. Asserting power can be risky because a failed power attempt can endanger your goals, your relationships and your credibility.

At first sight, it might appear that teachers of EIB are in the unenviable and powerless position of knowing less about business and management than their group of learners. Most EIB teachers have a language teaching background and do not have first-hand experience of business. They can not claim, for example, to have set budgets, negotiated deals or chaired company meetings.

We suggest that teachers of EIB do not need this experience. However, they do need to understand:

- what business people do in their jobs
- fundamental business concepts and attitudes
- what and how business people communicate
- how language is used in business situations.

There is one situation in which the power relationship is strongly on the side of the trainer and it needs careful handling. This situation may occur with very small groups or with one-to-one teaching (see also unit 3, chapter 8).

The one-to-one situation can be very common in companies where some employees have a very specific need, for example: the important presentation, the important meeting or specific sales negotiation. In the one-to-one classroom, what is often required is not a teacher but a partner to work with. Creating a rapport is vital and to do this, an awareness of the power relationship is necessary. One way a teacher can reduce the power imbalance is to share decision-making and information with the learner. The same is true of very small groups. Dudley-Evans and St John (1998) suggest that:

> The one-to-one teaching situation is much more personal than the class situation. In one-to-one the aim is to establish an interpersonal learning dialogue. Interpersonal because communication is essentially personal; learning because both participants will be learning: the teacher about the individual, their work, their communication style, their language and style; the student about language and language use; and dialogue because it is a two-way process of negotiated give and take. (Dudley-Evans and St John, 1998)

3.6: Marketing Yourself as the EIB Professional

The quality of the service offered by EIB institutions and university departments is often bound up with the perceived quality of the teacher. In other words, your performance will shape perceptions of both the service and the product quality. EIB teachers, therefore, need first-rate training skills and highly developed interpersonal skills in order to create the "right" professional impression (for more on services marketing see unit 1, chapter 9).

We have already mentioned that the teacher's appearance and interpersonal skills are crucial. The suit, the outgoing but tactful personality, and a genuine interest in business issues are some of the important characteristics of the successful EIB trainer.

Furthermore, in any correspondence with actual or potential customers, letters, the letter-head, and type of paper can convey the quality of your service. The same is true of any worksheets or handouts that are produced by the trainer. For company work, these must be of the highest standard and should be as tailored as the course itself. The company name, the date and the place of training must be clearly marked.

Price is also a clue to the quality of service, and EIB trainers, perhaps new to the corporate world, should not place their prices too low. This may be seen as an indicator of poor quality.

Networking is a vital marketing tool for the EIB trainer and is another reason why you will need the highly-developed interpersonal skills mentioned above. Word of mouth and personal recommendations are powerful promotional tools in the service industry and you and/or your institution should endeavour to take advantage of them.

Finally, trainers should always be sensitive to the learning styles of their students (see also unit 3, chapter 9). We suggest that you identify the learning styles and strategies of your learners and do your best to accommodate them. For more on marketing and management in EIB, and what this means for teachers, see unit 1 chapters 8 and 9.

3.7: TEIB in the Academic World

In principle, the qualities associated with corporate EIB teachers should also be developed in EIB teachers in the academic world. However, there are significant differences between the corporate and academic situations. In many colleges and universities, trainers and teachers will be dealing with undergraduates with little or no experience of the business world. Furthermore, whereas in the corporate environment EIB trainers have little or no direct experience of their learners' context, almost all EIB teachers in colleges and universities have studied in an academic environment.

In the corporate world, the trend is towards short and job-specific courses with an emphasis on skills and language. In addition, intercultural issues are increasingly a component of such courses. Dudley-Evans and St John (1998) make the point that for those involved with company language training, acquiring knowledge of, and/or developing skills in, five areas is vital. These areas are:

➢ the communicative functioning of English in a business context
➢ business people's expectations and learning strategies
➢ personal and interpersonal interactions in cross-cultural settings
➢ management theory and practice
➢ first-class training skills.

In the academic world, there may well be short courses designed as pre-sessional or even in-sessional courses, but the emphasis will be on helping learners cope with their future studies. Furthermore, undergraduates with no business experience may not fully appreciate such topics as interpersonal interactions in cross-cultural settings. The exact nature of any pre-sessional course will depend on the nature of the university course learners are to follow. For example, I worked at Manchester Business School's (MBS) Language Centre and we ran courses for non-native speakers who were to do the MBA programme. The MBS MBA has a hands-on, learning-by-doing approach to study, and this was reflected in the pre-sessional course. We concentrated, for example, on group decision-making and problem-solving and used case-studies and simulations which enabled learners to practise these skills.

Perhaps the most significant difference between the corporate world and the academic world is assessment procedure. In many corporate EIB situations, tests may be inappropriate. On short courses, the time is needed for input and practice. Furthermore, the results of such courses often reveal themselves some time after the event. Having said that, many companies will want to use assessment as part of a present situation analysis, to help with course design and as a tool for allocating learners to groups. However, it is unlikely that EIB trainers in the corporate world will ever have to immerse themselves in the type of formal assessment carried out in large academic institutions.

Finally, there is the question of culture. In the UK/US academic world, the learners usually have to adapt to language and the cultural expectations of the British/American university. In the corporate world, learners may use English language but not adopt the cultural values that go with it.

3.8: Conclusions

In this chapter, we have attempted to give you an overview of some of the environments in which EIB is taught. We have focused on the corporate world because it is in this world, perhaps, that the General EFL teacher will find the greatest need to adapt. We have omitted the area of English for General Business Purposes (EGBP) because the difference between General EFL teaching and EGBP is not always very marked.

Professionals in the business world expect high quality, value for money and professionally delivered courses. We have mentioned the trend towards courses which mix both language and skills. Although many courses focus on speaking skills, others focus on writing.

Unit 1: The Environment and Scope of EIB

Personal computers dominate today's offices, and business people are obliged to write their own e-mails, letters and reports. In the global world, most of this correspondence will be in English.

The professional demands placed on EIB teachers are high. But then so are the rewards. For those of you who are willing to take the plunge and become freelance trainers, you may find that your life is more risky but that your salaries rocket.

3.9: Answers to Questions

Question 1
For EFL learners, group sizes will probably be variable. Hours will also be variable but probably no more than 3 hours per week on an extensive course. Materials and handouts will probably be photocopies and/or textbooks, and the classroom will probably have standard school furniture. Assessment may well be by formal exam, and the appearance of the teacher will probably be informal.

Corporate learners will expect small groups of between 1 and 10 participants, and the course is likely to be intensive, i.e. 6-8 hours per day. Materials are probably tailor-made and contained in a folder. Many of these courses will be run in a hotel with conference facilities and modern teaching aids. There are rarely exams or any form of assessment. The teacher will be smartly dressed.

Question 2
1. Communication skills, presentation skills, negotiation skills, meeting skills, writing skills - letters and e-mails, and report-writing.
2. By shadowing, by attending meetings and presentations, and getting authentic examples of learners' written work.

Question 3
1. No
2. Verbal – words and the way they are strung together. Vocal – the way you say and emphasise the words, pausing and so on. Visual - facial expression, gestures, clothes and so on.

Chapter 4

The Intercultural Scope - 1

4.1: Introduction
4.2: Objectives
4.3: Culture Explained
4.4: The Need for Intercultural Sensitivity and Skills
4.5: Single-Dimension Models of Culture
4.6: Conclusions
4.7: Answers to Questions.

4.1: Introduction

This chapter and chapter 5 introduce you to standard models of national culture and attempt to assess their value in making comparisons between cultures. Chapter 4 deals with single-dimension models of culture and chapter 5 looks at multiple-dimension models of culture.

A thorough and complete understanding of these models is a vital foundation stone for any approach to understanding other cultures and their behaviours. Understanding, however, is not enough. We should all learn how these models can be applied in practice. Cultural differences are real, and how they are expressed can fundamentally influence the workplace, whether it is the office or the classroom.

The two chapters can only give you an overview of the main

thinking that has informed scholarly models of culture. Further and continuous reading is recommended. We suggest that you begin with Hofstede (1991). This work is, in our opinion, the most comprehensive, certainly the most accessible, and should be standard reading for any teacher of EIB.

At no point in this book do we imply that culture is the only determinant of behaviour, and we suggest that you view the models and their implications as tools amongst others which you can use to understand the environment in which you work. For example, within the world of business, behaviour might well be influenced by culture, but there may also be other factors to consider. For example:

- market factors
- national and international economic factors
- available technology
- industry values
- company culture
- national and international laws and regulations
- individual character.

However, the importance of culture can never be underestimated. Its influence may often be indirect. Some organisations and some people may choose to ignore the challenges posed by multicultural workplaces. We suggest that, given the continuing globalisation process, this is a risky alternative. For the teacher of EIB, ignorance is not an option.

4.2: Objectives

The objectives of this chapter are to:

- sensitise you to the importance of intercultural awareness
- identify key single-dimension models of national culture.

Pre-reading task

Before you begin, consider the questions in the shaded box below. These questions are designed to focus your thinking on some of the main issues concerning intercultural awareness.

Unit 1: The Environment and Scope of EIB

> 1. We are all individuals. Models of national culture are interesting but they can also be dangerous because they may encourage stereotyping. What is your opinion?
> 2. Teaching cultural differences is not really appropriate at lower language levels. Cultural differences are only important to those who can already communicate effectively. What do you think?

4.3: Culture Explained

Pause for thought

> 1. Before we go any further, make a list of those aspects of your culture which people believe to be "good" or desirable. Why might someone from another culture perceive these as not "good" or desirable? What does this tell you about the person from the other culture?
> 2. Now make a list of those aspects of your culture that people believe to be "bad" or undesirable. Why might someone from another culture perceive these as "good" or desirable? What might this tell you about the person and/or the culture s/he comes from?

There are many definitions of culture. For example, Trompenaars (1993) suggests that culture is the way in which a group of people solve their problems.

Hall and Hall (1990), speaking of cultural communication, suggest that, "...the essence of effective cross-cultural communication has more to do with releasing the right responses than with sending the right messages."

National culture is defined by Fukuyama (1995) as inherited ethical habit. Such a habit can consist of an idea, a value or a relationship. Patterns of ideas, values or relationships make up the ethical code by which societies regulate behaviour. This code is reinforced by repetition, tradition and example, and by images, habits and social opinions.

For those who view culture as an explicit social construct, the emphasis will be on such things as art, literature, education, religion

Unit 1: The Environment and Scope of EIB

and the food we eat. However, for those who view culture as an implicit feature of social life, the emphasis will be on how values, beliefs and attitudes influence behaviour within a culture group. These views of culture are not mutually exclusive. It is simply a question of emphasis.

Pause for thought

> *What did you include in your lists of "good" and desirable aspects of your culture? Did you focus on implicit aspects of culture or on culture as an explicit social construct? If you focused on culture-as-explicit, then you probably included religious books, works of literature, and recipes for your national dishes and so on. Which underlying social values did you include?*

We all carry within ourselves patterns of thinking and of feeling. We acquire these during our lifetimes. When these patterns have become established and internalised, they become what Hofstede (1984) describes as "mental programmes". Hofstede (1984) thus defines culture as:

> The collective programming of the mind which distinguishes the members of one human group from another... Culture in this sense, includes systems of values; and values are among the building blocks of culture. (Hofstede, 1984 p.21)

There are three implications of this. The first implication is that culture includes a system of values.

Pause for thought

> 1. How do you define cultural "values"?
> 2. How do these differ from attitudes and beliefs?
> 3. Are value systems always explicit? For example: if I introduce myself to a class of EIB learners as Robert, (not Mr Goddard) what is the underlying value expressed? If I answered the "pause for thought" above, I would have included as "good" in British society that subordinates in

Unit 1: The Environment and Scope of EIB

> *an organisation are usually consulted. What is the implicit value expressed here?*

Values, according to Hofstede (1991), are tendencies within social groups to prefer some states of affairs over others. Values deal with good and evil, dirty and clean, ugly and beautiful, unnatural and natural, abnormal and normal, paradoxical and logical, and irrational and rational.

The second implication of the definition is that values are learned and they are learned most intensively in early life. This means that many values remain unconscious to us, but they are second nature and hugely influence our behaviour and how we react to our environment. Because they are so deep rooted, the causes of many intercultural disputes and conflicts are never properly identified. The job of the intercultural trainer is to bring these differences to a level where they can be consciously investigated. This implies that the prerequisite for understanding the cultural conditioning of others is to fully understand our own.

Finally, the definition implies that culture is particular to a specific social group and not to others. Culture is shared with those who live in the same environment in which it was learned.

Pause for thought

> *The notion that culture is specific to one group and not another raises some important questions. How accurately can we talk about an American culture, for example, when the US contains so many groups claiming Black, Hispanic, or Indian sub-cultures? And what about Northern and Southern Italy or the former East and West Germany – can these be described as sharing the same cultural values?*

Cultural relativism

One vital question we need to address in this section is the question of normality. In other words, does one culture own the absolute criteria for judging the activities of another?

Unit 1: The Environment and Scope of EIB

Pause for thought

> 1. In the UK, it is considered good manners to queue. In fact the British are famous for it. Imagine a British man travels abroad and, finding he has to fight his way on to a bus, complains loudly about the absence of manners in the host country. Is he justified in doing this? Why? Why not?
> 2. Many cultures around the world consider it "normal" to do favours for members of the in-group or family. This may occur both in the private and the public spheres. This means that the CEO of a company may appoint his son or cousin to a position of power or influence in that company. Other cultures around the world may consider this to be corrupt. Which culture is right?

Perhaps your answer to the question concerning the Englishman and queues was that he should adapt to local conditions and fight his way on to the bus like everyone else. We think that this answer misses the point. The really important question to ask is how he feels inside when he realises he can not behave as "normal". What is the man's emotional reaction to his surroundings, and can he change this reaction even if he wants to?

And what about US or UK business people who sign a contract with an Arab country? What do they do when they find that their Arab colleagues do not attach the same value to a signed document as they do? In fact, the Arab partners appear to interpret and adapt the document as the need arises. Just because the UK values signed contracts highly and considers them binding, does this mean they should apply those values to everyone else? If the answer is yes, what right do they have to do this?

Furthermore, Hofstede (1991) comments that theories of culture and prescriptions of behaviour are as culture bound as anything else. Theories or prescriptions reflect the values of the culture that produced them. Consequently, there can be no certainty that management theories and theories of culture which are produced in one society can be usefully applied to another.

Unit 1: The Environment and Scope of EIB

Pause for thought

> *Think about this last sentence. The models of culture we examine in chapters 4 and 5 all originated within the cultural context of one country. Does this mean we can not apply these theories to other countries?*

4.4: The Need for Intercultural Sensitivity and Skills

Hofstede (1991) points out that the world is full of conflicts and confrontations between peoples, groups and nations who think differently. And yet, these groups, peoples and nations have common problems which require co-operation for their solutions. Hofstede (1991) points to AIDS, climate change, and economic problems as examples of these. After September 11 2001, we would add international terrorism to this list. Understanding the differences between the ways national leaders and their followers around the world think and feel is a necessary condition for bringing about workable and lasting solutions to common problems. We need global co-operation on a scale that has never before been needed. As Hofstede (1991) says, "A new level of intercultural co-operation is the only alternative to common doom."

In the business world, activities are increasingly global in their scope. Morden (1995) suggests that all managers engaged in global activities need to be sensitive to cultural differences. In particular, he mentions its importance in effective entry into new markets and new countries, the effective running of programmes for international human resource development, and the development of appropriate skills and competencies on which the achievement of corporate success depends.

Ridderstråle and Nordström (2000) point to a borderless world, in which communicating with other cultures is a necessity and not a luxury. Car manufacturers, for example, are increasingly becoming assembly plants, with the component parts coming from a wide range of different countries. This means that contracts are negotiated across cultures, meetings are held across cultures and presentations are given across cultures, and so on. In such a world, the ethnocentric manager who is unwilling or unable to deal with members of another culture will find that his or her career opportunities are limited.

As Mead (1994) points out, "Effective cross-cultural management means working with members of the other culture, tolerating differences...and recognising their priorities when developing shared priorities."

And what about the teacher of EIB? How important are intercultural skills and intercultural awareness for classroom practice? To answer this question, let's consider an example.

Imagine you are teaching on a pre-sessional EIB course at a British university or business school. You students will go on to study for an MBA. Most of the learners are Chinese. How far will the teacher take cultural factors into account when designing and implementing the course? Can the teacher afford to ignore these differences?

If we accept, for the moment that schools and other educational institutions reinforce and reflect the values of the society in which they operate, then we should assume that educational values will differ in the same way as national values.

Pause for thought

> *What do you identify as the key features of academic culture in your country? Compare them with the academic cultures of any other country with which you are familiar.*

As far as the UK is concerned, the Dearing report (1997) specifies that higher education in the UK should, "Sustain a culture which demands disciplined thinking, encourages curiosity, challenges existing ideas and generates new ones."

In order to succeed in this academic culture, Gent et al (1999) suggest that students need the following characteristics:

- disposition to enquiry
- self-awareness and reflection
- analytical approach
- depth of study
- effective communication of results.

So, what are the typical prior educational experiences of the Chinese students on our pre-sessional MBA programme? Richards (2000) suggests that the following are typical.

- Courses are based on one or two prescribed texts.

Unit 1: The Environment and Scope of EIB

- The content of these texts is rarely challenged.
- Learning is teacher-oriented and teacher-dependent.
- Students face pressure to conform to expectations.
- Success is attributed to effort rather than to ability.
- Students (typically) have never written more than 150 words in English.

There is clearly a mismatch here between what makes a "good" education, and what makes a "good" student. The mismatch raises a series of interesting questions to which we (as teachers of EIB) must attempt to find answers. For example, who should or can adapt to whom? Shen (1989) writes:

> In order to write good English, I knew that I had to be myself, which actually meant not to be my Chinese self. It meant that I had to create an English self and be that self. And to be that English self, I had to accept the way a Westerner accepts himself in relation to the universe and society.

The implications of cultural differences for the TEIB classroom will be dealt with in detail in chapters 6 and 7 of this unit and in unit 3. However, we would point out now that ignoring these differences is another option which is not open to us.

4.5: Single-Dimension Models of Culture

High- and low-context cultures

Hall (1960, 1976, and 1990) makes a distinction between high-context and low-context cultures. Context is defined as the way individuals and their society seek information and knowledge.

In high-context cultures, the external environment, situation and non-verbal behaviour are important elements in the communication process, i.e. sending, receiving and interpreting messages. Knowledge is often expected to be in (or within reach of) an individual. Consequently, little information needs to be made explicit. The spoken word may, therefore, be used to imply or infer. Messages are rarely explicit and subtlety is valued. In order to operate in such an

Unit 1: The Environment and Scope of EIB

environment, high-context people will gather a vast amount of information from their personal networks of friends, acquaintances and contacts. Because of the importance of this network, relationships are extremely important and tend to be long-lasting. Two people from such cultures may speak a lot but say little. When I lived in Italy (high-context) people often talked to me about football. They rarely asked me directly if I had heard of "Juve" or "Inter" or the players who graced those teams. They simply paid me the compliment of assuming I already had the information. As a typical product of a low-context culture (England) I admit to being often confused!

In low-context cultures, the environment, situation and non-verbal behaviour are relatively less important and information is more explicit. A direct communication style is valued. Low-context people tend to speak less but say more. They may also assume that their high-context colleagues are being deliberately vague or unhelpful (Lewis, 2006). High-context cultures tend to have the following characteristics.

- Relationships between individuals are relatively long lasting, and individuals feel deep personal involvement with each other.
- Much is communicated by a shared code so communication can be fast and efficient.
- Those in authority are personally responsible for the action of subordinates.
- Agreements tend to be spoken rather than written.
- Insiders and outsiders are tightly distinguished.
- Cultural patterns are slow to change.

Low-context cultures tend to have the following characteristics.

- Relationships between individuals are relatively short and, in general, deep personal involvement with others is valued less.
- Messages must be explicit, and the sender can depend less on the receiver inferring the message from the context.
- Authority is diffused throughout the system.
- Agreements tend to be written rather than spoken, and contracts are final and legally binding.
- Insiders and outsiders are less closely distinguished.
- Cultural patterns are faster to change.

High-context cultures would include Japan, China, Southern Europe

Unit 1: The Environment and Scope of EIB

and the Middle East. Low-context cultures could include the US, Scandinavian countries, Germany and Switzerland. High- and low-context cultures will appear frequently in this book, notably: unit 1, chapter 10 and unit 4, chapters 8 and 9).

Question 1

> *In a well-known global computer manufacturer based in Germany, the new HR director was French. His German subordinates were soon pulling their hair out in desperation. Their main complaint was that the new director did not tell them what they had to do in order to perform their duties. The French director was also complaining that his subordinates lacked initiative. How far can Hall's (1990) model explain this problem and what would you do about it if you were a consultant brought in to solve the problem?*

Monochronic and polychronic cultures

Lewis (2006) suggests that differing attitudes to time can be a constant irritation to those who work in an international context. Monochronic cultures use linear-active time in which a person:

> ...does one thing at a time in the sequence he has written down in his date book. His schedule that day said 8.00 A.M. get up, 9.00 breakfast, 9.15 change into tennis clothes, 9.30 drive to the tennis court, 10.00-11.00 play tennis, 11.00-11.30 beer and shower... (Lewis, 2006)

Polychronic cultures, on the other hand, use a multi-active time system in which many things are done at the same time and sometimes in an unplanned order. Lewis (2006) writes:

> Multi-active people are not very interested in schedules or punctuality. They pretend to observe them, especially if a linear-active person insists. They consider reality to be more important than man-made appointments.

We suggest that polychronic or monochronic tendencies are neither good nor bad, and both have strengths and weaknesses. Lewis (2006)

Unit 1: The Environment and Scope of EIB

supports this view.

> A study of attitudes towards time in a Swiss-Italian venture showed that, after some initial quarrelling, each side learned something from the other. The Italians finally admired that adherence at least in theory to schedules, production deadlines and budgets enabled them to clarify their goals and check on performances and efficiency. The Swiss, on the other hand, found that the more flexible Italian attitude allowed them to modify their timetable in reaction to unexpected developments... (Lewis, 2006)

Kaufman-Scarborough and Lindquist (1999) suggest that monochrons would be best suited to workplaces which require the establishment of well-planned schedules; for example, the establishment of repetitive programmes or activities whose success depends on structured time. Conversely, polychrons would be expected to do well in jobs that require the juggling of tasks, such as tour directors, secretaries, developers of products and emergency room personnel (for more on monochrons and polychrons, see unit 4, chapter 8).

Question 2

Imagine a negotiation between a monochronic German and a polychronic Italian. Assuming typical behaviour, what problems may occur in the conduct of the negotiation?

Pause for thought

Once again, assuming typical behaviour, what problems may occur in a formal meeting between the French and German managers of a global corporation?

Fukuyama's analysis of trust

Fukuyama (1995) suggests that high trust cultures can organise themselves on a more group-oriented and flexible basis with considerable responsibility being delegated to lower organisational levels. Low trust cultures, on the other hand, tend to be bureaucratic with many rules and regulations that govern relationships. Fukuyama

Unit 1: The Environment and Scope of EIB

(1995) claims that low trust societies will tend to:

- have a strong family business sector
- have a strong state sector and a strong state
- display low levels of interpersonal trust
- have difficulty in associating with others in groups
- prefer basing interpersonal relationships on formalised and centralised rules.

The correlation between hierarchy and the absence of trust is an interesting one that we shall come across again when we look at Hofstede's (1991) dimensions of culture. Fukuyama (1995) suggests that hierarchies are necessary because not everyone in the community can be depended on to live by implicit rules alone. They must, ultimately, be forced to behave by the use of explicit rules. In contrast, high trust societies will tend to:

- have strong organisations in the middle – that is, between the family and the state
- be characterised by high levels of social trust
- organise themselves on the basis of shared ethical values
- allow a variety of social relationships to emerge.

Interestingly, high trust cultures do not need to coerce their members with rules. Fukuyama (1995) suggests that supervision will be replaced by identification, participation and commitment.

Pause for thought

> *I would describe my own culture (UK) as being a high trust culture, and this is reflected, generally speaking, in UK management style. It is also reflected in my teaching style. How would you define your country? How does the tendency manifest itself?*

Culture and power relationships

Research by Laurent (1983) and later by Adler et al (1992) suggests that attitudes towards organisational power differ across cultures, and that managerial status may be viewed very differently. Cultures that value a hierarchical structure as a way of maintaining cohesion in organisations may impose severe restrictions on communication flow. This will influence what is communicated, how it is communicated, by whom and to whom.

Cultures with a preference for hierarchical structures include China, Italy and France. Cultures with a preference for flatter structures include Sweden, the Anglo-Saxon cultures and the US.

Question 3

> 1. Is there a relationship between Laurent's (1983) hierarchical cultures and Fukuyama's low trust cultures?
> 2. Imagine that a Swede, working in an Italian company, ignores the hierarchy and goes directly to the source of information he needs. The Swede might do this for the sake of efficiency. How do you think the Italian managers would view this type of behaviour?

4.6: Conclusions

In terms of content, this is an intense chapter. We have introduced some of the most important single-dimension models of national culture, and you will need to have a good understanding and appreciation of these as you read the rest of this book.

We would stress again that in order to understand and appreciate other cultures, you should begin by understanding and appreciating your own cultural conditioning. This is not always easy to do. It is far more comfortable to perceive of ourselves and our own cultures as the "norm" against which all other cultures are somehow deviant - in other words, we are right and they are wrong. There is no doubt that this is the easy route to take.

If you reject the easy route, then you are starting on a difficult but rewarding journey of self-discovery that will, we hope, take you beyond cultural awareness and tolerance. After all, tolerance alone is not enough. It is merely a stepping-stone towards the main goal, which is an appreciation of the mystery of other people's thoughts and feelings.

Unit 1: The Environment and Scope of EIB

4.7: Answers to Questions

Question 1

Germans (low-context) tend to appreciate direct and unambiguous instructions. They like to be told exactly what they have to do and then get on with it. The French (high-context) will assume that subordinates are able to see what is required of them by interpreting the messages that are sent to them. These messages are often implicit. In this situation we have an example of two different styles of communication clashing with each other. Perhaps, nobody is to blame, but both "sides" need intercultural awareness training.

Question 2

Perhaps the most obvious problem would be the tendency of monochrons to take the negotiation one step at a time, while polychrons might take an approach whereby everything is negotiated at the same time. The two approaches do not go well together.

Question 3

Yes. Hierarchical cultures tend to be low trust cultures.
The Italian might see this as insubordination.

Unit 1: The Environment and Scope of EIB

Chapter 5

The Intercultural Scope - 2

5.1: Introduction
5.2: Objectives
5.3: Multiple-Dimension Models of Culture
5.4: Conclusions
5.5: Answers to Questions.

5.1: Introduction

In chapter 5 we further examine national culture and the models you can use in order to approach it. The main focus of this chapter is multiple-dimensions of national culture. We also look at Asian management systems.

We repeat here that a thorough and complete understanding of these models is a vital foundation stone for any approach to appreciating other cultures and their behaviours. Such an appreciation will help us deal, not only with the world of international business, but also with our students, their learning needs and requirements.

Unit 1: The Environment and Scope of EIB

5.2: Objectives

The objectives of this chapter are to:

➢ identify key multiple-dimension models of national culture
➢ outline the influences on Southeast Asian Management.

Pre-reading task

Before you begin, consider the tasks in the shaded box below. These are designed to focus your thinking on some of the main issues in the chapter.

> 1. *If the teacher of EIB teaches in the right way, there is no need to understand models of national culture. Good teaching is good teaching no matter who is in the classroom. Consider this view.*
> 2. *How far can the models of culture examined in chapters 4 and 5 be applied to China? Is China somehow different? If the answer is "yes", then how is it different?*

5.3: Multiple-Dimension Models of Culture

Kluckhohn and Strodtbeck's (1961) six basic orientations

We include an overview Kluckhohn and Strodtbeck's (1961) model because you will later see that it has been widely influential. The authors suggest that culture groups show different orientations towards the world, and that these can be compared. The model has six basic orientations, and each asks questions about the culture group's perceptions of the human condition. The six orientations and their variations (a-b-c) are:

What is the nature of people?
a. good
b. a mixture of good and evil
c. evil.

What is our relationship to nature?

Unit 1: The Environment and Scope of EIB

a. dominant
b. in harmony
c. subjugation.

What is our relationship to other people?
a. hierarchical
b. collectivist
c. individualistic.

What is the focus of human activity?
a. doing
b. being in becoming
c. being.

What is the time focus of human activity?
a. future
b. present
c. past.

What is our conception of space?
a. private
b. mixed
c. public.

In the opinion of the writer, dominant UK culture sees people as:

➤ a mix of good and evil
➤ having a desire to control nature or human psychology
➤ individualistic
➤ pragmatic/doing
➤ acknowledging that there is a tension between past, present and future
➤ living and working in private spaces.

Pause for thought

> *How would you describe the dominant orientations of your culture? Keep in mind that we are talking about social orientations and not personal ones.*

Unit 1: The Environment and Scope of EIB

The model described above has a number of weaknesses so far as managers are concerned since its implications for management have never been fully explored. Further, the orientations described are vague and imprecise. Lastly, any interpretations will almost certainly be subjective. Nevertheless, we hope that its influence on later comparative models of culture will become obvious to you.

Hofstede's dimensions of culture

Hofstede's work shows how the values of a culture can influence relationships, and permeate through to both work and social situations. Hofstede (1984, 1991) suggests that national cultures and values can be categorised on the basis of four dimensions. These are:

1. **Power distance**. This dimension considers hierarchies (political and institutional) and what these might mean for management style, educational style and communication. Essentially, the dimension indicates how a society faces the fact of inequality and what it does about it.
2. **Uncertainty avoidance**. This dimension deals with how different cultures cope with ambiguous situations and tolerate uncertainties about the future. Essentially, is the culture comfortable or uncomfortable with risk?
3. **Individualism and collectivism**. This dimension deals with the relationship between the individual and the group to which the individual belongs. It concerns issues about individual motivation, and about the functioning of society as a whole.
4. **Masculinity and femininity**. This dimension concerns the sexuality of social roles and the degree to which society allows overlap between the roles of men and women.

We strongly advise you to read Chapters 2-5 of Hofstede (1991) or to look at http://www.geert-hofstede.com/ where you will find a fuller description of Hofstede's work.

Question 1

Look at the situations below and try to answer the questions. Compare your responses with our suggested responses in the Answer to Questions section. Approach the questions with reference to Hofstede's (1991) dimensions.

1. *In Greece, the CEO of a Greek company appoints his son to a position of power and authority in the company. How do think Greek employees would tend to react?*
2. *Imagine the same situation occurred in Sweden. How would Swedish employees tend to react?*
3. *You have a class of Japanese learners. They do not react when you try to elicit responses from the whole class. In fact, your questions are received by a wall of silence. Can you think of any reasons why this should be the case?*
4. *You are English and working for a German company in the Frankfurt area. When you make a serious mistake, you decide to come clean and admit your mistake to your colleagues. In the UK, you know that this admission will be seen as a sign of strength (as long as you show willingness to learn from it). However, your German colleagues are both angry and contemptuous. Why is this?*
5. *In South Korea, you begin a presentation with, "Hi, my name's Robert." You then decide to tell a joke in order to break the ice. How do you think the Korean managers would react? Why?*

Hofstede's work is, perhaps, weak on a number of points.

- It assumes that national territory and culture groups correspond.
- The research itself is culture bound.
- The findings in some cases are out of date (think of Yugoslavia).
- Informants for the research came from one company.

Furthermore, we should be careful not to interpret Hofstede's findings in a mechanistic way. For example, Schramm-Nielsen (2000) suggests that a low score on the uncertainty avoidance dimension can not necessarily be interpreted as a low need for certainty and a high score as a need to avoid uncertainty. What the author suggests is that we look closely at the environment of the respondents before coming to conclusions. However, Hofstede's work is hugely important and is still used as the basis for much scholarly research. See, for example: Jeanquart-Barone and Peluchette (1999) and Ardichvili and Kuchinke (2002). Despite its weaknesses, Hofstede's (1991) model is the best we currently have, and we recommend that you fully familiarise yourself with it.

Trompenaars' analysis

Trompenaars (1993) suggest that a culture will distinguish itself from another by the way it solves its problems. The solution chosen might help identify seven fundamental dimensions of culture. Here is a brief overview of each.

1. **Universalism and particularism.** The universalist approach tends to apply the "one good way" to all situations. The particularist approach pays greater attention to the obligations of relationships and to unique circumstances. Universalists tend to focus on rules and legal contracts. The person who honours that contract is trustworthy. Particularists, on the other hand, tend to focus on relationships and modify legal contracts as necessary. The person who honours the relationship is trustworthy. Evolving relationships are vital.
2. **The group and the individual.** This dimension considers the conflict between the needs of the individual and the interests of the group. Individualistic cultures tend to make frequent use of the word "I", and decisions are often made with little or no consultation with HQ. Personal responsibility and lone achievement are valued highly. Collective cultures tend to make more frequent use of the word "we". Decisions tend to be referred back to HQ, and group achievement and joint responsibility are valued.
3. **Affective and neutral cultures.** Affective cultures tend to freely show emotions whereas neutral cultures tend to remain more controlled. The former tend to reveal their feelings quite readily and to value heated and animated exchanges. The latter tend to conceal their feelings and self-possessed behaviour is respected.
4. **Specific and diffused cultures.** This dimension concerns whether we engage others in specific areas of our lives or whether we engage people diffusely in many areas. Specific cultures tend to have a direct and blunt communication style and to have consistent moral stands which are independent of the person being addressed. Diffuse cultures, on the other hand, tend to be indirect and evasive and their moral stands depend on the situation and person being addressed.

5. **Ascribed and achieved status.** This dimension concerns how a society ascribes status - on the basis of achievement or on the basis of age, class or education. Achievement-oriented cultures tend to frown on the use of titles, give respect on the basis of efficiency and promote managers on the basis of proficiency rather than on age. Ascription-oriented cultures tend to use titles extensively and give respect to older managers. Respect for superiors is seen as a measure of personal commitment to the organisation.
6. **Managing time.** This dimension concerns whether or not a culture is past, present or future oriented, and whether or not it is monochronic or polychronic.
7. **Relating to nature.** Do cultures let nature take its course or do they attempt to control it? External-oriented cultures tend to display a flexible attitude with a willingness to compromise. They tend to be comfortable with "riding out" difficult times and seek harmony with the environment. Internal-oriented cultures, on the other hand, often tend to display an aggressive attitude towards the environment and are uncomfortable when the environment seems out of control.

Pause for thought

> *From what you have so far read, how much of Trompenaars' (1993) work derives from previous research?*

We need to ask ourselves whether or not Trompenaars is telling us anything new or whether he is just serving up old wine in new bottles. The origin of the first five of his dimensions is to be found in Parsons and Shils (1951), and the origin of the last two dimensions is clearly to be found in Kluckhohn and Strodtbeck (1961). In addition, Hofstede (1996) remarks that the data-bank used by Trompenaars (1993) has serious shortcomings with regard to its content-validity. Further, Hofstede (1996) claims that Trompenaars (1993):

> ...does ride the waves of commerce: he tunes his message to what he thinks the customer likes to hear. The result is a fast food approach to intercultural diversity and communication.

Whether or not we agree with Hofstede (1996), Trompenaars (1993) offers an interesting interpretation and we recommend that you read it.

Unit 1: The Environment and Scope of EIB

Lessem and Neubauer's analysis

The main focus of Lessem and Neubauer's (1994) analysis is management systems. Lessem and Neubauer (1994) categorise the impact of national culture under four interrelated criteria. These are, the tension between pragmatism and idealism on one hand, and the tension between a rationalist approach and a humanist approach on the other hand.

Pragmatism is:
- empirically oriented
- competitively focused
- individualistic
- action oriented.

Idealism is:
- systems oriented
- co-operative
- developmental
- focused on public and private partnership
- sensitive to the organisation and the environment.

The pragmatic approach is a dominant influence in the Anglo-Saxon world and focuses on the enterprise and its ability to develop into a learning organisation. Idealism is directly opposed to this in the sense that it sees the organisation as an integral part of a greater whole.

Rationalism is characterised by:
- a scientific outlook
- a focus on organisations as structures
- professional and impersonal management
- a belief in planning.

Humanism is characterised by:
- an emphasis on the family and community
- a sense of duty and personal obligation
- flexibility and change
- personalised style of management
- fashion, feeling and sentiment.

Unit 1: The Environment and Scope of EIB

Question 2

> *Can you find any conceptual links between Lessem and Neubauer's (1994) analysis and any of the other models we have looked at in this chapter?*

Southeast Asian management

Chen (1995), Cragg (1995) and Seagrave (1995) suggest that there are a number of key, and mainly Chinese, historical influences on the development of management in Southeast Asia.

Morden (1999) identifies and summarises eight major influences. The first influence is Taoism. Taoism focuses on the interconnectedness of things. Each entity has the opposing forces of yin and yang, and harmony must be achieved between them. This harmony will ensure the quality of oneness. However, oneness is subject to change. According to the rules of nature, nothing is static, and to pursue stability is to pursue an illusion.

The second influence is Confucianism. Confucius was a Chinese sage, who stressed the importance of man as a social being. His doctrines became a moral and religious system upon which a structure of social principles developed. These principles are based on the concept of *ren* and the achievement of social harmony. The concept of *ren* involves humaneness and benevolence in the treatment of others. Social harmony should be established within a hierarchical framework. According to Confucius, mankind is divided between the weak/inferior and the strong/superior. The strong have an obligation through *ren* to take care of the weaker members of society. The weak, in return, have an obligation to work hard in order to pursue a greater and communal good.

The third influence is the role of the mandarin. Mandarins were state functionaries, a sort of professional meritocracy. They developed as a reflection of the Confucian principle that leaders and managers should work hard and, at the same time, demand hard work from their subordinates. Together, mandarins and subordinates would serve the needs of the wider community. In return, the community would support them. The development of this principle has become the basis of the work ethic we can see in the economies of Southeast Asia.

The fourth influence concerns personal relationships or *guanxi*. *Guanxi* means developing and maintaining social relationships on the

Unit 1: The Environment and Scope of EIB

basis of exchange of favours. Seagrave (1995) suggests that the many overseas Chinese communities and their trading links have held together because of the strong interpersonal bonds based on *guanxi* and *shinyung* or trust.

The fifth influence is the concept of face. Face concerns the dignity, self-respect, status and prestige of an individual. Negotiations and other social interactions should be conducted in such a way that nobody loses face.

The sixth influence is what Chen (1995) refers to as the five cardinal relations. While Confucius identifies many kinds of human relationships, five are fundamental. These are:

- sincerity between father and son
- righteousness between ruler and subject
- separate functions for husband and wife
- order between older brother and younger brothers
- faithfulness among friends.

These five relationships are based on the Confucian principle of social hierarchy and they stress the importance of the group. It means that the Chinese perceive of themselves as members of a group rather than as individuals. As members of a group, the Chinese tend to value restraining their individuality in favour of group harmony.

The seventh influence is the thinking of Sun Tzu. Sun Tzu's book, The Art of War, described the way in which effective wars are to be fought. For the Chinese, the concept of war and the concept of strategy are the same. As a result, Southeast Asians tend to see the marketplace as a battlefield. It follows that strategies for waging war have been applied to "waging" business.

As far as management style is concerned, Sun Tzu's thinking is reflected in the following principles.

- Strategic management means avoiding head-on confrontation.
- Strategic management means careful attention to planning.
- Objectives are shared between manager and subordinates.
- Leadership should be wise, sincere, benevolent, brave, and strict.
- Leaders should have absolute authority.
- Leadership should have the flexibility to implement strategy in response to changing conditions.
- Training is vital for efficiency.

Unit 1: The Environment and Scope of EIB

The final influence is the influence of the taipans. The taipan is defined by Cragg (1995) as supreme ruler or big boss. The first taipans were British. Today, many taipans are overseas Chinese. Cragg (1995) describes the taipans as being:

- autocratic
- entrepreneurial
- risk-takers
- rapid decision-makers
- keen network users
- supporters of creative ideas and innovation
- focused on detail
- skilled at managing face
- capable of working in the east and West.

5.4: Conclusions

The content of the last two chapters is crucial, both for an understanding of international business and for an understanding of the teacher's role in the classroom. We would stress again that you must get to grips with the model developed by Hofstede (1984, 1991) and be thoroughly familiar with its main ideas and applications.

5.5: Answers to Questions

Question 1
1. Greece is a high power distance culture so the employees would probably consider this promotion as relatively normal and not worthy of comment.
2. Sweden is a low power distance culture. Employees would probably be quite critical of such a promotion.
3. Japan is a collective culture. Personal opinions are considered illogical. You would need to put the class into groups and elicit group responses.
4. Making mistakes in a strong uncertainty avoidance and masculine culture is a sign of weakness and to admit it is even worse.
5. High power distance Koreans would expect you to introduce yourself and your titles in a way that suggests your senior position. First names would probably embarrass them. Further, the joke would probably appear flippant and not worthy of a senior manager.

Unit 1: The Environment and Scope of EIB

Question 2

Pragmatism could be linked to individualistic, low power distance and weak uncertainty avoidance cultures, for example: the UK and the US.

Idealism may be linked to low power distance, strong uncertainty avoidance, and individualistic cultures, for example: Germany and Switzerland.

Rationalism is typically French and therefore associated, perhaps, with high power distance cultures.

Humanism seems linked to polychronic and high-context cultures.

Unit 1: The Environment and Scope of EIB

Chapter 6

Culture and the Classroom - 1

6.1: Introduction
6.2: Objectives
6.3: Culture, Education and Methodology
6.4: Conclusions
6.5: Answers to Questions.

6 1: Introduction

Although the need for cross-cultural awareness and communication skills training is increasingly recognised, there still seems to be a scarcity of trainers, training designs and training materials. In part, this chapter and chapter 7 represent an attempt to alleviate these last two difficulties, although at no point do we claim to be writing a training manual.

Culture training can be divided into three distinct areas. The first area is pre-departure training for people who are about to go and live abroad for an extended period of time, for example: experts and volunteers in development work, diplomats and military personnel. We should also include spouses and children in this category. The author is acquainted with several people whose foreign assignments were cut short because their spouses were unable to cope in their new

Unit 1: The Environment and Scope of EIB

environment. The second area concerns acculturation programmes after arrival, for example: workshops for students on how to cope with local conditions, study skills and so on. The third area is teaching members of multicultural groups to become more aware and sensitive towards their colleagues' values, norms and behaviour patterns. Most teaching of cross-cultural communication within the context of EIB falls into this third category.

This chapter will examine the extent to which cultural differences can influence both the teacher-student relationship, and the extent to which the cultural background of the learners might influence the methodology adopted by the teacher.

Chapter 7 will consider some guidelines for designing training programmes in general before going on to examine specific examples of classroom activities. We can not possibly offer a comprehensive guide to activities that can be used in all types of intercultural training. Such an endeavour would take up several volumes. We do hope, however, that the examples we have included will inspire you to write or develop your own material.

6.2: Objectives

The objectives of this chapter are to:

➤ sensitise you to the ways in which national cultural values can influence educational values
➤ suggest how you may better adapt your teaching methods to suit the cultural values and expectations of your students.

Pre-reading task

Before you begin, consider the statement in the shaded box below. When you have finished the chapter, come back to this task and approach it again. Have your opinions changed in any way?

> *Communicative methodology is based on sound research and on a thorough understanding of how languages are best learned and taught. It can be used anywhere and with anybody.*

6.3: Culture, Education and Methodology

Hofstede's (1984, 1986, and 1991) research into cultural differences can be usefully applied to educational settings. This relevance is based on, "...the assumption that role patterns and value systems in a society are carried forward from the school to the job and back." (Hofstede, 1984). Hofstede (1986) argues that:

> As teacher/student interaction is such an archetypal human phenomenon, and so deeply rooted in the culture of a society, cross-cultural learning situations are fundamentally problematic for both parties.

Those of us in the field of intercultural education may sometimes be blind to these different perceptions of teacher-student interactions. For example, the low power distance British/American Business English trainer may give a talk about high and low power distance cultures and insist on treating their high power distance students as equals and confuse them in the process.

Holliday (1994a and 1994b) suggests that EFL teachers and EIB teachers and trainers are cross-cultural performers involved in training their students to be able to communicate cross-culturally using English. Teachers should, therefore, think and behave cross-culturally in the classroom. This need for cross-cultural sensitivity extends beyond language, literature, customs, festivals and gestures. It applies equally to methodology.

Holliday (1994a) suggests that communicative methodology is the product of a particular set of cultures. He terms these cultures the private-sector British, Australasian and North American (BANA) model of English language education. He contrasts this model with public-sector, non-Western ELT teaching situations which he terms Tertiary, Secondary and Primary (TESEP). If Holliday is correct and BANA-produced communicative methodology is culture bound, then its usefulness in TESEP situations should be questioned. For Holliday, it is clear that BANA methodology and TESEP classroom realities are often mismatched (see also unit 1, chapter 3 and unit 3, chapter 1). We can extend this debate by looking at Hofstede's (1991) dimensions of culture and how they can be applied to educational settings. You might also want to look at Richards and Rodgers (2001).

Hofstede (1984, 1991) uses his four dimensions of culture to identify

Unit 1: The Environment and Scope of EIB

a number of educational characteristics. Perhaps the most rewarding of these result from the power distance (PD), the individualist/collectivist (I/C) and uncertainty avoidance (UA) dimensions. In order to appreciate how the four dimensions can impact on student-teacher interactions, we shall look at the extreme differences between the dimensions while recognising that in many countries, the situation may be closer to the centre.

Question 1

From your own experience and your understanding of the power distance dimension, make a list of the characteristics of the student-teacher relationships in both high PD cultures and low PD cultures. What implications do these relationships have on appropriate methodology? When you have finished, compare your answers with the suggested answer in the Answers to Questions section.

These tendencies should encourage us to consider the extent to which the low power distance communicative methodology of BANA cultures is appropriate in high power distance TESEP situations. If it is appropriate, the assumption must be that either all students who study English as a foreign or second language share low PD communicative methodological values or that the values themselves have some kind of objective reality which transcends national culture. My own experience of working with high PD students (e.g. in Russia, Ukraine, Macedonia and with Chinese students in the UK) confirms the belief shared by Holliday and others that this is not the case. There is often a mismatch between communicative methodology and the expectations of high PD learners. If methodology is to be relevant to teachers, then the values underlying that methodology must be shared by the learners in the classroom.

Hofstede's (1984) findings about the educational characteristics resulting from the individualist/collectivist (I/C) dimension can be added to the picture gained from the PD dimension.

Question 2

From your own experience and your understanding of the collective/individualist dimension, make a list of the characteristics of individualist and collectivist classrooms. What implications do these characteristics have on methodology? When you have finished, compare your answers to our suggested answers in the Answers to Questions section.

Question 3

Repeat questions 1 and 2 above but this time, consider the masculine/feminine dimension and the strong/weak uncertainty avoidance dimension. Check your answers with the sample answers given in the Answers to Questions section.

We suggest that Hofstede's analysis of educational characteristics has clear implications for the teacher of EIB. The BANA situations, which we mentioned above, may be characterised by low power distance, individualist and weak uncertainty avoidance values. Communicative methodology is therefore also clearly linked to the same low PD, individualist and weak UA cultures. The converse is also clear. TESEP situations often exhibit high PD, collectivist and strong UA elements and may be linked to more traditional methodologies. We therefore suggest that teachers of EIB give serious thought to the methodology they adopt. Blindly teaching according to the dictates of a particular methodology could well lead to disruptive learners and ineffective learning.

Adapting material for other cultures

The following is a brief description of part of a lesson designed to develop reading skills in Business English.

- In groups, learners brainstorm ideas about a company and its products on the basis of its brochure illustrations.
- Groups give the teacher their ideas which are then presented on a flip chart.
- Teacher gives learners the name of the company.
- Individually, learners then modify their ideas about the company and its products.
- Individuals compare their ideas with a partner and the pair picks the best five ideas.

Unit 1: The Environment and Scope of EIB

> Learners read the brochure and decide which of the five ideas still seem appropriate.

Question 4

> *With regard to the lesson outline above, consider the following:*
> - *the function of the teacher*
> - *what is expected of the learners*
> - *student groupings*
> - *lesson results*
>
> *What are the cultural values underlying this part of the lesson as it is at the moment?*

Question 5

> *As it stands, the lesson might work well in Sweden, the UK, and the US. Now imagine you want to give a similar lesson in South Korea. How would you adapt the lesson and why?*

6.4 Conclusions

In this chapter we have tried to indicate how you should adapt materials in order to suit the culture in which you are working. Of course, some of you will be working with a cultural mix, and this mix will complicate matters. The important thing is, therefore, to be aware of the different educational values present in your classroom and to try and involve everyone in the teaching and learning process by using a variety of procedures and techniques. In my experience, the wide variety of cultures is likely to be present in classrooms in the UK, and I have found that most learners tend to be more flexible abroad than they are when at home. We suggest that you repay that flexibility by demonstrating your own.

6.5: Answers to Questions

Question 1
Low PD educational situations tend to be less formal, more participatory and more student centred than in high PD situations. Moreover, low PD situations are

inclined to favour communicative methodology while high PD tend to favour more traditional methodologies.

High PD educational situations tend to be characterised by teacher-centred education, in which teachers transfer their wisdom to the students. Students are not expected to initiate communication. Teachers tend to be respected in and out of classroom and are not to be openly contradicted. Formal lectures are appreciated.

Question 2
Hofstede (1984) claims that individualist classrooms tend to be more competitive with a willingness on the part of students to articulate personal opinions. Teachers who expect active participation from students may be disappointed when confronted with students from collectivist cultures. According to Hofstede, students in collectivist cultures conceive of themselves as being part of a group, and thus, it is illogical for them to speak up unless sanctioned by the group to do so. The elicitation of student responses is a feature of individualist cultures, where personal opinions are valued and everyone is expected to have one. In collectivist cultures, on the other hand, Hofstede claims that opinions are predetermined by group membership. Inexperienced teachers who are unaware of these cultural differences may be mystified and frustrated at their students' reluctance to participate in lessons.

It may seem that some techniques which are central to communicative methodology, for example, collaborative pair and groupwork, would be well suited to collectivist classrooms. This assumption may be misleading since it equates such activities with a collectivist mindset. However, research (e.g. Slavin et al 1985; Cowie and Rudduck 1988; Bennett and Dunne 1992) suggests that collaborative pairwork is as much a product of individualist cultures as other aspects of communicative methodology. Hofstede maintains that in individualist classrooms, the task prevails over the group structure arranged to achieve the outcome, i.e. groups are formed on an ad hoc basis depending on the task itself, student skills, personalities and levels. Conversely, in collectivist cultures, group structures prevail over the task, i.e. groups are formed on a more fixed basis depending on loyalties to family, religion and race. Thus, teachers whose methodology is based on ad hoc groupings may be disillusioned by the group inflexibility of students in collective classrooms.

Question 3
According to Hofstede, classrooms in feminine cultures tend to be characterised by student modesty, and friendly, approachable teachers. On the other hand, classrooms in masculine cultures tend to be characterised by student assertiveness and more distant teachers. Communicative methodology displays characteristics common to both aspects of the F/M dimension. It favours the friendly, approachable teacher of feminine cultures and the assertive student of masculine cultures. We might also add that in masculine cultures, teachers may encourage competition and openly praise the winners.

With regard to the uncertainty avoidance (UA) dimension we can say that low uncertainty avoidance learners tend to dislike too much structure and strict timetables. They also tend to dislike precise objectives and favour descriptive analysis and open-ended learning situations. The high uncertainty avoidance learner, on the other hand, tends to prefer structured activities and strict timetables. They also tend to favour precise objectives and prescriptive analysis, and prefer situations where there is one

Unit 1: The Environment and Scope of EIB

clear answer. Moreover, the favoured methodology of the low UA classroom is communicative whereas the high UA classroom tends to prefer more traditional approaches.

Question 4
- The teacher functions as facilitator (low PD) rather than as "guru" (high PD).
- Students are expected to speak up (individualist) and groupings and pairings are on an ad hoc basis (individualist).
- Activities are open ended with little resolution (low UA).
- All these characteristics conform to those of communicative methodology.

Question 5
South Korea can be characterised by the following dimensions:
- high power distance
- collective
- strong uncertainty avoidance.

In high PD classroom cultures, there may need to be more teacher-managed learning, e.g. through the provision of "correct answers" and clear tasks. In collectivist classroom cultures, because the lessons may need to be more teacher centred, there may be a reduced role for elicitation, and a need for greater sensitivity in the arrangement of collaborative work. In strong UA situations, open-ended tasks may be inappropriate, and grammar, vocabulary and correct pronunciation may need to be taught more overtly.

In practical terms, the lesson might be approached in the following manner if taught in South Korea. The teacher:
- gives students a copy of the company's brochure complete with name
- gives students five possible summaries of the company and its products
- asks students to decide which of the five possibilities represents a summary of the company
- gives students the vision statement and ask them to skim read to confirm which of their predictions are accurate
- gives students the correct answer.

Unit 1: The Environment and Scope of EIB

Chapter 7

Culture and the Classroom - 2

7.1: Introduction
7.2: Objectives
7.3: Designing Programmes - General Considerations
7.4: Designing Programmes - Ideas and Specific Workshops
7.5: Conclusions
7.6: Answers to Questions
7.7: Appendices.

7.1: Introduction

In the previous chapter we looked at how the cultural background of students can influence the methodology adopted by the teacher. This chapter goes a stage further by considering some guidelines for designing training programmes in general. We then examine specific examples of classroom activities.

7.2: Objectives

The objectives of this chapter are to:

Unit 1: The Environment and Scope of EIB

- suggest frameworks in which your intercultural training can take place
- give some examples of training workshops which will spark off your own creative ideas.

Pre-reading task

Before you begin, consider the questions in the shaded box below. The questions are designed to focus your attention on some of the main points in the chapter.

> 1. *A good intercultural trainer needs only to have a detailed understanding of the various models of national culture. What do you think?*
> 2. *Role-play, simulations and case studies are too open ended to use effectively in the training room. Learners need good lecturers who are able to give the "right" answers. What is your opinion?*

7.3: Designing Programmes - General Considerations

Cross-cultural training courses can be long or short, deep or shallow, for multicultural or monocultural groups, internally or externally focused, free-standing or part of a longer programme. In fact, they can be so flexible that it is hard to define them. From a theoretical point of view, the development of intercultural skills in EIB should focus on:

> ...the manager's ability to engage in effective cross-cultural interactions to the extent that such interactions are effective and misunderstandings and inappropriate behaviour are minimised, if not eradicated altogether. (Harris and Kumra, 2000)

The challenge for those wishing to prepare managers for this task is to determine which skills or competencies will enable them to do it. Ruben (1989) suggests that there are three key dimensions to intercultural competence. These are: building and maintaining relationships, transferring information and gaining compliance. Hofstede (1984) builds upon this analysis and proposes seven key

Unit 1: The Environment and Scope of EIB

cross-cultural skills. These are:

1. the capacity to communicate respect
2. the capacity to be non-judgmental
3. the capacity to accept the relativity of one's own knowledge
4. the capacity to display empathy
5. the capacity to be flexible
6. the capacity for turn-taking
7. tolerance for ambiguity.

Pause for thought

> *Think carefully about Hofstede's (1984) seven key skills. Can these skills really be taught? Maybe some of them can be taught. Which ones?*

There are a number of challenges with regard to teaching Hofstede's seven key skills. For example, some learners can be actively antagonistic to the notion that their cultural values are not the norm. Therefore, these learners may never develop the capacity to accept cultural relativity. Further, some learners may be resistant to the idea that self-awareness is a first step towards learning how to operate in other cultures. On top of this, tolerating ambiguity, for example, is not something that can be learned in a few days. Perhaps it can never be learned at all. The challenge may be all the more difficult if, as Grahn and Swenson (2000) point out:

> ...more managers are selected for cross-cultural assignments based on their technical and past managerial ability, rather than adaptiveness and ability to mobilise local resources to solve problems.

These challenges call for care and sensitivity on the part of the trainer. Oomkes and Thomas (1992) identify the following traits and skills for the successful intercultural trainer:

- acceptance of other people and a genuine desire to help them
- an ability to observe and understand social and group processes
- organisational ability
- the ability to inspire others

Unit 1: The Environment and Scope of EIB

- considerable experience of living abroad.

So what approach do you take to your training programmes? Gudykunst and Hammer (1983) see approaches as extending along two axes: experiential versus didactic, and culture-specific versus culture-general.

The experiential approach is based on the view that people learn best by doing (Kolb et al, 1991). Individuals are provided with situations and experiences that resemble as closely as possible the situations and experiences they are likely to encounter when dealing with people from other cultures. The types of approach used here would include role-play, simulation and self-assessment. The advantage of this approach rests in moving participants away from being information receivers to being active participants in a planned set of behaviours.

The didactic approach is based on the belief that a cognitive understanding is necessary before people can effectively interact with those from other cultures. This understanding can be developed through more traditional approaches to information-giving, for example: lectures, videos and group discussions.

Culture-general training concerns providing people with information they can use when finding themselves in any new culture. Culture-specific training aims to provide information to individuals about a single culture.

Clearly, the approach you adopt will depend on the particular group you are dealing with. My own intercultural training programmes tend to mix the experiential and the didactic approaches. The exact nature of the mix will depend on, for example: the group, the mix of cultures and learning styles, the time available and the needs of the participants.

Whichever approach you decide to take, there are a number of useful frameworks that can help you to structure your training sessions. Trompenaars (1993) suggests the following framework.

- It begins by recognising differences.
- It continues by the search for similarities.
- It creates solutions which involve synergy.

Trompenaars' framework is included in that of Estienne (1997). This approach consists of three elements.

1. Developing a mindset which is global.

Unit 1: The Environment and Scope of EIB

2. Working through a model of cross-cultural reconciliation.
3. Emphasising relational skills.

Another technique for creating cultural synergy is proposed by Adler (1991). This technique consists of six elements.

1. Describing the situation.
2. Determining the underlying cultural misconceptions.
3. Assessing cultural overlap.
4. Creating culturally synergistic alternatives.
5. Selecting alternative.
6. Implementing the selected alternative.

These three techniques are by no means mutually exclusive and they can form useful frameworks for your future intercultural communication skills courses. What the techniques above have in common is a familiarity with the models of cultural diversity, and learners need to be fully conversant with, for example, the work of Hofstede (1991) and Hall (1990).

The next step will depend on the specific needs of the learners. However, given that cross-cultural skills in EIB centre on the manager's ability to engage in cross-cultural interactions, the minimum recommendation is that learners become aware of non-verbal behaviour and learn some basic phrases in the local language. However, this will not be enough for those who have to chair meetings, negotiate or give presentations in a new cultural environment.

In the next section we shall focus on the needs of the international manager who is required to work abroad or who works from "home" but who interacts regularly with people from other cultures. We shall therefore look at:

➢ raising awareness of cultural differences
➢ introducing key cross-cultural frameworks (e.g. Hofstede, 1984)
➢ providing guidelines for specific cross-cultural training programmes.

7.4: Designing Programmes - Ideas and Specific Workshops

According to Hofstede (1991), the acquisition of intercultural communication skills passes through three phases.

1. Awareness that we all carry around with us a particular mental software because that was how we were brought up.
2. Knowledge about other cultures and their software.
3. Skills - this means, awareness plus knowledge, plus practice.

In this section, we shall, to a large extent, follow Hofstede's (1991) three phases. This means that we will:

- look at activities that help break the ice before we begin
- consider ways of presenting models of culture
- look at techniques that will help develop intercultural awareness and communication skills.

Breaking the ice

When people meet for the first time, there is usually a degree of nervousness. All societies have developed greetings rituals. These rituals may be brief or elaborate, but they have common purposes. These purposes are:

- to create a favourable impression
- to make time to observe the other person's behaviour
- to confirm one's own self image and place in society
- to help the formation of the relationship.

The same things happen in new classroom groups, and you can help facilitate the purposes above. To do this, you should offer class members the chance to engage in icebreaking activities. You should give your class:

- a safe, clear and acceptable structure
- conversation subjects that are relatively harmless but interesting
- enough opportunity for making and receiving first impressions
- something to relieve the tension

Unit 1: The Environment and Scope of EIB

➢ the chance to laugh.

Before starting any complex icebreakers, you may want to try a simple introductory exercise. For example, you could have participants go round the room to exchange names and introduce themselves. If the group is heterogeneous, you might ask them to demonstrate how people greet each other in their culture.

The following exercise, which has been adapted from Oomkes and Thomas (1992), is more complex. It is a good example of an activity than can be used to introduce cultural differences and to show how these differences can influence individual values and behaviour.

➢ Arrange participants in a circle, and ask them to write down the first five words that come to mind when they think of their country. You then ask the participants to read out their lists and to give some explanation where necessary.
➢ Ask participants to introduce themselves in their own language, and to behave as they would in their own countries. You can then ask them to demonstrate any differences in behaviour when they meet, for example, older or younger members of their society, men or women. You could also ask them to explain these differences.
➢ Ask participants to work in sub-groups. They should then explain aspects of their culture to each other. You can decide on the topics. These may be, for example: how children are raised, how old people are cared for, how responsibilities are divided between family members.

I have used this exercise several times with heterogeneous groups and it works very well, especially if you use it to spark off a discussion about cultural values and norms. This will then lead in to your presentation of models of cultural differences. Clearly, this exercise can be adapted in many ways in order to suit the particular cultural mix of your group.

Pause for thought

> *How could you use the three small role-plays below as icebreakers?*
>
> *1A You recently saw a film (choose any film you know) and want to tell your partner everything that happened. You only have*

Unit 1: The Environment and Scope of EIB

about 5 minutes, so it is important that your partner listens while you tell the story. Tell them all about the film. Be aware of how you feel about your partner as you communicate.

1B
Your partner wants to tell you all about the film they have just seen, but your purpose in this activity is to interrupt them as much as possible. Do not worry about being rude - just talk about anything you like - the weather, football, even fashion if you can't think of anything else, but keep interrupting them!

2A
Talk to your partner about something you have in common that will help you establish rapport with him/her - football, relationships, even the weather if you can't think of anything else. While you are talking, stand very close and touch your partner as much as possible. Keep this up for about 5 minutes.

2B
Talk to you partner about something of interest to you both. Be aware of how you feel about your partner as you communicate.

3A
Talk to your partner about something you have in common that will help you establish rapport with them – football, relationships, even the weather if you can't think of anything else. While you are talking, keep constant eye contact with your partner. Don't be afraid of staring. Keep this up for about 5 minutes.

3B
Talk to you partner about something of interest to you both and try and establish some rapport. Be aware of how you feel about your partner as you communicate

Oomkes and Thomas (1992) include many more ideas for icebreaking activities. You are recommended to consult the book and Hofstede et al (2002) and use or adapt the activities as necessary.

Presenting models of culture

When you present models of national culture, you will probably find that it is not too difficult to engage the interest of the participants, especially if you ensure that your presentation is focused on the cultures represented in your group. However, you can expect to come up against a variety of obstacles and challenges. The first of these is prejudice - a shared "we/they" contrast in which "they" are always wrong. This makes "we" feel better about ourselves. Discussing prejudice in the training room is a risky business. It places a question mark against a person's self image and view of the world, and can sometimes provoke resistance or hostility.

If prejudice is an attitude, then discrimination is behaviour. Oomkes and Thomas (1992) define discrimination as, "...subordination of persons or groups on criteria that are irrelevant to the situation, and which may offend moral criteria as well."

The third obstacle you are likely to encounter in the classroom is stereotyping. A stereotype is a fixed idea or opinion based on limited or false evidence. Frequently, the characteristics of one person are attached to all the people of the same nationality or race. It seems that people need stereotypes for several reasons.

- They offer security and safety. You no longer need to make up your own mind about where you belong and where your enemies are.
- They satisfy a need to feel superior and to be part of a superior group.
- They confirm first impressions (usually made in childhood).

You will encounter prejudice, discrimination and stereotyping in the training room. You will recognise it by:

- inaccurate statements
- statements not based on facts
- statements directed against people who are different
- statements that testify to an inflexible belief or position.

When you present models of national culture, you may have to spend some time discussing prejudices, discrimination and stereotyping. Many of us are unaware of them but, once aware, we would be willing to change our behaviours and our attitudes. However, be prepared for the deep-seated prejudices that can not be changed. Your training programme may be able to highlight them but it can not be expected to remove them.

I have found, over the years, that the majority of participants on my courses favour a direct lecture-style approach to the presentation of models of national culture. At various times, I have tried all sorts of exercises (for example, matching, elicitation) but the most effective way is often the simplest, that is, just tell them. This is not to be prescriptive. You will find the method that best suits you, your group and your teaching style.

You can vary the straight lecture by giving a brief explanation of the four dimensions and then getting the participants (in groups) to show how the dimensions might manifest themselves in, for example, management, chairing meetings or communication style. You would then give them your suggested answers.

Another effective way of presenting models of culture (but more time consuming) is to give participants a questionnaire designed to focus on the aspects of culture you have decided to elicit. Such a questionnaire is shown in appendix 1. This questionnaire was adapted from the one used by Hofstede (1984) in his original research with IBM. The presentation consists of the following steps.

➢ E-mail the questionnaire to the participants before the start date and ask them to fill it in and bring it with them on the first day of training. In theory, this should work. In my experience it sometimes does not. Participants forget the questionnaire or they do not fill it in. Some even claim they did not receive it. It is, therefore, probably more realistic to administer the questionnaire in class.
➢ When the participants have finished the questionnaire you can collect the scores and plot them on a flip chart - one flip chart for each dimension. You can then pin the flips to the wall. In my experience, this exercise creates curiosity and interest, and is a great preparation for the presentation of cultural models.

Developing skills

This may be the most challenging part of your intercultural seminar. If you have a heterogeneous group, we recommend that you take account of the notion that different cultures will have different preferred ways of learning (see also unit 3, chapter 9). These learning styles have developed and have been rewarded over many years and they will not easily change (Berger, 1998). As a rough guide, the three most common preferred learning styles you are likely to encounter are:

1. instructional – lecture-based
2. consensus building - working in teams to achieve a collective view

Unit 1: The Environment and Scope of EIB

3. individualistically based debate and the giving and receiving of feedback.

Those who prefer the lecture-based style of learning may expect the teacher to impart information while the role of the students is simply to absorb that information. There may well be resistance to such activities as role-play, simulations and case studies. There is a danger that, improperly handled, such activities can lack focus and direction, and can be perceived as being a waste of class time. If you decide to use an activity-based learning approach, we strongly advise you to clearly specify the learning outcomes and to state why the approach you are using is the most effective way of achieving those outcomes. Having said that, there may still be considerable resistance to classroom simulations, role-plays and case studies in, for example: Germany, China and Japan. For more on using role-play and simulations in the classroom, see unit 3, chapter 6.

Many case studies can also be used as role-plays or simulations and vice versa. Rees and Porter (2002) suggest that using case studies and/or role-plays will have a number of benefits.

- They help develop diagnostic skills - that is, they can develop effective problem-solving skills. In particular, they can help participants learn to identify the problem itself and to distinguish it from the symptoms.
- Cases and role-plays foster a depth of learning that is not easily achieved by other methods.
- They enable learners to apply their knowledge by involving them. This in turn will motivate them.
- Using cases and role-plays is an effective use of class time.
- They will help develop teamworking.
- Post-case analysis can be used to highlight any number of intercultural communication problems or team-working problems.

One of the challenges that you may face when you want to use role-plays, cases and simulations is that while you may consider it appropriate to use, for example, a case study, there may not be one available. One solution is to write your own. Another solution is to adapt what is already available. Whatever you do, make sure that:

- you know which aspects of communication you wish to focus on

Unit 1: The Environment and Scope of EIB

- the case is relevant to your group of learners
- you write them in international English.

Question 1

> *Look at the case study and the observation sheets in appendix 2. This has been adapted from Hofstede (1991). I used this case successfully in a training programme I ran for a heterogeneous group of managers in Frankfurt, Germany. I used the case study after I had presented Hofstede's dimensions of national culture. I adopted the following procedure.*
> - *I divided the group of fourteen into two groups of seven.*
> - *To each group I attached two observers who were to give feedback on the activity.*
> - *I appointed a chairperson to each team.*
> - *I gave them about fifteen minutes to individually read the case and to think about it.*
> - *I gave them thirty minutes to solve the problem as a group.*
> - *I asked the chairpersons for feedback.*
> - *I asked the observers to give their feedback.*
> - *General discussion.*
>
> *What do you think I used the case to focus on?*

The case study described above is rather lengthy and may not be appropriate in all situations. You might also consider using short role-plays as critical incidents. Mead (1994) includes several examples of these and you can adapt his to suit your situation or you can make up your own. The aim of these critical incidents should be to:

- spotlight situations which are relevant to learners
- spotlight differences between cultures
- encourage learners to practise appropriate behaviour in intercultural situations.

You should explain the exercise before assigning roles. Preparation should take about five minutes and the role-play itself about ten minutes. The discussion and analysis afterwards, perhaps with examples of behaviour taken from a video, should take longer. You can encourage the participants to talk about how they felt during the role-play while other members of the class should be encouraged to

Unit 1: The Environment and Scope of EIB

comment on what they observed.

Question 2

You have decided to use the situation below (in smaller print) in your programme. Your class consists of Europeans, Americans and Chinese managers from a multinational IT company. Which aspects of intercultural differences could the situation be used to focus on?

Situation
You have been working on a foreign assignment for six months now and you have identified some problems in your department. Staff are not highly motivated and you feel this is due to overwork and low pay. You think you have some really good suggestions for improvement and you have decided to talk to your line manager. Your proposal concerns a new overtime system and a new system of pay rewards which, you feel, will greatly improve the efficiency of the department. Furthermore, you think that some of the people in the department are not up to the job. Some of them are at an age where they might be encouraged to take early retirement. When you are ready, speak to your boss. What will you tell your boss, how will you say it, where will you say it and how will you structure what you say?

Pause for thought

Here is another critical incident - one that is close to home for lecturers and teachers. I have adapted this from Oomkes and Thomas (1992). Which aspects of intercultural communication skills would you focus on here?
Students.
You are not very happy with your lecturer/teacher. He is:
➤ *too friendly*
➤ *speaks with a strong Scottish accent*
➤ *speaks too fast*
➤ *never gives the structure of the lecture*
➤ *never gives handouts or lecture summaries.*
The lecturer once said, "If you have any problems please speak to me directly." Well, you and two other students decide to do just that.
Lecturer
You are new to the university and you are not used to working with international students. You find your students attentive but

Unit 1: The Environment and Scope of EIB

> *rather passive. For example, they never ask you questions after the lecture. Also, you have difficulty understanding some of the Asians because of their strong accents. One day, a group of Asians comes to you - they clearly want to say something.*

Critical incidents are a very useful tool for the intercultural trainer. Other short activities can also be used to great effect. Such activities can be used to focus on the particular needs of a group of learners.

Question 3

> *Look at the following questions. I gave them out to groups of participants to discuss before presenting models of culture. The group was heterogeneous. What, in your opinion, was the focus of the class?*
> - *What is a manager?*
> - *What is a leader?*
> - *Is there a difference between managers and leaders?*
> - *What are the functions of a manager? Make a list and then prioritise the functions.*

One aspect of intercultural communication skills that I have been frequently called upon to teach is intercultural presentation skills. The way I teach this is similar to the way I adapt lessons, lesson content, and teaching style when teaching other cultures.

In Germany, I was often asked to suggest ways in which Germans could make more effective presentations to Americans. The classes were usually monocultural (Germans) and these are the steps I followed.

1. I asked the Germans to prepare a short presentation about their jobs.
2. I asked the Germans to make a list of the elements of a good presentation in Germany. We usually ended up with a list that looked something like this. A Good presentation in Germany:
   - focuses on content
   - is factual and logical
   - has detailed visual aids
   - is very formal
   - is serious
   - has a direct beginning

- has detailed explanations.
3. I then presented the relevant parts of Hofstede's (1991) dimension of culture - uncertainty avoidance.
4. The next step was to ask the class to make a list of items that would make a good presentation in the US. We usually ended up with a list that looked something like this. A Good Presentation in the US:
    - focuses on the listener
    - is personal and enthusiastic
    - has simple visual aids
    - uses personal examples
    - is humorous
    - starts with a joke
    - has short and simple language.
5. The next step was to ask the class to deliver the presentation they gave at the start of the session but to adapt it to suit an American audience.

For the experienced trainer, we urge you to try out some of the commercially available business games. For example, you might want to look at Smith and Golden (1994a); Smith and Golden (1994b) and Keys, Edge and Wells (1991). Finally, you might want to look at Hofstede et al, (2002). This volume presents training that uses all of Hofstede's dimensions.

7.5: Conclusions

All trainers collect material, and I am no exception. Many exercises I use have been taken from other sources. Others I have written myself. Most, if not all of these have been adapted over the years and changed in the light of experience. Almost all of them will have to be adapted again to suit the requirements of the next course and the one after that.
What we have attempted to do in this chapter is to stimulate your own ideas and to give you a basic framework which you can use to prepare materials for your group.

Unit 1: The Environment and Scope of EIB

7.6: Answers to Questions

Question 1
I used the case to focus on intercultural teambuilding, and to highlight how differences in values can impact on the conduct of a meeting. In particular, I focused on problem-solving, and how different cultures may see different problems. After the case, we went on to consider how the team could learn to work together more effectively. For this purpose I used Adler's (1991) model of cultural synergy.
- Describe the situation from one's own cultural perspective.
- Determine the underlying cultural assumptions.
- Assess the cultural overlap.
- Create culturally synergistic alternatives.
- Select an alternative.
- Implement the culturally synergistic solution.

Question 2
With so many different cultures represented in the group, this would be an ideal opportunity for you to highlight the differences between high- and low-context cultures and to discuss the implications of this for teamworking. The Asian students may even tell you that it would be inappropriate to speak directly to the boss, and that a third party should be involved - someone who has influence at managerial level. Good! This is exactly what needs to be brought out into the open and discussed.

Question 3
The questions were designed to focus on management style and how this may be influenced by culture. We also considered communications between managers and subordinates, giving feedback to managers and how all of this can cause difficulties in multinational companies.

Unit 1: The Environment and Scope of EIB

7.7: Appendices

Appendix 1: value orientations - a questionnaire

The questionnaire below consists of FOUR parts. Each part contains five statements. Each statement is followed by a scale from 1 - 5. For each statement, circle the number that, in general, describes your home community. Please remember to describe your country and its values. Please do NOT describe company culture.
For example:

Relationships at work are informal and people use first names (e.g. Tom, Pierre, Antonio).

1_____2_____3_____4_____5

If you choose 1, the statement accurately describes your home community.

If you choose 2, the statement is partly true of your home community.

If you choose 3, the statement is not really true of your home community.

If you choose 4, the statement is mostly untrue of your home community.

If you choose 5, the statement is completely untrue of your home community.

When you have finished each part, add up the numbers that you have circled and put the final number in the space marked "score."

Unit 1: The Environment and Scope of EIB

Part 1

Statement 1
In school, students treat their teachers informally and as equals.

1_____2_____3_____4_____5

Statement 2
Decision-making in institutions is democratic.

1_____2_____3_____4_____5

Statement 3
In schools and universities, teachers will negotiate course content with their students.

1_____2_____3_____4_____5

Statement 4
Bosses and subordinates, teachers and students will usually call each other by their first names.

1_____2_____3_____4_____5

Statement 5
Large income/salary differences in society are thought to be bad.

1_____2_____3_____4_____5

SCORE_____

Unit 1: The Environment and Scope of EIB

Part 2

Statement 1
People are generally comfortable in situations where there is no clear answer.

1_____2_____3_____4_____5

Statement 2
Students are concerned with good discussions and not with correct answers.

1_____2_____3_____4_____5

Statement 3
Teachers and managers can say, "I don't know."

1_____2_____3_____4_____5

Statement 4
There should not be more rules and regulations than are absolutely necessary.

1_____2_____3_____4_____5

Statement 5
There is a tolerance of different people and ideas. What is different is interesting.

1_____2_____3_____4_____5

SCORE_____

Unit 1: The Environment and Scope of EIB

Part 3

Statement 1
Children learn to think in terms of "I" and adults value personal development.

1_____2_____3_____4_____5

Statement 2
Personal opinions are highly valued and everyone is expected to have one.

1_____2_____3_____4_____5

Statement 3
Hiring and promotion decisions are based on skills and rules only.

1_____2_____3_____4_____5

Statement 4
Management is management of individuals.

1_____2_____3_____4_____5

Statement 5
The job/contract/task is more important than the relationship between people.

1_____2_____3_____4_____5

SCORE_____

Unit 1: The Environment and Scope of EIB

Part 4

Statement 1
The dominant values in society are material success and progress.

1_____2_____3_____4_____5

Statement 2
Teachers and managers are expected to be decisive and assertive.

1_____2_____3_____4_____5

Statement 3
Conflicts are resolved by fighting them out.

1_____2_____3_____4_____5

Statement 4
We live so that we can work.

1_____2_____3_____4_____5

Statement 5
There are only a few women in positions of managerial authority.

1_____2_____3_____4_____5

SCORE_____

Unit 1: The Environment and Scope of EIB

Appendix 2: case study situation – Eisenmann GmbH

You are a group of consultants who have been called in on an emergency assignment by the general manager of the company below. You have been asked to report your initial findings after just one day in the factory. This is what you have found.

Eisenmann GmbH is a middle-sized, textile-printing company south of Stuttgart. It is having a hard time at the moment, and the future looks bad. Cloth, usually imported from China, is printed in multicoloured patterns according to the requirements of customers. Most of these are firms producing fashion clothing for the local market in Southern Germany. The company is run by a general manager, to whom three functional managers report: one for design and sales, one for manufacturing and one for finance and personnel. The total work force numbers about 350.

The working climate in the firm is poor. There are frequent arguments and confrontations between the sales and manufacturing managers. The manufacturing manager is interested in developing a smooth production process and he does not take kindly to product changes. He has a preference for grouping customer orders into large batches. Being obliged to change colour and/or design means that the machines have to be cleaned. This takes production time away and also wastes costly dyestuffs. For the manufacturing manager, the worst scenario is when he has to change from a dark colour-set to a light colour-set. Just one bit of dark-coloured dye will show on the cloth and ruin the product quality. Therefore, the manufacturing planners try to start on a clean machine with the lightest shades and gradually move towards darker ones, postponing the need for an overall cleaning round as long as possible.

The design and sales manager is under a lot of pressure. He has to attempt to satisfy his customers in a market which has become almost impossibly competitive. Most of the customers are fashion-clothing firms, and they are well known for constant short-term planning changes. As their supplier, the printing company often receives requests for rush orders. Even when these orders are small and unlikely to be profitable, the sales manager hates to say "no". The customer may go to a competitor and then, the printing firm will miss that big order which the sales manager is sure will follow. He simply can not afford to act like this in such a business environment. If he does, he thinks that sooner or later, they will all be out of a job. The problem is that rush orders usually upset the manufacturing manager's schedules. These orders oblige him to print short runs of dark colour-sets on beautifully clean machines. He is thus required to have the production operators constantly cleaning the machines.

There are frequent arguments between the two managers over whether a certain rush order should or should not be taken into production. The conflict is not only limited to the department heads; production personnel publicly express doubts about the competence of the sales people and vice versa. In the cafeteria, production and sales people will not sit together, although they have known each other for years.

The general manager wants your initial findings. He is expecting you to provide him with the following.

➢ A clear identification of the problem with the information you have at this time.
➢ Suggested options for solving the problem and your preferred group solution.

At the end of the time, you will be expected to give a one-minute summary of your conclusions.

Unit 1: The Environment and Scope of EIB

Observation Sheets for Eisenmann GmbH

Observer 1 will look at group proceedings and give feedback on the following.

- How the group reacted to the lack of information.
- How the group communicated.
- Whether there was a clear and explicit structure to proceedings.
- The role of the chairperson, for example: was s/he impartial, a facilitator or dictator?
- How well people listened to others.
- Whether expert information was given and/or used.
- Whether all the information was used.
- Whether there was an efficient procedure chosen for hearing all solutions and for discussing them.
- Whether a process for making the decision was agreed on, for example: consensus? Majority voting?

Observer 2 will look at proceedings from a cultural point of view.

- Did the chairperson act according to his/her cultural conditioning, for example: high/low power distance?
- Did you notice a connection between the solutions presented by delegates and their cultural conditioning?
- Was there a struggle for power among group members or did they show a willingness to compromise? Is there a relationship to cultural conditioning here?
- Did group members show sensitivity to possible differences in culture or did they simply seem to think that others were wrong or stupid? In other words, was the impression given that there is only one way to do things around here and we have it and you do not?
- Did group members show interest in knowing why other people thought differently? Did they simply try to change other opinions?

Unit 1: The Environment and Scope of EIB

Chapter 8

Management of Programmes

8.1: Introduction
8.2: Objectives
8.3: The Nature and Peculiarities of the ELT/EIB Product
8.4: Educational Management and Business Management
8.5: Theories of Organisations
8.6: Conclusions
8.7: Answers to Questions.

8.1: Introduction

Essentially management in EIB in particular does not differ greatly from management in ELT in general. This is partly because most of the institutions in which EIB programmes take place will be ELT schools or ELT departments in further education colleges and universities. There are a few schools which focus on specialised language courses for international business but, as this chapter argues, the nature of these schools and their products differs little from the nature of ELT schools and their products. The most important distinction that needs to be made is between EIB programmes in private commercial organisations and EIB programmes in the public sector. Although these differences are not central to this chapter, where the differences occur, they are pointed out.

We argue that management skills that are taken from the world of industry are not necessarily appropriate to ELT institutions. We suggest that these institutions have special characteristics and that their management should reflect them.

There are probably hundreds of books on management. Despite these books and despite their promises, there is no such thing as perfection in management. Like teachers, managers have to continually strive to improve what they and others do together.

Schools and colleges are highly complex organisations. They contain two sets of people - staff and students, and these people interact in different ways. In addition, there is the relationship between the school or college and its social, political and economic environment. School management is, therefore, concerned with getting practical results in a context that is subject to these internal and external forces. This greatly complicates the manager's job.

This chapter does not attempt to provide simplistic answers to complex issues. It does attempt to introduce some of the major themes within the area of educational management and to encourage you to read around the topic. Finally, many of the ideas presented here reflect the views of this particular writer. It is hoped that you will challenge these views and develop your own.

8.2: Objectives

This chapter aims to sensitise you to:

- the nature of the EIB product
- educational and business management - similarities and differences
- the theory of organisations.

Pre-reading task

Before you begin, consider the questions in the shaded box below. They are designed to focus your attention on the topic.

> 1. What are the main objectives of the institution you work for?
> 2. What are your main reasons for working within this institution?

Unit 1: The Environment and Scope of EIB

> 3. *Consider your answers to questions 1 and 2 above. Do your own personal objectives conflict with the objectives of your institution? If the answer is yes, how do you deal with this conflict?*

8.3: The Nature and Peculiarities of the EIB Product

Pause for thought

> ➢ *What are people buying when they spend their money on a language course?*
> ➢ *Why should they go to your institution rather than another?*

The broad differences between services and goods

A school or university language department exists to provide an educational service to its students and/or other stake-holders, for example: employers, governments and parents. But what exactly is the nature of this service and how does it differ from goods?

Berry (1984) describes a good as an object, device or thing. When a good is purchased, something tangible is acquired, something that can be touched, seen and perhaps smelled.

Kotler (1967) defines a service as an act or performance that one party offers to another. This performance is essentially intangible and does not result in the ownership of anything. Its production may or may not be tied to a thing. For example, a meal in a restaurant combines both the intangible service element and the tangible food. On the other hand, a visit to a psychoanalyst results in nothing tangible, except perhaps, the psychoanalyst's visiting card.

Services are thus consumed and not possessed, although most market offerings are a combination of both tangible and intangible elements. It is whether the essence of what is being bought is tangible or intangible that determines its classification as a good or service.

Zeithaml et al (2005) suggest that the crux of service knowledge is to define the perceptions that characterise the service in the eyes of the various customer-groups. The determination of these perceptions should be a priority for all those involved in the ELT industry. This implies that both teachers and management must rely heavily on the tools and skills of psychology and sociology. Familiarity with these tools helps the tangible-product industry to determine the intangible product image; for example, consider advertising that promotes the image of a particular car or hamburger. For the ELT industry, the skills and tools of psychology and sociology must be applied in order to determine a fundamental and tangible reality.

> Ask yourself how much of the anticipation is for the course, and how much for other possible pleasures - leisure, people, a break from your usual job and home routine, good food and drink, new sights, sunshine, sports, etc. The point is that it is easy to think that what you are selling is the language course. However, in fact what the student is buying is not just the course, but the school, the town/region/..., and the whole experience. (Underhill and Impey, 1994)

Customer involvement in production and the structure of distribution

Generally, goods are produced first, then sold and then consumed. Services are usually sold first, then produced and consumed at the same time. When performing a service, customers are often actively involved in helping to create the "product". Within the context of ELT/EIB, this means co-operating with service personnel in the school.

The tangible-product industry stresses distribution; that is, distributing products to the right place at the right time and at the right price. Within service industries, it is more important to distribute them in the right way. It is essential for EIB/EFL teachers and managers to understand this difference. Services, especially ELT services, are bound up with their human representatives. Thus, for many clients of language institutions, the teacher may often be perceived as the service itself, or at least, a very important part of it. The implications of this for EIB management and marketing management are far-reaching and profound.

Quality control and evaluation

We noted above that the teacher and student in ELT institutions are integral parts of the experience and together, their performance makes up a large part of the service or "product". This makes it difficult for the provider to offer consistency. It also makes it difficult for both the provider and the consumer to evaluate quality of service. Bovee, Houston and Thill (1995) identify three ways that consumers may evaluate services.

1. Products with tangible attributes (e.g. restaurants and hotels) are high in search qualities, attributes that can be evaluated prior to purchase.
2. Experience qualities can only be assessed after the product has been consumed. Most services, including ELT/EIB services, are high in experience qualities.
3. Product attributes known as credence qualities can not be evaluated even after consumption. Services are accepted partly on faith by customers. Moreover, customers can not be entirely sure that the service has been effective. This may be particularly true of, for example, intermediate students of English (whether or not the course is business related) who are often heard to complain about their inability to measure progress.

Furthermore, the quality of teaching and the teacher's ability to satisfy the customer depends not only on how well the teacher performs but also on how well the consumer performs. Zeithaml (1984) and Zeithaml et al (2005) suggest that consumers will attribute some of their dissatisfaction to their own inability to perform their part of the service. Consumers may well complain less frequently about services than about tangible products due to the belief that they are partly responsible for their dissatisfaction.

Question 1

> *Consider the points raised by Zeithaml (1984) and Zeithaml et al (2005) and think about the following questions. Check your answers with our suggested answers in the Answers to Questions section.*
> 1. *How can any educational institution try to ensure that the consumers' performance will be satisfactory?*
> 2. *How effective are the course evaluation forms filled out by learners at the end of a course?*
> 3. *If you were marketing your school, would you promise high quality before the learners arrive? Why/why not?*

Unit 1: The Environment and Scope of EIB

The peculiar nature of the ELT/EIB product; namely, the involvement of the student in the production process, and difficulties with quality control and evaluation present a number of implications for the management of these services. It is to these that we will now turn.

8.4: Educational Management and Business Management

In order to understand what educational management is, we need first to consider what management is. Then, we need to consider what management is in an educational context. Rather than give answers to these questions, this section will ask you to develop your own responses and opinions.

There are many definitions of management. Consider the following definitions.

> Management is an activity involving responsibility for getting things done through other people. (Cuthbert, 1984)

> ...the management process is concerned with helping the members of an organisation to obtain individual as well as organisational objectives within the changing environment of the organisation. (Gray, 1979)

> Management is a continuous process through which members of an organisation seek to co-ordinate their activities and utilise their resources in order to fulfil the various tasks of the organisation as efficiently as possible. (Hoyle, 1981)

> ...school management is a highly practical activity concerned with creating effective organisational means to ensure that educational values, goals and intentions are put into practice. (Glatter et al, 1988)

From the above, you can see that different writers focus on different aspects of management. However, there is a frequent distinction between organisational aims and individual aims.

The traditional view of management is that it is something done by some people to other people. Adair (1988) suggests that managers have

Unit 1: The Environment and Scope of EIB

to maintain a balance between three broad sets of needs. These needs are task needs, group needs and individual needs.

Task needs are those which have to be satisfied in order for the organisation to successfully meet its objectives. Such tasks might involve managers in recruitment, marketing, financial planning and allocating resources.

Group needs are concerned with the organisation as a social unit. In order to meet task needs, group maintenance is vital and might involve managers in team-building, motivating, disciplining, delegating and training. Furthermore, if individual needs are not met, then the team or group is likely to be ineffective. Satisfying individual needs might involve the manager in motivating, praising, rewarding and developing.

Pause for thought

> ➢ *Can you recognise this traditional view of management in the management of the organisation you work for?*
> ➢ *Are you involved in any managerial tasks?*
> ➢ *How do you define success in your organisation?*
> ➢ *Does this fit with your school's definition of success?*

A significant proportion of ELT/EIB work is carried out in private institutions, and it may be argued that business management principles and the traditional view of management are applicable within these institutions. Furthermore, even within the public sector, many ELT/EIB departments in FE colleges and universities have a notable commercial orientation and increasingly reveal similarities to institutions in the private sector.

Everard and Morris (1990) suggest that, in the development of educational management, theorists and practitioners have drawn heavily on business management. Everard and Morris were writing of state sector education. However, the reasons for the reliance of educational management on business management are equally relevant to ELT/EIB institutions and may be explained as follows.

Handy and Aitken (1986) state that essentially, educational organisations and institutions are like any other organisations and as such, the theories and findings of organisational research may be appropriate to the running of schools.

Furthermore, the influence of free-market theories is infiltrating many aspects of our lives, and education is not excluded. If efficient running of the nation's economy is promoted by effective management, then it might seem appropriate to some ELT school managers to apply business management theory to their schools. This perceived appropriacy might be reinforced by the fact that education has little management theory of its own. This is particularly true of ELT/EIB. Until White (1991), there were no books dedicated to management in ELT.

Borrowing from the theory and practice of business/commercial management is not necessarily a bad thing. It is vital, however, that the borrowings fit comfortably with the educational enterprise. When the borrowings fail to respect any special characteristics which ELT/EIB institutions may have, good educational practice may be undermined and staff enthusiasm dampened by the imposition of an alien management structure.

Pause for thought

> ➢ *Are educational organisations different from business organisations? If so, how are they different?*
> ➢ *As an EFL/EIB teacher, do you see yourself as part of the educational community or as part of the business community? Where does ELT/EIB fit?*

Differences between business organisations and educational organisations

Most business organisations, in the final analysis, have one purpose: to make an acceptable level of profit. Some ELT organisations may also have this profit aim as their main objective. However, state sector colleges have a range of expectations placed on them. Some of these expectations may include: a custodial role, a certificating role, a socialising role and a role which aims to develop the whole person.

Pause for thought

> *Do you share these expectations? Do you feel that the ELT industry shares these expectations?*

Partly because of these expectations, it is not easy to identify criteria for monitoring success in a school. A commercial firm can discontinue an activity if it is unprofitable. But what about the poor performance of

Unit 1: The Environment and Scope of EIB

a fee-paying student of EIB at a British university? Can s/he be "discontinued"?

Another major difference between educational and business organisations is the way they perceive their roles. For commercial and industrial organisations, plant is investment while people are an expense. For educational organisations, the reverse in true. People are investment and plant is expense. Is this the case in your institution? Is there an important difference here between private, commercially run ELT organisations and public-sector ELT?

A further difficulty is the categorisation of the participants in education. Are learners workers, clients or products? Who are the customers? And what about teachers? Are they workers or managers? What about heads of departments? If teachers are managers, and learners are clients, then who are the workers?

Teachers have a variety of managerial tasks to perform. In the course of one lesson they are likely to present information, record activity, analyse progress, motivate, lead, assess, and control. Outside the classroom they will prepare, report, monitor, communicate with other staff, and act as part of a team. Teachers are also classroom managers in the sense that they practise the basic management skills of leadership, communication and decision-making. Once again, this raises the difficulty of categorising them in terms of business usage.

In addition, how are the learners to be seen? Are they workers who are participating in some kind of joint-venture? Are they clients who can be regarded as people being served by the organisation? Are they simply products, an output somehow shaped and developed by the organisation?

Pause for thought

> - *How do you view your students?*
> - *How do you view yourself?*
> - *Think about one working week. How much of your time is spent on management tasks?*
> - *Do you think that a good teacher will make a good manager? Where should ELT managers come from?*

To conclude this section, one of the problems we meet when discussing management within an educational context is that schools in general tend to differ from the business organisations in which most management theory and practice are grounded. In comparison with commercial organisations, the aims of a school are difficult to define, whereas the aims of a commercial organisation are relatively clear.

Within ELT, we must make a distinction between the public and private sector. The measurable outputs of the former tend to be in terms of academic achievement. The measurable outputs of the latter tend to include the financial as well as the academic. The issue is further complicated by the argument that the most significant objective of both public and private sector schools can not be quantified, and that their importance lies in long-term rather than short-term outcomes.

Another problem concerns the teachers themselves. They share a common professional background and they claim a measure of autonomy in the teaching and learning process. As professionals, teachers expect participation in the decision-making process within the organisation in which they work. It is to these organisations that we will now turn.

8.5: Theories of Organisations

Different management models within an organisation will give rise to different styles of management. Management style will, in turn, lead to different kinds of organisational culture. Handy (1978) suggests four types of organisational culture and he has applied his ideas to the characterisation of schools as organisations (Handy and Aitken, 1986).

Handy (1978) stresses that no culture is completely good or completely bad, and that few organisations have only one culture. They are more often a mix of all four, and what makes organisations different is the mix they choose. Handy's (1978) classification is important if we wish to consider in what ways organisational culture helps or hinders the achievement of objectives. Handy's four cultures are:

1. the power or club culture
2. the role culture
3. the person culture
4. the task culture.

The power culture is, perhaps, best imagined as a spider's web with the power at the centre and surrounded by circles of influence. The main priority of such a culture is meeting the aims and objectives of its head. Such a culture is led rather than managed. Owner-managed schools in the ELT industry tend to have a club culture.

Question 2

> *Within the ELT industry, what are the advantages and disadvantages of the power culture?*

The role culture resembles the stereotypical organisational chart in which role boxes are detailed with aims and objectives and are independent of the person who occupies the "box". This culture encourages stability and predictability and attracts those people who work best in secure and predictable environments. It may be that mature organisations, perhaps, have a lot of the role culture within them. There are many tasks in a school that require the routine and the uniform handling of a role culture.

Question 3

> *Which tasks within an ELT organisation might need a role culture?*

The third type of culture as defined by Handy (1978) is the **person culture**. The priority in the person culture is the individual and his/her talents rather than the organisation. Those who work in such cultures probably see themselves as independent professionals, who loan themselves to the organisation. Management in the person culture is management by consent. It is difficult to imagine an effective school operating as a person culture because schools depend on teams and people working together for a common purpose.

Finally, Handy describes the **task culture**. Management here is concerned with the continuous solving of problems. The task culture is therefore oriented towards groups of individual talents and resources being applied to a particular problem or project. The group can be disbanded or changed as the task changes. Handy suggests that such a culture thrives in situations where problem-solving is the job of the organisation. There are team leaders rather than managers.

Unit 1: The Environment and Scope of EIB

Pause for thought

> ➤ Which type of Handy's organisational culture would you like to work in?
> ➤ Which (if any) of these organisations would be best suited to EIB? Think about both the private sector and the public sector.

Handy and Aitken (1986) suggest that it is important that all members of a school need the motivation of feeling they are partners in the organisation. Teachers in particular need to feel valued as professional people. Thus, they think that schools should move towards task cultures.

> This will require different philosophies of management from the ones currently prevailing in most…schools. Interestingly, however, most modern businesses are moving away from hierarchies towards networks in response to the need for more flexibility and in order to give more room to the individual. It may be that in aping the bureaucracy of large businesses…schools have been adopting a theory of management that is already out of date. (Handy and Aitken, 1986)

This is a view supported by White (1991), who suggests that a task culture is essential for school management.

> …a task culture provides an exciting work environment and it may well be the case that a good school is one in which a task culture predominates. Indeed, some small, specialised schools, such as those offering tailor-made courses for specific clients or groups, would tend to require a task culture, since no two courses will be the same and small, flexible teams of staff would be needed to respond to constantly changing client needs. (White 1991, p. 21)

Underhill and Impey (1994) echo these views. They suggest that the top-down hierarchy is turned through ninety degrees so that instead of being at the bottom of the diagram, the front-line people, those who interface with the customers, are at the sharp end. All the other employees are behind them. The authors argue that front-line people are mainly teachers but also include all those who deal directly with the clients. Such an approach emphasises that teachers are crucial to an organisation. It also removes the hierarchy of superiors that places a manager above a teacher, and it emphasises the fact that we may all have different jobs but we are all working towards a common goal.

> So what do front-line people have to do with management? With a shared sense of purpose, and a clear sense of their own role in achieving that purpose, they are the management. It may not be only to the benefit of the individual teacher's professional development to ask more, know more and contribute more to the direction and management of the institution, it will be ultimately to the benefit of the organisation as a whole. (Underhill and Impey, 1994)

Similarly, Drucker (1955) focuses on the importance of front-line managers.

> The mangers on the firing line have the basic management jobs - the ones on whose performance everything else ultimately rests. Seen this way, the jobs of higher management are derivative; are in the last analysis, aimed at helping the firing-line manager do his job... it is the firing line manager in whom all authority and
> responsibility centre... (Drucker 1955, p.138)

Drucker points out, however, that although the objectives of a professional's job have to remain professional objectives, s/he must also make a contribution to the enterprise and know what the enterprise is. In other words, teachers should have a maximum of managerial vision and know and understand the business. If teachers are capable of seeing the objectives of the business they will understand better what the business demands of them as employees.

> Teacher training, both before and during the teaching career, will surely begin to include more material on management and organisations. (Handy and Aitken, 1986)

Thus, the onus should not be placed solely on current school management. Teachers must understand that in order to participate fully in the running of a school, their time and commitment will be required. In other words, participation in management is not something that can be accepted if and when a teacher feels like it. It is not enough for teachers to concern themselves entirely with their next class. They need, for example, to understand the efforts that have been made to get the students in the classroom in the first place, and to understand the contribution each person in the room has made to the school's finances.

It is argued that for the UK ELT industry to compete effectively in this new millenium, the industry needs a new type of teacher/manager who is skilled in teaching, sensitive to the learning process, is able to make a contribution to the management of the organisation and who understands how the school/department functions as an organisation.

Pause for thought

> *It could be argued that the views expressed by Underhill and Impey, White, Handy and Drucker reflect the cultures in which they work(ed). These cultures could be described as being low power distance, weak uncertainty avoidance, masculine and individualistic. Look again at the chapters on cultural differences. Do you think that the ideas expressed by these writers would be acceptable in all cultures?*

8.6: Conclusions

In order to remain competitive, the ELT industry needs to attend to its management so that it reflects the peculiarities that the industry has. It is suggested that ELT institutions pay particular and careful attention to the needs of students, their learning styles and cultural background.

It is also suggested that in order to promote a genuine orientation of the organisation to the customer-satisfaction process, the industry restructures its management and invites teachers to participate fully in the management process.

Experienced teachers can bring a range of skills to management; namely and among others: organisational skills, decision-making skills, leadership skills and communication skills. Perhaps management training of teachers should be the responsibility of existing professional

Unit 1: The Environment and Scope of EIB

bodies within the world of ELT. Such bodies as ARELS (Association of Recognised English Language Skills) and The British Council do offer workshops in aspects of management. These are steps in the right direction. They are needed and they are needed now if the ELT industry is to be prevented from going the same way, perhaps, as the British motor cycle industry.

8.7: Answers to Questions

Question 1
1. By careful selection.
2. Without some form of training in what to look for - not very effective.
3. No - you can never be entirely certain how the service provider and the consumer will interact.

Question 2
Advantages can include: quick decision-making, exciting place to work if you belong to the club, convenient way of running small organisations, personal culture with charismatic leader. Disadvantages can include: no good if you do not belong to the club, no good when the organisation gets bigger, and no good if the head is weak. There may also be problems with succession i.e. when a particularly charismatic central figure is replaced by one who lacks the leadership skills of the retiring person.

Question 3
Any part of the organisation which is set up to operate routine procedures might require a role culture. For example: registration of students, the collection of fees, ordering and payment of school materials, payment of staff and payment of gas, electricity, water and so on.

Unit 1: The Environment and Scope of EIB

Chapter 9

Marketing the EIB Product

9.1: Introduction
9.2: Objectives
9.3: Marketing Management
9.4: Conclusions.

9.1: Introduction

In this chapter we argue that marketing skills that are taken from the world of industry are not necessarily appropriate to ELT institutions. In the previous chapter we suggested that these institutions have special characteristics. It therefore follows that their marketing strategies should reflect these characteristics. Further, it is suggested that adoption of these strategies will require a re-evaluation of the roles of teachers and management, and a greater focus on students' learning styles and cultural backgrounds.

9.2: Objectives

At the end of this chapter you will have a better understanding of:

Unit 1: The Environment and Scope of EIB

- marketing services in general and the EIB service in particular
- how to customise the service
- accommodating learning styles.

Pre-reading task

Before you begin, consider the questions in the shaded box below. These are designed to introduce the main ideas in the chapter.

> - *Does your school have a policy for marketing?*
> - *Who is responsible for marketing in your school and how do they go about their job?*
> - *Do you think that a good teacher will make a good marketer?*

9.3: Marketing Management

What is marketing?

For the purposes of this chapter, marketing is here described as requiring:

- a genuine attention to customers' needs and wants
- satisfaction of those needs at a profit
- orientation of the whole organisation towards the customer-satisfaction process.

In chapter 8 we noted the broad difference between services and goods, and the nature and peculiarities of the EIB product. Those peculiarities included the involvement of the learners in the production process, and difficulties with quality control and evaluation (Zeithaml et al, 2005). These peculiarities present a number of important implications for the marketing of ELT/EIB programmes. (Before continuing, you might like to scan through the relevant sections of chapter 8).

The implications mentioned above concern: internal marketing, the managing of tangible evidence, the customisation of services, learning styles and cultural background.

Unit 1: The Environment and Scope of EIB

Internal marketing

Berry (1984) points out that in high-contact service businesses like ELT, the quality of the service is often inseparable from the quality of the service provider. As we noted earlier, the teacher is often perceived as the service provider. This means that the performance of the teacher has an enormous impact on perceptions of an institution's quality. Consequently, the ELT industry needs to pay special attention to the merits of employees and their performance. Marketers in the ELT industry should therefore be concerned with internal marketing as well as external marketing.

In essence, this means that the practice of marketing should be applied to the teachers in order to ensure that the best people are employed and retained, and that they do the best possible work. In this way, by satisfying the needs of the teachers, a school can upgrade its capabilities for satisfying the needs of the external customer. The successful school should first sell the job to employees before it can sell its services to customers.

Bovee, Houston and Thill (1995) mention five ways that can be used to motivate employees to perform well. These are described as: money, valuable rewards, symbolic rewards, celebrations and meaningful work.

We would add another fundamental element. That element concerns management style and management attitude. How school management looks upon its teachers, handles them, communicates with them and rewards them is fundamental to success in ELT marketing. White (1991) stresses the importance of all employees in ELT schools taking a customer-oriented approach. Good marketing, White maintains, is a matter of attitude and organisation rather than intelligence or ability. According to White, the essential fact for ELT marketers to grasp is that success lies in a real belief, which runs through the entire school, that it gives superior value for money. Internal marketing should strive to ensure that this commitment is achieved and that the most effective style of management is utilised to realise it.

Pause for thought

> *What motivates you at work? What de-motivates you?*

Unit 1: The Environment and Scope of EIB

Managing tangible evidence

Berry (1984) points out that because goods are tangible, they are easier to evaluate, prior to purchase, than services. The intangibility of an ELT/EIB course prompts prospective students to be attentive to tangibles associated with the school for clues of the institution's nature and quality.

A prime responsibility for the marketer in an ELT school or department is to manage these tangibles so that the proper signals are conveyed about the service (Zeithaml et al, 2005). Thus, if product-based marketers emphasise abstract qualities associated with the product, the ELT marketer should focus on, and enhance, realities through tangible clues. In other words, it is the marketing of evidence that has priority.

Environment is a good example. The appearance of the school can play a crucial role in influencing the reality of the service in the mind of the customer. The style of furnishing as well as the decor can play an important part. If learners are staying with families, a warm welcome is vital for both children and adults.

We saw earlier that in ELT/EIB institutions, the service is inextricably bound up with its human representation. The consumer is unable to distinguish between them. Thus, the appearance and behaviour of the service provider are crucial.

Other forms of evidence might seem trivial. For example, letters, the letter-head and the quality of the paper are often perceived as peripheral to the main marketing plan. But these can powerfully influence perceptions of service quality and can convey the reality of the service to the potential customer.

Price is also a clue to the quality of a service. The relative absence of material data with which to evaluate a school makes price an important indicator of quality. Setting the right price can be critical in selling the EIB service to multi-national companies. Prices which are set too low can be perceived as indicating poor quality.

Advertising and promotion of services present problems and opportunities to the ELT marketer. Service elements are abstract and the marketer should ensure that they are perceived as real by building a case from tangible evidence. It may be unwise to advertise an abstract service with more abstraction such as, "A sound needs analysis" or "The communicative approach." These abstractions may not help the potential student form a reality nor do they achieve credibility. The task of ELT/EIB marketers is to develop a tangible representation of the service and to make the service more easily grasped mentally. Making learners members of the organisation and giving them an identity card is one option.

Advertising and promotion are usually concerned with the customer, but these tools can be used to encourage employees to perform well. George and Berry (1984) write that advertising is an important tool for selling jobs, for motivating and for communicating with employees. This clearly relates to internal marketing and to creating the crucial yet intangible feeling that, "...there is something special about the place. The staff enjoy working there, feel committed to it..., in a sense that they own it and what is happening in it." (Underhill and Impey,1994)

Advertising and promotion should also capitalise on word of mouth. Potential students, who have few tangible clues with which to evaluate a school, will often seek the opinion of others who have appropriate experience of ELT schools. Marketers of such schools should appreciate how powerful a tool personal recommendation can be.

Customisation of service, learning style and cultural background

The simultaneous production and consumption characteristics of ELT/EIB services can provide opportunities for customising them. A fundamental marketing objective is to find a good fit between what learners want and what the school has to sell.

ELT institutions that offer Business English courses to clients from the corporate world will often tailor the content of their programmes. Content, however, may not be enough. Research into learning strategies and cognitive styles suggests that there are other opportunities for customising services (see also unit 3, chapter 9).

Nunan (1991) claims that accommodating learning styles and strategy preference in the classroom can result in improved learner satisfaction and attainment. Any suggestion that learner satisfaction can be improved will be of interest to marketers.

Learning style refers to an individual's preferred way of going about learning. Nunan (1991) suggests that this style results from personality variables, socio-cultural background and educational experience. He defines learning strategies as the mental processes which learners employ to learn and use the foreign language. He identifies four types of learner.

Unit 1: The Environment and Scope of EIB

1. **Concrete learners**. These tend to like games, pictures, films, video, using cassettes, talking in pairs and practising English outside the classroom.
2. **Analytic learners**. These like studying grammar, studying English books and reading newspapers, studying alone, finding their own mistakes and working on problems set by the teacher.
3. **Communicative learners.** These tend to like to learn by watching and listening to native speakers, talking to friends in English and watching television in English.
4. **Authority-oriented learners**. These prefer the teacher to explain everything. They tend to like studying grammar, to learn by reading and to write everything in a note-book.

It would be difficult to organise classes on the basis of learning styles. However, it is suggested that teachers are able to identify learning styles and that they can comfortably accommodate them. If they are not able to do this, there is the danger that unsuitable methodologies are adopted for particular classes. If teacher and student performance are bound together to create the service, the adoption of unsuitable methodologies may result in an unsatisfactory product and dissatisfied learners.

This concern with learning styles and preferences has been taken a stage further by Holliday (1994a and 1994b). We noted earlier (unit 1, chapters 3 and 6) that Holliday suggests the whole ELT curriculum is culture bound and not necessarily appropriate in all ELT/EIB classrooms. Inexperienced teachers may experience a gap between the methodological principles of their training course and their teaching realities. They may find that learners from some cultures do not react well to certain key features of communicative methodology, for example: pairwork, role-play and simulations, and the technique of elicitation.

We suggest that teachers are sensitised to both learning style and to the (in)appropriacy of particular classroom methodologies. Without this sensitivity, it is argued that student satisfaction with the service will be a hit-or-miss affair. Further, teachers will not fully comprehend why some students seem dissatisfied with a course. Finally, dissatisfied students may blame themselves for their dissatisfaction as Zeithaml et al (2005) suggest. If one of the functions of marketing is to attend to customer needs and to satisfy those needs at a profit, then the desirability of focusing on the issues of learning style and cultural background is urgent and compelling. For an approachable account of learning styles and how to personalise learning, see Prashnig (2006).

9.4: Conclusions

The ELT industry needs to attend to its marketing strategies so that they reflect the peculiarities that the industry has. First, we suggest that those responsible for marketing fully grasp the nature of their products. Second, we argue that these marketers pay particular and careful attention to the needs of students, their learning styles and cultural background. For more on services marketing and access to a variety of service marketing case studies, see Lovelock and Wirtz (2006).

Unit 1: The Environment and Scope of EIB

Chapter 10

Language, Communication and Culture

10.1: Introduction
10.2: Objectives
10.3: The Relationship between Culture and Communication
10.4: High- and Low-Context Cultures
10.5: Power, Certainty and Communication Style
10.6: Conclusions
10.7: Answers to Questions.

10.1: Introduction

We noted in chapter 3 of this unit that the global business environment requires excellent leadership and management skills. Furthermore, increased global interaction, whether that be face-to-face or in telephone conferences, requires managers and leaders to have highly developed skills in communicating interculturally in the world language of English.

In this chapter we argue that linguistic skills alone will not prepare Business English students for such intercultural encounters. We suggest that the development of cultural awareness and adaptability is crucial for those who work in a global environment. For teachers of EIB, we propose that intercultural skills training should be an integral part of their teaching.

We begin by looking at the relationship between communication and culture, and how the latter can influence the former. Next, we look at models which will help us better understand how cultural differences can influence communication and language.

This chapter revisits and develops some of the issues raised in unit 1, chapter 4; notably Hall and Hall's (1990) discussion of high- and low-context cultures. Furthermore, this chapter should, perhaps, be viewed as introductory. The whole of unit 4 will build on the points raised in the following pages.

10.2: Objectives

At the end of this chapter you will:

- be able to critically evaluate the link between culture and communication
- be able to identify and assess the challenges posed by communication across cultures
- be able to identify some of the factors which influence intercultural communication.

Pre-reading task

Before you begin, look at the questions in the shaded box below. The questions are designed to focus your mind on some of the issues raised in the chapter.

> 1. *The effectiveness of the spoken word depends not so much on how people talk but mostly on how they listen. Consider this opinion.*
> 2. *Communication is about using language accurately. What do you think?*
> 3. *"Companies are there to make money. All forms of communication should focus on the data to be communicated. The rest is time wasting and, consequently, money wasting." What is your opinion?*

10.3: The Relationship between Culture and Communication

Leeds-Hurwitz (1989) suggests that communication is a process by which information is exchanged and has relevance and meaning for at least one of the participants involved.

In a similar vein, Nixon and Dawson (2002) argue that communication is an interactive event during which people give meaning to messages and jointly create a social reality. According to Nixon and Dawson (2002) effective communication takes place when the expression of the message-sender matches the impression of the message-receiver. In order for this to happen, the rules and expectations of both sender and receiver should be followed. However, in cross-cultural communication, the rules and expectations may differ according to the cultural conditioning of the participants. This implies that messages may be misinterpreted and that, as a consequence, communication may be ineffective. The challenge for people engaged in cross-cultural communication is to develop an awareness of the fact that what is "meaningful and relevant" may vary according to the cultural values of the people involved. Culture, therefore, functions as a frame of reference or a context in which all that occurs is understood.

Other research evidence supports this view by suggesting that there are culturally based differences in conversational style (Clyne, 1994; Scollon and Scollon, 1995; Ting-Toomey and Korzenny, 2002). These differences in style have their origins in the social norms, the beliefs and values of different peoples. Further, the differences can often result in miscommunication or non-communication (Gumperz, 1982). Wei et al (2001) point out that this miscommunication becomes particularly acute in professional settings when the interacting parties use the same linguistic code (i.e. English) but not the same cultural style.

White (1997) argues that although linguistic competence is an important basis for communication, communicative competence in terms of intercultural communication needs to be defined more broadly. Canale (1983) and Canale and Swain (1980) propose three sub competencies.

1. Sociolinguistic. This concerns the individual's perceptions and understanding of social relations. Further, it concerns the potential impact this understanding has on communication, and on choosing the appropriate thing to say.

Unit 1: The Environment and Scope of EIB

2. Discourse. This concerns the user's knowledge of the rules of discourse, and of how spoken and written texts are organised.
3. Strategic. How language users, when faced with a communication problem, negotiate their way to a solution.

Bachman (1990) proposes a further competency - pragmatic competence. This consists of illocutionary competence (the communication of the speaker's intention) and sociolinguistic competence (appropriateness). Thomas (1984) suggests that it is differences in pragmatic competence which may cause problems in intercultural communication. In other words, Thomas (1984) is suggesting that pragmatic failure will have more of an influence on communication than grammatical or lexical failures. Thus, in theory, it is possible to achieve a high level of linguistic proficiency while having a low level of pragmatic proficiency. The result is language which although grammatically "perfect" may be perceived as somehow inappropriate.

Pause for thought

> *In your work environment, is it possible to teach language that is appropriate in all situations? Do you think it can be taught at all, or is appropriateness something that each individual must learn through experience?*

Thomas' view is supported by Kameda (2001) who, discussing the Japanese, writes:

> I believe that linguistic capability and communication competence are two entirely different things. The Japanese people must first realise the differences in the styles of communication between the two languages to acquire communicative competency in English. They should change their communication style when they communicate in English with foreigners...

Language has many functions. In particular, language can have both an information function and a relationship function. This means that when we communicate with others, we not only convey a certain amount of information but we also reveal our expectations and feelings about the

Unit 1: The Environment and Scope of EIB

relationship with the person or persons with whom we are communicating. Cultures can vary with regard to the importance they attach to one function of language over the other.

Watzlawick (1967) refers to these functions as substantive and relational. For Watzlawick (1967) the relational element has more of an impact on communication than the substantive element. The substantive component transmits the data. The relational component indicates how the data should be interpreted. Every interpersonal relationship therefore takes place on two levels: a rational level and an emotional level. Watzalawick (1967) claims that if an atmosphere of harmony is not first established between two participants in a conversation, then it is not even worth the trouble of dealing with the content.

Conversations, according to Watzlawick (1967) do not, therefore, merely consist of a factual exchange of information. In every conversation, the social, interpersonal relationships between the sender and receiver also play a major role. Communication therefore takes place on two levels which are constantly interacting. First, there is the factual/content level, and second, the relational level of emotions, sensations and moods. This second level characterises the relationship between the interlocutors and determines the substantive component. Each interlocutor influences these social relationships by:

1. the way they speak
2. the time at which they speak
3. their choice of words and how they string the words together
4. facial expression and body language
5. finality of statements.

Pause for thought

> Look at statements 1-5 above. The statements represent behaviours that can influence the relational component of communication. To what extent do you feel that differences in cultural values will influence these behaviours?

Problems at the emotional level are usually only visible and active as problems on the factual level. This means that problems on the factual level are often displaced problems of relationship. Communication problems can occur:

Unit 1: The Environment and Scope of EIB

1. when the factual component is unclear
2. when misunderstandings happen on the relationship level
3. when factual and relationship levels are interchanged
4. when prejudices dominate the discussion (perception is restricted to those things which reinforce the prejudice and no attempt is made to understand the other person)
5. when the other person is insulted in their sense of values or feelings.

Pause for thought

> *Look at statements 1-5 above. Once again, from your current understanding of cultural differences, to what extent could culture be behind these reasons for communication problems?*

There are clearly a multitude of factors which influence behaviour in intercultural communication. However, White (1998) offers a useful summary of these factors. This summary is given below.

Language
- choice of words
- choice of grammar
- matching of function and form.

Culture
- styles of communication
- ways of relating to others
- beliefs, perceptions, attitudes and values
- world view.

Question 1

> *Below you will see examples which you should now list under one of White's (1998) four "__culture__" headings above. The examples are in no logical order. When you have finished, check your answers with the sample answer given in the Answers to Questions section. Do you agree with White (1998)? Is there something missing from his summary?*
>
> *turn-taking*

Unit 1: The Environment and Scope of EIB

> *relative status*
> *maintaining/challenging status*
> *loyalty*
> *high- and low-context communication*
> *direct versus indirect communication*
> *politeness*
> *rights and obligations*
> *human nature*
> *time and temporal focus*
> *certainty/uncertainty*
> *collectivism/individualism*
> *solidarity/deference*
> *formal/informal*
> *face-to-face versus written communication*
> *personal domains*
> *harmony*
> *collaboration.*

White (1998) emphasises that language is not simply a product of these elements, even though the elements do influence language choices and communication style. Rather, language itself is used to establish, maintain and change communication styles, values, and, perhaps, culture itself. In other words, the relationship between language and culture is both complex and intricate. As you work through this chapter, we suggest that you keep White's (1998) summary in mind. There is a lot to consider.

However, we suggest that White (1998) has either omitted or is vague about one important factor. Look at this example which has been taken from Tannen (1992).

> A Greek man married to an Englishwoman accused her of speaking in an irritating monotone, especially when their tempers were strained... It never occurred to either of them that he found the tone of her talk monotonous because he was looking for the extreme shifts in pitch typical of Greek speakers, especially Greek women.

Trompenaars (1993) makes a distinction between affective cultures and neutral cultures (see also unit 1, chapter 5). The former tend to show their emotions plainly by, for example, shouting and laughing, and by sending their voices up and down in pitch. Neutral cultures tend to hold on to their emotions and keep them controlled. Tannen (1992) suggests that changes in pitch in the speech of people from affective cultures reveal the attitude of the speakers to what they are saying, how much they care and how involved they are.

This amount of display of feelings can differ greatly across cultures. Each culture will have norms with regard to how much emotional expression is acceptable. For Tannen (1992):

> ...conversational signals can get crossed when well-intentioned speakers have different habits and expectations about using pacing and pausing, loudness and pitch to show their intentions through talk - in other words, different conversational styles.

With regard to pausing, Trompenaars (1993) suggests that for the Anglo-Saxons, when one speaker stops the other starts. It is not, according to Trompenaars (1993), polite to interrupt. Latin people tend to interrupt a speaker. These interruptions show how interested each is in what the other is saying. Trompenaars (1993) also claims that in oriental cultures, frequent silences between utterances can be disturbing for the Westerner - silence being an indication that there has been a failure in communication.

Trompenaars (1993) supports Tannen's (1992) view that tone of voice can also cause cross-cultural problems. For neutral societies, the variations in pitch displayed in some affective cultures can appear threatening or exaggerated. Oriental societies tend to have a more monotonous style. This implies self-control and respect for the listener.

Pause for thought

> *Imagine you have a group of Spanish students. How do you think they would react if you raised your voice in class? What about a group of Japanese - how do you think they would react to your raised voice?*

To conclude this section, we quote Kramsch (2001) who neatly sums up much of that which we have so far discussed. Kramsch (2001) suggests that, "Success in business transactions and diplomatic negotiations is not dependent on grammar alone; one has to know how to say what to whom at the right time in the right place."

10.4: High- and Low-Context Cultures

We have already described high- and low-context cultures in chapter 4, section 5 of this unit. We would like you to try the questions below. If necessary, you should re-read the relevant section in chapter 4 again. For more on high- and low-context, see unit 4, chapters 8 and 9.

Pause for thought

> *Imagine you are about to begin a class. A student comes in and says, "It's a hot day today." How would you identify the speaker's intended (illocutionary) meaning?*

The answer to the question above depends on the social and situational environment. How well do you know this particular student? Did she once complain about being too warm in the classroom? So, is she really asking you to open the window? Has she complained about the cold weather recently? Is she simply telling you a fact? Does she want to begin some small talk before your class or before asking you if she can leave the class early?

The point is that we interpret and create communication with reference to the context in which the communication occurs. For Hall and Hall (1990) the context is inextricably bound up with the meaning of the event (i.e. the communicative act).

However, it is not a simple as that. If we look at events and context as the ingredients that combine to give meaning, we shall see that different cultures attach more importance to one ingredient than the other. Hall (1976) refers to cultures which tend to focus more on the context as high-context (HC) cultures. Cultures which tend to focus more on the event are called low-context (LC) cultures. Chapter 4, section 5 of this unit lists the characteristics of HC and LC cultures. How much do you remember? Test yourself by doing the following question.

Unit 1: The Environment and Scope of EIB

Question 2

> *Below you will see some tendencies that characterise high- and low-context cultures. Look at each tendency and decide whether you think it is a characteristic of a low-context (LC) culture or a high-context (HC) culture.*
> 1. *Relationships have priority over tasks or contracts.*
> 2. *There is deep personal involvement between individuals.*
> 3. *People say exactly what they mean.*
> 4. *Agreements are written rather than spoken.*
> 5. *Insiders and outsiders are tightly distinguished.*
> 6. *Managers are personally responsible for their subordinates.*
> 7. *People need and give as much information as possible.*
> 8. *People talk around the topic and do not easily come to the point.*

We should point out that no country or culture can be found exclusively at one end or the other of the HC-LC continuum. However, we should expect to find HC tendencies in Japan, China, Korea and other Asian countries, countries around the Mediterranean and in the Middle East. LC countries include the US, the Anglo-Saxon countries and Scandinavia. However, all countries are likely to include groups that differ from the cultural norm.

Pause for thought

> *Consider the army, the family, and a football team. You are likely to find these or similar groups all over the world. Which sort of communication style would typify these groups: high- or low-context communication? Consider also a loose grouping such as youth culture. Is it not the case that young people deliberately create their own (HC) communication style in order to exclude their parents? Does this happen in your country?*

Korac-Kakabadse et al (2001) usefully describe the term high- and low-context culture as:

> ...the cultural rules around information exchange and, in particular, the degree to which information in a culture is explicit, vested in words or precise and unambiguous

meaning (low context), and the degree to which it is implicit, vested in shared assumptions and conveyed through verbal and non-verbal codes (high context).

In LC communication, the listener is assumed to know very little and must, therefore, be told almost everything. In HC communication, the listener should already be "contextualised" and does not need much information. High-context people tend to talk around the topic and expect others to have the sensitivity to understand the crucial point.

Pause for thought

> *Think about presentations, meetings, negotiations and telephone conferences. With regard to information exchange, what communication problems might occur (assuming typical behaviour) between a high-context Italian and a low-context German?*

In HC cultures, gestures and tone of voice may be an important part of communication. Furthermore, communication in HC cultures may take some considerable time because trust, family, friends and personal needs will all have to be taken into account. Conversely, people in LC cultures tend to get straight to the point and do not attach so much importance to relationship building; or at most, they may consider relationships only after any deal has been negotiated.

Hall (1976) observed that a preference for HC or LC communication is closely related to how people view time and space. Low-context cultures tend to function within a monochronic time mode while high-context cultures tend to function in a polychronic time mode (see also unit 1, chapter 4, section 5 and unit 4, chapter 8, section 6).

Monochronic time focuses on schedules, segmentation and promptness while polychronic time focuses on doing several things at the same time and emphasises the importance of relationships over the obligations of pre-arranged schedules. Look at the anecdotes in the "pause for thought" box below. These anecdotes have been taken from Mole (1995). Do you think that HC or LC patterns can explain the two situations?

Unit 1: The Environment and Scope of EIB

Pause for thought

> 1. My staff meetings are very annoying. It is hard to get them to stick to the agenda. And they insist on discussing every point until everyone has had their say (French manager of an Italian company).
> 2. You have the impression that the French don't realise that they are at a meeting. They don't pay attention or they interrupt or they get up and make a phone call (English director of a Franco-British company).

Question 3

Look again at the anecdotes above. Imagine you are a consultant called in the deal with these problems. How would you deal with them? When you have thought about this, compare your answer to our suggested answer in the Answers to Questions section.

Hall (1976) also suggests that the lives of people in LC cultures tend to be fragmented and individualised with little or no involvement with others. Conversely, people in HC cultures tend to be guided more by long-term relationships. This may mean that they will expect more from other people. Hall (1976) argues that HC people are deeply involved with each other and that they live and work in environments where information flows freely and is available to almost anyone.

10.5: Power, Certainty and Communication Style

Mead (1994) suggests that when planning communication, we should select from the following options.

- Who will communicate?
- To whom?
- What will be communicated?
- What is the appropriate medium?
- What is the appropriate time?
- What is the appropriate place?

Unit 1: The Environment and Scope of EIB

According to Mead (1994) communication may be ineffective with regard to one or all of the options above. White (1997) gives the following example of cross-cultural ineffectiveness in communication.

Question 4

> *A Canadian manager has been sent to the Athens office of his company. He is assigned a Greek secretary. Every day, he gives work to her. One day, she complains to a colleague, "I wish he would just tell me what to do instead of asking me. After all, he's the boss and I'm here to do what he wants me to do." What has gone wrong in this situation?*

Pause for thought

> *Now look at the following situations in smaller font below and say whether you think the behaviour is appropriate or inappropriate in its cultural context. You may need to look again at Hofstede's (1991) dimensions of power distance and uncertainty avoidance. For each of the situations give reasons for your decisions. Each situation carries a clue concerning the cultural dimensions you should be considering.*
> You are on a tour of your company's European subsidiaries.
> You go to Germany to give a presentation about your company's latest technology. You decide to focus your presentation on the benefits your product will have for the Germans and to spend little time on the technical details. Germany is a strong uncertainty avoidance culture - what do you think Germans value in a presentation?
>
> You then go to France to find out how they do business there and to understand how your subsidiary is run. You have not got much time so you decide to get right down to business and keep small talk to a minimum. France is a high-context culture - how do you think they would view this no-nonsense, straight-down-to-business style of communication?
>
> Still in France, you have some criticisms to make about the production manager and the way he handles his department. You decide to speak to him directly. France is also a high power distance culture and therefore steeply hierarchical. How do you think the production manager's boss would feel about your direct and personal intervention?
>
> Now you are back in Germany. You are to attend a meeting in which you will be expected to make an important contribution concerning global marketing policies. You have had little time to study the details of the plan but you feel you will be able to waffle your way through the meeting. Germany is a strong

> *uncertainty avoidance and a low-context culture. What sort of communication style will they tend to value?*
>
> *You are back in America and you have to write a report about your European trip. The report will be read by top management so you decide to make your writing as complex as possible. Your thinking is that the more difficult it is to understand, the more valuable are the ideas inside it. The US is low-context and low power distance. How do American's tend to like their written communication?*
>
> *You send a mail directly to the French production manager in order to confirm what was agreed at your private meeting. France is a high power distance culture and high-context culture. What would be their preferred communication style? And to whom should you communicate?*

10.6: Conclusions

In this chapter, we have given you an overview of the way in which culture, communication and language interact. For the teacher of EIB, an appreciation of this interaction is essential if s/he is to help learners communicate in an international business context.

We will take all the issues raised in this chapter a stage further in Unit 4. In the meantime, we suggest that you get to grips with the work of Hall and Hall and thoroughly familiarise yourselves with the characteristics of high- and low-context cultures. If you want to know more about the history of culture teaching and/or proposals for a framework to develop a transnational language and culture pedagogy that aims at the education of world citizens, see Risager (2007).

10.7: Answers to Questions

Question 1
The answer below is the (almost) complete list of the factors which, according to White (1998), influence intercultural communication.

Styles of communication:
topic control
turn taking
speaker's rights
taboo areas
direct versus indirect
deductive versus inductive

Unit 1: The Environment and Scope of EIB

formal versus informal
listener/reader responsibility
speaker/writer responsibility
face-to-face versus written
one-way versus two-way communication
non-verbal communication.

Ways of relating to others:
relative status
maintaining/challenging relative status
face and mutual face needs
politeness
solidarity/deference
imposition
personal domains
definitions of communicative event
conventions associated with that event.

Beliefs, perceptions, attitudes, values:
power and dependence
loyalty
motivation
rights and obligations
harmony
collectivism/individualism
assertiveness
competition/collaboration
certainty/uncertainty.

World view:
assumptions regarding the world and its peoples
high- and low-context
human nature
time and temporal focus
space
causality
fate.

Question 2
1. HC
2. HC
3. LC
4. LC
5. HC
6. HC
7. LC
8. HC

Unit 1: The Environment and Scope of EIB

Question 3
You need to sensitise the participants to each other's way of running, and participating in, meetings. This could, perhaps, be done by running short role-plays and then getting feedback from everyone involved. For example, what did they like/dislike about the meeting? What did they think of the way the meeting was chaired? How do they view the purpose of an agenda? Next, participants need to understand the underlying cultural values which produce certain behaviours, so present Hall's theories of high- and low-context cultures. Then you could look for cultural overlaps and get agreement on what meetings are, how they should be run, the purpose of an agenda, and what the role of the chairperson should be.

Question 4
Assumptions about power relationships have been confused. The Canadian (low power distance) and the Greek (high power distance) have not yet negotiated a shared set of norms. The Greek secretary accepts the power difference between her and her boss but the Canadian has taken his set of norms into another cultural setting where his norms are inappropriate. Communication is ineffective on the "who, whom and what" options above.

Unit 1: The Environment and Scope of EIB

Unit Bibliography

Adair, J. (1988) Effective Leadership. London, Pan.

Adler, N. (1991) International Dimensions of Organisational Behaviour. Boston, MA., PWS-Kent Publishing.

Adler, N.J., Campbell, N. and Laurent, A. (1992) "In search of appropriate methodology: from outside the People's Republic of China looking in," in Journal of International Business Studies, Spring, 61-74.

Ardichvili, A. and Kuchinke, P. (2002) "Leadership styles and cultural values among managers and subordinates: a comparative study of four countries of the former Soviet Union, Germany, and the US," in Human Resource Development International, Vol. 5, No. 1.

Bachman, L. (1990) Fundamental Considerations in Language testing. Oxford, Oxford University Press.

Badger, I. and Menzies, P. (1993) The MacMillan Business English Program. Hemel Hempstead, MacMillan.

Bennet, N. and Dunne, E. (1992) Managing Classroom Groups. Hemel Hempstead, Simon Schuster.

Unit 1: The Environment and Scope of EIB

Berger, M. (1998) "Going global: implications for communication and leadership training," in <u>Industrial and Commercial Training,</u> Vol. 30, No. 4.

Bernstein, B. (1971) "On the classification and framing of educational Knowledge," from Young, M. (ed), <u>Knowledge and Control</u>. London, Collier Macmillan.

Berry, L. (1984) "Service Marketing is Different," from Lovelock, C. (ed.), <u>Services Marketing</u>. New Jersey, Prentice-Hall, Inc.

Bhagat, R., Kedia, B., Crawford, S. and Kaplan, M. (1990) "Cross-Cultural Issues in Organisational Psychology: Emergent Trends and Directions for Research in the 1990s," in Cooper, C. and Robertson, T. (eds.), <u>International Review of Industrial and Organisational Psychology: Volume 5</u>. New York, Wiley.

Bovee, C. Houston, M. and Thill, J. (1995) <u>Marketing</u>. New York, McGraw-Hill, Inc.

Brown, P. and Levinson, S. (1978) "Universals in Language Usage: Politeness Phenomenon," in Goody, E. (ed.), <u>Questions and Politeness: Strategies in Social Interactions</u>. Cambridge, Cambridge University Press.

Canale, M. and Swain, M. (1980) "Theoretical bases of communicative approaches to second language teaching and testing," in <u>Applied Linguistics</u>, Vol. 1. No. 1.

Canale, M. (1983) "From communicative competence to communicative language pedagogy," in Richards, J. and Schmidt, R. (eds.), <u>Language and Communication.</u> London, Longman.

Casse, P. (1981) "Training for the Cross-Cultural Mind," in <u>Society for Inter-cultural Education, Training and Research</u>. Washington DC, Intercultural Press.

Unit 1: The Environment and Scope of EIB

Catterick, D. (1995) Approaching Appropriacy: The case for a culture-sensitive approach to methodology in the People's Republic of China. Unpublished MEd (TESOL) dissertation, CELSE, University of Manchester.

Chen, Min (1995) Asian Management Systems. London, Routledge.

Clyne, M. (1994) Intercultural Communication at Work. Cambridge, Cambridge University Press.

Cowie, H. and Rudduck, J. (1988) Cooperative Group Work: An Overview. London, BP Educational Services.

Cragg, C. (1995) The New Taipans. London, Century Business.

Crystal, D. (1997) English as a Global Language. Cambridge, Cambridge University Press.

Cuthbert, R. (1984) The Management Process. E234. Management in Post-Compulsory Education. Block 3, Part 2. Milton Keynes, Open University Press.

Dearing Report (1997) National Committee of Inquiry into Higher Education in UK p.6.

Drucker, P. (1955) The Practice of Management. Oxford, Heinemann Professional Publishing Ltd.

Dudley-Evans, A. and St John, M. (1998) Developments in English for Specific Purposes. Cambridge, Cambridge University Press.

Ellis, M. and Johnson, C. (1994) Teaching Business English. Oxford, Oxford University Press.

Estienne, M. (1997) "The art of cross-cultural management: an alternative approach to training and development," in Journal of European Industrial Training, Vol. 21, No. 1.

Everard, B. and Morris, G. (1990) Effective School Management. London, Paul Chapman Publishing.

Unit 1: The Environment and Scope of EIB

Fukuyama, F. (1995) <u>Trust: the social virtues and the creation of prosperity</u>. London, Hamish Hamilton.

Gent, I. Johnston, B. and Prosser, P. (1999) "Thinking on your feet in Undergraduate Computer Science: a constructivist approach to developing and assessing critical thinking," in <u>Teaching in Higher Education</u>, Vol. 4, No. 4 pp511-522.

George, W. and Berry, L. (1984) "Guidelines for the Advertising of Services", from Lovelock, C. (ed.), <u>Services Marketing</u>. New Jersey, Prentice-Hall, Inc.

Glatter, R. et al (eds.), (1988) <u>Understanding School Management.</u> Milton Keynes, Open University Press.

Glenn, E. (1981) <u>Man and Mankind</u>. Norwood, Ablex.

Graddol, D. (2006) <u>English Next</u>. British Council.

Grahn, J. and Swenson, D. (2000) "Cross-Cultural Perspectives for Quality Training," in <u>Cross-Cultural Management – An International Journal</u>, Vol.3

Gray, H.L. (1979) <u>The School as an Organisation</u>. Nafferton, Nafferton Books.

Gudykunst, W. and Hammer, M. (1983) "Basic Training Design: Approaches to Intercultural Training," in Landis, D. and Brislin, R. (Eds) <u>The Handbook of Intercultural Training</u>, New York, Pergamon.

Gudykunst, W., Ting-Toomey, S. and Chua, E. (1988) <u>Intercultural Communication Theory, Interpersonal Communications.</u> Beverley Hills, Sage.

Guirdham, M. (1990) <u>Interpersonal Skills at Work</u>. Hemel Hempsted, Prentice Hall International.

Gumperz, J. (1982) <u>Discourse Strategies</u>. Cambridge, Cambridge University Press.

Unit 1: The Environment and Scope of EIB

Hall, E.T. (1960) "The Silent Language of Overseas Business," in Harvard Business review, May-June.

Hall, E.T. (1976) Beyond Culture. New York, Anchor Press.

Hall, E and Hall, M. (1990) Understanding Cultural Differences. Maine, Intercultural Press, Inc.

Hamp-Lyons, L. (2001) "English for Academic Purposes," from Carter, R. and Nunan, D. (eds.), The Cambridge Guide to Teaching English to Speakers of Other Languages. Cambridge, Cambridge University Press.

Hampden-Turner, C. and Trompenaars, F. (1994) The Seven Cultures of Capitalism. London, Piatkus.

Handy, C.A. (1978) Understanding Organisations. Harmondsworth, Penguin.

Handy, C.A. and Aitken, R. (1986) Understanding Schools as Organisations. Harmondsworth, Penguin.

Hargie, O. (ed.), (2006) The Handbook of Communication Skills. London, Routledge.

Harris, H. and Kumra, S. (2000) "International manager development – Cross-cultural training in highly diverse environments," in Journal of management Development, Vol. 19, No. 7.

Hofstede, G. (1984) Culture's Consequences: International Differences in Work-Related Values. Beverley Hills, Sage.

Hofstede, G. (1986) "Cultural differences in teaching and learning," in International Journal of Intercultural Relations, Vol. 10.

Hofstede, G. (1991) Cultures and Organisation. London, McGraw-Hill International.

Unit 1: The Environment and Scope of EIB

Hofstede, G. (1996) "Riding the Waves of Commerce: A Test of Trompenaars' Model of National Cultural Differences," in International Journal of Intercultural Relations," Vol. 20, No.2.

Hofstede, G.J., Pedersen, P. and Hofstede, G.H. (2002) Exploring Culture. London, Nicholas Brealey Publishing.

Hollett, V. (1991) Business Objectives. Oxford, Oxford University Press.

Holliday, A. (1994a) Appropriate methodology and Social Context. Cambridge, Cambridge University Press.

Holliday, A. (1994b) "Student culture and English language education: an international perspective," in Language Curriculum and Culture Vol.7, No. 2.

Hoyle, E. (1981) The Process of Management. E323. Management and the School. Block 3, Part 1. Milton Keynes, Open University Press.

Hughes-Wiener, G. (1995) "The learning how to learn approach to cross-cultural orientation," from Jackson, T. (ed.), Cross-Cultural Management. Oxford, Butterworth-Heinemann.

Hutchinson, T. and Waters, A. (1987) English for Specific Purposes. Cambridge, Cambridge University Press.

Jeanquart-Barone, S. and Peluchette, J. (1999) "Examining the Impact of the Cultural Dimension of Uncertainty Avoidance on Staffing Decisions: A Look at US and German Firms," in Cross Cultural Management, Vol. 6, No. 3.

Jenkins, J. (2003) World Englishes: A Resource Book for Students. London, Routledge.

Jenkins, J. (2007) English as a Lingua Franca: Attitudes and Identity. Oxford, Oxford University Press.

Johnson, R. (1995) "ESL Teacher Education and Intercultural Communication: Discomfort as a Learning Tool," in TESL Canada Journal, Vol. 12, No. 2.

Kameda, N. (2001) "The implications of language style in business communication: focus on English versus Japanese," in Corporate Communications: An International Journal, Vol. 6, No. 3.

Kaufman-Scarborough, C. and Lindquist, J. (1999) "Time management and polychronicity," in Journal of Managerial Psychology, Vol. 14, No. 3-4.

Keys, J.; Edge, A. and Wells, R. The Multinational Management Game: A Simuworld of Global Strategy. Little Rock, Micro Business Publications.

Kluckhohn, F. and Strodtbeck, F. (1961) Variations in Value Orientations. New York, Peterson.

Knoke, W. (1996) Bold New World: The essential road map to the twenty first century. Kodansha International.

Kolb, D., Rubin, I. and Osland, J. (1991) Organisational Behaviour: An Experiential Approach, 5th ed., Englewood Cliffs, Prentice-Hall.

Korac-Kakabadse, N., Kouzmin, A., Korac-Kakabadse, A. and Savery, L. (2001) Low- and High-Context Communication Patterns: Towards Mapping Cross-Cultural Encounters," in Cross Cultural Management, Vol. 8, No. 2.

Kotler, P. (1967) Marketing Management. New Jersey, Prentice-Hall, Inc.

Kramsch, C. (2001) "Intercultural communication," in Carter, R. and Nunan, D. (eds.), Teaching English to Speakers of Other Languages. Cambridge, Cambridge University Press.

Laurent, A. (1983) "The cultural diversity of Western conceptions of management," in International Studies of Management and Organisations, Vol.13, Nos. 1. & 2.

Unit 1: The Environment and Scope of EIB

Leeds-Hurwitz, W. (1989) Communication in Everyday Life: A Social Interpretation. Norwood, Ablex.

Lessem, R. and Neubauer, F. (1994) European Management Systems. London, McGraw-Hill.

Levine, D. (1985) The Flight from Ambiguity. Chicago, Chicago University Press.

Lewis, R.D. (1992) Finland: Cultural Lone Wolf – Consequences in International Business. Helsinki, Richard Lewis Communications.

Lewis, R.D. (2006) When Cultures Collide. Leading Across Cultures – 3rd ed. London, Nicholas Brealey Publishing.

Lovelock, C and Wirtz, J. (2006) Services Marketing. Prentice Hall.

Marin, G. (1987) "Attributions for tardiness among Chilean and United States students ," in Journal of Social Psychology, Vol. 125, No. 5.

Mead, R. (1994) International Management. Oxford, Blackwell Publishers Ltd.

Mehrabian, A. (1971) Silent Messages. London, Wadsworth.

Mole, J. (1995) Mind Your Manners: Managing Business Cultures in Europe. London, Nicholas Brealey Publishing.

Moran, P. (1990) A Framework for the Teaching of Culture. Vermont, School for International Training.

Morden, A.R. (1995) "International Culture and Management," in Management Decision, Vol. 33, No. 2.

Morden, A.R. (1999) "Models of National Culture – A Management Review," in Cross Cultural Management, Vol. 6, No. 1.

Morley, D. and Shockley-Zabalak, P. (1987) "Conflict Avoiders and Compromisers: Towards and Understanding of Their Organisational Communication Style," in Group and Organisation Studies, Vol. 11, No. 4.

Nelson-Jones, R. (2006) Human Relationship Skills. London, Routledge.

Nixon, J. and Dawson, G. (2002) "Reasons for cross-cultural communications training," in Corporate Communications: An International Journal, Vol. 7, No. 3.

Nunan, D. (1991) Language Teaching Methodology. Hemel Hempsted, Prentice Hall.

Oomkes, F. and Thomas, R. (1992) Cross-Cultural Communication: A Trainer's Manual. Aldershot, Gower Publishing.

Parsons, T. and Shils, E. (1951) Towards a general theory of action. Cambridge, MA, Harvard University Press.

Penner, J. (1995) "Change and Conflict: Introduction of the Communicative Approach in China," in TESL Canada Journal, Vol. 12, No. 2.

Peoples, D. (1997) Presentations Plus. Techniques That Work From the Experts' Expert. New York, John Wiley.

Prashnig, B. (2006) Learning Styles in Action. Network Educational Press.

Rees, W. and Porter, C. (2002) "The use of case studies in management training and development," in Industrial and Commercial Training, Vol. 34, No. 1.

Richards, R. (2000) How does the development of critical thinking relate to the demands of academic writing in higher education? in Thompson, P. (ed.), Patterns and Perspectives: Insights into EAP writing practice. Reading, Centre for Applied Language Studies.

Richards, J. and Rodgers, T. (2001) *Approaches and Methods in Language Teaching*. Cambridge, Cambridge University Press.

Ridderstråle, J. & Nordström, K. (2000) *Funky Business*. Harlow, Pearson Education Ltd.

Risager, K. (2007) *Language and Culture Pedagogy: From a National to a Transnational Paradigm*. Multilingual Matters Ltd.

Robinson, P. (1991) *ESP Today: a Practitioner's Guide*. Hemel Hempstead, Prentice Hall International.

Ruben, B. (1989) "The study of cross-cultural competence: tradition and contemporary issues," in *International Journal of Intercultural Relations*, Vol. 3.

Schramm-Nielsen, J. (2000) "How to Interpret Uncertainty Avoidance Scores: A comparative study of Danish and French firms," in *Cross Cultural Management*, Vol. 7, No. 4.

Scollon, R. and Scollon, S. (1995) *Intercultural Communication*. Oxford, Blackwell.

Seagrave, S. (1995) *Lords of the Rim: The invisible empire of the overseas Chinese*. London, Bantam Press.

Seidlhofer, B. and Jenkins, J. (2003) "English as a lingua franca and the politics of property," in Mair, C. (ed.), *The Politics of English as a World Language*. Amsterdam, Rodopi.

Sharma, P. and Barrett, B. (2007) *Blended Learning*. Macmillan Education.

Shen, F. (1989) "The classroom and the wider culture: Identity as a key to learning English composition," in *College Composition and Communication*, Vol. 40, pp 459-466.

Shostack, G. (1984) "Breaking Free from Product Marketing", from Lovelock, C. (ed.), *Services Marketing*. New Jersey, Prentice-Hall, Inc.

Servaes, J. (1989) "Cultural Identity and Modes of Communication," in Anderson, J. (ed.), Communication Yearbook 12. Newbury Park, Sage.

Simintiras, A. and Thomas, A. (1998) "Cross-cultural sales negotiations," in International Marketing Review, Vol. 15, No. 1.

Slavin, R. et al (eds.), (1985) Learning to Co-operate, Co-operating to Learn. New York, Plenum Press.

Smith, J. and Golden, P. (1994a) Airline: A strategic Management Simulation. Englewood Cliffs, Prentice-Hall.

Smith, J. and Golden, P. (1994b) Corporation: A Global Business Simulation. Englewood Cliffs, Prentice Hall.

Strevens, P. (1988) "ESP after twenty years: a re-appraisal," from Tickoo, M. (ed.), ESP: State of the Art. Singapore, SEAMEO Regional Language Centre.

Sun Tzu (1971) The Art of War. Translated by S.B. Griffith. Oxford, Oxford University Press.

Swales, J.M. (1990) Genre Analysis: English in Academic and Research Settings. Cambridge, Cambridge University Press.

Tannen, D. (1984) Conversational Style: Analysing Talk Among Friends. Norwood, Ablex.

Tannen, D. (1992) That's Not What I Meant. London, Virago.

Thomas, J. (1984) "Cross-cultural discourse as 'unequal encounter': towards a pragmatic analysis," in Applied Linguistics, Vol. 5, No. 3.

Time, April 13, 1998.

Ting-Toomey, S. (1985) "Towards a Theory of Conflict and Culture," in Gudykunst, W., Stewart, L. and Ting-Toomey, S. (eds.), Communication, Culture and Organisational Processes. Beverley Hills, Sage.

Unit 1: The Environment and Scope of EIB

Ting-Toomey, S. and Korzenny, F. (eds.), (2002) Language, Communication, and Culture: Current Directions. Sage Publications.

Trompenaars, F. (1993) Riding the Waves of Culture. London, Nicholas Brealey Publishing Ltd.

Underhill, N. and Impey, G. (1994) The ELT Manager's Handbook. Oxford, Heinemann English Language Teaching.

Unger, C. (2006) Genre, Relevance and Global Coherence: The Pragmatics of Discourse Type. Palgrave Macmillan.

Watzalawick, P. (1967) Pragmatics of Human Communication. New York, Norton and Company.

White, R. (1991) Management in English Language Teaching. Cambridge, Cambridge University Press.

White, R.V. (1997) "Closing the Gap between Intercultural and Business Communication Skills."
http://www.rdg.ac.uk/AcaDepts/cl/slals/closing.htm

White, R.V. (1997) "Going Round in Circles: English as an International Language, and Cross-Cultural Capability."
http://www.rdg.ac.uk/AcaDepts/cl/SLALS/circles.html

Wei, L., Hua, Z. and Yue, L. (2001) "Conversational Management and Involvement in Chinese-English Business talk," in Language and Intercultural Communication, Vol. 1, No. 2.

Zeithaml, V. (1984) "How Consumer Evaluation Processes Differ between Goods and Services", from Lovelock, C. (ed.), Services Marketing. New Jersey, Prentice-Hall, Inc.

Zeithaml, V., Bitner, M. and Gremier, D. (2005) Services Marketing. McGraw-Hill Education.

Unit 1: The Environment and Scope of EIB

Computer-based corpora

Wordsmith
http://www.oup.com/elt/global/isbn/6890/

Hong Kong University of Science and Technology – Vocabulary Trainer http://uvt.ust.hk/about.html#n4

Links to places where Concordances Corpora and text analysis software are available
http://www.ruf.rice.edu/~barlow/corpus.html.

Readware - a text analysis program
http://www.readware.com/

More Links to text analysis software
http://www.intext.de/TEXTANAE.HTM

A summary of text analysis tools for PC windows and Apple Mac
http://info.ox.ac.uk/ctitext/enquiry/tat01a.html

UNIT 2

Needs, Materials and Course Design

UNIT 2: Needs, Materials and Course Design

Chapter 1

Course Design - 1

1.1: Introduction
1.2: Objectives
1.3: Terminology and Key Concepts
1.4: The Elements of Course Design
1.5: The Syllabus
1.6: Theories of Learning
1.7: Conclusions
1.8: Answers to Questions.

1.1: Introduction

Chapters 1 to 3 of this unit examine the principal elements of course design. Chapter 1 looks at the syllabus, descriptions of language and learning theory (see unit 3, chapter 9 for more on learning theories). Chapter 2 examines needs analysis in some detail, and chapter 3 considers how we can put all the information together and come up with a viable course.

Hutchinson and Waters (1987) argue that designing a course is fundamentally a matter of asking the right questions in order to provide a foundation upon which the subsequent processes can be built. These processes are: syllabus design, materials selection, classroom teaching and course evaluation.

If we pause to consider these processes, it will become clear that course design is closely related to other topics in this book. Chapter 10 of unit 3, for example, considers testing and evaluation. At the same time, course designers and/or teachers will need to ask themselves how to approach classroom teaching. In other words, which learning theory will underpin the course, and what methodology will be employed? You will find that these are dealt with in unit 3.

We examine course design from a practical angle so that, at the end of this unit, you will be better prepared to design your own courses. We do not aim to be prescriptive. There are probably as many different approaches to course design as there are course designers and teachers. We can, however, identify the main elements and approaches to course design so that you can decide for yourself what works for you in your situation.

1.2: Objectives

The aims of this chapter are to:

- raise awareness of the elements of course design
- clarify the uses of a syllabus
- outline descriptions of language and learning theories.

Pre-reading task

At the end of the chapter we hope you will be better able to approach the questions in the shaded box below.

> *What are the main elements of course design?*
> *What do you understand by the term syllabus?*

1.3: Terminology and Key Concepts

Course design is a process that interprets the information we get from a needs analysis and transforms the information into a series of lessons that lead learners to a desired set of skills and/or knowledge. A syllabus identifies what the content of the course will be. The selected

UNIT 2: Needs, Materials and Course Design

methodology will determine how teachers and learners work with that content. The content and methodology will directly influence the materials that are chosen for the course. Evaluation procedures will also be put into place in order to measure progress towards the specified aims.

Even when we have collected information from a needs analysis and looked at theories of learning, the data we have still needs to be interpreted. There is not always a clear link between needs analysis and course design. For example, imagine a situation in which a learner is sent by his/her company to participate in a course designed to develop negotiation skills. Perhaps the learner has other needs or wants. For example, s/he needs a break from work or perceives the course as a sort of holiday, a reward for hard work.

There will certainly be other factors to consider. For example, is the course to be intensive or extensive? Are the learners' needs immediate needs or delayed needs? Are the learners experienced in their fields or are they still students? Is the course one-to-one or a group course? If it is a group course, is the group made up of learners from one particular profession or not?

Some of these factors are beyond the control of the course designer. If a course is designed some time before it takes place, it may well be that details will have to be revised during the course itself. An experienced teacher of EIB may wish to negotiate the course content with the learners and react quickly to needs and to changes in needs as they occur. Course design can therefore be described as:

> ...a dynamic mix of juggling and doing jigsaw puzzles. Juggling because there are a lot of different aspects to keep in mind...jigsaw puzzles because we are taking different pieces and shifting them around until they fit to make a satisfactory picture. (Dudley-Evans and St John, 1998, p 162)

Essentially, course designers should be aware of the options open to them and to be flexible with regard to approaches.

In the next sections we will examine the different elements of course design, that is, the jigsaw pieces and the balls that are being juggled. We will examine these balls and pieces discretely, but only because it is convenient to treat them discretely. In practice the course designer will look at the elements of course design concurrently before deciding on a

UNIT 2: Needs, Materials and Course Design

particular approach to designing a course.

1.4: The Elements of Course Design

At the beginning of this chapter, we suggested that, in essence, designing a course concerns asking questions in order to provide information that can help us in the subsequent process of syllabus design, materials selection classroom teaching and evaluation.

Pause for thought

> *Consider which questions you would need to ask before you begin to design a course in EIB. How would you get the answers? Make a list of your questions.*

We will need to ask a lot of questions. Some of the questions can be answered by effective needs analysis. Others can be answered by looking at available theoretical models of learning. Sometimes, teachers and/or course designers will have to fall back on intuition and experience.

Hutchinson and Waters (1987) outline the basic questions that need to be asked and answered.

1. Why does the learner need to learn?
2. Who will be involved apart from the learner? Employers?
3. Where will the course take place? Does this place have any obvious disadvantages?
4. When will the learning take place? How much time do we have? How will that time be distributed?
5. What does the learner need to learn? What language level needs to be achieved? How can we describe the aspects of language needed?
6. How will learning take place? What methodology will we employ?

The answers to questions 1, 2, 3 and 4 concern needs analysis. This will be discussed in chapter 2. Question 5 concerns the syllabus and will be examined in this chapter. Question 6 deals with learning theory and methodology. We will look at these topics in this chapter and in unit 3.

We emphasise again that we discuss these elements of course design separately in order to clarify them. In practice, they are interdependent.

UNIT 2: Needs, Materials and Course Design

Their relationship may be represented in the figure below.

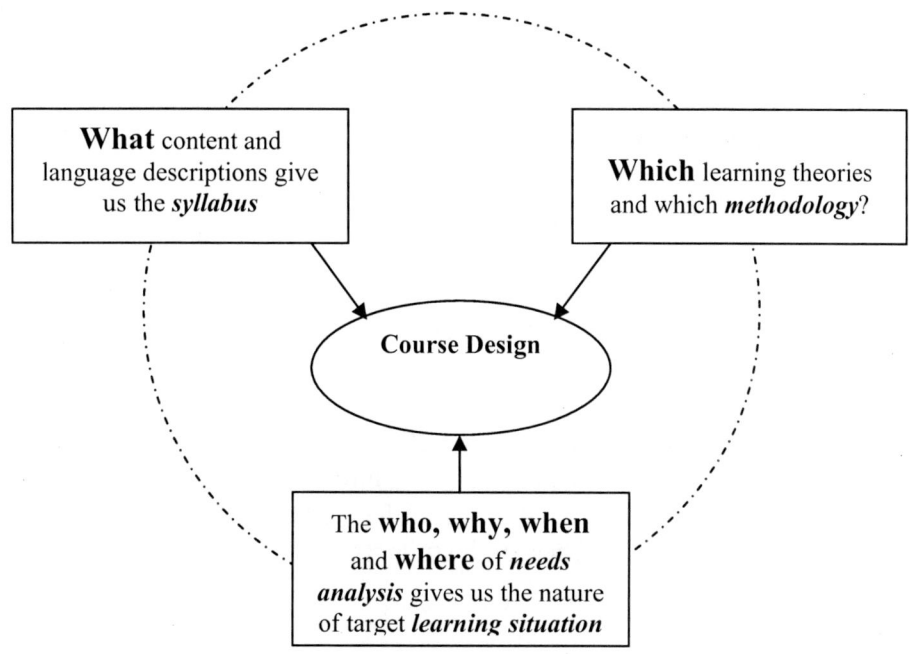

Question 1

Imagine that you work in the Efficient and Effective Language School (EELS) in Central London. You offer courses in EIB to anyone who needs them. It is Friday afternoon and you have just come back from lunch. Your Director of Studies (DOS) has left you an e-mail before hurrying away for the weekend.

Apparently EELS was contacted that very morning by a business school in London. They want to know if you can offer a programme to upgrade the business communication skills of two Japanese students before they embark on a programme leading to an MBA. Your DOS has left a telephone number for you and is expecting you to organise and teach the course. The course starts on Monday.

You ring the number and you get through to the business school and a rather stressed-sounding course administrator. In order to prepare your course you will need some information from him.

UNIT 2: Needs, Materials and Course Design

> *What questions will you ask? Make a list. Imagine that the course administrator only has some of the answers you need. For example, he does not know exactly what the learning needs are. How will you handle the situation on Monday?*

1.5: The Syllabus

Pause for thought

> *Why do we need a syllabus?*
> *How can a syllabus be organised?*

Any syllabus is a plan of what is to be achieved through teaching and learning. It is part of...a course which is made up of four elements: aims, content, methodology and evaluation. The syllabus identifies what will be worked upon by the teacher and students in terms of content... (Breen, 2001)

It would be a mistake to think of a syllabus as document which must be prepared by ministries of education or by the management of an educational institution. All teachers will follow a syllabus. This syllabus may well be a pre-prepared document, but it may also be a day-to-day choice of content for a particular group of learners. In this case, the syllabus unfolds as the course progresses.

Whatever the type of syllabus teachers follow, Breen (2001) suggests that any syllabus should provide the following.

- A list of knowledge and skills within the framework of overall aims.
- A sense of direction for teachers and learners.
- A record of what has been done in the classroom.
- A basis for learner evaluation.
- A basis for course evaluation.
- Content appropriate to the learners' needs.

Breen (2001) goes on to consider four principles which define a syllabus. These principles are expressed as questions.

UNIT 2: Needs, Materials and Course Design

- What knowledge and skills should be focused on? Should we focus simply on linguistic knowledge or on more communicative knowledge? Should we focus on all four skills or only one?
- What should we choose as appropriate content? If the focus is linguistic, what structures should be covered? If the focus is communicative, which particular uses of language should be chosen and which types of task?
- How should we divide up the content into manageable chunks?
- How should the content be sequenced?

A syllabus, therefore, represents our attempts to break down the mass of information we have concerning the learners and to transform it into manageable chunks. The way we choose to segment that information will reveal what we believe to be the nature of language, and how the language should be described.

Descriptions of language

Hutchinson and Waters (1987) acknowledge six principal means of describing language.

1. Traditional grammar – in which descriptions of language are based on an analysis of the role played by each word in a sentence.
2. Structural linguistics - in which language is described in terms of the structures which carry fundamental propositions, for example: statements, negatives and interrogatives. The most obvious application of structural linguistics is the syllabus whereby items are graded so that simpler forms precede the more complex ones. Learners are exposed to a systematic description of the core of language.
3. Transformational generative (TG) grammar - whereby it is argued that an understanding of structure is superficial and that these structures do not necessarily reflect the thoughts behind the words. The most important effect of TG on language teaching has been to establish the distinction between language performance and language competence; in other words, the distinction between what we do with language (performance) and what it is that enables us to do it (competence). This idea of competence is directly linked to work into language as communication and the functional/notional description of language.

UNIT 2: Needs, Materials and Course Design

4. Functional/notional grammar - whereby communicative acts are performed through language. For example: ordering a meal, hiring a car, and making travel arrangements.
5. Language variation and register analysis - whereby language can vary according to context. This has led to attempts to identify the kinds of language associated with a specific context, for example: presentations, negotiations and chairing meetings.
6. Discourse analysis - in which language is studied independently of the notion of the sentence. Discourse analysis usually involves studying longer spoken and written texts and, especially, the relationship between the text and the situation in which it occurs (see also unit 4 chapter 2).

We would like to emphasise at this point that there is no single source from which a syllabus should derive its linguistic content. The developments described above are not separate bodies. They inform and inspire one another. In essence, the descriptions are descriptions of the same thing. Further, they are complementary in the sense that all communication has a structural level, a functional level and a discourse level.

Question 2

> *Look at the lists below. They are examples of the content of some EIB courses. On what criteria are the lists organised? In other words, can you see any implicit of explicit assumptions about language descriptions?*
>
> *Example 1*
> *Location*
> *Measurement*
> *Property and shape*
> *Processes 1*
> *Frequency.*
>
> *Example 2*
> *Making arrangements*
> *Travelling*
> *Chairing meetings*
> *Participating in meetings*

UNIT 2: Needs, Materials and Course Design

Negotiating
Presenting facts and figures
Writing e-mails.

Example 3
Presentation skills
Negotiating skills
Meeting skills
Writing reports
Writing business letters and e-mails
Improving reading efficiency.

Example 4
Company results
Present perfect simple and continuous.
Systems and processes
Passive voice and sequencers.
Describing trends
Prepositions, cause and effect connectors.
Company presentation
Present continuous and present simple. To have.

Example 5
Human resources
Recruitment
Selection
Motivating personnel
Marketing
The marketing mix
Promotion
Retailing and merchandising
Finance
Raising capital
Investing
Accounting.

It is highly likely that you can easily identify the criteria on which these lists were organised. However, most syllabi will operate several other syllabi at the same time. One will almost certainly be dominant, but elements of the others will also be present. For example, every function is realised by structures. Thus, any functional syllabus will contain structural elements. Furthermore, texts will be written or spoken about something. Therefore, all syllabi will have topics.

Hutchinson and Waters (1987) suggest that course design should reflect all descriptions of language and that course designers take a varied approach to syllabus design. A syllabus that is framed in only one view of language description may well be ineffective. The real challenge is not which language description to select but how to integrate them all so that they make up a sensible teaching programme.

Pause for thought

> *Look at any EIB coursebook with which you are familiar. On what criteria has the content been organised? Does the author(s) take an integrated approach?*

1.6: Theories of Learning

We begin this section by making a clear distinction between language descriptions and learning theory. As we have seen, language description concerns the way in which language is broken down and described. The terms we have examined, for example: structural, functional and notional, belong to the area of language description and how language may be analysed. These terms say nothing about how language should be learned or taught. Approaches to learning come from a view of learning and not from descriptions of language. It is the learning theory that should underpin our classroom methodology.

Learning theories are dealt with fully in chapter 9 of unit 3, and we recommend that you read the relevant parts of the chapter in order to review the main developments in learning theory. In order to assess the relationship between learning theory and methodology we suggest you look at Lightbown and Spada (2006).

UNIT 2: Needs, Materials and Course Design

Pause for thought

> *Identify the main developments in learning theory and make a note of the basic teaching techniques associated with these theories. In your opinion, is there a place for all these teaching techniques in course design, or should we focus only on current theories and current techniques?*

Hutchinson and Waters (1987) point out that developments in learning theory have followed a similar pattern to developments in language description.

Pause for thought

> *Look again at question 2 and the lists of content for some EIB courses. In your opinion, is there a causal link between language description and learning theory? In other words, does a cognitive learning theory, for example, go hand in hand with a functional view of language?*

We still have much to learn about learning, and we suggest that it would be unwise to base any approach to teaching on one theory. It is probably better to take what is useful from each theory and to trust in your own judgement as a teacher and/or course designer. There are: behaviourist, cognitive and affective aspects to learning a language, and all of them should be seen as a resource. You may find that a behaviourist approach works well with some classes and with some aspects of language, and that a cognitive approach works better with other classes and other aspects of language.

Hutchinson and Waters (1987) suggest that there is no causal link between a particular theory of learning and a particular theory of language description. There may well be a historical connection, but a behaviourist theory of learning does not necessarily go naturally with a structural view of language. Nor is there a logical connection between cognitive learning theory and a functional view of language.

For the course designer, we suggest that language descriptions and learning theory should be selected according to the principle of what is appropriate for the group of learners you have in mind.

UNIT 2: Needs, Materials and Course Design

1.7: Conclusion

We have offered a standard approach to course design. However, for those who are interested in more extensive studies, you are recommended to consult Hewings and Dudley-Evans (1996), which looks at course design for EAP at British universities. Nunan (1988) is a standard reference for learner-centred courses. You may also like to look at Breen and Littlejohn (2000) for more input on syllabus design, and Long and Crookes (1992) who look at task-based syllabus design. Richards (2001) is excellent on all aspects of course design including: situation analysis, needs analysis, goal setting, syllabus design, materials development, teaching and evaluation. For an excellent introduction to theories of first and second language learning, you should consult Lightbown and Spada (2006). The authors make the connection between the main theories of learning and classroom methodology and practice.

The elements of course design that we have examined in this chapter should all be seen as resources at your disposal. Which resource you decide to adopt for your course and how you do it will depend, to a large extent, on your needs analysis. It is to needs analysis that we now turn.

1.8: Answers to Questions

Question 1
You can group your questions under two headings; the course and the students. Among the questions you should ask are:
The course: Why is it needed? What is the content? What does it require of the learners?
The students: Why are they studying in London? How old are they? What is their level of English?

You should aim to do a needs analysis during the first lesson. This could consist of fairly detailed questioning, either on a face-to-face basis or by using a prepared questionnaire (or both). You should be prepared to negotiate course content and to change it as the course progresses and needs become clearer or change.

Question 2
Functional/notional syllabus
Functional/task-based syllabus
Skills-based syllabus
Structural/situational syllabus
Topic-based syllabus.

UNIT 2: Needs, Materials and Course Design

Chapter 2

Course Design - 2: Needs Analysis

2.1: Introduction
2.2: Objectives
2.3: What is a Needs Analysis?
2.4: Getting Information about Target Needs
2.5: The Present Situation, Learning Needs and Means Analysis
2.6: Where Do We Get Data for Needs Analysis?
2.7: Conclusions
2.8: Answers to Questions.

2.1: Introduction

This chapter continues our examination of course design and focuses on needs analysis. We saw in chapter 1 that needs analysis is only one element of course design. The others concern language description and learning theory, syllabus design, materials selection, classroom teaching and course evaluation.

It is useful to point out once more that these are not linearly-related activities. They are interdependent. For example, needs analysis attempts to establish the *what, who, why* and *where* of a course, while evaluation is the process of establishing the effectiveness of a course. However, both need to be ongoing so that the one continuously informs

UNIT 2: Needs, Materials and Course Design

the other.

2.2: Objectives

This chapter aims to further develop your sensitivity to:

➢ the information you require for your needs analysis
➢ where to get that information.

Pre-reading task

Before you begin, look at the questions in the shaded box below. Make a note of your answers now. When you have finished the chapter, answer the questions again and compare your two sets of responses.

> 1. Where would you get the information for your needs analysis?
> 2. How would you get this information?
> 3. What would you do with it once you have designed your course?

2.3: What is a Needs Analysis?

Needs analysis concerns the collection of data. This data can usefully be categorised under the following headings.

➢ Target situation analysis (TSA).
➢ Learning situation analysis (LSA).
➢ Present situation analysis (PSA).

Question 1

> Imagine you have the following statements. They were given to you during an interview with a group of learners on an EIB course. Would you categorise these statements under the TSA, LSA or PSA heading?
> 1. I need to negotiate contracts with US suppliers.
> 2. I need to give presentations to European counterparts.

UNIT 2: Needs, Materials and Course Design

> 3. *I did grammar at school – I just need practice with spoken English.*
> 4. *I don't like role-plays.*
> 5. *I have problems with conditionals.*
> 6. *I need to know the structure of English.*
> 7. *I want to speak correct English.*
> 8. *I need to know how to write e-mails.*
> 9. *I take clients out for meals.*
> 10. *I want the teacher to correct all of my mistakes.*

Dudley-Evans and St John (1998) further break down the categories above. The TSA includes objective or perceived needs. These needs come from facts, from what is known by outsiders. The TSA also includes product-oriented needs. These come from the goal or target situation. The LSA includes subjective needs or wants, and process-oriented needs. Process-oriented needs come from the learning situation. A PSA includes information about learners' strengths and weaknesses in language, skills and learning experiences. We could add means analysis. Means analysis considers the environment in which the course takes place and acknowledges that what works well in one situation may not work so well in another.

Dudley-Evans and St John (1998) suggest that needs analysis means collecting data about the following.

1. The target situation - objective needs. We need to know what activities learners will be doing in English.
2. Students' wants - subjective needs. We need personal information about the learners. We need to know about their previous learning experiences, cultural expectations and reasons for attending the course.
3. The present situation. We need to know about the learners' level of English and their current skills ability. This will enable us to assess:
4. The learners' lacks. This is the gap between 3 and 1 above.
5. Learning needs. Effective ways of learning the language and skills in 4.
6. Linguistic analysis. Knowledge about how language is used in 1.
7. Means analysis. We need information about the environment in which the course will be run.

UNIT 2: Needs, Materials and Course Design

2.4: Getting Information about Target Needs

Essentially, an analysis of the target needs is a matter of asking the right questions about the target situation. The simple framework below (adapted from Hutchinson and Waters, 1987) outlines the kind of information course designers need to gather.

Why is the language needed?
1. For use in meetings.
2. For negotiating.
3. For chairing meetings.
4. For presenting.
5. For study, for example: an MBA programme.
6. For writing reports.
7. For some other reason.

How will the language be used?
1. Speaking, writing, reading, listening.
2. Telephone, face-to-face, one-to-one, one-to-many.
3. Type of text, for example: informal discussions, formal discussions, reports, lectures and so on.

What will the content be?
1. Topics, for example: marketing, HRM, finance.
2. Level, for example: student, manager, technician.

Where will the language be used?
1. Office, lecture theatre, conference room.
2. Human context, for example: meetings, telephone, alone.
3. Linguistic context, for example: abroad, at home.

When will the language be used?
1. At the same time as the course or after it?

In the ideal scenario, the answers to these questions should be obtained from a variety of sources. Needs are a matter of perception, and perceptions can differ. For example, learners' views may well conflict with the views of their sponsors, their teachers and/or course designers.

We should never ignore the wants of the learners even if their wants conflict with the wishes of their sponsors. For example, a company may well have a need for employees who can communicate confidently (not necessarily accurately) with employees from other countries. However, learners may well feel that they need to communicate accurately rather than fluently. They may perceive mistakes in English grammar as a weakness and personally unacceptable.

2.5: The Present Situation, Learning Needs and Means Analysis

The analysis of target needs gives the course designer information about what learners need to do in English in certain specified situations. This information may be recorded in terms of language items, skills and subject knowledge.

However, course designers still need to know how they should best approach the learning of these items, skills and subject knowledge. To analyse learning needs, the present situation and the potential or constraints of the environment, course designers will need to ask more questions.

The following question framework has been adapted from Hutchinson and Waters (1987).

Why are the learners taking the course?
- Is it obligatory or optional?
- Does the course involve status, promotion or money?
- What do learners think they will achieve?
- What is their attitude to the course? Do they resent the time they are spending on it?

How do the learners learn?
- What is their learning background?
- How do they perceive teaching and learning?
- What methodology will appeal to them?
- What sort of teaching techniques will appeal to them?

What resources are available?
- Number of teachers and their experience.
- Attitude of teachers to the world of business.
- Teachers' knowledge of business and management.
- Teaching/learning aids.

UNIT 2: Needs, Materials and Course Design

Who are the learners?
- Age, sex, culture.
- What is their level of English?
- What is their level of subject knowledge?
- What are their interests?
- What teaching styles are they used to?
- What is their attitude to English and the cultures of the English-speaking world?

Where will the course take place?
- What are the surroundings like?
- Can you change the surroundings?
- What resources do you have?

When will the course take place?
- Time of day.
- Every day, once a week.
- Full-time, part-time.
- Concurrent with need or pre-need.

Clearly, there are a lot of questions to ask. However, the way in which a needs analysis is actually carried out will depend on the situation. The amount of data collected, and when it is collected, may vary considerably. For example, if a course is repeated on a regular basis and includes large numbers of learners, advance needs analysis may be possible. However, many EIB courses in which the writer has been involved have been held at very short notice. Furthermore, the number of learners may be as low as one and pre-course information may be limited or non-existent. When this is the case, the needs analysis may have to be done in the first lesson and consist simply of asking pertinent questions or having learner(s) fill out a questionnaire. Certainly, it would be advisable to maintain a flexible attitude to course design and negotiate it with learners as the course progresses.

2.6: Where Do We Get Data for Needs Analysis?

In order to collect data you might consult some or all of the following sources.

UNIT 2: Needs, Materials and Course Design

- The learners.
- Past learners.
- Other people who are working in the same field as your students.
- Documents which are relevant to that field.
- The clients or sponsors.
- Colleagues.
- EIB research.

You can select from the following methods of data collection.

- Questionnaires.
- Discussions with learners and/or clients.
- Structured interviews with learners and/or clients.
- Analysis of authentic texts.
- Observations/shadowing.

If you decide to use a questionnaire, you will need to think carefully about its construction. An ideal questionnaire should be:

> ...clear, unambiguous and uniformly workable. Its design must minimise potential errors from respondents...and coders. And since people's participation...is voluntary, a questionnaire has to help in engaging their interest, encouraging their co-operation, and eliciting answers as close as possible to the truth. (Davidson, 1970)

When constructing the questionnaire, there are some types of question that should be avoided. For example, try to avoid leading questions; that is, questions which are worded in such a way as to suggest to respondents that there is only one acceptable answer. For example: *"Do you prefer grammar-based courses or courses which are practical, related to your day-to-day work and which will benefit you in the future?"*

Avoid questions which are too jargon-based. For example: *"Do you prefer a behaviourist or a cognitive approach to language learning?"*

You should also avoid complex questions or questions which might irritate in some way. For example: *"If you are over forty, please state the last time you attended a language course."*

Questions should also be of the closed type, requiring a yes/no response or a tick in a box. For more detail on questionnaire design, see

UNIT 2: Needs, Materials and Course Design

Cohen and Manion (1980, pp 90 – 95).

Informal discussions during a course can be a useful way of gaining insights into both learner needs and learner satisfaction with a particular course. However, it is important to distinguish between views that represent the whole group and those which represent the views of a vocal minority.

Structured interviews can also be a valuable way of gathering information for needs analysis. Structured interviews consist of questions that have been prepared beforehand and are put to all the learners. However, there are weaknesses associated with interviews. Cohen and Manion (1980) suggest that some of these weaknesses may concern:

> ...the characteristics of the interviewer, the characteristics of the respondent, and the substantive content of the questions. More particularly, these will include: the attitudes and opinions of the interviewer; a tendency for the interviewer to see the respondent in her own image; a tendency for the interviewer to seek answers that support her preconceived notions; misperceptions on the part of the interviewer of what the respondent is saying; and misunderstandings on the part of the respondent of what is being asked. (Cohen and Manion, 1980)

Analysing authentic texts is a vital part of needs analysis. The texts may be written or spoken. For example, recordings of telephone interactions, negotiations, meetings and presentations are of particular interest to EIB course designers. The analysis may be for TSA purposes or to determine the linguistic features of a communicative event. It could also be that the texts are samples of participants' language and therefore help towards carrying out a PSA.

Observation for the purposes of needs analysis can cover a range of activities. Most observation is for TSA purposes but could also be for PSA. Observation may involve shadowing - following everything a person does for a specific period of time. For example, the writer was once asked to sit in on in-company meetings so that he could observe the chairperson and how he chaired meetings. This can be a sensitive issue. We first had to explain exactly what it was I was doing in the room, and we also had to ask permission from the other participants. The subsequent observation was extremely interesting from a number of perspectives - language, communication, decision-making skills, intercultural issues and chairing skills.

2.7: Conclusions

We conclude this chapter on needs analysis by again stressing that it is a complex process and involves much more than simply looking at what learners will have to do in the target situation. Behind every successful course in EIB is a continuous process of questioning. This questioning leads initially to what a course should contain and how it should be run. Further questions should lead to a possible revision of objectives and a modification of teaching methods and materials. This basic process should be ongoing. We would point out that the data collected from needs analysis has no intrinsic value. The information we have needs to be interpreted in some way. How we interpret the data will depend on our approach to course design. These approaches will be dealt with in the next chapter. For those of you who would like to read more about needs analysis, we recommend Long and Richards (2005). This book examines needs analysis in a variety of sectors and contexts, and the authors discuss the methodology employed.

2.8: Answers to Questions

Question 1
1. TSA
2. TSA
3. LSA
4. LSA
5. PSA
6. LSA
7. LSA
8. TSA
9. TSA
10. LSA

UNIT 2: Needs, Materials and Course Design

Chapter 3

Course Design - 3: Putting It All Together

3.1: Introduction
3.2: Objectives
3.3: Principal Approaches to Course Design
3.4: Materials Selection
3.5: Course Evaluation
3.6: Conclusions
3.7: Answers to Questions.

3.1: Introduction

We have already mentioned that there are probably as many approaches to EIB course design as there are course designers. However, we can identify three main approaches to course design. These are:

➢ A language-centred approach.
➢ A skills-centred approach.
➢ A learning-centred approach.

In this chapter we will give you an overview of each of these approaches. Having decided on your approach, you will need to make sure that it is working effectively; in other words, you will need to set

UNIT 2: Needs, Materials and Course Design

up a process of evaluation to determine which (if any) aspects of the approach you have chosen need changing.

3.2: Objectives

The aims of this chapter are to:

- introduce the main approaches to course design and to evaluate their strengths and weaknesses
- suggest ways in which we can evaluate whether or not the course is meeting the needs it was designed to satisfy.

Pre-reading task

> *Imagine that you have collected the data from your needs analysis. You have reviewed the theories of learning and descriptions of language. Now, you have to decide what you will do with the information you have. How will you interpret it?*

3.3: Principal Approaches to Course Design

Language-centred approach to course design

This is, perhaps, the simplest type of course design process. It aims to connect the analysis of the target situation and the content of the EIB course as directly as possible. This can be shown diagrammatically. The figure on page 180 has been adapted from Hutchinson and Waters (1987).

Question 1

> *A language-centred approach to course design has advantages and disadvantages. What are some of these advantages and disadvantages?*

UNIT 2: Needs, Materials and Course Design

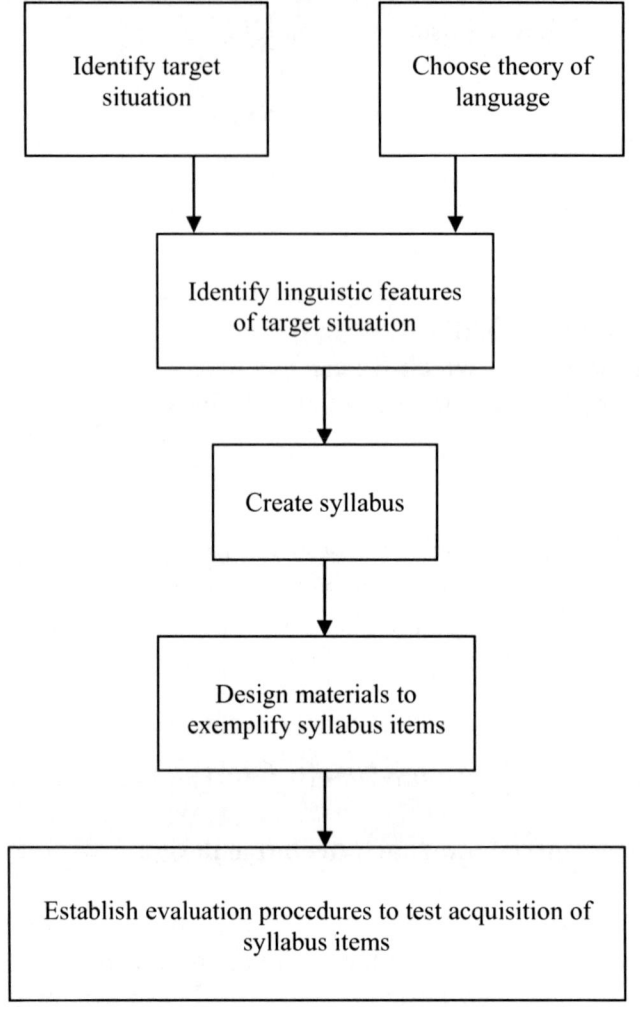

Skills-centred approach to course design

Essentially the skills-centred approach to course design presents its objectives in terms of language performance and language competence. For example, the performance level may state that students will be able to negotiate deals. The competence level may state that students will be able to make and respond to suggestions and to confidently handle the first and second conditionals. Furthermore, a skills-centred approach can be seen as a process approach. This means, for example, that learners on a course designed to improve presentation skills, do not

UNIT 2: Needs, Materials and Course Design

finish the course as perfectly proficient presenters. Instead, the course is viewed as an important part of a constantly evolving process which has no final end.

Hutchinson and Waters (1987) present the approach diagrammatically.

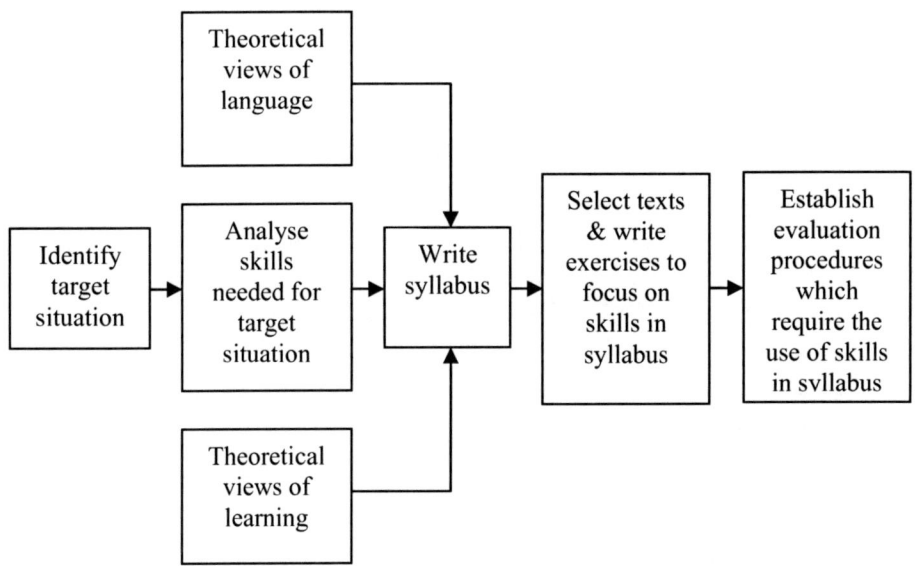

Question 2

Like the language-centred approach to course design, the skills-centred approach has its advantages and disadvantages. What are they? Make a list and then compare it with the answers we suggest in the Answers to Questions section.

Learning-centred approach to course design

Proponents of the learning-centred approach to course design claim that it is both dynamic and interactive in the sense that it considers, at all stages of the design process, the interests of the learners and the learning process. Furthermore, no single element is the determiner of course content. The syllabus, the selected materials, the methodology and evaluation process are all influenced by the EIB learning situation and by the target situation. Similarly, each element of course design

UNIT 2: Needs, Materials and Course Design

will influence and be influenced by the other elements.

Therefore, the learning-centred approach is not a linear process. Instead, it is dynamic and recognises the fact that needs and resources can change over time. The course design, therefore, needs to have feedback channels built in to it so that designers and/or teachers can respond to developing needs. Hutchinson and Waters (1987) represent the learning-centred approach diagrammatically.

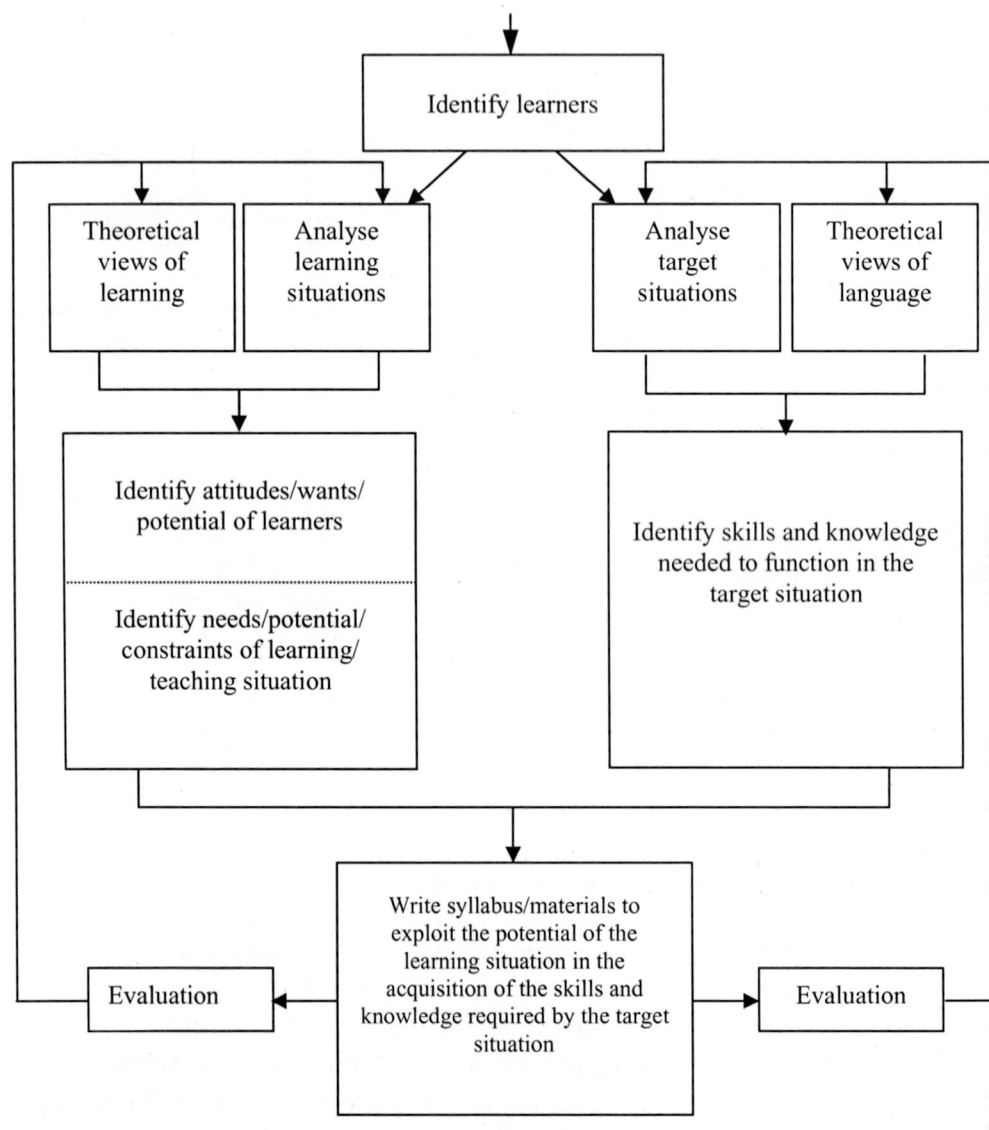

UNIT 2: Needs, Materials and Course Design

Question 3

> *How does the learning-centred approach to course design differ from the language-centred approach and the skills-centred approach? What is the main disadvantage of the learning-centred approach?*

3.4: Materials Selection

We will examine EIB materials evaluation and selection in the next chapter. However, in this section we shall outline some basic principles you may use when selecting good materials for EIB.

Essentially, materials do not teach anything. They should encourage and motivate learners to learn by providing interesting texts and enjoyable activities. They should also provide a stimulus to activate thinking capacities.

Furthermore, materials should provide a clear course structure that helps both teacher and learner negotiate the complicated mass of language they are faced with. On the other hand, materials should not be so tightly structured that they become monotonous and de-motivating.

With regard to the teacher, materials should suit an individual teacher's style of teaching and embody his/her view of what language is and how it can best be learned. For both students and teacher, materials should be balanced and make the learning process appear manageable. Finally, materials should provide a model of appropriate language usage. This is particularly important if access to native-speaker language is difficult for the learners.

The writing of materials from scratch is something that should probably be done only as a last resort. There are many sources of materials and there is no point in reinventing the wheel. Material can be modified and adapted to suit a particular situation.

Whether you decide that you have to write your own materials from scratch or you decide to modify existing material, your decisions will ultimately depend on the aims of the course, the language level of the learners, and your overall approach to teaching and learning.

UNIT 2: Needs, Materials and Course Design

3.5: Course Evaluation

It is useful to identify two types of evaluation - evaluation of learners and evaluation of the course. This chapter will look at course evaluation while chapter 10 of unit 3 examines testing and assessment of learners. You might want to scan through that chapter before you tackle this section.

The origins of most EIB programmes lie in satisfying a need. Evaluation helps us to assess how well the needs that created the demand for our course in the first place are being met.

Pause for thought

> *If you were asked to evaluate your own EIB course, what will you decide to evaluate and how will you go about it?*

What exactly is evaluation? There are many definitions. Dudley-Evans and St John (1998) define evaluation as, "...a whole process which begins with determining what information to gather and ends with bringing about changes in current activities or influencing future ones."

Genesee (2001) defines evaluation as, "...a process of collecting, analysing and interpreting information about teaching and learning in order to make informed decisions that enhance student achievement." Genesee (2001) describes the process as having four major components.

1. Articulation of the evaluation purpose.
2. Identifying and collecting relevant information.
3. Analysis and interpretation of that information.
4. Decision-making and action.

Pause for thought

> *Imagine that you are still working at EELS in London. One of your most successful courses has been your programme in oral and written EIB. Learners on this course are adult, non-native speakers of English whose employers want to transfer them to international operations. EELS have decided that they want to introduce a new set of materials for this course. This material includes new textbooks and new audio-lingual teaching aids. You*

UNIT 2: Needs, Materials and Course Design

> *will use this material for one year before determining its effectiveness. Then you can decide whether to continue using it for a second year. Think about the points we have mentioned above. How would you use this framework for your evaluation?*

Evaluation in EIB concerns the effectiveness and efficiency of learning and the achievement, or not, of objectives set by the needs analysis. We need to know whether learning potential has been fully exploited and whether resources have been effectively deployed. Evaluation is therefore formative (ongoing) evaluation and takes place within the lifetime of a course in order to modify it if necessary.

Evaluation should, in an ideal scenario, be part of the course design. Evaluation should also focus at different times on different course components, for example: evaluation of materials, evaluation of classroom activities, and evaluation of methodology.

Many EIB courses are one-off, short courses. Evaluation of these programmes may take the shape of asking questions during the break or at the end of the day. These questions should focus on change that is viable. It is at this point that evaluation and on-going needs analysis overlap. For courses that are longer in duration, evaluation may be more structured and have a wider range of purposes.

How do we evaluate the course?

There are many ways in which a course can be evaluated. These ways range from simulations to suggestion boxes. However, most EIB programmes can be evaluated by using one or more of the following techniques.

- Test results.
- Questionnaires.
- Discussions and/or structured interviews.

We have already looked at some of the drawbacks of questionnaires and interviews in chapter 2 of this unit. The techniques you decide to use will depend on the situation you are in. However, gathering information is only the first step in the process. The information should be summarised and discussed with all the interested parties. Then, the conclusions you come to should be used as a basis for decision-making and action.

UNIT 2: Needs, Materials and Course Design

Where do we get information for evaluation purposes?

The involvement of the different groups will vary with every course. However, it is likely that the parties most interested in course evaluation will be: the institution, the teachers, the learners, and the course sponsors. Evaluation is concerned with perceptions of value and perceptions of value can differ according to interests and concerns. We have already noted in unit 1 chapter 8 (Management in EIB) that it can be difficult to get useful feedback from learners. They will often blame themselves for inefficient learning and poor results. Having said that, course evaluation needs to involve all those who share in the learning process and who have an interest in making the course as satisfying as possible.

Question 4

> *Imagine you have just finished a two-day course in presentation skills. The company was run at the insistence of managers who saw a need to upgrade the presentation skills of employees who regularly presented to US colleagues. You now have to evaluate the course.*
> 1. *How could you articulate the purpose of the evaluation?*
> 2. *How would you get the material for evaluation?*
> 3. *Who would you involve in the evaluation process?*
> 4. *What would you do with your conclusions?*

Student achievement is an important focus of evaluation because teachers and others need to know what, and how much, students have learned in order to make appropriate advancement or placement decisions. In collaborative programme evaluation, teachers along with researchers and/or ministries and/or HR departments engage in research to evaluate the programme (Burns 1996). Teachers are primary agents in planning, managing and carrying out formative evaluation (Genesee and Upshur 1996).

However, there are sometimes difficulties in reconciling teacher-driven evaluations with state- or company-mandated evaluations (Brindley 1998). The problem is how to incorporate the (often) informal evaluations of the classroom with the standardised evaluations often required by ministries or companies. Resolving the issue involves both technical and socio-political considerations.

UNIT 2: Needs, Materials and Course Design

Mention should be made here of the trend towards classroom-based evaluation that is linked to classroom teaching. This trend is often confused with a movement towards "alternative assessment" but in fact it involves issues of evaluation. The approach is characterised by the following.

- Multiple types of information, for example: student achievement, attitude, learning style, needs and aspirations.
- Alternative methods of information collection to complement tests, for example: dialogue journals and student-teacher discussions.
- Concerns for both the processes and the products of teaching and learning. We are often quite good at evaluating the processes of a course, but how can we effectively evaluate the product? For example, how do we evaluate how well learners present, negotiate or chair meetings long after the course has finished?

3.6: Conclusions

In this chapter we have looked at how the information we get from a needs analysis can be used to design an effective EIB course. We have suggested that course design should be as dynamic and interactive as possible, and factors concerning learning should be brought into play at all stages of the design process. We have also stressed the necessity for on-going or formative evaluation procedures where possible.

However, we would also stress that a lot of energy can be saved if we learn from other examples of course design. In the same way that materials need not necessarily be written from scratch, past courses can be adapted and modified to suit other situations.

3.7: Answers to Questions

Question 1
Advantages include the following.
- It is logical and straightforward.
- It is the simplest kind of course-design process.
- It is likely to be familiar to teachers.

Disadvantages include the following.
- It does not really consider the learners. Learners are useful in order to identify the target situation.

UNIT 2: Needs, Materials and Course Design

- It is a static and inflexible procedure with no real feedback channels and with little tolerance of error built in to it.
- Its analysis of the target situation reveals little about language competence.

Question 2

Advantages
- It takes into account both language performance and language competence.
- It tries to build on the positive factors that learners bring to the classroom and does not simply focus on "lacks."
- Its objectives are open-ended so that learners can always achieve something and continue to develop skills after the course.

Disadvantages
- Like the language-centred approach, it sees the learner as a user of language rather than as a learner of language and does not fully consider learners other than to analyse the target situation needs.

Question 3

The learning-centred approach is different because it considers the learning process at all stages of course design. It is, therefore, more flexible and dynamic than the other two approaches and attempts to maximise the potential of the learning situation. The main disadvantage is that it is much more complex than the other two approaches.

Question 4

1. To determine the effectiveness and usefulness of course.
2. Teacher observation, learner observations, post-course questionnaires for participants and managers, post-course discussions with participants and management.
3. Learners, management.
4. To restructure/refocus course design if necessary and to decide on future action.

UNIT 2: Needs, Materials and Course Design

Chapter 4

Materials for EIB

4.1: Introduction
4.2: Objectives
4.3: Terminology and Key Concepts
4.4: The Purpose of Materials
4.5: Evaluation and Selection of Available Material
4.6: Being Creative with Available Material
4.7: Supplementing Material - Teacher-Generated Material
4.8: Supplementing Material - Learner-Generated Material
4.9: Conclusion
4.10: Extracts
4.11: Answers to Questions.

4.1: Introduction

Tomlinson (2001) writes that development of materials can be viewed from two separate but inter-related perspectives. The first perspective views development of materials as a discipline, a field of study in its own right. The second perspective views development of materials as something practical, something which potentially takes up a great deal of teachers' time.

As a discipline, development of materials can involve studying the

UNIT 2: Needs, Materials and Course Design

principles and procedures of designing, implementing and evaluating language teaching materials. As a teacher-activity, it involves producing, evaluating and adapting language teaching materials for classroom use. In an ideal world, these two aspects of development are interactive in the sense that the one informs the other.

Tomlinson (2001) argues that studies of materials development did not receive serious consideration from teacher educators and writers until the 1990s. He gives two reasons for this change in attitude. The first reason was a growing awareness that providing practice in materials development was an effective way of helping teachers to understand and apply theories of language learning. Furthermore, provision of this experience helped teachers achieve more personal and professional satisfaction - in other words, it increased motivation.

The second reason was the realisation that no one coursebook is ideal for all classes. The logical consequence of this was that teachers should be able to efficiently evaluate, adapt and produce materials in order to match them to the needs and requirements of the learners.

Within the context of EIB, many courses are tailor-made to suit the requirements of a particular company. Furthermore, the company might expect to receive nothing less than specially written materials and handouts. For the company, such material can represent value for money.

We hope that this chapter will also be of value to you in the sense that it will be of practical use when you are faced with the task of preparing and/or designing material for a particular group of learners. Tomlinson (1998) is recommended additional reading for this chapter and it offers important insights into materials development. Both this chapter and the recommended reading will give practical guidance with regard to the criteria you might use when selecting, evaluating, adapting and supplementing materials.

4.2: Objectives

The aims of this chapter are to:

- identify what we mean by the term "materials"
- examine the purpose of materials
- identify criteria for evaluating and selecting material
- consider the reasons for adapting materials

UNIT 2: Needs, Materials and Course Design

- suggest various means by which materials can be adapted
- suggest situations in which new materials should be considered
- suggest how this new material can be developed.

Pre-reading Questions

At the end of the chapter, we hope you will be better able to approach the questions in the shaded box below. Make a note of your ideas and opinions and do not worry if you are unsure about your answers at this stage. At the end of the chapter you should go back to this section and answer the questions again. You should then compare your two sets of responses.

> - *What are "materials" in EIB?*
> - *What is the purpose of materials?*
> - *What criteria do you use when you select material for a class?*
> - *Have you ever incorporated materials brought into the classroom by learners? How have you done this?*
> - *Have you ever supplemented a course with additional material? Why and how did you do this?*
> - *Have you ever written material completely from scratch? How long did it take to write it? Was it worth the effort?*
> - *If you have written material from scratch, how did you evaluate its effectiveness?*

4.3: Terminology and Key Concepts

All teachers use materials. For the purposes of this chapter, the term material covers everything which is used to help teachers to teach and learners to learn. So, materials can be linguistic, visual and auditory. They can be presented in print, through performance on cassettes, video, CD-ROM, DVD or the internet. Furthermore, materials may be used to give information about language, to provide exposure to language, and to stimulate language use. Most teachers will use paper-based materials. It is highly likely that the paper-based material with which you are most familiar is the coursebook.

UNIT 2: Needs, Materials and Course Design

Question 1

> *What, in your opinion, are the main advantages and disadvantages of using a coursebook? Make a list of the advantages and disadvantages, and then compare it with the suggested answers in the Answers to Questions section at the end of the chapter.*

Other examples of materials you might use for EIB courses include: magazine articles, recordings of television or radio business programmes, and company information provided on the internet.

Any discussion of materials selection should clarify the role of content. The concepts of carrier content and real content are essential to grasp if teachers are to effectively evaluate, select and adapt materials for classroom use.

Within the context of EIB, consider the use of a table of statistics to teach a lesson on the language used to make comparisons. The aim of the exercise is to present and practise the language of comparisons. The exercise makes use of the table of statistics in order to present this language. It is not the aim of the exercise to teach statistics, although certain lexical items might well be useful. The table of statistics is the carrier content used to teach the specific language that the teacher wants to introduce. The table is thus the vehicle used for the real content of the lesson, the language of comparisons.

Question 2

> *Look at the profit and loss account for IBM on the following website*
> *http://www.ibm.com/annualreport/2006/cfs_earnings.shtml*
> *Imagine you have decided to print it and use this as carrier content. What real content could you use this as a vehicle for?*

4.4: The Purpose of Materials

Pause for thought

> *You have been asked to teach a two-day seminar on presentation skills. The course will be held in-company in Germany and is*

UNIT 2: Needs, Materials and Course Design

> *intended to help German employees present to their American counterparts. You have been told/asked to use the in-house produced materials in 4.10: extract 1. What exactly is the purpose of these materials? Would you prefer to add any further materials? Why? Why not?*

Dudley-Evans and St John (1998) argue that there are four principal reasons for using materials in an EIB context.

1. As a source of language.
2. As a learning support.
3. For motivation and stimulation.
4. For reference.

Dudley-Evans and St John (1998) expand on these reasons in the following way. In situations where English is a foreign language, the authors suggest that the training room may be, for practical purposes, the only realistic source of language. Learners may well have access to one of the global television channels or to English magazines and newspapers. However, the materials provided by the teacher are vital in order to expose learners to the language they will need.

As learning support, the authors argue that materials need to be consistent and to have a recognisable pattern. Materials should encourage learners to think about the language they need, and activities should stimulate cognitive rather than mechanical processes. Furthermore, the material should be challenging but not so difficult that it demotivates. The provided material should reflect the experiences and/or the aspirations of the learners so that it encourages creativity. The input should be familiar and grounded in the needs of the learners; but at the same time, it should offer something new, so that learners get involved and are stimulated to participate.

For reference purposes, material should be well-presented and self-explanatory. It should be suitable for revision, self-study and reflection.

We would add to the purposes suggested by Dudley-Evans and St John (1998). Firstly, we view material as a tool for teachers. Materials are a convenient way to help in the preparation of lessons and in the presentation and practice of new language. For the learner, materials offer a sense of cohesion and continuity. In addition, we see materials as an important tool for marketers. In the ELT industry, the only tangible evidence that anything at all has happened may be the material kept by the learners. Materials are a vital clue with which customers and prospective customers evaluate the quality of the product. Within the context of EIB, where the customers are often professionals from the corporate world, well-presented and well-prepared materials can be a crucial indicator of quality (for more on services and services marketing see unit 1, chapters 8 and 9).

All this places great demands on the teacher of EIB. Finding suitable carrier content, matching real content to the requirements of the learners, and designing meaningful activities can take up a great deal of time. Dudley-Evans and St John (1998) argue that designing new materials from scratch for every new course is simply not practical. Further, they suggest that one of the myths within ESP in general is that teachers have to write their own materials, and that a good ESP teacher is a good designer of materials.

We would agree that designing materials from scratch should not be the main concern of EIB practitioners. However, teachers of EIB do need to be good providers of materials. In essence this means that the teacher of EIB needs to:

➢ evaluate and select from what is already available
➢ be creative with what is available
➢ supplement materials where necessary
➢ present it in an acceptable professional manner.

In the following section we shall examine some criteria to use when evaluating available materials.

4.5: Evaluation and Selection of Available Material

Pause for thought

> *Consider the materials you are using at the moment. Did you choose them? If the answer is yes, which criteria did you use to select these materials? If you did not select the material, think about the criteria that you would use. Make a note of your answers.*

Before looking at why we should evaluate material in the first place, we should make a distinction between situations where we have a choice of

UNIT 2: Needs, Materials and Course Design

material, and situations where materials are chosen for us by, for example, a ministry of education. In the first situation, there is a wealth of material specially written for EIB. We have noted already that writing material from scratch may be time-consuming and not necessarily cost-effective, so that the ability to evaluate what is available is a very important professional ability for all those engaged in EIB.

For teachers who are working with materials given to them by a ministry, the evaluation of material may not, in practice, be productive. I once conducted a teacher training course in the Former Yugoslav Republic of Macedonia. The course was intended to introduce aspects of communicative methodology to local EL teachers. Although participants found the course very interesting, they frequently complained that they would not be able to use the ideas in the classroom because of restrictions imposed upon them by their government. We hope that current readers will not be so limited and will have the freedom to adapt material to suit their particular situation.

In order to evaluate material and to decide what to use and what not to use, teachers have to make choices. In order to make choices, teachers need criteria on which to base decisions. Dudley-Evans and St John (1998) suggest three initial questions to ask when selecting material. These questions clearly relate to our discussion of the purpose of materials.

1. Does the material motivate and stimulate?
2. Does the material match the teaching/learning objectives?
3. Will the material support that learning?

We may be evaluating a complete textbook, a unit of a textbook, simply one activity in a unit, or some other material such as a magazine article or a recorded television programme. Essentially, teachers will need to consider whether the carrier content is suitable for their particular course and whether the real content matches course objectives.

McDonough and Shaw (1993) examine what they call external and internal evaluation of material. Although they are writing principally of ELT coursebooks, the criteria they discuss can usefully be applied to the evaluation of EIB materials.

The external evaluation looks at the claims made for the material by the author and/or the publisher. These claims are usually found on the

UNIT 2: Needs, Materials and Course Design

back cover and/or in the introduction. Teachers need to know whether the materials are targeted at experienced or pre-experience learners. It may well be that the topics that motivate one audience will not motivate the other. Teachers will also need to know at which language level the material is aimed and whether or not the material is intended for specific business purposes or general business purposes. Furthermore, the date of publication may be important as it could be a good indication as to the subject matter and skills covered. For example, a coursebook published in the early nineties is unlikely to provide suitable coverage of writing e-mail.

Teachers will also need information on the presentation of language items, whether the materials are core materials or supplementary materials, the use of visuals, the role of a teacher's book, the cultural specificity of the materials, the provision of audio-visual material and inclusion of tests.

This external evaluation will help the teacher decide whether or not the material or some of the material is potentially appropriate for adoption or adaption for a particular group.

Pause for thought

> *Look at the publisher's information (blurb), the introduction and the contents' page of the material you are currently using. What kind of information do they give you?*

The information in italics in the box below has been taken from Hollett (1991). Imagine you are considering using part or all of this material for your group of lower intermediate learners. These learners are studying EGBP and are on an extended course in, say, Italy. They come to classes three hours per week and have enrolled for one academic year. This book was published in 1991. Consider which aspects of the material you might, on first sight, have to adapt to suit the needs of learners in 2007.

> *Business Objectives is a course for managers and students of business who have reached a lower intermediate level of English. Based on a carefully constructed grammatical syllabus, the sixteen units also tackle the key functional areas of business interaction, such as telephoning, meetings, socialising, presentations, and project briefings. While offering opportunities*

UNIT 2: Needs, Materials and Course Design

> *to practise all four language skills, the exercises in Business Objectives focus particularly on those listening and speaking skills most needed by business people. Business Objectives gives students the chance to do both controlled grammar practice and challenging role-play activities, and to relate the language used to their own work experience. Other features include:*
> 1. *business authenticity ensured by use of authentic materials from real companies*
> 2. *full glossary of business terms*
> 3. *full grammar summary.*
>
> *An audio cassette and a Teacher's Book, including classroom notes for each unit, answers to all exercises, and tapescripts, also form part of the Business Objectives package.*

If the external examination shows the material to be potentially appropriate for a particular group of learners, teachers can go on to carry out a more detailed internal evaluation. Such an evaluation may concern an investigation into the following.

- How are the skills presented? Are they taught discretely or in an integrated way? Do all the skills receive equal attention? How are the skills treated?
- Are the texts suitable for our learners or will they have to be adapted or modified in some way?
- Are the listening passages (if any) authentic or obviously contrived?
- Are the reading passages up to date and what sort of vocabulary is in them? The business world is adept at creating its own lexis, for example: *downsizing* and *on a going forward basis*. Such words and expressions go out of fashion as easily as they come into fashion.
- Do the speaking activities practise what we know about speaking skills?
- Do the exercises and activities relate to the needs of our particular group?
- Is the material suitable for different learning styles and cultural expectations?
- Will the material motivate and stimulate?

Having looked at the external and internal aspects of the material, we are now in a position to make an overall evaluation. Teachers should consider how far the material can be integrated into their course. Parts of the material may be useful while others are not. Teachers need to consider which parts of the book can be used as they are and which parts require adapting or supplementing. For example, it may be that some reading passages are suitable for carrier content, but they need updating or shortening. Perhaps the carrier content is suitable but the activities do not match real content so that new activities will have to be devised.

Pause for thought

> *At the beginning of this section you were asked to make a note of the criteria you would use to evaluate material. Now refer back to those criteria. Do they match with the ones you have read about in this chapter so far? Are there any which are different?*

For more information on evaluating and selecting materials you are recommended to read Cunningsworth (1996) and Hidalgo et al (1995).

4.6: Being Creative with Available Material

Pause for thought

> *Do you feel that the materials you are using at the moment need to be adapted in any way? Note down the main aspects of change that you would like to see. Are your materials commercially produced or are they given to you by a ministry? Perhaps your materials are produced in-house. Do you have much time to adapt materials? Do you have easy access to a word processor so that you can actually re-write materials?*

In this section we will show that adapting material is essentially a process of matching. This means that material is adapted so that it is more appropriate for a particular teaching/learning situation.

The reasons for adapting material will depend on a range of variables operating in one particular teaching situation. The following are some possible reasons for adapting materials.

➢ There is not enough grammar coverage.
➢ Grammar is presented in an unsystematic way.

UNIT 2: Needs, Materials and Course Design

- ➤ The reading passages contain too much new vocabulary.
- ➤ The content of reading passages is out of date.
- ➤ The questions on reading passages are too easy.
- ➤ Listening passages are inauthentic.
- ➤ The subject matter is inappropriate.
- ➤ The role-plays and simulations are too complicated/too easy.
- ➤ There are no role-plays or simulations.
- ➤ There is not enough provision for groupwork.

No doubt you could add to this list. However, the examples chosen give a useful indication of the range of areas that can be adapted.

Despite this wide range, the reasons for adapting material may simply concern modification of content. By content we mean, for example: exercises, texts, instructions, and activities. The focus will always be on comparing what the materials contain with the requirements of a particular teaching situation. In other words, the situation may oblige the teacher to make changes that lead to greater appropriacy. This appropriacy can be expressed in terms of:

- ➤ personalising the content
- ➤ individualising the content
- ➤ localising the content
- ➤ modernising the content.

Personalising content refers to making the content more relevant to the professional backgrounds of the learners, in other words, making changes to carrier content. Individualising refers to changes that make the material more appropriate to the learning styles represented in the class. Localising takes into account the fact that what works well in one culture may not work well in another. Modernising refers to changing materials that are out of date either from the point of view of content or from the point of view of language usage. Techniques that we shall look at are:

- ➤ adding material
- ➤ deleting material
- ➤ modifying material - rewriting or restructuring
- ➤ simplifying.

UNIT 2: Needs, Materials and Course Design

Pause for thought

> *You are running a two-day programme in negotiating skills. You are running the course for eight employees of a car manufacturer in France. Your students are supposed to be at an intermediate level. Look at the material you want to use for a role-play (4.10: extract 2). You found this material in an EIB coursebook. How would you adapt it to suit the needs of the learners? Think about the criteria we have considered above.*

Adding material can simply involve extending or giving more of the same. This means that material is added within the framework of the original model. For example, look again at Question 2. If you have used this carrier content to contrast the present perfect with the simple past (e.g. overheads have increased this year. Last year overheads stood at…), it may be that your learners are having difficulty with this and need more practice material. On the other hand, you may think that your learners need more carrier content to reinforce the key vocabulary, so that a second reading passage may be appropriate.

Adding material can also involve expanding or moving outside the framework of the original model by developing something new. For example, we could add a skill or a new practice component. It may be that we want to add a listening comprehension that mirrors the vocabulary and grammatical structures contained in a reading passage.

Deletion of material is clearly the opposite of adding material. For example, learners of EIB on a short course may be using communicative materials because of the instrumental nature of the course aims and objectives. The communicative material you have chosen may be accompanied by lengthy grammatical exercises which you may feel to be inappropriate. You would, therefore, delete them.

Modifying material can be divided into two areas. The first concerns rewriting material and the second concerns restructuring material. Rewriting materials refers to making the materials more appropriate to the needs of the learners. This could relate to both carrier content and real content. For example, we may decide that the material in extract 2 is suitable from the point of view of real content and language level. However, we may wish to modify the material so that it suits the needs of another industry sector.

Restructuring refers to classroom management. For example, you may have a suitable role-play in mind for a group of learners, only to

UNIT 2: Needs, Materials and Course Design

discover (because of no-shows) that you have more roles than learners! You may be forced to take a role yourself or assign two roles to one learner.

Pause for thought

> *Look at the extract in smaller font below. It has been taken from a coursebook for EIB. The book was published in 1994. The exercise was designed to help develop writing skills in a business context. Although you feel the real content is OK, you have decided to adapt the material. Think about the criteria we have discussed above and decide how you would adapt it.*
>
> *A fax or a telex is quicker than a letter, but a letter is more formal and confidential. What would you send in the situations below? How would you begin and finish your communication?*
> - *You have heard that Mrs Parker is visiting your offices next month. You want to offer to book a hotel for her.*
> - *Signor Fracassini has asked you how to get to your office from the airport. You have promised to send him a map.*

Because it involves rewriting, simplifying material, strictly speaking, is a technique of modification. However, we consider simplification as a separate procedure because it is such an extensive activity and deserves attention in its own right.

Many aspects of material may be simplified, for example: instructions, explanations of grammatical structure, and activities. Texts, usually reading texts, are commonly the main focus of simplification. The emphasis is often on changing the text so that it better matches the proficiency level of the learners. We can simplify the following.

- Sentence structure - sentences may be reduced in length, or a complex sentence may be re-written as a number of shorter sentences.
- Lexical content - the number of new words can be controlled.
- Grammar - for example, past tenses can be changed to present tenses and passives can be turned into actives.

Another way to simplify is not to change the content, but to present the text in a different way. For example, we can lead the learners through the text in a number of simple and graded stages.

UNIT 2: Needs, Materials and Course Design

Question 3

> *Below you will see four reasons for adapting materials. For each reason suggest how you would adapt the material.*
> 1. *The activities that practise real content are repetitive and mechanical.*
> 2. *The reading text you have chosen is out of date.*
> 3. *You have found a good role-play for your group of learners but the role-play instructions are more difficult than the role-play itself.*
> 4. *The activities focus too strongly on carrier content.*

So far, we have looked at adapting existing materials to suit the needs of a particular group of learners. We now need to look at supplementing existing material by providing extra input and activities.

4.7: Supplementing Material - Teacher-Generated Material

We would suggest that the dividing line between adapting material and providing new material from scratch is very unclear. It is, perhaps, rather a question of degree. Suppose we rewrite a business article so that it better suits the needs of our group of learners. Does this mean we have adapted it or have we provided something new? Suppose we go further and use this material for a jig-saw activity and follow it up with a small report? Have we provided new material? Dudley-Evans and St John (1998) suggest that in order to write materials, practitioners of EIB need to be able to:

- match carrier content to real content
- provide variety
- grade activities to language level and learning level
- present the material in a professional fashion.

Matching carrier content to real content

The development of new materials can come from two different directions. The first direction is the availability of suitable carrier content. This may come from the learners, or be something we have

UNIT 2: Needs, Materials and Course Design

found. This carrier content might be, for example: a magazine article, an in-company publication, financial documents or a video of the television business news.

The next step is to look carefully at this carrier content and decide whether it could be exploited to teach the real content of our course. The second direction is when we see that there is a gap in the course material. In other words, we have some course objective, some real content for which we have no suitable carrier content.

After we have matched real content and carrier content, the next step is to devise activities. While devising activities, teachers should consider the resources available, the group size, and approaches to learning. Teachers should also ensure that the activities are suitable for their particular learning situation.

Providing variety

When we are devising activities, we should make sure that we provide enough variety in our class. We should vary the skills and the micro-skills practised, we should consider a range of activity types, and we should vary the types of interaction that take place in the classroom.

It may be that we have been asked to do a seminar in report-writing. Even if our class has development of this one macro-skill as its aim, we suggest that the use of other macro-skills will help the learning of the target skill and provide variety for the class. In the same way, we suggest that a course, for example, in reading or listening skills, does not focus on one micro-skill such as deducing meaning from context. We should focus on a variety of micro-skills, for example: predicting skills, recognising discourse markers, and reading or listening for specific information. As teachers of EIB we should also focus on key business vocabulary.

Furthermore, Beaumont (1983) suggests that apart from micro-skills, exercises should be developed which help learners understand:

- ➢ text structure - how it is linked together
- ➢ text purpose - who is it for, what does it do?
- ➢ topics - the main idea and the supporting ideas
- ➢ the opinions and stance of the writer/speaker.

The range of activities that can be used to develop the skills is enormous. However, among activities you should consider for reading skills, for example, are: literal comprehension questions, reorganisation of text activities, inferring meaning activities, and evaluation questions.

For listening skills, you might consider, for example: completing diagrams and charts, predicting what comes next, inferring opinions and gap-filling. Consider also introducing a visual element. Visuals for EIB might include, flow-charts, diagrams, bar and pie charts, matrices and sketches. Visuals like these may be used as a comprehension check on a reading or listening activity. They may also be used to generate conversation or written work - perhaps a report or a summary to be sent as an e-mail to a colleague.

Pause for thought

> *Look at the textbook you are using or one which you have used in the past. Examine the activity types that are adopted and see whether or not visuals are used. Do the same with any in-house material you are familiar with. Do you think that there is sufficient variety? Would you add any activities?*

Apart from activity type, the nature of interactions in the EIB classroom should be considered. Interactions can vary between teacher-input, individual work, groupwork and pairwork, and role-plays and simulations. Much depends on class size and learner expectations about what a "good" lesson is. For example, some cultures do not place much importance on role-plays. Although this will always depend on the individual and the particular group, the writer's experience in Germany suggests that role-play is not a very popular activity in many Germany companies. The same is true of Chinese students with whom the writer has worked at three British universities. At DaimlerChrysler, for example, participants made it clear to me that they would only consider doing a negotiation role-play if the objectives of the exercise were made absolutely clear and not left vague and open-ended. Furthermore, at the end of the activity, it is advisable, in a situation like this, to draw out all the learning outcomes and write them as bullet points on a flip chart.

Grading activities

Many in-company courses in which the writer has been involved have consisted of mixed-ability groups. Often, we have no control over who is in our courses, but we may be left to deal with the consequences - a potentially difficult teaching situation.

One way of handling the situation is to present each task, activity or exercise at different levels. These levels may correspond to unsupported, partially supported and fully supported. Thus, learners at different levels may be engaged with the same material but working on graded tasks or activities. For more on this, see section 4.8 and framework activities.

Presenting the material

When presenting the material, consistency is vital. By consistency we mean:

- consistency of terms
- consistency in the prompts used in rubrics
- consistency of layout
- consistency of font and font size.

For material written for company work, the quality of presentation is vital. Binders may be used and photocopies should be of the highest quality.

Pause for thought

> *Look at any commercially-produced EIB material and consider the points concerning consistency above. Make a list of the key words and prompts used in the rubrics and consider using them if/when you have to write your own material.*

4.8: Supplementing Material - Learner-Generated Material

Sometimes, learners will provide materials for use in the EIB classroom. If the material they provide represents the group's needs and interests, teachers can decide whether or not to make use of this material. It may be the case, for example, that learners participating on a course designed to develop their negotiating skills will want to practise these skills in areas that are directly relevant to them, for

UNIT 2: Needs, Materials and Course Design

example: sales contracts, servicing arrangements or negotiations with suppliers. Alternatively, it may be that learners on a course designed to polish their presentation skills have a particular presentation which they have to practise and the slides that go with it.

The advantages of learners providing carrier content are that they are often more committed to the content and have a sense of ownership. In short, it can increase their motivation. Teachers should bear in mind, however, that it is not sufficient to satisfy carrier content criteria and that real content criteria should also be considered.

In fact, Dudley-Evans and St John (1989) suggest that one of the principal problems faced by materials designers is precisely this achievement of the right balance between carrier content and real content. They suggest that one solution to this problem is to provide what they call framework material. Framework material provides neither carrier content nor language input. What it does provide is a framework or a context within which learners put their own carrier content and language.

Framework material takes visual representations and uses them for language production. Examples of frameworks are: classification trees, flow charts and problem-solving models. Diagrammatically represented presentation structures can also be very helpful. With such a framework, the topics presented could be: a new product, the company, or reasons for implementing a particular decision. In other words, the same framework can be used by professionals with widely different backgrounds. Furthermore, the language used will be from the learners' own level of competence so that the framework can be used with mixed ability groups.

Frameworks can also be used to generate particular language such as comparisons, or they can be used to generate particular interactions such as presentations or problem-solving.

Question 5

> *Look at the framework below. It shows a model for problem-solving. How could you use this in the EIB classroom? How might you use it with a mixed-ability group?*

UNIT 2: Needs, Materials and Course Design

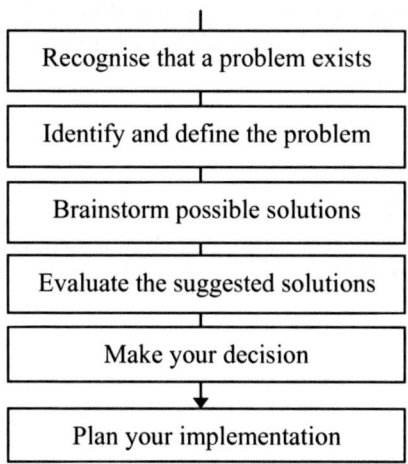

Question 6

Look at the fourth point in the problem-solving model - "Evaluate the suggested solutions." Devise a framework for learners to evaluate two possible solutions, and to look at the strengths and weaknesses of each solution.

4.9: Conclusion

Teachers of EIB should see themselves as good providers of material. Writing material from scratch is probably best perceived as something teachers should do only as a last resort.

It may be possible to use existing material for our group. However, it is important to keep in mind that some learners or their sponsors will expect specially written material. Even in this situation, it is usually possible to adapt existing material. This may mean selecting units from a coursebook or adapting some exercises or texts to suit the needs of the group.

There has been little published research into materials development and not much work on theories of materials evaluation. Tomlinson (1998) provides a framework for teachers to use when developing materials. Hidalgo et al (1995) include several chapters on how textbooks are written. Byrd (1995) is also worth looking at for views on materials' writing.

UNIT 2: Needs, Materials and Course Design

Finally, for those teachers who feel that they have to write new materials from scratch, the following points should be born in mind.

- Use existing material as a source of ideas.
- Work in a team.
- Do not expect perfection the first time round.
- Writing materials is time-consuming.
- Make sure the materials look professional.

4.10: Extracts

Extract 1: Presentation Skills
Background
A presentation is a prepared talk given by a speaker (the transmitter) to one or more listeners (the receivers). It is probably better if your talk encourages two-way rather than one-way communication. So - encourage the audience to provide feedback. Remember that the talk is given for the benefit of the audience and not for the speaker's. So, what are the elements of an effective presentation?

1. Good organisation of the information.
2. Good delivery of information.
3. Good use of language.

Organisation of information.
- Have a clear beginning, middle and end.
- Identify main points and supporting points.
- Start in the audience's area of interest.

Delivery of information. Think about:
- Your image.
- Audience features.
- Non-linguistic techniques, for example: eye-contact, body and facial movements.
- Linguistic techniques, for example: the use of short and long sentences.
- Technical support.

Use of language.
- Vocabulary (choose the right word in the spoken language and not the written language - think about culture differences).
- Grammar - assemble the sentences correctly in terms of language forms.
- Pronunciation (stress words and sentences correctly).
- Fluency - vary your sentence length and your sentence structure.
- Link your ideas and do not talk too quickly.

Pre-preparation.
Think about your objectives.

UNIT 2: Needs, Materials and Course Design

- What will be the change you bring about in your audience?
- Do you want to inform them, amuse them, persuade them or train them?

Think about the audience.
- What type of people are they?
- How many people will there be?
- What mood will they be in?
- What do they know about the topic?
- What is their level of English?

Think about the time.
- How much time do you need?
- How much time does the audience have?
- How long can they concentrate?
- What can they remember?

Think about the location.
- Where will you stand?
- How far away from the audience will you be?
- Do you intend to use visual aids? Will the equipment work?

Planning your presentation
- Why do you want to speak to this audience?
- What will they expect to get out of it?
- What main points do you want to make?
- What is the best order to present them in?
- What sort of relationship do you want to establish with the audience? Think about culture here.
- How do you want them to react?

Preparing the presentation
- Collect your material.
- Select the points which seem most relevant to the situation you have defined.
- Group the points which have some common threads.
- Sequence these groups into a structure.
- Consider ways of linking the groups together, by a common idea.

Making and using notes.
- Consider placing your groups of information as headings horizontally arranged on the page, with the points listed vertically underneath. If the points are arranged in order of importance, this will allow omissions from the bottom of each column if time is short.
- Make a note on the plan of the position of any audio-visual material.
- Make sure that your visual are VISUAL, and arrange them in such a way that they will have visual impact.
- Make a list of all the practical requirements and make sure these are available.
- Decide what kind of notes you are going to work from on the day. Use as few as possible. Use large writing and colours where suitable.

UNIT 2: Needs, Materials and Course Design

The Introduction
Prepare your introduction. Include at least four pieces of information.
1. What you are going to talk about.
2. How long you will take.
3. What your main groups or sections are.
4. Whether you will take questions during or after the talk

When your introduction is ready, practise speaking it into a tape recorder and listen to yourself.

Structure and language
There is a standard structure
- Greeting
- Introduce yourself
- Introduce the topic
- Give the agenda
- Present main points
- Summarise main points
- Conclude talk
- Invite questions

The Introduction
First impressions are important, so let the audience see your best qualities. In particular, try to be:
- Organised. Make the plan of your talk transparent.
- Human. Make some reference to the immediate situation and relax.
- Fluent. Learn the introduction by heart.

Linking ideas
It is vital to signal to your audience what you are going to do. This means giving a commentary on your recent and planned progress, so that the listeners know exactly where they are. You can choose from a list of linking sentences that the trainer will give you. Explore the possibilities and choose the ones that suit you best.

Language
Below are some phrases you may find useful in helping to structure your presentation.

Opening
Good morning ladies and gentlemen...
Hello everyone...
It's a great pleasure for me to welcome you all here at...
My name is...
I am...and I'm responsible for the...
For those of you who don't know me, I am...
I have been with the company for...

The purpose
The purpose of my presentation today is to talk about/ outline/ describe/ examine...
Today we'll be looking at...

UNIT 2: Needs, Materials and Course Design

What we'll be doing this morning is looking at...

The agenda
I have divided my talk/presentation into two/three parts. First, we'll look at ... Second we'll examine..., and finally we'll discuss...

Inviting questions
If you have any questions, or if my English is not clear, please don't hesitate to interrupt.
If you have any questions, I shall be pleased to answer them at the end of the talk.

Bridging
That leads us to...
So, having looked at A... NOW let's turn our attention to B.
That covers A...NOW let's turn to B.
So much for A...NOW let's move on to B.

Summarising
So, then, to sum up...
So, to summarise the main points...

Closing
Well, that's all I have to say about A, but if there are any questions...
And that brings us to the end of my presentation. Now if there are any questions...

Taking questions
Acknowlege the question
- That's a very good point...
- Thanks for bringing up the point...

Clarify them
- If I understand you correctly, what you're asking is...
- So, what you'd like to know is...

Answer them

Check
- Does that answer your question?
- So, is that OK?

Using visuals
- Is the visual necessary?
- Would a visual help? Why?
- Is the visual "visual" or is it verbal?
- Is there too much on the visual?
- Does the visual clarify/illustrate the point?

UNIT 2: Needs, Materials and Course Design

The Cultural Dimension
Below you will find a summary of some differences between German and American cultures. Think about how these differences will influence the presentations you give in the US.

German
- Long planning phase.
- Decisions are firm and plans are changed reluctantly.
- Flow of information should be organised.
- Explanations supported with background and assumptions.
- Opinions change through persuasive argument.
- Conversationalists are very involved in the subject matter.
- Mistakes should be avoided.
- Scepticism and critical thinking are basic attitudes.
- The more difficult an idea is to understand the more important it is.
- Product orientation.
- No criticism is good news.

American
- Short planning phase.
- Plans are changed and revised if necessary.
- Information flows freely.
- Explanations limited to current topic and future-oriented.
- Opinions change through dialogue.
- Conversationalists maintain an emotional distance from the subject.
- Learning through mistakes is respected.
- Optimism – there are no problems, only challenges and opportunities.
- Content must be presented in an easily understood way.
- Market orientation.
- No praise is bad news.

Extract 2: Negotiation - Robert's Robots
Rob 1 is an industrial robot produced by Robert's Robots, a Swedish engineering company based in Stockholm. Rob 1 has begun to gain considerable market share in Europe's increasingly robotised manufacturing industries. In particular, it has been successful with the European car industry. British car manufacturers, however, are reluctant to invest, and Robert's Robots is hoping to gain a foothold in Britain and build up a strong brand image before the Japanese and the Germans can dominate the market. The Swedes are also working on two new powerful models (Rob 2 and Rob 3) which are to be launched within the next 18 months. Last winter, there was an engineering trade fair in Milan and representatives from Europe's car industries were there to see Rob 1 in action.

Chris Wood, the production manager with a fast developing sports-car manufacturer (Tiger plc) based in Reading England, was at the fair. He was very impressed by what he saw and thought the growth of Tiger plc justified investment in such modern technology. On his return to Reading, Chris spoke to Jim Cleary, his managing director. Chris stressed the need to invest in the most up-to-date technology if Tiger plc was to survive and prosper in a bitterly contested market.

UNIT 2: Needs, Materials and Course Design

Jim Cleary was also impressed. He had been looking closely at the competition in France and Germany. BMW's Z3 and the new Mercedes sports model were direct competitors. Furthermore, Jim knew that many of Britain's car companies collapsed because of lack of investment. Jim was determined not to make the same mistakes as Morris, Wolseley and Austin.

Chris and Jim flew out to Stockholm to have a better look at Rob 1 and to examine how it could be programmed to perform the tasks needed for the production of Tiger cars. They also spent two mornings with the Swedish sales director. They discussed prices, maintenance, training facilities and so on.

About one month later, Jim Cleary e-mailed Robert's Robots and asked them to draw up a quotation for the purchase of four Rob 1 robots. Full robotisation of the Reading plant would require 16 robots but Jim thinks that it would be safer to order in stages. The next day, Jim received the quotation. It was clear that the negotiators would need to discuss the following points.

- price
- discounts
- delivery date
- delivery point
- guarantee provision
- length of guarantee
- training facilities
- after-sales service
- supply of spare parts
- buy-back arrangement

Robert's Robots – role card
Your robots are perfect for Tiger plc. On the other hand, Jim Cleary knows how much you want to enter the British market. After all, the Reading plant can be your showroom in Britain, and Tiger plc will provide you with a good entry into the UK market. Robert's Robots recently began offering a leasing arrangement. This means that customers can hire robots with an option to buy. You have not yet mentioned this to Jim Cleary. At this stage, you would prefer to make a cash sale. You can introduce new variables into the negotiation. Remember to try and obtain Jim Cleary's list of variables before the negotiation begins. He will negotiate hard, and you must try and obtain concessions in exchange for those you give.

Jim Cleary – role card
You are aware of Rob 1's qualities but you are not satisfied with the Swedish quotation as it is. You intend to negotiate every point. You are also worried about Robert's Robot's after-sales service and would like further details. For example, do they offer a quick and efficient breakdown service or will you have to wait a long time for repairs to be carried out? Another concern is whether or not Robert's Robots operate a buy-back arrangement. In other words, will they take back ageing robots at a future date at a guaranteed price?

UNIT 2: Needs, Materials and Course Design

4.11: Answers to Questions

Question 1
Advantages of a coursebook can include that:
- it is a convenient form of presenting material
- it helps consistency
- it helps continuation
- it gives learners a sense of system
- it gives learners a sense of progress
- it helps learners revise and reflect.

Disadvantages of a coursebook can include that:
- it may be superficial
- it may not be suitable for all learners and their diversity of needs
- the syllabus design may be uniform.

Question 2
The most obvious real content that comes to mind is to use this carrier content as a vehicle to provide practice in contrasting the present perfect, (sales have gone up this year) with the simple past, (sales fell last year). You could also the carrier content to practise the language of comparisons, (sales this year are better than last year). It could also be used to practise presentations.

Question 3
1. Change the content/focus of the activity or drop it.
2. Rewrite it.
3. Change/simplify the role-play and/or the rubric.
4. Rewrite them.

Question 4
You could use this as a case study or as a problem-solving activity. As a case study you could ask participants to work individually or in pairs before coming together as a group to discuss the suggestions or to come up with a solution. Alternatively, pairs could present their solutions to the group. A vote could then be taken as to the best solution. As a problem-solving activity, participants could practise problem-solving models, chairing and participating skills.

Question 5
You could group learners according to their language level and have them work together to define the problem. Possible answers could be presented to the whole group. A similar technique could be used with the other stages of the model.

UNIT 2: Needs, Materials and Course Design

Question 6

	Strengths	Weaknesses	Opportunities	Threats
SOLUTION 1				
SOLUTION 2				

UNIT 2: Needs, Materials and Course Design

Unit Bibliography

Beaumont, M. (1983) "Take it from the Text: an Approach to the teaching of Reading," from Jordan, R.R. (ed.), Case Studies in ELT. London, Collins.

Breen, M.P. and Littlejohn, A. (eds.), (2000) Classroom Decision-Making: Negotiation and Process Syllabuses in Practice. Cambridge, Cambridge University Press.

Breen, M.P. (2001) "Syllabus Design," from Carter, R. and Nunan, D. (eds.), The Cambridge Guide to Teaching English to Speakers of Other Languages. Cambridge, Cambridge University Press.

Brindley, G. (1998) "Outcomes-based assessment and reporting in second language programmes: A review of the issues." Language Testing 15(1).

Burns, A. (1996) "Collaborative research and curriculum change: Australian Adult Migrant English Programme." TESOL Quarterly 30.

Byrd, P. (1995) Materials Writers Guide. New York, Newbury House.

Cohen, L. and Manion, L. (1980) Research methods in Education. London, Croon Helm Ltd.

UNIT 2: Needs, Materials and Course Design

Cunningsworth, A. (1996) <u>Choosing Your Course Book</u>. Oxford, Heinemann.

Davidson, J. (1970) <u>Outdoor Recreation Surveys: The Design and Use of Questionnaires</u>. London, The Countryside commission.

Dudley-Evans, A. and St John, M. (1998) <u>Developments in English for Specific Purposes</u>. Cambridge, Cambridge University Press.

Ellis, M. and Johnson, C. (1994) <u>Teaching Business English</u>. Oxford, Oxford University Press.

Genesee, F. and Upshur, J. (1996) <u>Classroom-based Evaluation in Second Language Education</u>. Cambridge, Cambridge University Press.

Genesee, F. (2001) "Evaluation," from Carter, R. and Nunan, D. (eds.), <u>Teaching English to Speakers of Other Languages</u>. Cambridge, Cambridge University Press.

Hewings, M. and Dudley-Evans, A. (1996) "Evaluation and Course Design in EAP." <u>Review of ELT</u>, vol. 6 no. 1. Hemel Hempsted, Prentice Hall Macmillan in association with the British Council.

Hidalgo, A.C., Hall, D. and Jacobs, G.M. (eds.), <u>Getting Started: Materials Writers on Materials Writing</u>. Singapore, SEAMEO Regional Language Centre.

Hollett, V. (1991) <u>Business Objectives</u>. Oxford, Oxford University Press.

Hutchinson, T. and Waters, A. (1987) <u>English for Specific Purposes</u>. Cambridge, Cambridge University Press.

Long, M.H. and Crookes, G. (1992) "Three approaches to task-based syllabus design." <u>TESOL Quarterly</u> 26 (1).

Long, M. and Richards J. (ed.), (2005) <u>Second Language Needs Analysis</u>. Cambridge, Cambridge University Press.

UNIT 2: Needs, Materials and Course Design

Lightbown, P. and Spada, N. (2006) <u>How Languages are Learned</u> – 3rd ed. Oxford, Oxford University Press.

McDonough, J. and Shaw, C. (1993) <u>Materials and Methods in ELT</u>. Oxford, Blackwell.

Nunan, D. (1988) <u>The Learner-Centred Curriculum</u>. Cambridge, Cambridge University Press.

Richards, J. (2001) <u>Curriculum Development in Language Teaching</u>. Cambridge, Cambridge University Press.

Sweeney, S. (1997) <u>English for Business Communication</u>. Cambridge, Cambridge University Press.

Tomlinson, B. (ed.), (1998) <u>Materials Development for Language Teaching</u>. Cambridge, Cambridge University Press.

Tomlinson, B. (2001) "Materials Development," from Carter, R. and Nunan, D. (eds.), <u>The Cambridge Guide to Teaching English to Speakers of Other Languages</u>. Cambridge, Cambridge University Press.

UNIT 3
Methodology and Classroom Practice

UNIT 3: Methodology and Classroom Practice

Chapter 1

What is Appropriate Methodology?

1.1: Introduction
1.2: Objectives
1.3: Examination of terms
1.4: Appropriacy in Appropriate Methodology
1.5: Conclusions
1.6: Answers to Questions.

1.1: Introduction

This chapter examines the influences on English Language teaching in general and suggests why it may be necessary to adapt existing approaches and methodologies so that they are more suitable for the non-Western teaching/learning situation. Chapter 2 takes us a stage further by going beyond method and looking at the thinking that has led to a postmethod pedagogy. Both chapter 1 and chapter 2 should be taken as a coherent whole and both tend towards the theoretical in the sense that they look at the whole issue of "appropriate" in the expression "appropriate methodology", how teachers should relate to it and how they might adapt their teaching accordingly.

The rest of the unit (chapters 3 – 10) is, perhaps, more practical in nature and explores what we teach, how we can approach teaching it

UNIT 3: Methodology and Classroom Practice

and how we can assess the effectiveness of what we have taught. All these chapters are designed to help you evaluate your role as teachers. Evaluation will lead, we hope, to development. By development, we mean that you might challenge what you take for granted and, by doing so, break your own teaching rules and traditional ways of doing things. In this way, we hope you will try out new ideas and incorporate some of them into your regular teaching. Above all, we hope that you will not only improve your classroom performance but also learn something more about teaching and about yourselves so that you continue to develop and grow, both personally and professionally.

Pause for thought

> *The paragraphs above contain some fine ideas. Since you have embarked on reading this book, can we assume that you are interested in self-development or is the notion of self-development only a Western ideal? How far is your interest in this book governed by more instrumental desires - for example, promotion, status and an increase in salary?*

1.2: Objectives

At the end of this chapter, you will be able to:

- critically examine popular teaching methodologies
- critically evaluate the usefulness of these methodologies for your own situation
- better understand why some methodologies may not be suitable for your teaching situation.

Pre-reading task

While you are engaged with this chapter, you are asked to work on the activity in the shaded box below. The activity is designed to stimulate your thinking and to focus your mind on the main ideas in the text.

> *Below is a list of criteria for evaluating lesson effectiveness (Ur, 1996).*
> - *Learners were active all the time.*

UNIT 3: Methodology and Classroom Practice

> ➢ *Learners were attentive all the time.*
> ➢ *Learners were motivated.*
> ➢ *Learners seemed to be learning the material.*
> ➢ *The lesson went according to plan.*
> ➢ *The language was always used communicatively.*
> ➢ *The learners were constantly engaged with the language.*
>
> *We now want you to prioritise these criteria and to justify why you have ordered it in the way you have. (You can, of course, add criteria if you feel these are necessary).*

1.3: Examination of Terms

In this section, we shall define the terms that are commonly used throughout this chapter and, indeed, the rest of the unit. The terms are: method, approach, procedure, technique and model. We shall also briefly review the main components of EIB.

Any discussion of methodology can be confusing due to lack of clarity concerning the terms we mentioned above. What exactly is the difference between an approach and a method? How does a technique differ from a procedure? Before attempting to shed some light on this shadowy area of definitions, we would like to emphasise that the most important thing for you to do is not necessarily to correctly define these terms, but to ask yourself two questions. First, is your current teaching practice appropriate and effective for your classroom situation? Second, are the activities you are using effective and satisfying for both you and your students?

Harmer (2001) argues that the term "approach" refers to descriptions and theories of language and language learning, and how these descriptions and theories inform the practice and principles of language teaching. We noted in unit 2, chapter 1 that descriptions of language may be:

- ➢ classical or traditional
- ➢ structural
- ➢ transformational generative
- ➢ functional/notional
- ➢ concerned with language variation and register analysis
- ➢ discoursal.

UNIT 3: Methodology and Classroom Practice

Question 1

> *You might want to look again at unit 2, chapter 1 and our explanations of these terms before attempting the following question. In what ways (if any) do language descriptions carry implications for language learning?*

Theories of language learning have been influenced by:

- behaviourism
- mentalism - often associated with Chomsky (1964)
- theories of cognition (see e.g. Ausubel et al., 1978)
- the affective factor - learners as emotional beings
- theories of acquisition (Krashen, 1981).

An approach makes a statement about how people acquire knowledge of a language and the conditions which best promote successful language learning (Harmer, 2001).

Question 2

> *Is there a link between theories of learning and language descriptions?*

Question 3

> *Is there one theory of language learning, in your opinion, that is better than the others and on which you prefer to base your teaching? Check your answer with our suggested answer in the Answers to Questions section.*

A method is the approach put into practice. A method will usually prescribe the types of activities, roles of the teacher and learners, the materials to be used and a model of syllabus design. Methods will often prescribe the techniques and procedures that should be adopted by the teacher in order to foster learning.

Procedures are ordered sequences of techniques. For example, a procedure for introducing new language might look like this.

- Lead-in activity.

UNIT 3: Methodology and Classroom Practice

- Elicitation of the new language (if possible).
- Explanation of the form of the new language.
- Accurate reproduction of the new language - by, for example, drilling.
- Immediate creativity.

Techniques are single activities rather than sequences. For example, you may have discovered a new technique for effectively explaining a language item.

Models are sets of procedures which you may have come across in your teacher-training. Models are abstractions of real world practice, for example: the presentation, practice, production model for language teaching or the six-step model for problem-solving in the business world (see also unit 2 chapter 4 section 4.8). The model looks like this.

- Recognise the existence of a problem.
- Identify and define the problem.
- Brainstorm possible solutions.
- Evaluate the possible solutions.
- Decide.
- Implement.

Having looked at some terminology, we now have to decide on the 'what' of EIB.

Question 4

So what are the main elements of EIB?

Having decided on the 'what' of your particular class, you still have to decide on your approach or method of teaching. It is to these considerations that we shall now turn.

1.4: Appropriacy in Appropriate Methodology

Approaches to language teaching in the West have changed dramatically in the last 150 years or so. The major historical influences that impact on ELT today spring from:

UNIT 3: Methodology and Classroom Practice

- the grammar-translation approach
- the direct method
- audio-lingualism
- the communicative approach
- second language acquisition (Krashen, 1981)
- experiential learning (Kolb, 1984)
- task-based learning (Willis, 1996)
- the lexical approach (Lewis, 1997).

For a more detailed account of these influences, you might want to look at Harmer (2001). Harmer (1991) is particularly good in his description of the communicative approach. Richards and Rodgers (2001) offer a good discussion of approaches and methods, while Williams and Burden (1997) concisely describe audio-lingualism. Byrne (1986) is good on the presentation, practice, production model while Flowerdew (1998) and Littlewood (2000) show the dangers of cultural stereotyping within educational contexts. Lightbown and Spada (2006) are excellent on how language learning theories relate to classroom methodology.

With so many approaches and methods to choose from, many teachers may well be unsure as to which to choose and how to go about making their choice. In this section, we look at the cultural implications of methods and approaches. We shall then be in a better position to assess the term "appropriate" in the expression "appropriate methodology."

The fact is that many of the approaches and methods we have mentioned are based on Western ideas about what makes good learning, how good learners should behave in the classroom and how teachers should relate to their students. This may mean that these approaches are limited in their effectiveness in non-Western situations. For a fascinating account of native English speakers teaching English as a global language in non-English speaking countries, we recommend that you consult Luk and Lin (2006).

Question 5

> *Why is an appreciation of the limitations of Western methodology important for teachers of EIB?*

It may sound like a strange comparison, but we feel that there are similarities between burger outlets and TEFLers (i.e. teachers of EFL).

UNIT 3: Methodology and Classroom Practice

Both promote themselves through the use of well-known icons - the famous yellow arches of the drive-through and the introductory TEFL certificates. Furthermore, both the burger industry and the ELT industry are international and internationalising concerns. In part, the reputation of both industries is based on their rapid production of reliably good products for their international markets: fast food and TEFLers respectively.

Much scepticism has accompanied the internationalisation of the burger industry - are its products really suitable for all parts of the world? Similar voices (e.g. Holliday, 1994a, 1994b and Alptekin, 2002) can now be heard about the ELT industry - are certificate-trained TEFLers really appropriate for every English language classroom? A glance at any TEFL jobs database (e.g. TEFL.com) indicates that many EIB jobs require a TEFL certificate and several years experience. Thus, we suggest that the question we have raised above is equally relevant for many teachers of English for International Business.

Most certificate courses attempt to integrate teacher-training, which we understand to mean immediate skills development, and teacher education, which we understand as awareness-raising for long-term development. Courses aim to bridge the gaps between trainee knowledge, awareness and skills prior to the programme and the knowledge, awareness and skills required by the actual classroom realities they are likely to encounter once in work. In order to bridge these gaps between trainees' entry and exit proficiency, it is usually necessary to make assumptions about post-certificate classroom realities.

Until the early 1990s, most trainees went to teach in countries such as Spain, Italy, Greece and France. Assumptions about classroom realities were based on such destinations. However, by 2007, the vast majority of jobs seem to have relocated to Eastern Europe and the Far East. Informal and admittedly unsystematic feedback from participants (certificated on a course with which the current writer was involved) suggests that many trainees experienced a gap between the course principles and their subsequent training realities. For example, some trainees who later worked in Japan and China found that the technique of elicitation was less straightforward than course methodology suggested.

The trainees further suggested that their training had not adequately prepared them for tendencies within Japanese and Chinese classrooms. They wanted guidelines to help them make their practice more

UNIT 3: Methodology and Classroom Practice

appropriate to the classrooms in which they worked. For example, they asked questions such as, "Why don't my students say anything?"

These factors suggest that certificate-trained teachers of EIB need to be able to handle a wide range of classroom realities. Trainees need to be prepared for situations where, for example, they might be discouraged from setting up pair and groupwork (too noisy) or be required to present grammar in a decontextualised manner, where reading aloud and translation may still be popular techniques, where mother-tongues may still be forbidden in the classroom and where the teacher is supposed to behave in an authoritarian manner and to have all the answers.

In each of the above examples, there is a potential mismatch between the methodologies learned and the educational culture and classroom practices trainees may be expected to follow afterwards.

Look at the following comments made to me by two would-be Ukrainian teachers of EIB during recorded interviews (1996) for my own MEd dissertation. The "course" I mention near the end of the extract was a course designed to help Ukrainian EL teachers develop their skills in communicative approaches to teaching EIB.

RG - Robert Goddard. UT1 - First Ukrainian teacher. UT2 - Second Ukrainian teacher.

RG: What about your training as a teacher?
UT1: My training as a teacher?
RG: Can you remember what you did at university?
UT1: My training? It was...I don't remember...1965 and for two years. Not in Vinitsa, in Kiev at the Pedagogical...now it's the university...we studied mostly Galsworthy. We learned some accent by heart...
RG: And did you do any linguistics?
UT1: Yes, you see, my investigation was the use of the article.
RG: For your training?
UT1: Yes, it was very interesting by the way and er the use of the article and the construction, for instance, a cup of tea. It's because the problem of the article is very interesting and very difficult for us. A...cup...of...tea and I found some 20 variants or combinations of articles and so I had some 50 odd thousand examples er...from again Galsworthy. I named my daughter Irena because Irene of that Galsworthy. I called her Irene when she was a child.

UNIT 3: Methodology and Classroom Practice

RG: This course that we are doing now is a bit different.
UT1: I enjoy it. First of all, it's something new, it's very interesting. They relax. It's interesting for me. I was never interested in marketing but certainly they don't know the language of marketing.

UT2: I saw...very sad sometimes that teachers work with these new courses which predetermine the communicative approach but they work in a very traditional manner with a lot of translation which is not the main idea of the communicative approach, and it is taught in the traditional way...eighty percent translation, choosing words and translating them.

Pause for thought

> *The training and experiences revealed in the interviews above were not untypical of many Ukrainian teachers I talked to. Clearly, the educational culture here is not very welcoming for teachers armed with, for example, TBL, or the not-very-authoritarian role of teachers used to adopting a communicative approach. Nor is the educational culture above confined to Ukraine. In such a situation, would you:*
> - *try to convince your local colleagues that they are misguided and need to update their teaching skills and become familiar with modern methodologies?*
> - *adapt your own teaching style to suit local conditions?*

We would suggest that you adapt your teaching style. Both trainees and experienced teachers need to develop a critical appreciation of the various approaches and methodologies we mentioned at the beginning of this section. The strengths and weaknesses of each "method" or components of each method need to be considered in the light of the particular learning situation. Decisions can then be taken as to what is appropriate.

We are not suggesting that this is an easy task. It is very difficult to come to conclusions about which approaches and methods are most appropriate for any given teaching situation (Harmer, 2001). We shall offer guidelines to help you in approaching this task in chapters 3 to 9 of this unit. For the moment, let us consider some theoretical background.

UNIT 3: Methodology and Classroom Practice

Theoretical background

In unit 1, chapter 3, section 3 we noted that teacher-groups often form professional/academic cultures and that Bernstein (1971) identifies two basic types of academic culture. These are described as collectionist and integrationist. Holliday (1994b) argues that English language education is divided between these two cultures and that an understanding of this division is necessary if teachers working in other cultures are to find an appropriate methodology. For the sake of convenience we again list the features of the collectionist code and the integrationist code. The collectionist code is characterised by:

- separate subjects
- strong subject boundaries
- didactic, content-based methodology
- rigid timetabling
- hierarchical departmental structure
- staff identities, loyalties and notions of specialisation oriented to knowledge of subject
- classroom practice invisible to most other staff
- oligarchic control of institution.

The integrationist code is characterised by:

- inter-disciplinary subjects
- blurred subject boundaries
- skills-based and discovery-oriented
- flexible timetabling
- staff identities, loyalties and notions of expertise oriented to classroom skills
- classroom practice is open to observation
- democratic control.

We also noted in unit 1, chapter 3, that Holliday (1994a and 1994b) suggests that the professional academic culture of the TESEP (non-Western, Tertiary, Secondary and Primary education) situation is essentially collectionist.

Holliday (1994b) also argues that the British, Australasian and North American (BANA) model of ELT may be inappropriate in the TESEP situation by suggesting that:

UNIT 3: Methodology and Classroom Practice

> ...the professional-academic culture of the BANA English language teaching group is essentially integrationist. In the last twenty years it has taken on a skills-based, and more recently a discovery-problem-solving, heuristic approach... which the learning group ideal embodies. (Holliday, 1994b)

Thus, the educational environment that produced BANA methodologies is very different from the TESEP environment in which many teachers of EIB are working. Without delicacy of approach and intercultural sensitivity, BANA teachers of EIB may well come up against difficulties and experience conflict from both local teachers and learners. What are the reasons for this?

First, there is a potential difference in values. BANA teachers often value their knowledge of, and skills in, methodology. In the TESEP situation, mastery of the subject content may well be the measure of professionalism and status. Holliday (1994b) points to the dangers of a naive acceptance of BANA methodologies as being somehow the "best" way to teach. He writes:

> Unexplained violations of the expected norm by teachers enthusiastically embracing communicative approaches may lead to the diminution of their status and perceived competence in learners' eyes. (Holliday, 1994b, citing Cortazzi)

Further, we noted above that in TESEP situations like Ukraine, for example, it is not unusual to see teachers using textbooks based on communicative methodology, heavily relying on the textbook and without a real understanding of the approach.

Secondly, there is the potential problem of disruption caused by the introduction of BANA integrationist codes in collectionist cultures. As Bernstein (1971) puts it, "...a move from collection to integrated codes may well bring about a disturbance in the structure and distribution of power, in property relationships and in existing educational identities."

Holliday (1994b) maintains that there may often be a lack of respect on the part of BANA practitioners towards collectionist subject boundaries and the didactic approach of TESEP English language education. Further, as Bernstein points out, "The openness of learning under integration may produce a culture in which neither staff nor pupils have a sense of time, place or purpose."

UNIT 3: Methodology and Classroom Practice

Question 6

> *While in Germany and teaching in-company, I was once discussing a course in foundations of business communication for German employees with the manager of the company's education unit. My suggestion that we introduce intercultural awareness into the sessions was met with an almost incredulous, "No!" The manager was adamant that intercultural issues should be done in the intercultural communication seminars and that there could be no crossover with other courses. I had forgotten that Germany was a collectionist culture. Does this anecdote tell you anything about the geographical spread of TESEP/BANA cultures or was the difficulty I experienced due to simple personality differences?*

Indeed, it could be argued that the methodologies we briefly examined at the beginning of this chapter, methodologies which demand a certain type of student behaviour, are not adaptable for use in TESEP situations. The message is clear. English language teachers need to examine their methodologies in the light of the professional/academic cultures in which they are working. As Holliday (1994b) points out:

> In the case of English language education, where the new methodology may well be of a totally alien nature, coming from outside the local educational environment, the impact may well have a complex ripple effect throughout the whole host ecology of cultures... At the same time, the success of the innovation will depend on a deep understanding of this ecology. There is therefore a socio-moral implication in trying to introduce BANA integrationism into TESEP institutions in other people's countries, with possible effects that go far beyond the management of learning a second or foreign language.
> (Holliday, 1994b, p.102)

National culture and its influence in the classroom

There are enormous differences in the way people from different cultures think, act and feel, and we suggest that mutual understanding is only possible if there is a framework in which cultural awareness can be raised. Hofstede (1991) claims to have such a framework (see also

UNIT 3: Methodology and Classroom Practice

unit 1, chapter 5). He identifies four dimensions of culture, and these form the basis of his analysis of cultural variety. If you have not already done so, read chapters 2 to 5 of Hofstede (1991). Alternatively, look again at unit 1, chapters 5 and 6. His dimensions of culture are:

- the power distance (PD) dimension - from high to low
- the collective/individual (IC) dimension
- the uncertainty avoidance (UA) dimension – from high/strong to low/weak
- the femininity/masculinity (FM) dimension.

For Holliday (1994b), wide-scale, national cultural factors like Hofstede's dimensions, are over-generalised and, therefore, distorting. We agree that there is a real danger of applying Hofstede's general characteristics to every individual and every situation (see also Flowerdew, 1998 and Littlewood, 2000). However, as generalisations, they represent an interesting link with Holliday's (1994b) terminology.

We think that low power distance (Anglo) cultures are strongly linked to BANA countries and their associated methodological preferences; that is, integrationist, communicative teaching methodology. We could, therefore, argue that communicative methodology is based upon the national cultural values of BANA countries (low PD, individualist) rather than the high PD, collective values of TESEP countries like, for example, Ukraine, Japan and China.

With regard to low PD classrooms, Hofstede (1991) identifies several characteristics (see unit 1, chapter 6). The implication is that the values underlying communicative methodology (and TBL), the textbooks and the training that promotes them, are similar to those revealed in low PD societies which, in turn, can be associated with Holliday's BANA cultures.

Further, Hofstede's (1991) link between low PD and individualistic cultures indicates that education in individualistic societies may reveal the same characteristics as those revealed in low PD societies. For example, the desire to elicit responses - a key feature of communicative methodology - is a feature of individualistic societies. Personal opinions are valued and everyone is supposed to have one.

Further, Hofstede's analysis of the educational characteristics of the uncertainty avoidance situation reveals a similarity between low UA cultural values and values implicit in BANA methodology (see also

UNIT 3: Methodology and Classroom Practice

unit 1, chapter 6). However sound the linguistic and psychological principles on which many BANA methodologies are based, they are not necessarily appropriate for learners from high UA cultures like Japan. These learners may want to focus on accuracy, correct grammatical rules, correct pronunciation and they may expect the teacher to have all the answers.

We argue that to insist on BANA methodologies in TESEP countries, would be to enforce something that in many ways is alien to learners. We suggest that if a methodology is to have any relevance for learners, then the values that promote it must be shared by its recipients. However, we have indicated that communicative methodology, for example, is linked to Holliday's (1994b) BANA situations which in turn can be characterised by Hofstede's (1991) low PD, individualistic, and low UA values. Teachers need to think very carefully before applying such methodology in the TESEP situation with its high PD, collective and high UA values.

Question 7

> *Imagine you are teaching a group of Chinese students in a British University. It is language centre (and university) policy to ask students to fill in an end-of-term feedback form on which they are invited to comment on the course and its effectiveness. Is this the most appropriate means of getting feedback from Chinese students?*

To summarise so far, we are not suggesting that the imposition of a Western curriculum with Western standards and criteria of achievement represent an act of linguistic imperialism or oppression (see also Luk and Lin, 2006). We are arguing that if teachers do not take account of the differing interests and responses of different groups, their teaching will be less relevant and less appropriate to some pupils (see also Wringe, 1988).

The issue has been taken a stage further by Alptekin (2002), who attacks the validity of a pedagogy based on the native-speaker model of communicative competence (see Canale, 1983). Alptekin suggests that the insistence on the ideal that the language presented in the classroom should be authentic has always been one of the tenets of communicative methodology. However, the language which is authentic for native speakers may not be authentic for non-native

UNIT 3: Methodology and Classroom Practice

speakers. Alptekin (2002) asks:

> How relevant...are the conventions of British politeness or American informality to the Japanese and Turks, say, when doing business in English? How relevant are such culturally laden discourse samples as British railway timetables or American newspaper advertisements to industrial engineers from Romania and Egypt conducting technical research in English? How relevant is the importance of Anglo-American eye contact, or the socially acceptable distance for conversation as properties of meaningful communication to Finnish and Italian academicians exchanging ideas in a professional meeting?

Alptekin (2002) goes on to argue that communicative behaviour needs to be redefined in relation to the reality of English as an International Language. This means that we should consider not only the uses of English that are real for native speakers but also the uses of English that are real for non-native speakers. Further, Alptekin suggests that if language is embedded in native-speaker culture, the culture of the learners is pushed to one side or ignored completely. And yet, "this is the area where non-native speaker teachers are at their best, due to the linguistic background and life experience they share with their students" (Alptekin, 2002). For more on non-native speaker teachers, see chapter 2 of this unit and/or you might want to look at Arva and Medgyes (2000).

Alptekin (2002) concludes his attack on the native speaker model of communicative competence by stating that:

> The conventional model of communicative competence, with its strict adherence to native speaker norms within target language culture, would appear to be invalid in accounting for learning and using an international language in cross-cultural settings. A new pedagogic model is urgently needed to accommodate the case of English as a means of international and intercultural communication.

Alptekin's (2002) model has the following characteristics.

UNIT 3: Methodology and Classroom Practice

- The pedagogic model should be served by successful bilingual individuals speaking English as an International Language (EIL).
- Intercultural communicative competence should be developed among EIL learners.
- EIL pedagogy needs to be of global appropriacy.
- Instructional material and activities should involve local and international contexts.
- Instructional materials should include suitable discourse samples that deal with native and non-native interactions as well as non-native and non-native interactions.

Essentially, Alptekin is suggesting that ELT develops new pedagogies and instructional material that will foster the development of intercultural communicative competence among learners. Alptekin's work has been taken further by Risager (2007), who envisages a complete break with the view of language as something trapped within a tightly knit national world of history, culture and mentality.

The question remains, that with so many different approaches and methods available to us, and taking into account the potential mismatch between a particular methodology and the cultural values of a particular group of learners, on what basis can we decide on our approach to teaching? In addition, what criteria do we now use in order to define communicative competence?

1.5: Conclusions

Some answers to the questions above may be found in what Harmer (2001) refers to as a pragmatic eclecticism. This means that, essentially, decisions about what to teach and how to teach are based on what seems to work. However, before we look at pragmatic eclecticism, we need to examine the thinking behind the notion that methods are no longer relevant and that teachers should familiarise themselves with the idea of postmethod pedagogy. If you have the time, the inclination and a copy of the book to hand, you might want to read through the appropriate chapters of Harmer (2001) in order to broaden your understanding of the main ideas in this chapter. You might also access the article by Alptekin (2002) and skim through Risager (2007).

UNIT 3: Methodology and Classroom Practice

1.6: Answers to Questions

Question 1
Communication has a structural level, a functional level and a discoursal level. In other words, they are not mutually exclusive. Further, Stern (1983) argues that, "Whether techniques of linguistic analysis – however well they may lend themselves to linguistic research – are equally applicable to language teaching is of course open to question." Our answer is that descriptions of language do not necessarily carry implications for language learning.

Question 2
We can find no logical connection between a particular psychological theory of how grammar is learned and a particular theory of language structure. A behaviourist theory of learning does not necessarily go with a structural view of language. Nor does a functional view of language necessarily go with a cognitive learning theory.

Question 3
Our answer would be – probably not. After all, nobody knows for sure how we learn. We suggest that an eclectic approach – taking what is useful from each theory – would be a wise course of action.

Question 4
- Area-specific vocabulary - for example, the language of marketing and finance.
- Grammar, which gives us the forms to combine the words.
- Functions, which enable us to use language appropriately in a range of situations.
- Techniques and strategies for communication in typical business situations, for example, negotiations, presentations, meetings, giving feedback and dealing with conflict.
- Intercultural skills, which enable us to communicate effectively with people from other cultures.

Question 5
Because the value systems underlying this methodology may fly in the face of the educational values of learners. Given that more and more jobs are available in the Far East, teacher-training courses have to concern themselves with producing teachers who can deal with non-Western teaching realities.

Question 6
It may have been due to personality! But Germany is a collectionist culture. This shows us that the BANA/TESEP distinction is not simply Western versus Eastern.

Question 7
This type of feedback may be appropriate with low PD learners. High PD learners may be shocked at being asked for their comments. It is unlikely that learners will offer any constructive criticism of their teachers. Further, the Chinese (like other high context collective cultures) may prefer to offer spoken feedback indirectly through a third person. Written feedback may be another example of attempting to impose Western values.

UNIT 3: Methodology and Classroom Practice

Chapter 2

Method, Postmethod or Pragmatism?

2.1: Introduction
2.2: Objectives
2.3: Method, Postmethod or Pragmatism?
2.4: Conclusion
2.5: Answers to questions.

2.1: Introduction

In the previous chapter, we asked whether approaches and methods developed in the West are suitable for non-Western teaching and learning situations. This chapter takes us a stage further and suggests that the concept of "best" method is an illusory concept, and that the search for this "best" method is, therefore, unachievable.

We ask whether the whole notion of method is still relevant in the world of ELT today. If the answer is, "No," then how can teachers make decisions on what to teach and how to teach it?

We consider whether the answer to this question can be found in the world of postmethod pedagogy (Kumaravadivelu, 2005). In this world, teacher development is vital and ways to achieve that development are at the heart of this pedagogy.

UNIT 3: Methodology and Classroom Practice

2.2: Objectives

At the end of this chapter, you will be able to:

- better judge what is appropriate for you and your learners
- fully appreciate the usefulness of action research as a tool (among others) to further develop your professional skills.

Pre-reading task

While you are engaged with this chapter, you are asked to work on the activity in the shaded box below. This activity is designed to stimulate your thinking and to focus your mind on the main ideas in the chapter.

> *Choose an area of doubt or uncertainty in your own teaching (past or present). Decide how you would go about gathering data, analysing the data and what action to take in order to remedy the situation.*

2.3: Method Postmethod or Pragmatism?

The arguments concerning which method (if any) best encourages the learning of language is not new. Hutchinson and Waters (1987) argue that teachers should consider whether or not basing any teaching approach on one theory of language or learning is sound practice. "...it is wise to take an eclectic approach, taking what is useful from each theory and trusting also in the evidence of your own experience as a teacher." (Hutchinson and Waters, 1987)

The argument above is echoed in Harmer's (2001) call for teachers to base their decisions about what and how to teach on what seems to work. According to Harmer (2001), what seems to work may depend on, for example:

- the age of the learners
- the character-type of the learners
- their culture
- their level of proficiency
- the teacher's preferences
- the teacher's attitudes and beliefs.

UNIT 3: Methodology and Classroom Practice

Pause for thought

> *How often do you take a pragmatic course of action in the classroom, a course that goes against what you learned during your training as a teacher? How do you feel about this? Do you feel that you are doing something 'bad' or do you feel that are doing something positive, responding to your learners' needs and being innovative?*

If you feel 'bad' about doing things which go against the dictates of your training, you might take heart from Prabhu (1990) who writes:

> If...we view teaching as an activity whose value depends centrally on whether it is informed or uninformed by the teacher's subjective sense of plausibility - on the degree to which it is "real" or mechanical - it (methodology evaluation) becomes a worthwhile goal for our professional effort to help activate and develop teachers' varied senses of plausibility... Perhaps the best method varies from one teacher to another. (Prabhu, 1990)

Prabhu (1990) is therefore echoing Harmer's (2001) view by suggesting that:

> ...if we regard our professional effort as a search for the best method which, when found, will replace all other methods, we may not only be working towards an unrealisable goal but, in the process, be misconstruing the nature of teaching as a set of procedures that can by themselves carry a guarantee of learning outcomes. (Prabhu, 1990)

Prabhu concludes his article by suggesting that the search for an inherently best method is unachievable. Teachers are recommended to turn their attention instead to looking for ways to make their teaching real for their own situation. This does not mean that anything goes. An individual teacher's perceptions of what makes "good" teaching should always be informed by sound theory and reflection.

This reflection, according to Harmer (2001) and Kumaravadivelu (2001) could take the form of action research. By constantly monitoring

UNIT 3: Methodology and Classroom Practice

their classes, teachers can adjust what they do in their search for methods and techniques which are best for them in their particular situation.

Action research is just one of several ways in which teachers can foster their own development.

Question 1

> *In the postmethod world, teacher development, as we shall later see, is crucial. Action research is one way to achieve development. What other ways can you think of?*

Pause for thought

> *How many of the suggestions we mention in our answer have you tried out? If your answer is "None of them," we suggest you start immediately by writing down your thoughts about lessons you have taught and lessons you will teach. Keep your notes in a note-book and refer back to them at a later date.*

Action research is the name given to a series of procedures teachers can engage in. Their reasons may be that:

- they want to improve certain aspects of their teaching
- they want to evaluate the success (or failure) of certain activities
- they want to evaluate the effectiveness and/or appropriacy of certain classroom activities.

The classic action research model has seven steps (Ur, 1996).

1. A problem is identified.
2. Relevant data are collected and recorded.
3. Practical action is suggested that might solve the problem.
4. A plan of action is put into practice.
5. Results are recorded.
6. If the problem is solved - fine.
7. If not the problem is redefined and the cycle is repeated.

For a fuller and more detailed description of action research, you might want to look at Edge and Richards (1993) or Harmer (2001).

UNIT 3: Methodology and Classroom Practice

Action research (as part of teacher development) is also at the heart of Kumaravadivelu's (2001) theory of postmethod pedagogy, which we would like to describe in some detail.

Pause for thought

> *As you read through our description of Kumaravadivelu's theory we would like you to consider whether the values supporting postmethod pedagogy are as culture-dependent as those that support communicative methodology?*

Kumaravadivelu (2001) takes some of the issues raised by Prabhu (1990) several steps further. First, Kumaravadivelu addresses the limitations of the concept of method. Second, he emphasises the need to go beyond a transmission view of teacher education (see chapter 1.4 of this unit and our description of burgers and TEFLers). However, the main focus of the pedagogy is, in Kumarvadivelu's (2001) words, "...a long-felt dissatisfaction with the concept of method as the organising principle for L2 teaching."

Postmethod pedagogy consists of three interacting pedagogic parameters. These are:

1. particularity
2. practicality
3. possibility.

Let us examine them in turn.

Particularity refers to a pedagogy that is sensitive to a particular teaching situation. This means that it is sensitive to:

- a particular group of teachers with
- a particular group of learners attempting to reach
- a particular set of goals
- in a particular institution
- in a particular socio/cultural environment.

The essence of particularity is that it focuses on a critical awareness of local needs. Teachers are required to constantly observe their teaching, evaluate its outcomes, identify problems, find solutions and try them out again. It is this action research that is at the heart of postmethod

UNIT 3: Methodology and Classroom Practice

pedagogy.

Pause for thought

> *Do you feel that your teacher-training prepared you for the particularity as it is described above? Are there any local needs to which you have been obliged to react on your own initiative?*

Particularity interacts so strongly with practicality that it can not really be understood without it. Practicality concerns the relationship between theory and practice.

Pause for thought

> *How do you relate to your training as a teacher? Do you see yourself merely as an implementer of the theory you learned on your course?*

The essence of practicality is that it aims for a, "teacher-generated theory of practice," (Kumaravadivelu, 2001). Kumaravadivelu points to an unhealthy dichotomy between professional theories generated by experts, and teacher theories generated while on the job. The reality is that the former often have immense value while the latter are sometimes ignored. Kumaravadivelu is calling for a context-sensitive pedagogy that emerges from teachers as autonomous individuals who are able to develop their own theory of practice, which is generated through practice. In this context:

> ...pedagogical thoughtfulness simultaneously feeds and is fed by reflective capabilities of teachers that enable them to understand and identify problems, analyse and assess information, consider and evaluate alternatives, and then choose the best available alternative, which is then subjected to further critical appraisal. In this sense, a theory of practice is an on-going, living, working theory involving continual reflection and action. (Kumaravadivelu, 2001)

Good teachers, according to Kumaravadivelu, know by instinct what works and what does not work. Essentially, he is echoing Harmer's (2001) view here and Prabhu's (1990) sense of plausibility.

UNIT 3: Methodology and Classroom Practice

The idea of a pedagogy of possibility essentially seeks to harness the social, political and economic character of the learners' environment so that it may directly shape the nature of classroom input and interaction. In the process:

> ...pedagogy of possibility is also concerned with individual identity. More than any other educational enterprise, language education provides its participants with challenges and opportunities for a continual quest for subjectivity and self-identification. (Kumarvadivelu, 2001)

Question 2

What are the implications of postmethod pedagogy for both learners and teachers?

One outstanding area of particularity, perhaps, is the issue of native and non-native teachers (NESTS and non-NESTS) in the classroom (see e.g. Medyges, 1994; Arva and Medyges 2000).

Pause for thought

NESTS and non-NESTS both have strengths and weaknesses as teachers. What do you think these strengths and weaknesses are?

Medyges (1994) claims that NESTSs and non-NESTs are two "different species." He bases his claim on the following arguments.

- They differ in terms of language proficiency.
- They differ in terms of teaching behaviour.
- Language proficiency is responsible for most of the differences in teaching behaviour.
- Both are equally good as teachers in their own terms.

Some of the differences between NESTs and non-NESTs are listed below.

UNIT 3: Methodology and Classroom Practice

Pause for thought

> *How far do these differences relate to Bernstein's (1971) integrationist and collectionist educational cultures?*

According to Arva and Medyges (2000) NESTs tend to:

- speak better English
- use real language
- adopt a more flexible approach
- are more innovative
- are less empathetic
- attend to perceived needs
- are less committed
- focus on fluency, meaning and oral skills.

Non-NESTS tend to:

- speak poorer English
- use language which is somehow "bookish"
- adopt a less flexible approach
- are cautious
- are more empathetic
- attend to real needs
- are more committed
- focus on accuracy, form and grammatical rules.

Question 3

> *If you were the Director of a school in which NESTs and non-NESTs worked side by side, what would you do to ensure that any differences and problems between the two were not only minimised but used productively?*

2.4: Conclusions

It is clear that there is a connection between Prabhu's (1990) concept of plausibility, Kumaravadivelu's (2001) theory of particularity, practicality and possibility, and Harmer's (2001) pragmatic eclecticism.

UNIT 3: Methodology and Classroom Practice

All three embrace the idea of basing what and how we teach on what seems to work. However, this does not mean that anything goes. The opposite is true. Teaching practice needs to be constantly scrutinised to see that it is working and why it is working. Furthermore, learners have a right to expect the teacher to have some purpose in mind and a right to know why they are being asked to do certain things. We will finish with Harmer's conclusions about teaching practice.

- Learners need exposure to language.
- Learners need help to notice language facts.
- Learners need to learn how to communicate and for this some task-based, communicative activities can be beneficial.
- Anxiety should be lowered in order for effective learning to take place.
- Learners should be encouraged to discover certain things for themselves.
- Lexis and grammar should not be ignored.
- Any teaching practice should take account of the socio-cultural aspects of the learners' environment. Compromise will probably be necessary.

Pause for thought

> We began this chapter by asking you whether or not self-development was a Western ideal. How far are the ideas represented in this chapter simply more manifestations of Western thought - thought that can not be applied in other cultures?

2.5: Answers to questions

Question 1
- Reflection after each class.
- Sharing and reflecting with a colleague.
- Airing problems (and successes) during in-house staff meetings.
- Peer teaching, peer observation.
- Attending conferences and workshops.
- Reading.
- Doing further study.
- Informal teachers' groups.

UNIT 3: Methodology and Classroom Practice

- Joining teachers' associations (e.g. IATEFL).
- "Talk" to colleagues and exchange ideas on the internet.

Question 2

The postmethod learner is an autonomous learner. By autonomous, Kumaravadivelu means: academic autonomy, social autonomy, which encourages learners to be collaborative partners and to work in teams, and liberatory autonomy, which encourages critical thinking. Essentially, this means recognising the social, political and economic impediments to full human development and providing tools to overcome those impediments.

The postmethod teacher is also an autonomous person. The autonomous teacher can only become fully autonomous by embarking on a process of self-development. Teacher research is at the heart of this assertion. Action research, for example, can help teachers assess what works, what does not work, for what reasons, and deciding what to do about it. Apart from action research, Kumaravadivelu also points to teacher-training and how such training should not simply develop ready-packaged TEFLers. Effective teacher-training should lay strong foundations for future development, that is, teacher-training should foster the conditions necessary for change.

Question 3

I would set up a system for NEST/non-NEST collaboration. Both have strengths and weaknesses. The JET and the Koto-ku projects could serve as models of effective NEST/non-NEST collaboration (see Brumby and Wada, (1990) and Sturman, 1992).

UNIT 3: Methodology and Classroom Practice

Chapter 3

Teaching by Principles

3.1: Introduction
3.2: Objectives
3:3: Teaching by Principles? What Principles?
3.4: Conclusions
3.5: Answers to Questions.

3.1: Introduction

In the previous two chapters, we saw that the concept of method in ELT is, at least with some researchers, out of favour. The diversity of language learners in diverse contexts with diverse needs necessitates an eclectic mixture of tasks. These tasks should be fashioned for a particular group, studying in a particular place with its own particular opportunities and challenges. There probably never will be one method which will be suitable for everyone. We suggest that teachers think in terms of possible methodological options open to them, options which can be tailored to a particular group and which may change over time as a result of reflection and/or feedback from colleagues and learners.

In this chapter we will continue our search for methodological appropriacy. We shall consider some principles which will inform your approach to classroom practice. Formal and informal feedback should

UNIT 3: Methodology and Classroom Practice

encourage you to take risks in your teaching and foster dynamism and growth. Action research should reveal new understandings and fresh perspectives on your classroom practice. These insights should inspire you to change and to experiment.

We are well aware of situations around the world in which your choices may well be limited by a number of institutional factors. Among these may be regulations which demand a certain curriculum content, budgetary constraints, which will dictate class size and number of hours, an old-fashioned textbook, or an obligation to teach in a certain way (grammar-translation "method" for example). We do not underestimate these challenges. In fact, if you are a new and inexperienced teacher, these may be the biggest hurdles to overcome. Having said that, once you are settled, feeling comfortable, and have found ways to compromise, you can begin to take risks and teach creatively, and make use of some innovative techniques that we shall consider in this chapter. For a more detailed analysis of the areas we outline in this chapter, you are recommended to look at Harmer (2001) and/or Douglas Brown (2001).

3.2: Objectives

At the end of this chapter, you will be able to:

➢ critically evaluate the principles by which you teach.

Pre-reading task

Before you begin, try the activity in the shaded box below. The activity is designed to focus your thinking on the main ideas in the chapter.

> *Consider the influences on your approach to teaching (for example, maybe your own experience as a language learner is an important influence for you). If you can, make a list of about 10 of the most important influences. How could these be re-written/re-interpreted so that they describe an approach to language teaching?*

UNIT 3: Methodology and Classroom Practice

3.3: Teaching by Principles? What Principles?

In the conclusion of the previous chapter we observed that with regard to best approaches and methods, Harmer (2001) drew seven conclusions.

1. Students need exposure to language.
2. Students need the opportunity for noticing language or consciousness-raising in order to remember facts.
3. Students need communicative and task-based activities.
4. Students need a non-threatening environment.
5. Students need to be encouraged to be independent learners.
6. Methodology is often linked to cultural values.
7. Grammar and vocabulary should not be ignored.

Douglas Brown (2001) also points to twelve principles on which the essence of an approach to language teaching can be based. Together with good practice, these twelve principles can form the basis on which teachers can plan, carry out and reflect on their lessons. Douglas Brown (2001) outlines his principles under the following headings:

- Automacity.
- Meaningful learning.
- Anticipation of reward.
- Intrinsic motivation.
- Strategic investment.
- Language ego.
- Self-confidence.
- Taking risks.
- The connection between language and culture.
- The influence of the native language.
- Interlanguage.
- Communicative competence.

Pause for thought

> *As you read the following descriptions of these principles, compare them with Harmer's (2001) conclusions about language teaching. Are there any similarities?*

UNIT 3: Methodology and Classroom Practice

Automacity concerns the belief that language teaching should not focus entirely on pieces of language analysed in isolation. Teaching should also attempt to give learners the opportunity to practise language in authentic contexts and for meaningful purposes. In this sense, automacity implies that adults should aim to emulate the success of children who appear to acquire language subconsciously.

Question 1

What are the implications of automacity for you as a teacher?

The second principle of meaningful learning is closely linked to that of automacity. In essence, meaningful learning means that the language learned should be relevant to the goals and aspirations of the learner. Although learning by heart and mechanical drilling may have their uses in the classroom, students will learn more effectively when learning has some direct meaning for them.

Question 2

How can the principle of meaningful learning by applied in the EIB classroom?

The third principle, anticipation of reward, means paying attention to motivation and student purpose. It also means making sure that learners are clearly aware of the aims of the course, its content and its activities, and can see how the course will be of benefit to them.

Question 3

How can the principle of anticipation of reward influence learning and teaching?

The fourth principle, intrinsic motivation, concerns tapping into the motivations that lie within the learners, and encouraging behaviour that needs no external rewards. In other words, it is the learning itself that is motivating and rewarding. This is not to say that teacher-praise is out of place. Constructive feedback can play an important role in reinforcing learner autonomy and self-fulfilment.

UNIT 3: Methodology and Classroom Practice

Question 4

> *What activities can you use in the EIB classroom to capitalise on the principle of intrinsic motivation?*

The fifth principle of strategic investment focuses on the role of the learner in the classroom. This means that although the methods employed by the teacher are important, the methods used by the students to learn are of equal importance. In chapter 9 of this unit, we will examine the role of the learner and the characteristics of various learning styles (see Oxford and Green, 1996; Reid, 1995).

Six learning styles can be identified.

1. Visual learners – learners who, for example, prefer to see the words they are learning.
2. Tactile learners – learners who learn by touching.
3. Kinaesthetic learners – learners who, for example, prefer to learn by experience.
4. Auditory learners – learners who prefer to learn by listening.
5. Individual learners – learners who work best alone.
6. Group learners, who learn best when studying with others.

Question 5

> *How could an appreciation of different learning styles influence your classroom teaching?*

The language ego principle essentially concerns developing sensitivity towards learners as human beings, who may be feeling inhibited and defenceless in the classroom. It means offering emotional support to fragile egos.

Question 6

> *How can you give this emotional support to your learners?*

The principle of self-confidence is clearly linked to that of language ego. However, self-confidence emphasises the belief learners have in their own ability to accomplish the task regardless of the ego principle.

UNIT 3: Methodology and Classroom Practice

Question 7

> *How can you help learners develop and/or maintain their self-confidence?*

The principle of risk-taking concerns the belief that taking risks will help learners retain learning for longer periods. In order to encourage risk-taking, teachers will need to ensure that the tasks they choose are neither too hard nor too difficult. It is up to the teacher to create an atmosphere in the classroom that is conducive to risk taking, and when risks are taken, the teacher's response must be encouraging.

The connection between language teaching and culture has already been examined in unit 1, chapter 6. Teachers should always be sensitive to different cultures and their methodological preferences. For example, some learners may not react very well to groupwork. If this is the case, ask yourself whether or not they are used to this type of student grouping. If they are used to teacher-centred, whole-class teaching, then it might be wise to introduce groupwork and pairwork slowly at first. Similarly, many learners may be confused by peer evaluation and feedback. Learners may also need to be introduced slowly to these techniques.

Douglas Brown's tenth principle concerns the learner's native language and its effect on second language learning. Most teachers rightly focus on the interference of the native language, that is, learners' errors which originate from an assumption that English functions like their mother tongue.

Question 8

> *How can you use the native language effect in your classrooms?*

Douglas Brown's (2001) eleventh principle concerns the systematic acquisition of a second language. Adults, like children, manifest a progression through certain language stages in their development towards fuller competence. Internalising rules (correctly and incorrectly) is natural for both adults and children. For example, it might not be uncommon to hear a statement like, "Peter goed to the cinema," uttered by both non-native speaker adults and native speaker children. Douglas Brown calls this principle the principle of interlanguage, and it has significant implications for the feedback

UNIT 3: Methodology and Classroom Practice

teachers give to their learners.

Question 9

> *What are the implications of the principle of interlanguage for teachers of EIB?*

The final principle concerns what Douglas Brown (2001) believes to be the most important linguistic principle, that of communicative competence. This principle suggests that if confident and effective communication is the ultimate goal of language teaching, then teachers should ensure that they give enough attention to language use, fluency, authentic language and the context in which the language is spoken. In addition, it means that we pay adequate attention to the real needs and requirements of the learners.

Question 10

> *Imagine you are teaching presentation skills to a group of middle-level managers. How would/should the principle of communicative competence manifest itself in your teaching?*

Douglas Brown's (2001) twelve principles can form the basis of your teaching in that they can help you make choices about what to do in the classroom. They can also help you monitor yourself and assess what you have done so that next time you may be able to do things better. The principles may therefore be utilised to scrutinise your practice to see whether or not it is working, and if it is not working, why not?

The principles alone, however, are not enough. You can not even begin to think about planning lessons and the techniques you will use, without thinking about, for example:

- the age of your learners
- their language level
- their cultural background
- their motivation
- their learning styles
- the character of the group itself
- the syllabus
- the coursebook (if the class are using one)

UNIT 3: Methodology and Classroom Practice

- the group's expectations and previous learning experience
- any socio-political factors.

Pause for thought

> *Have we missed out anything here? Are there any other factors which you feel are equally important?*

3.4: Conclusions

At the beginning of this chapter we asked you to make a list of the things that have influenced you as a teacher. We then asked you to reinterpret these to describe your approach to language teaching. Have a look at that list again. Does the approach contain any of the principles we have discussed in this chapter? Would you now add anything to that list? If so what?

3.5: Answers to questions

Question 1
There may be many implications. Some that come to mind are that you should not focus too much on grammar and usage. Attention should also be given to fluency practice, encouraging your learners to communicate and giving them the confidence to experiment. This is not to say that grammar rules and usage are to be ignored. What we are saying is that attention to the language system should be balanced by encouraging fluency. Automacity also implies that fluency should be practised in a way that is as genuine as possible, given the limitations of the classroom.

Question 2
You can ensure that the content and the activities you choose are relevant to the goals of your learners. This means that you should be as familiar as possible with what your learners do and how they do it. Drilling activities may have no relevance for intermediate learners wishing to learn how to negotiate with the Chinese for example. However, some Chinese students may be poor communicators due to poor pronunciation. In this case, some pronunciation drills may be appropriate. Similarly, too much grammatical explanation may not be appropriate for learners wishing to develop confidence and fluency in giving presentations.

UNIT 3: Methodology and Classroom Practice

Question 3
It may be that learners have only an instrumental purpose in learning English – that is, they are only interested in language learning for the sake of their career or promotion. If this is the case, you can hardly expect them to show an intense interest in the language itself or the culture of those who speak it. This means that you should focus almost entirely on the purpose to which the language is put, whether or not you agree with this. Reward also means encouraging learners and getting them to encourage each other. This is not necessarily an easy thing to do. For example, peer review of presentations and/or reports can be unsuccessful owing to the attitude that "teacher knows best." Reward also implies that you should also show enthusiasm and interest.

Question 4
You should choose activities which appeal to the genuine interests and concerns of your learners and their careers. Further, you should make it clear exactly why you are choosing a particular technique or activity and what you want your students to achieve by doing it. For example, if you want learners to discover something for themselves, you could hint at what that something is. You should also ensure that the activity you choose is reasonably challenging and that you give adequate and constructive feedback at the end of the activity. Essentially, capitalising on intrinsic motivation means focussing on student needs and helping them to achieve their goals in a constructive and enthusiastic manner.

Question 5
You will need to employ a variety of techniques in order to ensure that you cover as many students and their learning styles as possible. You will need to mix individual and groupwork, and visual and auditory techniques. You will also need to sensitise yourself to any connection between culture and preferred learning style (see Rao, 2001).

Question 6
Clearly, you need to provide activities which are challenging but not too difficult for your learners. You also need to be sensitive to your correction techniques. How will you correct your learners? How hard will you be? You also need to be sensitive when/if you single out learners to answer questions. Would it be better to place students in groups and ask a student to volunteer the group answer? Which students should you group together? Which cultures prefer to work in groups and which prefer to work individually?

Question 7
You can start by giving plenty of assurance to the students - by reinforcing their abilities to do the tasks you give them. Sensitivity is needed here. There is a fine line between giving assurance to someone who needs it and being too soft on someone who needs a push. You can also make sure that you sequence activities from easy-to-accomplish to more challenging. In this way you can help build self-confidence. If you start with something difficult, you can be directly responsible for students building up some kind of defence mechanism instead.

UNIT 3: Methodology and Classroom Practice

Question 8

It can help if you understand something of the language which is native to your students. Of course, if you are teaching a multi-national class, this may not be easy. However, learners' errors can sensitise you to underlying problems. For example, if your Italian student says, "I am living here since one month," you may assume that this is what s/he says in Italian. If you do not know, then ask them. It will help you and your students to predict errors and deal with them. You might encourage your learners to think in English rather than translate, although this is easier said than done.

Question 9

You need to distinguish between interlanguage errors, which may be a good indication that language acquisition is taking place, and other errors. You need to make this distinction because some interlanguage errors should be tolerated. You do not want to make your students feel stupid when their mistakes simply indicate that language development is proceeding as it should. After all, inappropriate correction may discourage learners from speaking up. If you are working in an environment in which you are the only source of the native language, your insensitivity may have serious consequences - your learners will never have the chance to speak.

Question 10

Firstly, you should bear in mind that the aim of the learners is to give effective presentations. This may mean that explanations of grammar and/or drills are inappropriate. What you need to focus on is fluency and communication skills (discourse competence, organisational competence, and pragmatic competence). Some of these may be enhanced by training in pronunciation and intonation. Indeed, if communication is rendered difficult because of these aspects of language and/or grammar, it may be necessary to do some remedial teaching. However, the most important thing to focus on is the effectiveness of the presentations themselves, and students should not be constantly focusing on small mistakes. This is not to say that these mistakes should be ignored but that they can be dealt with at some other time.

UNIT 3: Methodology and Classroom Practice

Chapter 4

Balancing Techniques and Teacher Roles

4.1: Introduction
4.2: Objectives
4.3: Balancing Techniques
4.4: Teacher Roles
4.5: Conclusions
4.6: Answers to Questions.

4.1: Introduction

There are many techniques available to the teacher and many different roles the teacher can play in the EIB classroom - sometimes in the same lesson. There are no right answers as to what techniques to use and what role to adopt. What is important, however, is that teachers are sensitive to the learners and their requirements. What works well with a group of undergraduates may be entirely inappropriate with a group of managers on an intensive course in-company.

Culture may also play a role here. Learners who are used to a teacher-dominated classroom may be uncomfortable working on their own or in groups. Essentially, the techniques you decide to use and the role you play may depend on something apparently trivial, for example, the time of day or the mood of the class. We therefore suggest that flexibility in your planning is vital.

UNIT 3: Methodology and Classroom Practice

4.2: Objectives

At the end of this chapter, you will:

- be able to critically examine the usefulness of a variety of classroom techniques
- be sensitive to the need for balancing activities in the classroom.

Pre-reading task

Before you begin, try the activities in the shaded box below. These activities are designed to stimulate your thinking and to focus your mind on the main ideas in the chapter.

> - *How many different types of interaction can occur in the classroom during any one lesson?*
> - *Consider the roles you play in the classroom. How many different roles can you think of? Which of these comes most naturally to you?*

4.3: Balancing Techniques

In this section we begin by examining the criteria teachers may use to select from the plethora of activities that teachers have at their disposal for use in the classroom. Section 4.4 considers the extent to which the choice of activity will impact on the role teachers play in the classroom and on the resulting talk. Talk can be categorised as teacher-talking-time (TTT) or student-talking-time (STT).

It would be an impossible task to list all the techniques that teachers can use to develop all the four skills of speaking, listening, reading and writing. What we intend to do here is to lay the foundation for good practice by establishing some principles of our own. We suggest that, as you work through this chapter, you keep in mind the challenge of combining the techniques you examine in order to plan lessons that have an identity of their own. Lesson planning will be dealt with in the next chapter.

UNIT 3: Methodology and Classroom Practice

Fluency versus accuracy

The distinction between classroom activities which promote accuracy and classroom activities which promote fluency is an important one because it will influence the feedback we give our students. Our decisions on how to react to learner performance will be guided by whether the activity is non-communicative or communicative. Non-communicative activities may be designed to focus on a piece of grammar, vocabulary or pronunciation, for example. Communicative activities may be designed to focus on developing skills. Non-communicative activities usually require accuracy while communicative activities require fluency rather than accuracy. Both kinds of activity are important, and learners will normally need some kind of feedback on their performance whether they are engaged in accuracy work or fluency work.

Generally speaking, if learners are engaged in accuracy work, it is usually the teacher's function to point out any mistakes and to correct them. However, if learners are engaged in an activity to develop fluency, it is probably best if the teacher does not interrupt to correct and therefore break the flow of language.

Unfortunately, it is not as simple as that. Learners who are used to a transmission style of teaching, where the teacher is expected to have all the answers, may feel that unless teachers correct them, teachers are not doing their job properly.

Question 1

> *Imagine you have just run a business role-play with your learners. You chose the activity because you wanted to help your students develop their fluency in a real-life business situation. After the lesson a delegation comes to you and complains that you do not correct their mistakes. What will you do to remedy the situation?*

From controlled practice activities to free practice activities

Most techniques can be placed somewhere along a continuum of possibilities. The two extremes of this continuum may be characterised by manipulation at one end and free communication at the other. Activities which are manipulated are controlled by the teacher and the

UNIT 3: Methodology and Classroom Practice

students' responses are highly predictable. Drilling and choral repetition can lie at this extreme end of the continuum. At the other end are free and open-ended activities, in which students' responses are unpredictable. Examples of such techniques are: role-plays, simulations, case studies, and some games.

It is important to remember that some activities are difficult to categorise. They can fall almost anywhere along the continuum depending on the teacher's purpose. Some communicative tasks have a controlled element, while some controlled activities may have a communicative element. However, the essential thing for teachers to appreciate is that there is a wide range of techniques available for use in the classroom.

Ur (1996, p.84) suggests a useful description of activities which range from very controlled and accuracy-oriented to fluency activities, which give students the opportunity to practise grammar freely and in context. For more on aspects of grammar and grammar teaching with practical implications for the classroom see Bygate et al (1994) and Ur (1988).

Douglas-Brown (2001) makes some useful generalisations with regard to distinguishing between controlled and free practice. Controlled activities tend to:

➢ focus on the teacher
➢ be highly structured
➢ manipulate
➢ focus on predictable learner-responses
➢ have planned aims.

On the other hand, free activities tend to:

➢ focus on the learner
➢ help learners communicate fluently
➢ be open-ended
➢ be unpredictable
➢ have negotiated aims.

You might like to look at Douglas-Brown (2001, pp 134-135). You will find a list adapted from Crookes and Chaudron (1991) of 38 techniques for language teaching. These techniques range from controlled, through semi-controlled, to free practice. As you examine these techniques, do

UNIT 3: Methodology and Classroom Practice

keep in mind that the categorisation is indicative only.

Question 2

> *Look at the descriptions of classroom activities (in smaller font) below. They have been adapted from Ur (1996). Decide whether or not these activities tend to fall at the controlled or the free end of the continuum. Would you describe the activities as effective or ineffective? Make a note of your answers and compare them with our suggested answer in the Answers to Questions section. Think about and try to clarify any differences between them!*
>
> ***Activity 1.***
> The aim of the lesson is that learners will memorise a model telephone dialogue in the textbook so that they can adapt it for use in other business telephone situations. Teacher reads out the dialogue bit by bit with the students repeating in different ways: together in chorus, half the class taking one role while the other half takes the other role, one student to another student, one student to the rest of the class.
>
> ***Activity 2.***
> The aim of the lesson is to revise and practise business vocabulary.
> Teacher: Who can remember the meaning of the word liability?
> Student 1: A market study?
> Teacher: No...anyone else? Come on everyone, we did this last week.
> Student 2: A product study?
> Teacher: No, the word has nothing to do with studies. Come on, think!
> After a while, the teacher gives up and tells the students the meaning.
>
> ***Activity 3.***
> The students are told that they are a company advisory group and that they have been asked to advise the HR Manager on the recruitment of staff for a particular job. The group have a detailed job description and profiles of four interviewed candidates. The group should decide on the most suitable candidate for the post and present their recommendations to the CEO.

Student groupings – advantages and disadvantages

There are innumerable ways in which teachers can group their learners. These range from whole-class teaching on the one hand to students working on their own on the other. Between these extremes, students can work in pairs or larger groups depending on the aim of the teacher. Generally, deciding when to teach the whole class, when to put students into pairs or groups or when to let individuals study on their own will depend on a number of factors. For example, your decision may be based on the mood of the class, on your wish to introduce variety into the lesson, or the task at hand may demand a certain kind of student

UNIT 3: Methodology and Classroom Practice

grouping.

Question 3

> *What are the advantages and disadvantages of whole-class teaching? Make a note of your answers and compare them with our suggestions in the Answers to Questions section.*

Question 4

> *What are the advantages and disadvantages of students working alone? Once again, make a note of your answers and compare your ideas with our suggested answers in the Answers to Questions section.*

Question 5

> *What are the advantages and disadvantages of pairwork?*

The advantages and disadvantages of groupwork are similar to those of pairwork. Business English teachers will often put their classes into groups in order to carry out a negotiation role-play or to solve a problem in a simulated meeting, for example. Groupwork can foster the development of co-operative and social skills while at the same time allowing for individual differences in personality in the sense that reticent students, for instance, can choose when to speak without pressure from the teacher. Disadvantages of groupwork can include that they may be difficult to organise, or that some learners may take the opportunity to sit back and allow others to dominate the discussion.

Basic procedure for setting up pairwork and groupwork

Once you have decided to have your learners work in pairs or groups, you need to address what you are going to do before the activity, what you are going to do during the activity and what you are going to do after the activity.

Before the activity, you will need to tell the students what they are going to do, how they will do it and why you want them to do it. Frequently, you may need to give a demonstration of what you want. If you are setting up pairwork, for example, get two "good" students to do the activity as an example. Alternatively, you could ask the learners to repeat your instructions back to you. Essentially, if pairwork and groupwork are to succeed, learners must know exactly what they are to do and why, and how much time they have to complete it.

During the activity, you have a number of options available to you. Among these are the following. Stand back and watch from a distance. This may help you identify which groups are having problems. If you are using the activity to focus on accuracy work, you will probably want to intervene if students are making mistakes. If, however, you are focusing on fluency, it may be enough to ensure that learners are on track for completing the task at hand.

You may wish to take this opportunity to give personal attention to those students whom you have identified as needing your help. If your students are engaged in fluency work, you may still wish to make a note of the most common errors and give whole-class feedback on these after the activity.

When the activity is finished, you should give feedback. This may focus on both the content of the activity and the language used to accomplish the task. Whatever you do, make sure that your feedback is constructive.

Question 6

> *Imagine you have been teaching negotiating skills to your class of in-company adult learners. They are on a two-day seminar designed to develop their skills before an important (real-life) negotiation the following week. On what would you focus your feedback?*

For more on groupwork and pairwork, you might like to look at Wright (1987), Haines (1995) and Courtney (1996). For a good collection of activities that focus on the business world, Rosenberg (2005) is very useful.

4.4: Teacher Roles

In the classroom, our roles may change from one activity to another. Look at the following outline stages of a lesson.

UNIT 3: Methodology and Classroom Practice

1. Teacher elicits and/or explains the nature and purpose of presentations.
1. Teacher elicits and/or explains the structure of presentations.
2. Teacher elicits or explains the structure and language of the introductory part of the presentation. Teacher sets up preparation work.
3. Learners work alone to prepare the introduction of their presentation.
4. Learners give their presentations to the rest of the class.
5. Teacher elicits feedback from the class and gives own feedback.

Question 7

> *Harmer (2001) outlines eight roles for the classroom teacher. These are:*
> 1. *teacher as controller*
> 2. *teacher as organiser*
> 3. *teacher as assessor*
> 4. *teacher as prompter*
> 5. *teacher as participant*
> 6. *teacher as resource*
> 7. *teacher as tutor*
> 8. *teacher as observer.*
>
> *Look at the outline stages of a lesson above and decide which roles you would take in each of the stages.*

Connected to the roles a teacher can play in the classroom is the issue of teacher talking time (TTT) and student talking time (STT). Getting the balance right is often difficult. I once went to Russia, soon after Perestroika. I was the first English person the teachers and students had met. In the circumstances, they were simply happy to listen to me speaking, and my planned communicative lesson was thrown into the bin. It may often be the case that you are the only source of language input for your group of learners. However, the learners also need the chance to practise language. They may soon get bored listening to you, and it would be very tiring to be constantly "on stage".

If your lessons are generally well-balanced, and you have planned for adequate classroom interaction, you will find that the amount of STT and TTT finds its own equilibrium.

UNIT 3: Methodology and Classroom Practice

Question 8

> *Look again at the roles of the teacher in question 7. In which of these might TTT be inappropriate?*

4.5: Conclusions

In this chapter we have tried to give you an overview of the variety of techniques that are available to you for classroom use. We have also tried to give you an indication of the variety of roles that you can play during class time.

We recommend that you look at Douglas Brown (2001) and/or Harmer (2001) and/or Ur (1996). These books will give you more insights into theories, methods and techniques and give you more ideas with regard to techniques, managing classes and teaching the four skills. Above all, we suggest that you try out new ideas and take risks in the classroom. In this way, you will be able to build up a repertoire of classroom techniques and enrich, not only your own teaching, but also your students' learning.

In the next chapter, we examine the elements of a good lesson plan and how the techniques and roles we have looked at can be combined in order to give your plan coherence.

4.6: Answers to Questions

Question 1
You probably did not make your purpose clear before starting the activity. Next time, make sure that your students know exactly what your objectives are in choosing this type of activity. If your students insist on having feedback on their grammatical accuracy, you can write down students' mistakes and correct them after the activity. Alternatively, you can video the activity and, during playback, ask the students themselves to note down their errors.

Question 2
Activity 1
The aim of this activity is to present a dialogue and to get students to memorise it. It is, therefore, controlled. The resulting learning by rote may be satisfactory. However, nothing is done to make the dialogue meaningful to the learners and their situation. It does not engage the learners either intellectually or emotionally in any way. As it stands the activity breaks several of Douglas-Brown's (2001) twelve principles of language learning.

UNIT 3: Methodology and Classroom Practice

Activity 2
This practice session unfortunately happens. As a practice session, it (should) falls somewhere in the middle of the controlled-free continuum. In this case, learners do not remember the word and it should be re-taught and then practised through some kind of meaningful, contextualised situation.

Activity 3
Problem-solving activities like the one here tend to be at the free end of the continuum. These activities are particularly suitable for business learners because the activities will produce a high level of participation and motivation especially if the activity matches the goals of the learners themselves. The purpose of the activity here is to develop fluency in the context of HR Management. Feedback on accuracy can be given after the activity if this is necessary. Alternatively, the teacher can focus on aspects of communication, for example: effective questioning, effective responding, effective presentation structure and so on.

Question 3
Advantages can include:
- an increased sense of belonging among class members
- suitability for teacher-centred activities, such as explanation and instruction
- it allows the teacher to assess the mood of the class
- it may be the preferred style in many educational settings.

Disadvantages can include that:
- it is difficult to deal with individual students
- some students do not like participating in front of the whole class
- individuals may have little chance to say anything
- it encourages teacher-centred transmission of knowledge
- it is not the best way to encourage communicative language teaching.

Question 4
Advantages can include that:
- it develops independent learning
- teachers can respond to individual difficulties and challenges
- it may be less stressful.

Disadvantages can include that:
- it discourages cooperation and a sense of belongingness
- it takes time.

Question 5
Some advantages are that:
- it increases the amount of students talking time (STT)
- it encourages cooperation
- it allows the teacher to give individual attention while the rest of the class is working
- it is easy to set up
- it allows learners to work relatively independently.

Some disadvantages are that:
- it can be noisy

UNIT 3: Methodology and Classroom Practice

- students can often take the opportunity to do something else or talk in their mother tongue
- some students prefer to interact with the teacher and find it a waste of time to work with other learners, claiming that they do not want to learn other people's mistakes.

Question 6
Given that the seminar is in preparation for a real event, I would not wish to discourage the learners in any way. I would focus my feedback on the skill itself and areas that could be improved quickly (for example, preparation work, approach, cultural issues etc). I would restrict feedback on language to those areas that might interfere with the negotiation process itself. In my experience, this would probably be inappropriate use of the conditional (for example: if we offered a discount, would you be prepared to...).

Question 7
In stages 1 to 3 your role would be that of controller. As controller, you are in charge of the class and of the activity. At stage 3, your role also becomes that of organiser in the sense that you have to organise the learners to do certain tasks. In this case, they are to prepare for their presentations. However, in general, stages 1 to 3 are teacher-centred. In stage 4, the role changes to that of teacher-as-resource. The learners might need help, and you are the only person who can help them. In stage 5, your role changes again to that of organiser and perhaps that of prompter. As prompter, you might want to offer words or expressions that can be of some help. You need to do this sensitively and without taking the initiative away from the learners and their presentations. You are also an observer since you must watch what your students are doing and decide what feedback to give them. At stage 6, your role becomes that of assessor. The learners will want feedback on their performance.

Question 8
Teacher as prompter – here you should help but do it with discretion.
Teacher as observer – take notes, observe, but let learners get on with the task at hand.
Teacher as resource – be available and helpful, but do not interfere unless you are asked to.

UNIT 3: Methodology and Classroom Practice

Chapter 5

Lesson Planning

5.1: Introduction
5.2: Objectives
5.3: Lesson Planning -: Theory
5.4: A Sequence of Lessons
5.5: Lesson Planning -: Practice
5.6: Conclusions
5.7: Answers to Questions.

5.1: Introduction

In the previous four chapters of this unit we have looked at the principles you can use to teach by, techniques available to you for classroom use, and the variety of roles you can play in the classroom.

This chapter outlines how all these elements can be combined to help you form your lesson plan. We would add that lesson plans should always be written in pencil. By this we mean that you should be flexible and ready to change things. Your lesson plan should reflect your plan for a "best-case scenario," but you should also prepare for the worst. What happens, for example, if only half the class turn up for your beautifully prepared role-plays? What will you do if your group of learners is tired or listless and you have prepared something that requires active and alert participation? In other words, with regard to lesson planning, we suggest that you hope for the best, but prepare also for the worst.

5.2: Objectives

At the end of this chapter, you will be able to:

➢ evaluate the elements of a lesson plan
➢ plan a lesson or a series of lessons.

Pre-reading task

Before you begin, try the activity in the shaded box below. The activity is designed to stimulate your thinking and to focus your mind on the main ideas in the chapter.

> *Harmer (2001) describes lesson planning as, "the art of combining a number of elements into a coherent whole so that a lesson has an identity which students can recognise, work within, and react to..." Consider what these elements might be.*

5.3: Lesson Planning -: Theory

In the shaded box above, we quoted Harmer (2001) as saying that a lesson plan consists of a number of elements which are combined into a coherent whole, and that these elements should give a lesson its own identity.

Before beginning your own lesson plan, you will need to consider a number of factors. It is unlikely that all the information you might need will always be available to you. However, according to Harmer (2001) and Douglas Brown (2001) the factors you consider can include:

➢ the language level of the learners
➢ the number of students in the class
➢ their expressed needs (if any)
➢ their cultural background
➢ their motivation

UNIT 3: Methodology and Classroom Practice

- their learning styles
- the syllabus you are required to work to
- any exams the learners are going to take
- classroom constraints
- available materials
- available equipment
- any other institutional demands.

Once you have considered these factors, you should be in a position to attend to the lesson plan.

A good starting point is to ask yourself what it is, exactly, that you want the students to gain from your lesson. Perhaps the most effective classroom plans are those that are directed towards a specific aim and which can be measured. In other words, at the end of the lesson you can evaluate the success or otherwise of your lesson plan. You might want to begin your lesson aim with the words: "At the end of the lesson(s) students will be able to..."

Question 1

> Look at the following lesson aims and evaluate them.
> 1. Students will learn about conditionals.
> 2. Students will improve their speaking skills.
> 3. Students will give presentations.
> 4. To enable students to successfully practise (previously taught) language and skills of negotiations in a role-play.

Once you have decided on a clear objective, you can now consider the main body of your plan. Douglas Brown (2001) suggests that teachers identify a number of enabling objectives. These are interim steps that build on each other in order to achieve the final objectives. Most plans will consist of:

- an opening activity or warmer
- a variety of enabling activities directed towards your goal
- linking these activities logically
- the closure.

As you are writing the step-by-step outline of your lesson, you will need to look at how the lesson holds together. You will need to strike a

UNIT 3: Methodology and Classroom Practice

balance between:

- free and controlled practice
- teacher talk and student talk
- teacher-centred activities and learner-centred activities
- fun/serious activities
- input and practice
- fluency and accuracy
- the four skills.

Essentially, you will need to look at whether your plan has enough variety, the right pace, and whether you have given yourself enough time.

Successful lessons tend to engage learners in a number of activities, for example: listening to teacher input, working in pairs or groups, working alone, reading and speaking. You will also need to look at whether or not your plan is sequenced logically. Ask yourself whether or not all your enabling activities are leading towards your goal. If they are not, then ask yourself why the particular activity has been included. Generally, easier tasks should be put at the beginning of the lesson.

You should also look at the pace of a lesson. Does it flow smoothly? Is it "jerky", with learners moving too quickly from one activity to another? Can you easily move from one activity to another with little or no explanation? Ur (1996) has the following advice for ordering lesson elements and pacing.

- Put quieter activities before lively ones.
- Think about your transitions - do you need to include a brief transition activity or can you simply move immediately from one activity to another?
- Pull the class together at the beginning and at the end.
- End on a positive note.

Finally, you need to decide whether or not you have timed the lesson well. It is not unusual for very experienced teachers to get their timing wrong. Usually, teachers prepare too much but always have some backup activity ready should you once finish too early.

UNIT 3: Methodology and Classroom Practice

5.4: A Sequence of Lessons

Essentially, a sequence of lessons can be planned in the same way as one lesson. However, if you are planning a number of lessons, you should be prepared for the unpredictable. Your plan should, therefore, be flexible. Further, you will need to think about the long-term goals and the short-term goals. For example, your long-term goal might be for your learners to communicate effectively in negotiations with people from other cultures. A short-term goal (for one particular lesson) might be to enable your students to handle the language of bargaining. Another short-term goal might be to raise awareness of cultural differences and how these differences impact on negotiation skills. Generally, a sequence of lessons can hang together well if it has a theme running through it, for example: negotiating, participating in meetings, or topics, for example: marketing or finance.

5.5: Lesson Planning -: Practice

Question 2

The Efficient and Effective Language School (EELS) recently won an important contract with Multek – a multinational based near London. They have agreed to send a group of employees to you for a 3-hour trial course focusing on meetings. You senior teacher had been negotiating course content with Multek and has now gone on a one-week walking tour in Portugal before the trial course begins.

It is Friday afternoon and Multek have rung EELS to bring the trial course forward by a week. This means that the course will start on Monday next, and you will have to teach it. You have tried to contact the senior teacher on his mobile but he must have turned it off because he is not answering. He has left a few brief notes on his desk and this is all the information you have regarding the course and what Multek wants. The contents of the senior teacher's notes are summarised below.

➢ *6 middle managers from 4 different countries: China (1), Germany (2), France (1), Japan (1) and Italy (1).*
➢ *Level: intermediate plus - the Chinese student is a bit weaker than the others.*

UNIT 3: Methodology and Classroom Practice

> ➢ *Requirements: to further develop communication skills in English in the context of multinational meetings. The senior teacher has underlined the word, "chairing."*
> ➢ *Time: 3 hours.*
>
> *Outline your plan for the first lesson. Include your objectives, the steps you will take to reach those objectives and a brief description of the activities you will adopt. When you have finished, compare your answers with ours in the Answers to Questions section.*

5.6: Conclusions

In this chapter we have tried to give you some insight into the elements of a good lesson plan. In the space available, it has only been possible to outline the factors that you will need to think about. In other words, you will need to read a good deal more.

If the opportunity arises, observe what your colleagues are doing and discuss their plans both before and after a lesson. Asking and answering questions about a plan can often clarify things and highlight problems that had not previously been noted.

Above all, we suggest that your plans include new ideas so that you can take risks in the classroom and, by doing so, build up a repertoire of classroom techniques that work for you.

5.7: Answers to Questions

Question 1
The first three objectives are vague and difficult to evaluate. The first aim might be improved by stating something like: "At the end of the lesson, learners will be able to use the first and second conditionals in making offers and proposals in negotiations." The second aim might be improved by stating something like: "Learners will be able to use the language of agreeing and disagreeing when taking part in meetings." The third aim could be improved by stating something along the lines of: "Learners will be able to demonstrate that they can structure an effective presentation and deliver it fluently with the use of visual aids." The fourth objective states explicitly what learners will be able to do and can be evaluated.

Question 2
Objectives: At the end of the lesson participants will be able to effectively chair multicultural meetings in English.

UNIT 3: Methodology and Classroom Practice

Enabling/intermediate objectives
1. In pairs, students prioritise a list of characteristics of "good" meetings.
2. Students listen to a recording of a meeting and write down the main functions of the chairperson.
3. Students (individually) suggest phrases which could be used by the chairperson in the functions above.
4. Students hold brief meetings (role-plays) to practise the language above. For each role-play a different chairperson is chosen.
5. Open discussion about the different styles of chairing, for example: was the chairperson directive or controlling? How did this influence the participants? What did the participants expect from the chairperson? Was there a link between chairing style and cultural background? Teacher should have slides of Hofstede to briefly present his dimensions and how these can influence the chairing style.
6. In pairs, students work out a brief agenda from a list of given points.
7. Role-play. A meeting to discuss a company problem (see below) and to make recommendations to the Board. Students are given some time to prepare their roles and the chair must write an agenda. The meeting should be recorded so that feedback can be given.

The problem: The Company has money to spend on improving facilities for staff. Among the options are: a sports club with gym and bar, a crèche for employees' children, an internet café for staff and families and a swimming pool. You should decide on one of these options to recommend to the board.

After the meeting, teacher gives feedback on the language generated from 3 and 4 above. Teacher then hands out a brief questionnaire about the meeting and students complete this individually. The questionnaire is used as the basis of discussion and evaluation of the role-play (and, essentially, of the lesson itself). Questions might include:
1. Were the meeting's objectives clear?
2. Did you feel that your ideas were listened to?
3. What was the result of the meeting?
4. How do you feel about the result?
5. How do you feel about the chairing style?
6. Was the meeting too long or too short?
7. Did the meeting have a clear structure?
8. Did you keep to the agenda?

And for the chairperson
1. Do you think you were effective?
2. Did you summarise the meeting?
3. Did you try and listen to everyone's opinions?
4. Did you summarise opinions so that the others could understand what was said?
5. How could you have chaired the meeting better?

UNIT 3: Methodology and Classroom Practice

Chapter 6

Using Simulations and Case Studies

6.1: Introduction
6.2: Objectives
6.3: Defining and Clarifying Terms
6.4: Advantages and Disadvantages
6.5: Setting up and Running the Exercise
6.6: Examples and Sources
6.7: Conclusions
6.8: Answers to Questions
6.9: Appendices.

6.1: Introduction

Terminology will be discussed fully in section 6.3 of this chapter, but it would be useful to point out immediately that the expression Experiential Learning Activity (ELA) is adopted to cover the terms role-play, simulation, case study and game. ELA should not be understood to be in any way the "official" terminology. It is an expression that has been chosen to avoid tedious repetition of the whole range of terms.

ELAs are generally well established in both management training and the teaching of EIB, but there are many misconceptions about their benefits and how to best use them in the classroom. This chapter attempts to explain the potential benefits of using ELAs and to identify the skills needed to use them effectively.

We are not suggesting here that ELAs should ever be used exclusively. As with any technique, judgement is required about when to use them. What we are suggesting is that if the decision is taken to run, for example, a simulation or a role-play in class, then the activity should be used professionally.

There are both advantages and disadvantages in using ELAs. One advantage, for example, is that they may facilitate deep as opposed to surface learning. One disadvantage is that the techniques may be time-consuming whereas lectures can sometimes communicate a subject more efficiently. My own experience suggests that role-plays, simulations, games and case studies sometimes work and sometimes fail - often with the same group. Success or failure can be unpredictable. What you can do is to minimise the possibility of failure by preparing thoroughly for the activity. Preparation is perhaps the single most important factor for a successful ELA.

6.2: Objectives

At the end of this chapter you will:

- better understand the differences and similarities between role-plays, simulations, games and case studies
- be better able to evaluate the potential purposes of running ELAs
- better understand the advantages and disadvantages of using ELAs
- be able to evaluate the role of the teacher during the setting up and running of ELAs
- appreciate the importance of the preparation stage of ELAs
- be able to evaluate the criteria for producing your own ELAs for classroom use.

Pre-reading task

Before you begin, try the activities in the shaded box below. These activities are designed to stimulate your thinking and to focus your mind on the main ideas in the chapter.

UNIT 3: Methodology and Classroom Practice

> *Simulations and case studies are static (in the sense that while students make decisions, time stands still) and therefore lack realism. Furthermore, they are time-consuming and time-wasting. A student comes to the classroom in order to be taught and not to waste valuable class time listening to a class colleague speaking incorrectly. Consider these views.*
> *Some people might argue that case studies and role-plays bring the real world into the classroom. Well, why not bring in guest speakers? Do they not come from the real world? Alternatively, learners can be sent on company-based projects. Why simulate the real world when learners can easily have the real thing for themselves? It does not make sense. What is your opinion?*

6.3: Defining and Clarifying terms

Essentially, case studies, role-plays, games and simulations (ELAs) are techniques which involve a number of learners working together. ELAs require careful preparation, and they are usually set in a scenario outside the classroom. In this section we shall attempt to make a distinction between these frequently overlapping terms. This is no easy task. Even in the literature, definitions of role-play, simulation, game and case study tend to differ (Feinstein et al, 2002).

All four are usually forms of experiential learning (see chapter 9 of this unit) in which participants:

> …must be able to involve themselves fully, openly, and without bias in new experiences; they must be able to observe and reflect on these experiences from many perspectives; they must be able to create concepts that integrate their observations into logically sound theories; and they must be able to use these theories to make decisions and solve problems. (Kolb, 1984)

Feinstein et al (2002) suggest that, "…the basis for the definition of simulation must begin with its foundation, the model. We use the classic definition of model as a representation of the reality it is constructed to depict." The authors go on to say that, "...simulation can

UNIT 3: Methodology and Classroom Practice

be defined as the behaviour of the model."

Simulations tend to be constructed around elaborate scenarios. Klippel (1984) suggests that, "As a rule simulations are...highly structured and contain...diverse elements in their content and procedure." However, participants have no roles imposed upon them. Consequently, with no prepared parts to play, learners are free to behave as themselves and apply their own values and reactions to the task. Any conflict in a simulation tends to be between the participants themselves, and is directed at some external threat. Conflict is not between prepared roles.

Simulations may be classified in three ways.

1. They may be close or distant to an individual's own experience.
2. They may take place in both everyday and imaginary situations.
3. They may be realistic or fantastic.

Role-playing, on the other hand, allows participants to immerse themselves in a learning environment by acting out the role of a character or part in a particular situation. Participants follow a set of rules that define a situation and then interact with others who are also playing roles. Roles may be classified in three ways.

1. They may be close or distant to the player.
2. They may take place in both everyday and imaginary situations.
3. They may be realistic or fantastic.

Question 1

How important are the factors in the classification above for a successful role-play or simulation? In other words, does it matter if a role-play is distant, imaginary and fantastic or if a simulation is far from personal experience, imaginary and fantastic?

Question 2

Are there some cultures which tend to have difficulties, not only with role-play and simulations, but with any form of experiential learning?

UNIT 3: Methodology and Classroom Practice

The term case study is defined by Ross and Wright (2000) as:

> ...a hypothetical, though lifelike, narrative describing a situation in which embedded difficulties need to be identified, studied, and solved. The situation should also be conducive to discussion and interpretation in disciplines in which practical problem-solving is required.

Richardson (1994) defines a management case study as, "...a model of real life which serves to facilitate decision-making practice...and improve the managerial skills of students and practitioners of management."

Easton (1992) supports the definitions above by claiming that:

> Case studies are means to provide practice in problem-solving and decision-making in a simulated situation... The case method is primarily a vehicle for developing skills; skills which are a vital part of a decision maker's armoury...together these skills can be described in one phrase - creative problem solving.

The case study, as a model of real life can take a number of forms and be expressed through a number of media (Richardson, 1994).

- Text. This tells a story or describes a situation. These cases can range from a half-page illustration (vignette) to a 50-page and major case study. Richardson (1994) points out that, "Textual cases can also be used as springboards from which to launch into more active case media for management skills building, such as role-play..."
- IT simulations. These enable the modelling of "What if?" scenarios. Students will input a range of assumptions about the future. These may produce scenarios in the form of financial models.
- Video. This will bring a realistic situation into the classroom by way of the video screen.
- Raconteurs. They describe their own experiences of a real management situation and who respond to learners' questions.
- Case simulations. These involve learners in events which are designed to closely replicate real-life experiences, for example: disaster-management simulations.

UNIT 3: Methodology and Classroom Practice

- Role-play.
- A combination of all these.

Games usually consist of interactions among learners, who are under the constraints of a set of rules and procedures. Further, the setting is prescribed (Hsu, 1989). Hsu goes on to say that activities of this type usually, but not always, exclude taking roles. Teams are usually formed and then provided with information. This information may be of a financial or marketing nature or concern the allocation of resources. Decisions are then taken on certain topics, for example: marketing strategy, re-allocation of resources or pricing strategy. Games are typically turn-based or round-based where teams make decisions after reviewing a set of external or competitor variables. Decisions are taken to adjust these variables and a new round, based on these adjusted variables, is conducted. Teams compete against each other, and outcomes are usually rewarded for maximising profitability.

An example of such a game is Pizza Panic. Pizza Panic allows competing teams to run a pizza takeaway for a year. The year of the exercise is divided into 4 quarters and teams make decisions on running their business each quarter. Decisions are taken concerning quality of product, pricing, shop-fittings, and variety of pizza toppings. During later stages of the game, learners are invited to make decisions concerning the expansion of their product range. The teams' quarterly decisions are fed into a computer, which produces the results of their decisions in terms of number of pizzas sold and profit or loss for the quarter. In this sense, the computer programme can be seen as the market. The winning team is the one with the highest profit at the end of the year. The game is aimed at intermediate level and above, and is designed for students wishing to pursue courses in business, management and other related disciplines.

Although Pizza Panic is described as a game, there is an element of role-playing in the sense that learners are required to act the part of business people rather than students. However, team games such as Pizza Panic offer learning opportunities at the content and process levels. The content involves them in financial and marketing decisions while the process obliges them to apply their interpersonal skills, language skills and team-building skills. There may also be an element of intercultural awareness raising, depending on the composition of the groups.

UNIT 3: Methodology and Classroom Practice

Question 3

> *If you were the teacher involved in setting up and running Pizza Panic, on what would you focus your feedback?*

ELAs can also be aimed at learners with a lower level of language proficiency than that required by Pizza Panic. Two commonly adopted techniques are the cued dialogue or guided role-play (Porter Ladousse, 1987), and information-gap activities. These techniques allow the teacher to introduce an element of communication while retaining control over the language used. In this sense, the activities belong to that part of a lesson devoted to language practice rather than the development of oral skills. However, the introduction of a semi-communicative context will help lower level learners prepare for later, more spontaneous interactions.

6.4: Advantages and Disadvantages

Jennings (1996) suggests five major advantages of using case studies. We suggest that these advantages apply equally well to the other forms of experiential learning discussed in this chapter. The advantages can be discussed under five headings. The headings are:

- illustrative
- strategic analysis
- pedagogic expedience
- communication and interpersonal skills
- integrative.

Illustrative. Jennings (1996) is referring here to the use of case studies to provide descriptions of real-world situations and to introduce the methodology of real world decisions. ELAs are important media for introducing students to the theory which underpins good practice in management. ELAs will help learners to test the validity and usefulness of the theory.

Strategic analysis, for example: developing awareness of a problem area, providing practice in the analysis of a strategic context, and planning potential ways forward. ELAs can also be designed to focus on stages in the decision-making or problem-solving cycles.

UNIT 3: Methodology and Classroom Practice

Question 4

> *Look at the problem-solving cycle below and decide how you would integrate it into the activity in appendix 1.*
> - *recognise the existence of a problem*
> - *identify and define the problem*
> - *brainstorm solutions*
> - *evaluate solutions*
> - *decide on a solution*
> - *implement the solution.*

Pedagogic expedience. Here Jennings (1996) is referring to the use of cases to provide interest, stimulate discussion and to prevent boredom. Rees and Porter (2002) argue that one of the principal benefits of ELAs is the depth of learning that students may experience. The authors argue that this depth is not easily achieved through more traditional methods, such as lecturing. We suggest that a mixture of techniques is appropriate. However, a lecture on problem-solving or decision-making skills is likely to be much more effective if it is followed up by some form of ELA. Rees and Porter (2001) suggest that lectures alone lead to remarkably little information being absorbed. ELAs can allow learners to apply knowledge. In turn, this may motivate them to learn the theory and help them see how the theory can be put into practice.

ELAs will also help learners take a greater responsibility for their own learning. With adult learners this may mean that learning takes place by pooling the knowledge of both teachers and students. Tutors may need only to explain those issues that learners have not worked out for themselves. Learners may also learn from the presentations of others during plenary sessions. Further, presenters will have the chance to practise their presentation skills and their ability to deal with questions.

Question 5

> *Imagine you are using case studies, simulations and role-plays in-company. Is there a place for the all-knowing, authoritarian teacher in these situations?*

Communication and interpersonal skills. Apart from giving learners the opportunity to practise their presentation skills, ELAs can also be

UNIT 3: Methodology and Classroom Practice

followed up by report writing. Further, learners have the opportunity to develop their team-learning, team-building and chairing skills. One way of doing this would be for the teacher to appoint an observer to chart the flow of discussion and to give feedback on the effectiveness of the group during the activity. Alternatively, appoint two observers, one with the purpose of observing group effectiveness and the other with the purpose of, for example, observing the effectiveness of the chair. I have often run role-plays in this way with observers reporting back on the negotiation itself and the effectiveness or ineffectiveness of the participants' interpersonal skills.

Integrative. Here Jennings (1996) is referring to the integration of functional skills and to theory and practice. Within EIB, the language of such activities as marketing, process re-engineering, accounting, and supply-chain management can be practised using ELAs. These may also be used to introduce learners to the theory of management, which underpins good practice in the functional areas mentioned above.

Jennings (1996) concludes by claiming that although the primary objective for using ELAs is to develop ability in strategic analysis and strategic thinking, they are most effective as a means of developing communication and interpersonal skills. In this sense, we suggest that they are ideal for use in most EIB classrooms because they give learners the opportunity to practise spoken language in a business context. Two questions arise: what sort of language can we expect from the learners? What is the nature of spoken language?

Question 6

Why is it important for teachers of EIB to answer these questions?

Bygate (2001) suggests that speech production consists of four major processes:

1. conceptualisation
1. formulation
2. articulation
3. self-monitoring.

All this happens very fast and depends on automation. The four processes are also dependent on context, and most speech is produced

UNIT 3: Methodology and Classroom Practice

on-line. This means that speakers have to decide on their message and communicate it without taking time to check it over and correct it. In addition, speech typically expresses politeness and other face-saving devices. Further, on-line processing conditions produce language that is grammatically fragmented, uses more pre-fabricated phrases and tolerates repetition of words or phrases within the same stretch of discourse. Finally, there are inevitable adjustments. These include:

1. changing the message or its formulation
2. self-correction
3. various kinds of hesitation.

Question 7

> *Look at the statement below. Are these statements characteristics of written (W) language or of spoken (S) language? Write W or S beside each statement.*
> 1. *Produced in complete sentences.*
> 2. *Produced in incomplete sentences.*
> 3. *Generally produced in complex syntax.*
> 4. *Generally produced in simple syntax.*
> 5. *Generally produced in simple words.*
> 6. *Generally produced in less common words.*
> 7. *Information is generally presented logically and without repetition.*
> 8. *Information is poorly organised and rambling.*
> 9. *Generally produced with correct grammar.*
> 10. *Generally produced with broken grammar, hesitations and false starts.*
> 11. *Language is generally transactional (information carrying) rather than interactional (contributing to relationship building).*
> 12. *Language is generally interactional and transactional.*

UNIT 3: Methodology and Classroom Practice

Question 8

> *Bearing in mind the answers to question 7, can we expect learners engaged in ELAs to do the following?*
> 1. *Use extensive vocabulary?*
> 2. *Produce accurate language?*
> 3. *Produce "final draft" speech?*
> 4. *Be fluent?*

The implications are that spoken and written language are different and that oral language skills and oral language should be practised and even assessed under different conditions from written skills. Case studies, role-plays, gaming and simulations can provide those conditions. However, these activities should not be seen as miracle methods. They can work very well but they can fail miserably although in my experience they rarely fail for linguistic reasons. The most obvious reasons for failure are as follows.

➢ Time is lacking.
➢ Learners are not motivated by their roles or by the situation.
➢ The situation is too complex for the particular group.
➢ There is resistance to the use of experiential learning techniques by students who have been used to more conventional methods of education.

Question 9

> *Students from authoritarian cultures may often have difficulty in adjusting to experiential learning. They may be used to "right" answers and rote learning. In addition, there may well be an expectation that it is the teacher's responsibility to impart information, and that the role of the learner is to passively absorb information. What can you do with these learners?*

Having looked at some advantages and disadvantages of ELAs, we now need to consider how to run them. What skills do we need to get the most out of the activities we choose to run?

UNIT 3: Methodology and Classroom Practice

6.5: Setting up and Running the Exercise

Your role of teacher during ELAs may change according to the stage you have arrived at. In the main, you will be a facilitator, concerned with process activities. This means that you will:

- encourage discussion
- guide and manage group activities at all stages of the session
- coach individual participants
- observe
- present
- create an atmosphere conducive to learning.

Question 10

> *All of the above roles are important, but which is a vital prerequisite for successful learning to take place?*

Most ELAs can generally be divided into three distinct phases (Bygate, 1987). These stages are:

1. giving learners the necessary linguistic and contextual information - input
2. the task itself - output
3. feedback and follow-up work.

The input stage

Kerridge (1996) divides the input stage into distinct phases. These are:

- lead-in activities
- background details
- activities
- linguistic input.

Question 11

> *Look again at appendices 1 and 2. You have decided to use this situation for your class of adult learners in-company. Your intention is for them to role-play a business meeting so that they*

UNIT 3: Methodology and Classroom Practice

> can practise the language of meetings (appendix 2) and the language of marketing. Now look at the three questions below.
> 1. What sort of lead-in activities could you use?
> 2. How would you deal with the background details?
> 3. What type of other activities could you use and why?

Question 12

> It is clear that the preparation stage can be a lengthy process. What difficulties can you predict and what would you do about them?

The task

The first minute or so is crucial. In this minute you should be able to tell whether or not the preparation stage has been effective. You will need to be sensitive to learners and help and coach those who are having difficulties. If all is going well, then you should only intervene if there is a breakdown in communication.

This does not mean that you put your feet up and watch learners perform. The teacher has three main roles.

1. Time keeper. Learners should be aware of any time constraints and, at intervals, you should remind them how long they have had and how much time remains. You could also let them know whether or not they are where they should be.
2. Preparing for feedback. This means that you should note errors that you intend to correct later with the whole group. You can also note individual errors which you wish to correct on an individual basis later.
3. Recording the play. You should make a note of the counter number of the most interesting sequences and of those sequences you want to correct. You should also make a note of examples of good language usage.

Feedback

If you do your job correctly, you will find that you are very busy. At the end of the activity, you need to organise feedback and any follow-up activities. Feedback can come from the following.

UNIT 3: Methodology and Classroom Practice

- The participants themselves - for example, you can ask them to comment on the effectiveness of the chairperson and the effectiveness of the activity itself.
- The chairperson (if applicable).
- The observers - if you have assigned them.
- The teacher.

Generally, you should restrict your feedback to those areas which have been practised and to those areas which are within your area of expertise. This may be relative. For example, if you are running the activity with a group of finance managers, then you should comment on language and communication rather than their ability to make financial decisions. On the other hand, if you are teaching students, you may wish to comment on their decision-making skills and/or the accurate use of financial terminology.

Question 13

> *Imagine you have been running a simulation in which learners have been working in teams. Would you give feedback on effective team-building?*

With regard to language, I have often found it effective to write some errors on the flip chart and ask participants to correct them. It is also both useful and professional to write down the errors, photocopy them and hand them out to participants. This will mean working very quickly and efficiently during the task itself.

If you use a video recording, use only selected sequences for feedback. Various techniques can be used. For example, play a sequence, freeze frame and ask participants what should come next. Then, invite comments on what actually came next, for example, was the phrasing appropriate? What might have been better? What other examples of this language function can you think of? How would these have changed the meaning?

Follow-up activities could focus on an expansion of the activity itself. For example, learners can write reports, letters or e-mails. Alternatively, you may want to focus on a grammatical point, or area-specific vocabulary. You may also wish to have learners engage in small role-plays, for example, reporting the main points of the meeting/negotiation to their managers on a one to one basis or by way of mini presentations to their work teams.

6.6: Examples and Sources

ELAs can be long and take eight hours or more to complete, or short and take five minutes. Pizza Panic (see section 6.3) normally takes one day to run. A similar game is Lawn Trimmers. Lawn Trimmers is a computer game for groups of between three to six members and for up to six teams. The game needs between three and five hours to complete. Like Pizza Panic, team calculations are handled by the computer programmes. After each round, participants are told what happened as a result of their calculations and are asked to examine the data before making decisions for the next round. The objectives of the exercise are:

1. to improve participants' understanding of primary business relationships
2. to show how different functional activities fit together
3. to provide decision-making practice against a realistic background
4. to develop participants' interpersonal skills.

During the activity, participants:

- study written data about an imaginary company and its situation
- debate alternative strategies
- make decisions and enter these on a form
- analyse the computer-generated financial and operational reports
- observe the strategies of competitors
- try and frustrate their opponents.

Pause for thought

> What, in your opinion, are the biggest weaknesses of these longer games and simulations?

Perhaps the greatest disadvantage of games such as Pizza Panic and Lawn Trimmers is the length of time they take to complete. In the context of higher education, it is difficult to find one whole day to run such a game. I once ran Pizza Panic at the University of Reutlingen in Germany, and had to ask students to come in on a Saturday in order to

UNIT 3: Methodology and Classroom Practice

do it. The alternative is to run the game over a number of sessions, but this can result in a decline of tension and interest. It is easy to forget what happened two days previously.

One publication I have found very useful and useable is Casler et al (1989). The book, which is easily updateable, consists of a number of case studies. These integrate language, business content and culture in a way that is enjoyable and stimulating for both teachers and students. Furthermore, the materials can be used as a stepping stone to the simulation or as a self-contained course. Input includes documentary material such as, letters, memos, newspaper articles, company profiles and articles from business magazines. Further input includes a video sequence and audio material. There are also language and information-processing activities to help learners master this input material. For example, there are vocabulary building activities, and tasks designed to develop the communicative skills needed for each case. There are also reinforcement activities designed to follow each assignment. Finally, there are extensive teachers' notes for each case study. These set out the main points at issue and the possible solutions.

One of the problems with ELAs is that there may not be a suitable activity for your particular class. One solution would be to write your own. The material for appropriate ELAs can come from a variety of sources. These include:

- issues raised by students in the classroom
- issues reported in the media
- issues provided by the client organisation if you are working in-company
- adaptations of existing ELAs.

If you decide to write your own ELAs, the following techniques may prove useful (Rees and Porter, 2002).

- There are usually only two questions to ask at the end of an ELA. What are the problems and what should be done about them?
- Do not include the date. You may want to use the ELA with other groups at a future time.
- Make the initials of each character correspond with their job title. For example, the Marketing Director could be called Martin Davis. This can help learners remember who does what.

- Use a title that helps learners remember the content of the ELA. For example, "Sweet Success for Fielders," is likely to be more memorable than, "A change in Marketing Strategy."
- Test your ELAs before using them, if this is practicable.
- After using your activity, make a note of the answers. Future learners usually find it interesting to compare their solutions with their predecessors' efforts.
- Write your ELA in international English. There is nothing to be lost by writing in clear English and by avoiding unnecessary idiomatic or colloquial expressions.

If you need immediate access to examples of case studies, and case studies that can be used as role-plays or simulations, you might want to have a look at the following web site - http://www.thomsonlearning.co.uk and then have a look at Rees and Porter (2001). The website contains over forty management case studies and exercises and can be easily used as they are or adapted as necessary.

6.7: Conclusions

ELAs have come to play a major role in my own teaching of EIB. However, these activities should always be used together with other teaching techniques. For example, in some situations, lectures with discussion can be equally efficient in clearly communicating the subject matter. Similarly, tutorials can provide a range of views with learner participation.

The main drawbacks with regard to ELAs are that they can be time-consuming and demanding on staff resources. In addition, ELAs may not be appropriate in all classes. Teachers are increasingly obliged to teach students from a wide variety of cultural backgrounds and not all cultures will be as enthusiastic about using, for example, a role-play, as you are. Sensitivity is needed. Above all, a successful ELA depends on how well you and the students prepare.

Using experiential methods in EIB has many benefits that often go beyond more traditional forms of instruction. Student motivation tends to increase during role-plays and simulations because, in part, they are actively involved in learning. Furthermore, recent research in cognitive learning (see chapter 9 of this unit) supports the benefits of immersing

UNIT 3: Methodology and Classroom Practice

learners in interactive environments that replicate situations they might encounter in their professional lives.

6.8: Answers to questions

Question 1
Stuart and Binstead (1981) have identified three dimensions of reality for learners. These are:
1. content reality - is the task close to perceived real-world experience?
2. environment reality - does the task represent the world learners are intending to work in?
3. process reality - is the learning process comparable to the processes in which learners intend to engage in the real world?

If learners feel that their talk replicates the conditions of talk in the real world, they may overlook the limitations of a simulation or role-play which does not conform to the first two dimensions above. However, it is vital that teachers are sensitive here. What works with one group may not work with another.

Question 2
Rees and Porter (2002) suggest that students from authoritarian (high power distance) cultures may have difficulty in adjusting to experiential learning. These students may be used to learning by rote and the provision of prescriptive answers. Further, my own anecdotal experience suggests that cultures where needs to avoid uncertainty are large, often (but not always), have difficulty identifying with a role which is foreign to them.

Question 3
You have a wealth of material to choose from. You may decide to focus some of your feedback on the content of the game and the wisdom or not of the decisions taken. In my experience such an activity can be used before explaining any relevant theory concerning aspects of the game, for example, financial planning, the marketing mix, decision-making strategies or team working. Games and other forms of experiential learning can demonstrate the relevance of theory and motivate students to learn and understand it (Rees and Porter, 2002). Relevant theory can be discussed after the game in an informal and effective way, often on a question and answer basis.

On the other hand, you may wish to focus your feedback on language. If you have used a video recorder, make a note of the recorder number when you hear errors on which you want to focus. This will help enormously and prevent unprofessional time-wasting when trying to find the relevant part.

Question 4
First, you need to decide what sort of activity you are going to run here. You could run a role-play by writing role cards for the sons, Peter, John and Mark, and their father William. Conflicting opinions and points of view could then be written into the roles. The chair's role could then include instructions for an agenda based on the

UNIT 3: Methodology and Classroom Practice

problem-solving cycle noted in the question. Alternatively, you could use the situation as a problem-solving case study, where the learners are themselves. The problem-solving cycle could be taught before learners attempt the case. You could also ask learners to attempt to solve the problem first and then teach the cycle. The task could also be run as a simulation/role-play by asking learners to take on the roles of consultants but without giving them role cards.

Question 5
Probably not. Your role should be to:
➢ facilitate
➢ direct activities
➢ encourage discussion
➢ guide group activities
➢ observe
➢ create a climate conducive to open discussion and learning.

Question 6
Teachers need to know what is appropriate and what is inappropriate spoken language when giving feedback. Should we expect learners to be grammatically perfect? Why? Why not? Should teachers give feedback on each and every error? Why? Why not?

Question 7
1. W
2. S
3. W
4. S
5. S
6. W
7. W
8. S
9. W
10. S
11. W
12. S

Question 8
The answer to all four questions is no.

Question 9
Learners need to be aware that management and business are not areas in which prescriptive answers can easily be applied. However, you can ease the situation somewhat by specifying learning outcomes or by using a workbook in order to reassure learners that there is a valid structure to their programme. Rees and Porter (2002) suggest that workbooks, "…can easily be constructed to give details of the teaching programme, learning outcomes, case studies and other material to be used, hand-outs and appropriate reading references."

UNIT 3: Methodology and Classroom Practice

Question 10
It depends on the situation. In company, I have found that the appropriate atmosphere must be created early on. Appropriate here means an atmosphere conducive to learning. Participants must feel relaxed and respected and valued for their experience and potential. The teacher should encourage adult-to-adult relationships, joining in as an equal partner and not someone who knows all the answers. Participants do not want to feel that they are back at school. Within the context of higher education, this atmosphere is still crucial, even though the learners may need a little more authoritarian behaviour or guidance from the teacher.

Question 11
The lead-in questions are designed to focus the attention of learners on the topic and to bring up some of the main issues in the role-play and, if necessary, to pre-teach some vocabulary. It could be done as a simple question and answer session. At this stage, learners have not seen the text.
- Do you eat chocolate?
- What sort of chocolate do you eat?
- Where do you buy it?
- Where do you think most chocolate is sold?
- Which companies dominate the chocolate market?
- Do you ever give chocolate as a gift?
- What is an income statement?
- What does it tell you?
- What would you expect to see detailed on such a statement?

There are any number of ways you can present the text. The simplest way, perhaps, is to have learners read it in class in groups. You can focus their attention on the main points by writing questions on the board or on handouts. For example:
- How long has the company been operating?
- Describe the company's products.
- Describe the company management structure.
- Who dominates the chocolate market?
- How is most chocolate sold?
- Where do Fielder's sell their products?
- What is the company's problem?
- What do they need to do?

The last question should elicit that they should devise a new marketing strategy. In order to revise the language of marketing, you could initiate a question and answer session. For example:
- What are the elements of the marketing mix?
- Where could the company find new markets?
- How could the company change its image?
- How could it advertise and where?
- What about pricing policy?

Alternatively, you could prepare a text and delete the relevant marketing vocabulary and ask learners to complete the text. The missing words could be given in jumbled order at the beginning of the text.

Activities can also be devised to revise/practise the language functions you want learners to use in the activity. Appendix 2 contains a list of some of these functions. It

UNIT 3: Methodology and Classroom Practice

is probably not practical to expect learners to use all the examples here. What I often do is ask them to choose two or three phrases from the list and to use them during the role-play. Alternatively, you could use some form of gap-filling activity (listening or reading) in order to focus attention of these functions. You could also set up a brief pairwork exercise so that learners can practise the functions.

You should consider at this stage whether a role-play is the best activity for to meet your objectives. Sometimes it is better to use a situation for a case study or a simulation. Roles should be written in order for learners to focus on the issues you want them to focus on. In this case, you want them to focus on marketing strategy and the language of marketing. Conflict should therefore be built into the roles. However, you should allow a certain amount of freedom of movement for participants in the roles, otherwise they may feel under too many constraints. Further, if they simply can not identify with the role, they may be half-hearted in their approach. Look at our examples below. Are the roles too detailed?

William Fielder –: chairperson.
He has no role, but he must prepare aims and objectives for the meeting and prepare an agenda.

John Fielder -: production manager.
You think a lot more investment should be made in product research and development. You are very interested in developing a new, filled chocolate-bar to compete with Mars. You think that Fielder's should diversify out of solid chocolate and make a wider attack on the confectionery market. You think that the franchising operation has grown too quickly and is not a good idea anyway, as you believe that franchising offers a lower gross margin than retailing through Fielder's own shops.

Peter Fielder -: marketing manager.
When you took over responsibility for the marketing operation, your lack of experience was balanced by an enthusiasm to get business moving ahead. You felt that many important decisions had been neglected in the past. You feel that product standards have dropped and production convenience is taking precedence over marketing needs. Shop display and stock control standards have declined as a result of complacency and under-investment in shop-fitting and management. You have consulted various advertising agencies, and believe that a substantial investment in promotion is essential for future success. You would like to see an expansion of the franchise operation, which you think has huge sales growth potential. You think the company should open more shops in the south of England and you have a number of possible locations in mind.

Mark Fielder -: finance manager
You would like to slash expenditure on research and development, which you consider to be quite unnecessary. You are also unwilling to spend any more money on product promotion, which you consider to be ineffective from a costs perspective. You would prefer to reduce the advertising budget. You think that the company is in danger of breaking away from the traditional values which have always been its hallmark, and which have given it so much success. In general, you want to see rationalisation and consolidation. You would like to carry out a full financial appraisal

UNIT 3: Methodology and Classroom Practice

of each shop and close down those that are not making a satisfactory profit. You think the company should approach a large retailer with a good reputation for high quality (e.g. Marks and Spencer) and make own-brand chocolate for them.

We suggest that when you give out the role cards, ask the learners to note down the main points of their role (perhaps on a pre-prepared grid) and then take the role cards back. This will prevent learners from simply reading from their cards during the play itself.

If you have a large class, you will have to run several role-plays concurrently. During the preparation of roles stage, we suggest that you put those learners with similar roles together so that they can help each other and prepare together. You could also ask them to decide on common objectives so that after the play, they can compare results. I have found that this creates a positive atmosphere of competition and motivates learners. This is particularly true of negotiations and ensures that students listen to the feedback given by their classmates after the activity.

You may also need to decide what to do about the learner/s who are shy or who dislike role-plays. Such a non-participant can perform a useful role, for example, as the note-taker or the observer who will later give feedback. Non-participants can also be asked to operate the camera.

Question 12

In my experience, if you take too long over the preparation stage, learners may lose interest. For example, you may find that you can create suspense and motivate learners so that they want to do the play, only to lose their interest by doing a series of language practice exercises. You have to be sensitive to the class mood. On many occasions, I have dropped an exercise rather than lose the class. Remember that in the final analysis you want to give your learners oral practice. Another problem may be time. Ask yourself whether you can introduce the activity, run it and give effective feedback in the time you have. Work out how long you can spend on each stage of the activity and stick to it. You should also pre-empt problems by not having learners stumble over vocabulary difficulties or roles which are too complex for them. If you are using observers, make sure that they know exactly what they are looking at. Nothing will demotivate learners more than lack of clarity and uncertainty regarding their tasks.

Finally, you will need to start the activity. This may mean rearranging the furniture and having learners move around the class to form different groups. Consider having participants write the name of their role on a piece of paper, which can be pinned to their jackets.

Question 13

It depends on the group. If the learners are students of management with little experience of working in teams, then it might be appropriate to give them some feedback on the team-building process. However, if you are working in-company, and your students are experienced managers then they can probably teach you something about team-building. In this latter scenario it is your job to:
- ➢ create an environment where students work as a team
- ➢ encourage self-evaluation
- ➢ give students feedback regarding how their choice of language, intonation, and so on, influences their performance within a team

UNIT 3: Methodology and Classroom Practice

➢ discuss and explore compensation strategies. These strategies are ways students can manage with language or cultural differences. For example, students who have trouble with verb tenses can be encouraged to use lots of time markers.

In a similar way, if you are running a simulation that demands leadership skills, it may not be your job to teach experienced managers leadership skills. It is your job to let them know whether their choice of language and tone of voice are harming their ability to lead.

6.9: Appendices
Appendix 1: Fielder's Chocolates Ltd

Background

The company was founded in 1945 by William Fielder, who began by making hard-boiled sweets in his garden shed. After a trip to Belgium in 1950, he introduced his "Continental" range of dark chocolates, which were an instant success. By 1960, William had over 30 shops in the north of England, and by 1980, there were 250 Fielder's shops in the UK. The company has recently launched a franchise option, and there are now 14 franchisees operating in England and Wales.

Fielder's have justifiably acquired a high quality "exquisite taste" image. The company has continued to emphasise traditional values; their products and shops have changed very little over the years. There has been no major product innovation since the introduction of the Continental range.

William Fielder ran the company single-handedly until 1985, when he delegated some control to his three sons: Peter, John and Mark.

The confectionery market

This has been in decline for the past ten years. It is dominated by three large players - Cadbury-Schweppes, Rowntree-Nestle and Mars. It is highly competitive, and the most highly advertised of all products.

Sales of confectionery through the traditional outlets, small independent confectioners and newsagents, has almost halved in the last ten years, while supermarkets and superstores now account for 82% of purchases.

Apart from Fielder's, none of the major manufacturers have their own retail chain.

Income statement and budget

	2003	2004	2005
Sales	230,826	250,551	278,250
Direct costs	105,112	126,191	131,760
Gross profit	125,714	124,360	146,490
Wages and salaries	50,000	55,000	60,000
Distribution	5,000	6,000	8,000
Rents	6,000	8,000	10,000
Post, telephone, travel	1,500	2,500	3,000
Advertising	1,500	6,000	7,000
Legal & financial charges	2,500	3,000	2,500

UNIT 3: Methodology and Classroom Practice

Research	1000	1000	1,500
Total overheads	67,500	81,500	92,000
Trading profit	58,214	42,860	54,490

The future

The current situation looks all right, but there is no doubt that times are getting harder. Competition at home is stiffer all the time, as more and more global varieties find their way to the UK. Fielder's have never put much effort into winning export markets.

Some people have expressed concern that mistakes have been made on pricing policy (Fielder's are amongst the highest-priced chocolates on the market), advertising (which has always been meagre) and overhead cost control. It is felt that there is a need for a sound corporate strategy to provide a longer-term perspective than that of the annual budget.

Appendix 2: Useful Language for Participating in Meetings

Giving an opinion
- I'm convinced we should...
- I'm sure...
- I have no doubt...

- I think...
- As I see it...
- In my opinion...

- It seems to me...
- I tend to think...
- I feel...

Agreeing
- I totally agree.
- I agree entirely with Peter.
- I quite agree.
- Absolutely/Precisely.

- I agree with you.
- I think you're right.
- That's true.

- Maybe you're right.
- Perhaps.
- I tend to agree.
- I suppose so.

Disagreeing
- I don't agree with you at all.
- I totally disagree.

UNIT 3: Methodology and Classroom Practice

- It's out of the question.
- Rubbish/nonsense.

- I don't really think so.
- I can't see that, I'm afraid.
- I'm afraid I can't agree with you.

- I'm not sure.
- I tend to disagree.
- Is that a good idea?

- You have a good point but...
- I agree with you up to a point but...
- Maybe that's true but...
- That's very interesting but...

Suggesting
- I suggest that...
- I would suggest...
- My suggestion would be to...

- We could...
- Perhaps we should...
- It might be worth...
- What about...?
- Why don't we...?

Checking comprehension/reformulating
- If I understand you correctly, what you're saying is...
- Are you saying that...?
- Does that mean...?
- So what you're saying is...
- If I follow you correctly...

UNIT 3: Methodology and Classroom Practice

Chapter 7

Business Communication Skills

7.1: Introduction
7.2: Objectives
7.3: Common Distinctions between EIB and General ELT
7.4: Business Communication Skills
7.5: Conclusions
7.6: Answers to Questions.

7.1: Introduction

Chapters 7 and 8 focus on two common elements of EIB: business communication skills and one-to-one teaching. This chapter introduces business communication skills. It outlines the nature of these skills and how they are different from the language skills usually associated with General EFL teaching.

We hope that, for those with little or no experience of teaching business communication skills, the chapter will be extensive enough. For those who do have experience of Business English we hope that the chapter will encourage you think more deeply about how you can fit the skills more comfortably into your own teaching of EIB. We repeat that this chapter only introduces the topic. For a fuller analysis, look at unit 4, chapters 5, 6 and 7.

UNIT 3: Methodology and Classroom Practice

7.2: Objectives

At the end of this chapter, you will be able to:

- further clarify distinctions between teaching EIB and teaching EFL
- better appreciate key business communication skills and approaches to teaching them.

Pre-reading task

Before you begin, try the activities in the box below. The activities are designed to stimulate your thinking and to focus your thoughts.

> 1. The business person with no teaching experience is likely to make a better teacher of EIB than the good EFL teacher with no business experience. What is your opinion?
> 2. What are the advantages of teaching business communication skills?

7.3: Common Distinctions between EIB and General ELT

It might be argued that, essentially, the methodologies of general ELT and EIB are not very different. For example, some teachers might argue that the main language functions used in EIB are no different from those used in EFL. These teachers might give the functions of agreeing and disagreeing as examples. However, although most Business English trainers would probably agree that the EIB classroom is similar to the EFL classroom, they might add that it can also be very different.

Pause for thought

> So, what are the main differences between EFL and EIB teaching? Make a note of your answers before carrying on with reading the text.

The style and manner in which EIB is taught is, or should be, very different from general EFL teaching. Firstly, the way teachers present themselves and their material must be appropriate to the expectations of the business world. Essentially, teachers of EIB are often management trainers and need to look the part. In addition, materials need to be well produced, and classroom aids need to be used professionally. Essentially, business learners tend to appreciate evidence of good planning and a systematic delivery. Business courses need clear objectives and measurable outcomes. Further, business people expect to be asked for feedback and to see evidence that their feedback has been noted and acted on.

We would also expect to see the trainer of EIB showing at least some interest in business topics. This is not to say that the EIB teacher needs to be an expert in business and management. However, teachers do need to be experts in language, and how language is used in a business context. Some familiarity with business topics and their related vocabulary may also be a necessity. Such topics may cover, for example: marketing, financial planning or customer care. These areas can be used as the content for the further development of communication skills. It is to these skills that we now turn.

7.4: Business Communication Skills

The aim of this section is to introduce the field of business communication skills to those whose experience of teaching is centred largely on general ELT. In the introduction to this chapter, we suggested that business communication skills form a large part of EIB teaching and are, in addition to one-to-one teaching, one of the main differentiators between EIB and EFL.

So - what are the advantages of teaching business communication skills? The most important advantage is that they allow learners to develop proficiency in the activities in which they are most involved at work. Learners make progress in the particular language and skills that they need. Above all, they can measure their progress.

Many learners of EIB have unrealistic and unclear objectives. These objectives often revolve around the need to have simple conversations with native speakers or the need to understand what native speakers are saying.

Question 1

Why is this apparently simple objective of little use to the teacher of EIB?

UNIT 3: Methodology and Classroom Practice

If the objectives mentioned above are, perhaps, unrealistic and difficult to measure, focusing on business communication skills can help learners see real and achievable progress. The effectiveness of teaching can often be maximised by concentrating on one or two selected skills. Identifying these skills is therefore of central importance to the teaching of EIB.

Question 2

> *Peter Eitler is an executive for a leading car manufacturer based in the south of Germany. He has been appointed to a position in which he is responsible for the interiors of a new range of sports models.*
>
> *He has arrived at your school for a one-week intensive course because he and his superiors are seriously worried about his level of English. His language level is lower intermediate. He rarely communicates directly with suppliers, but spends a lot of time communicating orally and in writing with colleagues around the world and in Germany. Most of this communication is in English. What questions would you ask Peter in order to determine his business communication needs in English? Consider both oral and written needs.*

If we consider Business English communication from a linguistic point of view, we might see that some of these language skills can really be described as speech events. A speech event is the social setting or framework in which communication takes place. For example, debates, prayers, and performance appraisals are speech events. The limits of the event are defined by the participants themselves and the purpose of the interaction. Giving a presentation, negotiating a contract or solving a problem in a meeting are, therefore, speech events.

We suggest that a presentation is a clear example of such an event. The participants and the purpose are well defined. Further, the communicative purpose is distinct from what was happening in terms of communication before the presentation. We suggest that presentations are a specific kind of speaking and are, therefore, a Business English genre. By genre we mean a type of communication with its own distinctive identity (see also unit 4, chapter 4).

A vital element in the teaching of business communication skills is the distinction between skills and language. In other words, should we teach only the language associated with the skills or do we deal with the skills themselves?

Question 3

> *Peter Eitler has been asked to give a presentation to his superiors. The ten-minute presentation should outline in English the main points of Peter's strategy for the development and design of his car interiors. This is an important moment for Peter, and his strategy and English ability will come under close scrutiny. Peter has asked you as his teacher to go through his presentation with him, choosing every word carefully, so that he can subsequently learn the presentation by heart and deliver it from memory on his return to Germany. How do you respond to his request?*

Peter's situation is quite common, and it raises some important questions.

- Do we teach only the language of business communication?
- Do we teach only the skills themselves?
- Do we teach a combination of the two?
- Do we teach general communication skills but in a business context?
- Do we teach specific communication skills and in a business context?

It may be argued that an English teacher's expertise is in the area of language and that, therefore, the best approach to teaching business communication skills would be to focus on language. However, there are two fundamental difficulties with this.

1. The value of teaching content. By content here we mean subject matter. There is evidence to suggest (Prabhu, 1987) that students learn more English when they study another subject (content), while using English as the language of study.
2. Identifying real language. The language used for key business skills, for example, speaking at meetings, may not be so easy to identify as many teachers and writers would have us believe.

UNIT 3: Methodology and Classroom Practice

The value of teaching content

The pioneering work on the teaching of content was carried out by Prabhu (1987). Prabhu was interested in the idea that language could be acquired as a by-product of learning something else, something that was not directly related to language. He set up controlled research in various schools, and demonstrated that teaching another subject (content) but in the medium of English, was equally effective or more effective than teaching the language itself.

This research has since been challenged but nonetheless EIB teachers should seriously consider content teaching as an alternative to straight language teaching.

Pause for thought

> *How far do you agree with the idea of content teaching? Is it useful for the teaching of business communication skills?*

Identifying real language

We suggest that when trainers plan to teach the language of business, they need to be sure this language accurately reflects that used by business people. There is very little evidence to show that the language practised in classes and prescribed in coursebooks as the language of Business English (for example the language of meetings) is in fact the language business speakers really use. There are of course notable exceptions to this, and the work of creating corpuses of Business English goes on.

While I was working as a language consultant at Hewlett-Packard in Germany, I was frequently invited to attend business meetings as an observer. Usually my task was to give feedback to one of the participants after the meeting. All of these meetings were composed of mainly non-native speakers but with one or two native speakers. Although I did not collect or analyse data, it soon became clear to me that the language prescribed in textbooks was simply not good enough.

For example, the language of agreement and disagreement that we often see in textbooks suggests that speakers are likely to say, for example: "I agree with you up to a point, but...," or , "I absolutely disagree."

In reality, agreement and disagreement were much less explicit than the coursebooks suggested. Further, there were important cultural considerations, and the politeness strategies reflected in the language were often culturally inappropriate (Alptekin, 2002). Essentially, there was a notable mismatch between the language used in real meetings and the language used in the teaching materials.

What we are suggesting here is that language study need not be the principal focus when teaching business meetings. We suggest that there are two possible alternatives. These are:

➤ studying and teaching the strategies speakers use
➤ studying and teaching the actual skill of speaking at meetings.

The approach that now dominates EIB and, we suggest, is the most practical approach, is teaching the business communication skills themselves.

Specific business communication skills

If you decide to teach business communication skills you will find that a wide range of management training materials becomes available to you (see for example, Guirdham, 1990). This material may appeal to business learners because it is designed for their world. Such material might concern how to structure your utterances so that they have the most impact, how to use body language effectively or how to give feedback in a constructive and non-threatening manner. Watkins (2003) is very good on the skills needed for effective writing, oral presentations and one-to-one dealings with others. Furthermore, the book deals with such writing skills as drafting effective proposals and writing effective e-mails. Thomas and Inkson (2004) are very good on business communication across cultures. In particular, the book deals with decision-making, communicating across cultures, leadership and multicultural teams.

The purpose of this section is to give you an overview of the nature and content of business communication skills. In the space available here, there is no room to deal with all the skills that might be needed by your learners. To exemplify the principal points, we have chosen three skills. These are:

➤ presentation skills
➤ meeting skills

UNIT 3: Methodology and Classroom Practice

> negotiation skills.

Presentation skills

Pause for thought

> *What are the language skills needed for presentations?*
> *What other skills are needed to give effective presentations?*

While working in-company in Germany, I was called upon to teach two different classes in presentation skills. The first was called, "The Language of Presentations." The content of this was focused on the language you have seen in Unit 2, chapter 4, section 10, that is: greetings, opening the presentation, bridging and so on. The second was called, "Presentation Skills in English," and consisted, largely, of the language mentioned above and skills, for example: effective organisation of information, effective delivery and effective use of language.

Both courses were always fully booked. However, I found it increasingly difficult (if not impossible) to separate skills from language. Consequently, both types of course tended to be similar, but with a different focus.

Question 4

> *You have managed to persuade Peter Eitler that memorising his presentation is not a good idea. Given that his language is weak, on what would you focus your lessons?*

It might be useful here to compare two books on presentation skills, and we recommend that you look at them if you can get copies. The first (Sweeney, 1997) deals with presentations from a language point of view. The second (Hindle, 1998) is a text from the field of management training.

Sweeney (1997) is useful because although the work focuses on language, it integrates the language with the skills required for presentations. On the other hand, Hindle (1998) focuses on the aspects of presentation that are likely to be of interest to business professionals. These aspects are: researching material, content, eye contact, reading

UNIT 3: Methodology and Classroom Practice

the body language of the audience, and relaxing before the presentation. For example, with regard to content, Hindle writes:

> Every adult audience has a limited attention span of about 45minutes. In that time they will absorb only about one third of what was said, and a maximum of seven concepts. Limit yourself to three or four main points, and emphasize them at the beginning of your speech, in the middle, and again at the end to reiterate your message.

In coursebooks which focus on language, some or all of these topics will be left out in favour of language based activities. Nor do most language-based books deal with the issue of culture. Cultural differences can have an enormous impact on what constitutes a "good" presentation (see also unit1, chapter 2, section 3), and those people who work internationally will need to know how to adapt their presentations in order to suit the culture of the audience. For a good trainer's guide to presentation skills training you might want to look at Jolles (2005).

Meetings

There is a good selection of material on the market that deals with the language and the skills needed for participating in, and chairing, meetings, for example: Donna (2000) and Brieger (1997). There is also a wide range of techniques appropriate to the teaching of meetings in EIB. However, at some stage most teachers might want to use a simulated meeting (for example, see chapter 6 of this unit). We think that simulated meetings give the learners the opportunity they need to put what they have learned into action. Such meetings present an effective platform for demonstrating both business communication skills and language. They also provide a rich source of feedback and analysis, particularly if they can be recorded on video or a similar medium. For a fuller examination of meetings skills see unit 4, chapter 5.

Negotiating skills

Teaching negotiating skills (see also unit 4, chapter 6) will also provide learners with enormous potential for speaking practice. In order to introduce the topic of negotiation, I have found the following introductory questions useful.

Example questions

Look at the following possible outcomes of a negotiation. What are the advantages and disadvantages of each?
- lose/lose
- win/lose
- lose/win
- win/win.

Look at the following descriptions of a negotiator? Rank them according to order of importance.

Negotiators:
- try to develop a rapport with their opposite number
- discuss conflict and suggest ways of resolving it
- listen
- have clear objectives
- show respect for their opposite number
- compromise
- clarify what their opposite number is saying
- are determined to win
- repeat the main points
- have a range of objectives
- take the negotiation one step at a time.

The purpose of these questions is to give learners some theory about the topic of negotiations and then give them the opportunity to put theory into practice by using a simulation or role-play. The simulation would then be followed by feedback and analysis.

There are many approaches to negotiating skills themselves - this is a central topic for management training materials. One useful approach is given in Sweeney (1997). The author identifies the following negotiation skills.

Good preparation. This means:
- identify your minimum requirements
- prepare an opening statement
- decide what concessions you can make

- know what role you play in the negotiation team
- know your aims and objectives
- prepare any figures, calculations and support materials
- know your weaknesses.

Good bargaining. This means:
- be clear about the important issues and the less important issues
- give what is not so important for you but is valuable to the other side
- ask lots of questions to clarify positions
- listen
- build on common ground
- be brief but clear
- be flexible and keep a flexible attitude.

7.5: Conclusions

This chapter has introduced you to the field of skills training in EIB. For those of you who need to go further, we suggest that you have a look at material which focuses on the language connected to these skills and also at material which focuses on the skills themselves. Only you can judge how to combine these two elements in your teaching. However, there is no doubt that you will enrich your own teaching by combining language with communication skills and become a better (and better-paid) trainer. For those who want to know more about business communication, we suggest you look at Hargie (2006), Watkins (2003) and Thomas and Inkson (2004). Those of us who are experts in language and who also know something of communication skills are rare.

UNIT 3: Methodology and Classroom Practice

7.6: Answers to questions

Question 1
Because it takes months or even years of living in a country to be able to have "simple conversations." In addition, most business learners need achievable and measurable objectives. Most learners are not able to devote the time and resources to the language learning that will fulfil their initial expectations. This is news that has to be broken gently, and a clear strategy with concrete objectives provided to replace unrealistic expectations.

Question 2
Companies and schools may have their own needs analysis procedures that can be applied to a case such as Peter's. You might begin by asking Peter what he sees as being his needs. Next, you could find out what activities he carries out in English at work. This will form a starting point for deciding which business communication skills to work on. Some example questions could be:
- Do you speak at, or chair, meetings?
- Do you make presentations?
- Do you take part in negotiations?
- Do you speak on the telephone?
- Do you write reports?
- Do you write memos?
- Do you write emails and faxes?
- Do you write letters?
- Do you write promotional marketing material?

An analysis like this would give you an indication of the areas Peter needs to develop. It is only a first step, and you will need to ask further questions in order to get a clearer picture of Peter's precise needs.

Question 3
Memorising the presentation would seem to have advantages. For example, if Peter is not confident in his English ability, memorisation could be good for him in the short-term. However, we do not recommend it. For example, Peter can not memorise answers to the questions he will receive. Further, Peter would need a considerable amount of time to prepare, memorise and practise the presentation. In addition, memorisation has implications for pronunciation. Long extracts spoken from memory tend to be delivered in a flat and lifeless way which can obscure meaning and send the audience to sleep. Presenters are likely to be understood more easily when speaking naturally from notes than when speaking from memory. Finally, it is likely that Peter will want to present again in the future. In this case, considerable attention should be given to the skills of presenting as well as the language so that Peter can practise what he has learned at a future date.

Question 4
I would certainly begin by teaching him the structure of presentations and the language connected with that structure. I would then ask him to prepare a presentation so that he could practise the linguistic elements. I would then teach him some aspects

UNIT 3: Methodology and Classroom Practice

of the skill itself. For example: the use of body language, tone, using visuals and a structure for handling questions. If we had time, I would then give more input on presentation preparation. For example, I would ask him the following questions. What do you want your audience to think and feel at the end of the presentation? What do you need to tell them in order for them to think and feel in this way? This last question teases out the principal points that need to be presented. Last, but by no means least, I would ask Peter to practise, practise and practise and I would give him feedback on all the points taught.

Chapter 8

Teaching One-to-One

8.1: Introduction
8.2: Objectives
8.3: Advantages and Disadvantages
8.4: Techniques
8.5: Dealing with Relationships
8.6: Conclusions
8.7: Answers to Questions.

8.1: Introduction

Although one-to-one teaching is very common in the world of EIB, it is by no means unique to it. There is plenty of such teaching in general ELT, including teaching young learners.

However, we suggest that teaching one-to-one is often a major focus of language schools specialising in Business English and of in-company courses. Further, some courses with which I have been involved combine one-to-one with group sessions. These often require a learner to attend, for example, group classes in the mornings and personalised one-to-one classes in the afternoon. These afternoon sessions usually focus on an aspect of teaching which is specific to the particular person. For example, a learner might want to practise a

UNIT 3: Methodology and Classroom Practice

particular presentation, learn and practise very specific vocabulary or have a need to practise a specific communication skill, for example, giving a job appraisal in English.

For teachers, one-to-one teaching is a very different experience from whole-class teaching. We would suggest, for example, that social skills are as important as specialised teaching skills. We would also add that many of the skills teachers have learned in their training courses may not be particularly relevant in one-to-one courses. There is no need, for example, to set up groupwork or pairwork, to deal with quieter students or to repeat points for the benefit of those who were not listening. On the other hand, teaching one-to-one requires teachers to make a good impression and to quickly develop a working rapport with the student. Above all, perhaps, patience, empathy and sensitivity are needed if one-to-one sessions are to be effective and successful. For a good account of one-to-one teaching in ESP, including in-company work, we suggest you get a copy of Wilberg (1987).

8.2: Objectives

The main aims of this chapter are to:

- examine the advantages and disadvantages of one-to-one teaching for both teachers and learners
- establish some principles for one-to-one teaching
- outline the disadvantages and potential hazards of one-to-one teaching.

Pre-reading task

While you are working through this chapter, you are asked to work on the activity in the shaded box below. This activity is designed to focus your thinking on the main issues raised in the text.

> *Thomas Stein is a marketing executive from Frankfurt. Thomas speaks very good English, although his opinion of his language skills is low. He has been sent to your school for one week of intensive one-to-one training by his boss in Frankfurt. His boss wants Thomas to improve his business communication skills in English so that he can manage his global workforce more*

> *effectively. Thomas, however, has other ideas. He is more interested in perfecting his grammar and vocabulary and he is convinced that these are the keys to improving his English in any situation. He says he wants you to explain, amongst other things, the verb tense system in English and he wants plenty of traditional grammar exercises. Thomas is hard-working, motivated and anxious to show his superiors that he has benefited from his week in England, but he is determined to do things his way. You are his trainer. How will you deal with this situation?*

8.3: Advantages and Disadvantages

Below you will see some of the advantages of teaching one-to-one for teachers/trainers.

- You can design a finely tailored course which meets the needs of a particular individual.
- You do not need to deal with the pressures, stress and demands of a group of people with diverse needs and requirements.
- You can concentrate on responding to the specific needs of a learner rather than having to control or monitor a group.
- You can deliver material in a way which is appropriate for a particular learner and a particular learning style.
- You will have greater scope for utilising materials and situations that the learner brings to the sessions from his/her own working environment.
- You can estimate fairly accurately how much time to spend on highly individual and specific activities.
- There is plenty of scope for learners to be in control of activities and equipment in the classroom, for example, the video player or the white board.
- You can take advantage of the learner's first language even if you do not speak it. This is difficult in classes in which several different languages are represented.

And here are some of the advantages of one-to-one teaching for learners.

UNIT 3: Methodology and Classroom Practice

- Learners can expect to be involved in activities that have been tailor-made for them. With good dialogue between teacher and student, all activities can potentially be relevant and appropriate to the needs of one particular person.
- Learners can proceed at their own speed.
- Learners have more control over the nature of classroom activities.
- Learners can be active and participative in use of classroom space and facilities.

And what about the disadvantages for teachers? These are outlined below.

- Some teachers miss the stimulus that performing for a group can sometimes bring. This lack of a stimulus can be a source of monotony if not handled properly.
- Extended one-to-one teaching can often lack the variety of activities that group teaching can potentially provide.

And the disadvantages for the learner?

- Learners are usually unable to take advantage of the presence of other students in order to tune out for a few minutes. This can make the experience extremely tiring.
- Learners may find that they are expected to spend long periods of time with a person and personality they would not normally choose to be with. Sensitivity is required on both sides
- One-to-one training is much more expensive than being taught in a class.

Pause for thought

> *Think of ways in which these disadvantages may be minimised.*

8.4: Techniques

A comprehensive analysis of needs (see unit 2) is something that should be carried out in most learning situations. However, when teaching one-to-one, it is an activity that needs to be thorough and precise. An effective and ongoing analysis of needs ought to lead to a

UNIT 3: Methodology and Classroom Practice

programme that meets the needs of specific learners. However, the reality often (but not always) is that in many cases, there is a limited amount of time to make a thorough analysis of needs. The questions below might help you to determine the needs of your particular student.

What does the learner do in English when he/she is at work? Teachers need to clearly define the kinds of workplace interactions and activities in which the learner is involved. These interactions may concern something general, for example, socialising with clients. Conversely, the need may be very specific, for example, making a presentation to a potential customer in the car industry. Teachers need to question learners in order to elicit those activities in which development is most urgently required.

What is the language associated with the activities identified in question 1? Having elicited from the learners which activities they do in English at work, it is usually relatively simple to identify the language that is often associated with those activities. We would raise again, however, the issues dealt with in chapter 7 of this unit, about authenticity of language.

What activities can be chosen that will help practise the language derived from points 1 and 2 above? There are, of course, many coursebooks on the market, which focus on language functions, and these may often be useful. For example, the functions of making appointments, or showing guests around your work site are very common. Occasionally, however, teachers will have to write their own material or adapt material from existing textbooks (see unit 2, chapter 4). In these circumstances, it is not unusual, in my experience, to have one trainer working on materials while another trainer is using previously prepared material with the client. Whatever the case, it is advisable, when working with companies, to prepare all material individually, with the name of the client and the company, and the date written across the top of the pages used. The last in a long line of bad photocopies simply will not do.

Frequently, teachers will be required to help students update and polish versions of specific workplace interactions, and this can provide a major focus for language development. Considerable flexibility and creativity can be used in this. For example, many learners come to one-to-one classes with a presentation that they want to make as effective as possible for use on return to work. Some of the stages that teacher and learner may go through are listed below.

UNIT 3: Methodology and Classroom Practice

- Learner identifies the objective of the presentation.
- Learner defines the audience and outlines their possible attitude (friendly, hostile, indifferent, sceptical).
- Learner produces a version of the presentation which is recorded (video, audio).
- Learner and trainer work together to identify the changes that need to be made in order to improve the presentation.
- Trainer analyses the language of the presentation and produces a "correct" version of learner presentation.
- Learner produces and practises an improved or updated version of the presentation.
- Trainer and learner work to improve chosen aspects of the new version, for example: language use, delivery, body language, and cultural considerations.

The stages above can be repeated if necessary. The main advantage of this sequence is that it allows learners to focus on aspects of their presentation which, in consultation with the trainer, they have helped to identify.

8.5: Dealing with Relationships

Question 1

What can the trainer do to ensure that his/her relationship with the learner is productive?

In my experience, it is often the nature of the relationship between trainer and trainee that is the key to successful one-to-one sessions. Student and teacher may be with each other every morning and afternoon for up to two weeks. This length of time is unusual, but nonetheless, the relationship between the two is close and demanding.

It is, perhaps, true to say that in any relationship there is a need to be sensitive and responsive to the other person. This sensitivity may concern cultural differences, or aspects of the learner's behaviour. Changes in energy levels at different parts of the day or motivation may also be vital issues.

UNIT 3: Methodology and Classroom Practice

Question 2

> *Learners come on one-to-one courses for a variety of reasons. Whatever the reason, it will influence both the training itself and the relationship between teacher and learner. Why do people come on one-to-one training courses? Make a list and compare your answers with ours in the Answers to Questions section.*

Whoever they are, students will bring a variety of learning styles into the training room. Sensitivity to learning styles is vital in one-to-one teaching (see chapter 9 of this unit). There are methods you can use to identify the learning style preferences of students and this might be done during the first sessions. Teaching students in a way that does not match their learning style can damage the relationship between teacher and student. On the other hand, any attempt to persuade learners to change their style of learning may be met with hostile resistance. Furthermore, we might add that some teachers may be reluctant to change their teaching style, especially if this change goes against their principles. Once again, sensitivity is needed.

Question 3

> *Pierre works as a financial director in a Paris-based company. He has been sent to your school to improve his English because the company has just merged with a company in the US and all future communication is supposed to be in English. Pierre is due to travel frequently to the US for meetings with his counterparts there. He clearly needs to improve his spoken English but he constantly stops himself in mid-flow to ask you if what he is saying is correct. He simply will not believe you when you tell him that he needs to concentrate on fluency rather than accuracy. What do you do?*

Working at close quarters with learners for long periods of time can be dangerously claustrophobic for both teacher and learner. In order to alleviate this problem, the trainer can create physical and psychological space. In order to create this space the trainer can do a number of things.

➢ Divide the training room into different activity areas.

UNIT 3: Methodology and Classroom Practice

- Give the learner an area where s/he can work alone. This could be at a separate computer or at a smaller desk to one side of that used by the trainer. Learners can use this "private" area when working on, for example, writing tasks or listening with head phones.
- Furnish a part of the room with comfortable chairs. This part of the room could be used for activities like reading the newspaper or watching TV.

When one-to-one teaching becomes too intense it can help learners and teachers to focus their attention on something different. Inside the classroom, learners can be invited to engage in activities that do not directly or immediately involve the teacher, for example: writing, listening or reading. A separate space should be assigned for this. Activities outside the classroom could also be useful at this point.

The one-to-one environment can be quite tense and trainers need to be aware of the kinds of hazards that exist for both learners and trainers. One key issue concerns power. If trainers think that they are the experts in language and training and that they alone should control most aspects of the training, this can lead to serious problems in the relationship. Learners are usually successful professional people and often with a high degree of autonomy in their working lives. For a trainer to attempt to dominate in this way is unlikely to be well received. We mentioned above that trainers need to be responsive to learners. They also need to be aware of the role they are playing in the relationship and how they are perceived by the learner.

There is also the opposite possibility that learners will see themselves as better able than language trainers to take control of the learning programme. In my own experience, this hardly ever happens. Learners will usually acknowledge the trainer's expertise in training skills and language. The learner may, however, want to make it clear that in some areas they want to have control. These areas may concern a preference for some activities over others, or simply stopping something when they have had enough. For an excellent account of how to improve and repair relationships in a training environment, we suggest you look at Nelson-Jones (2006).

UNIT 3: Methodology and Classroom Practice

8.6: Conclusions

One-to-one teaching has great potential in the sense that it offers the freedom to negotiate course content and to deliver training in a very flexible way. My own experience of one-to-one, and discussions with colleagues over many years, suggest that there are some basic principles for successful training. Most of these have been dealt with in the various sections of this chapter.

It is important to make an ongoing effort to like the person with whom you are sharing a room for such a long time. Negative feelings are difficult to hide, and if your student becomes aware of them, an unpleasant experience may well be the result.

Finally, one-to-one teaching is not appropriate for every teacher and his or her teaching style. Although teachers can adapt and show sensitivity to the learner, they can not really change their teaching style preferences. In these circumstances, one-to-one teaching can become tedious very quickly. If this applies to you, you should consider what you can do to change the situation. Perhaps, you can use the sessions to experiment with techniques in which you are interested, for example, using cuisenaire rods, or playing music to create the appropriate atmosphere. Whatever you do, do it with a positive attitude and remain sensitive to your learners. They form 50% of a quite intense relationship, and you can not afford to ignore them if you are to deliver professionally.

8.7: Answers to Questions

Question 1
The trainer can:
➢ respond to the learner as an individual
➢ create physical and psychological space
➢ be aware of the things that can harm a good relationship.

Question 2
Some employees will have tried hard to get the training, and they will be highly motivated. They might see the training as a prelude to advancement in the company or to getting a pay rise. Sometimes, employees are sent whether they want the training or not. Other employees will come as a perk of the job and they will have no clear reason for learning. Worse, in such cases, they may not be highly motivated. All of these people will bring positive and negative points with them into the training room.

UNIT 3: Methodology and Classroom Practice

For example, the employee who has been sent as a perk of the job may not be highly motivated but may be fun to teach.

Question 3
I would try and compromise by telling him I would give him feedback on his language once he has finished the activity in which he is engaged. This would mean making a note of his mistakes and going through them with Pierre at the end of the activity. In this way we could build up a record of his weaknesses. Another alternative would be to record him and give feedback on the recording. In this way Pierre could practise fluency and also get feedback which would improve his accuracy.

UNIT 3: Methodology and Classroom Practice

Chapter 9

Learning and Learning Styles

9.1: Introduction
9.2: Objectives
9.3: Learning
9.4: The Learner
9.5: Introduction to Learning Styles
9.6: Conclusion
9.7: Answers to questions.

9.1: Introduction

Rubin (1975) suggests that good language learners have the following characteristics.

- They are willing to guess and accurate at guessing.
- They have a strong need to communicate.
- They are uninhibited and willing to make mistakes.
- They focus on form by looking at patterns.
- They utilise all practice opportunities.
- They monitor their own speech and that of others.
- They pay attention to meaning.

UNIT 3: Methodology and Classroom Practice

Behaviourists view the learner as a blank slate and emphasise a scientifically and carefully controlled approach to the study of behaviour. The responsibility for learning lies with the instructor. A stimulus from the environment is present, and then the learner reacts to the stimulus with some type of response. If the response is "correct" then it is reinforced through a reward mechanism. The pattern is repeated until the behaviour becomes automatic. This signifies that learning has occurred. Classical behaviourists will reject any attempt to explain human behaviour in terms of thinking and mental processes or intentions. They believe that behaviour must be submitted to measurable tests of observation or experiments (Pellone, 1991).

The main premise of Skinner's (1957) work is that the actions of animals and human beings depend entirely on rewards and punishments. For example, in teaching pigeons to peck complex patterns, Skinner included simple step-by-step procedures in which he rewarded success, usually with food and, in some situations, punished lack of success.

The simple directness of behaviourism has had an enormous impact on learning psychology and on language teaching. Behaviourism provided the theoretical foundation for the Audio-lingual method of the fifties and sixties. This method laid down a series of guiding methodological principles for teachers. These principles were based firmly on the stimulus-response concept and on the assumption that second language learning should imitate, as far as possible, the perceived process of mother tongue learning. For the teacher, these concepts developed into:

➢ never translate
➢ new language should always be dealt with in the sequence: hear, speak, read, write
➢ frequent repetition is vital for effective learning
➢ all errors must be corrected immediately.

In the language classroom, activities based on behavioural theory would be teacher-centred and include, for example: drilling and pattern practice or choral repetition, instructional games, and spelling. The learner is only required to recall basic facts, produce automatic responses, or perform tasks with well-defined procedures.

A teacher who respects the importance of the behavioural theory of learning tells students whether or not they have given the correct

UNIT 3: Methodology and Classroom Practice

answer (feedback), praises them for giving a correct answer (positive reinforcement), or prompts the ones who may need a hint to answer a question (cueing).

Question 1

> *Imagine you are working in-company. You have been asked to teach a series of courses on communication skills. In particular, you have been asked to teach presentation skills and appraisal skills in English. How far could you adopt a behaviourist approach to your courses?*

Cognitive theorists believe that learning is based on the thought process behind behaviour, and that there are "built-in" language-learning abilities in the human mind. This means that learners have a proactive role in their own learning. They therefore play an active role in finding ways to understand and process information that they receive and relate it to what is already known and stored in their memory.

Applying cognitive learning to teaching practice means that good teaching should progress from the known to the unknown, use analogies to explain new concepts, and make topics meaningful. Classroom activities based on this theory of learning would include small group discussions, reasoning, and classifying or chunking information into logical groups.

The basic teaching technique associated with a cognitive theory of language learning is the problem-solving task. In EIB, such exercises can often be modelled on activities associated with the learners' jobs.

Pause for thought

> *Consider the last sentence above. How many problem-solving activities can you think of that can be modelled on your learners' jobs?*

Contemporary cognitive psychologists have proposed models of learning which involve the gradual formation of conceptual schemata. Schematic learning implies that the use of previously learned ideas and concepts is a prerequisite for grasping new input. Schemata have a great influence in determining how new information is processed and how long it is retained (Pellone, 1991).

UNIT 3: Methodology and Classroom Practice

Rogers (1969) distinguished two types of learning: cognitive (meaningless) and experiential (significant). The former corresponds to academic knowledge such as learning vocabulary or multiplication tables while the latter refers to applied knowledge such as learning keyboarding in order to operate a computer. The vital distinction is that experiential learning addresses the needs and wants of the learner.

According to Rogers (1969), learning is facilitated when the student participates completely in the learning process and has control over its nature and direction. He believes that learning is primarily based upon direct confrontation with practical, social, personal or research problems. Learner self-evaluation is the principal method of assessing progress.

Rogers' (1969) theory of learning originates from his views about psychotherapy and the humanistic approach to psychology. For Rogers, experiential learning has the following qualities.

- Personal involvement.
- Learner-initiation.
- Evaluation by the learner.
- Pervasive effects on the learner.

For Rogers, experiential learning is equivalent to personal change and growth, and it applies primarily to adult learners. The importance of experiential learning is supported by Burnard (1989), who also sees experiential learning in terms of personal development. Burnard argues that nobody can learn, for example, interpersonal skills by rote-learning or by mechanically learning a series of behaviours. He stresses that we need time to reflect on our own behaviour and on the feedback given to us by colleagues and by the trainer.

Kolb et al (1974) see experiential learning as a circular and on-going process. The key stages in this process are:

- experience
- analysis of the main learning points arising from the experience
- consequent planning and testing of new behaviour.

Honey and Mumford (1983) have further refined this process and identify the types of trainee most likely to benefit from experiential learning. These types are as follows.

UNIT 3: Methodology and Classroom Practice

- Activists - people who are willing to try anything once.
- Reflectors - people who need time to think about things.
- Theorists - people who need to understand the interconnectedness of things.
- Pragmatists - people who need to put theory into practice.

Question 2

How far are theories of experiential learning incorporated into EIB?

Knowles (1980) takes a slightly different view of experiential learning by suggesting that it involves learners in sorting things out for themselves by restructuring their perceptions of what is happening. This view is clearly linked to discovery learning, which draws attention to aspects of behaviour we might refer to as insight.

Discovery learning can be understood as a reflection of the way in which people learn to recognise and define problems, and experiment to find solutions to those problems. Solutions may be sought through trial and error, by deduction, by seeking information or help, or by a combination of these.

So what is the role of the trainer in experiential learning? At different times during a session, the trainer may play a variety of roles. Generally, the trainer will act as a facilitator, and is concerned with process activities. This means that the trainer will:

- encourage discussion
- guide group activities
- coach individual participants
- observe
- give group feedback
- create a climate conducive to learning and encourage adult-to-adult relationships, joining in as an equal and not as someone who knows all the answers.

Question 3

Can you think of any cultures which might be resistant to experiential learning?

UNIT 3: Methodology and Classroom Practice

9.4: The learner

When faced with a group of learners, teachers are obliged to make decisions with regard to, for example, their style of teaching, the content of their teaching, the materials they use, classroom arrangement and the management of interaction between the learners themselves.

In order to make these decisions teachers will need to identify a number of important learner characteristics or variables. Some of the characteristics may be more or less predictable while others will be better assessed in the classroom itself. Some of the variables are interrelated. Stern (1983) identifies the following variables.

- Age: this may influence the topics chosen and the types of learning activity.
- Interests: this will also help in identifying topics and activities.
- Level of proficiency in English: is the class of mixed proficiency?
- Aptitude for language learning.
- Mother tongue: this may have an influence on error analysis as well as on topic selection.
- Academic and educational level.
- Attitudes to learning, and to the English language itself.
- Motivation.
- Reasons for learning.
- Preferred learning style.
- Personality.

Pause for thought

> *Think about your own teaching situation. Make a list of the characteristics of your learners. Which of these characteristics have the most influence on your teaching?*

We suggest that an understanding of learner characteristics is crucial if teachers are to adjust or vary their teaching to allow for individual differences in the classroom. However, some of the characteristics above do not necessarily always have an obvious effect on language learning, for example, personality. Other characteristics are more difficult to measure and are likely to change during the course itself. Motivation, for example, can be influenced by the style of language instruction, by perceived progress and by the personality of the teacher.

UNIT 3: Methodology and Classroom Practice

The most successful language learner I have ever met was a young Italian beginner who fell in love with his English teacher.

Question 4

> *How can a teacher respond to individual learner differences of the kind listed above?*

Learner autonomy

Autonomy and independence are used more or less as synonyms in language teaching. Both terms imply that students take a greater degree of control over the content and methods of learning than is usual in classroom language learning contexts. Taking control over learning also implies that students have, or develop, the capacity to learn independently, and that the institutional context in which they are learning allows them to do so. Further, it has been claimed that all learning is ultimately autonomous learning in the sense that it depends on the efforts of the learners themselves.

Individualisation in language learning is, perhaps, a consequence of the development of interest in learners and their individual needs. This is particularly true in the area of ESP. Skehan (1989) suggests that individualisation represents an important move away from the behaviourist, psychological approaches to learning and towards a revival of interest in cognitive approaches.

Pause for thought

> *Why should you want to individualise language learning?*

Most language learning takes place in groups. A major concern of all teachers should be, therefore, to ensure that the needs of individual learners are not suppressed by the constraints of the group. It will be clear to you that some of your learners prefer working in groups while others prefer working alone. Further, some learners will prefer studying in the evening while others prefer the early morning.

As important as these practical reasons are, individualisation is also important in order to help learners develop the ability to learn how to learn, in other words, to design and manage their own learning projects.

UNIT 3: Methodology and Classroom Practice

Question 5

> *How appropriate is individualised learning in cultures which see knowledge as objective or God-given, and which often view the teacher as the source of this knowledge? Such cultures would include China, Japan and Russia.*

So, how can we define individualisation? Brumfit and Roberts (1983) suggest that individualisation involves:

> ...the organisation of learning and teaching in such a way as to allow the abilities, interests and needs of the individual learner to be enhanced as effectively as possible; with the consequence that the traditional notion of the "average student" and "aiming for the middle" in teaching is abandoned.

The question arises, "Is individualised learning the same as autonomous learning?" After all, a teacher may identify an individual's difficulties and prescribe the measures to be taken in order to alleviate those difficulties. An individualised programme in this sense is very controlled. The opposite extreme would be a totally self-directed learning programme with no intervention from the teacher.

Pause for thought

> *How do you currently deal with individual learner needs in your classroom?*

Your answer to this question may begin with, "It depends." However, the majority of individualised learning lies somewhere between the two extremes mentioned above.

So, how can teachers implement autonomy and independence in EIB teaching and learning? One way of providing individual choice is to use self-access activities where learners choose the tasks and activities that they wish to pursue. Some teachers programme self-access work into their weekly teaching programme. This may be possible in a university or school environment, but it is more problematic in company training where resources may simply not be available.

It is true that there is an abundance of web-based material that teachers can choose from. However, in my experience, many business people do not have the time to study individually, and many learners simply do not like learning without a teacher. Further, people who have spent the day in front of a computer do not necessarily relish the thought of spending yet more time working from a screen. What is more, the type of training required by companies is often practical and oriented to immediate results, for example: presentation skills, negotiation skills and meeting skills. Autonomous learning does not easily lend itself to such requirements.

Electronic technology makes more information more easily accessible and more cheaply than ever before. It is the potential this has for boosting both the quantity and quality of learning that has created considerable interest in the past few years.

Amidst all this excitement, we need to remember that electronic learning is fundamentally another learning opportunity, the latest addition to many.

Pause for thought

> *Honey (2001) suggests that there is great room for improvement in e-learning. Look at his criticisms and suggestions below and decide whether or not you agree with them.*

- Stop pushing text down the telephone line and calling it learning.
- Have more sympathy for the learner. It is unrealistic to expect busy people to be motivated and disciplined to learn at their desks in what is, effectively, free time.
- E-learning is not the answer to everything. We need to work out the distinctive competence of the e-learning approach and how it can complement other forms of learning.
- Show more interest in learning as a process and in how to tailor information to meet the needs of the learners with different learning styles. Ask questions to find out the learning preferences of students and use e-technology to customise offerings accordingly.

UNIT 3: Methodology and Classroom Practice

9.5: Introduction to Learning Styles

In the introduction to this chapter, we mentioned that learning styles and learning strategies are not necessarily the same thing. What is the difference between them? According to Oxford and Green (1996):

> Learning styles are the broad approaches to learning a new subject or solving a problem, whereas learning strategies are specific behaviours that learners use to improve their own learning.

In other words, language learning strategies are specific actions, behaviours, steps, or techniques that students may consciously or subconsciously use in order to improve their developing second language skills. These strategies may help learners internalise, store, retrieve, and utilise aspects of the new language. Therefore, strategies are tools which can be used to develop communicative skills.

Pause for thought

> *My own experience when learning to speak Italian (while living in Italy) was that I learned best when I was able to put into almost immediate practice what I had learned while studying at home. In other words, I studied the details of grammar alone and then went out to practise it in the street. This worked well for me. I also found that I repeated patterns to myself and held imaginary conversations with people in certain situations, for example: the post office or at the bank. In your own experience of language learning, what worked for you?*

Pause for thought

> *What is your preferred learning style for foreign languages? Do you think that your preferred learning style has influenced your teaching style? If the answer is yes, how has it influenced your teaching?*

Many researchers, including Reid (1987) and Nunan (1989) believe that identifying and accommodating the learning style preferences of our students may have wide-ranging implications in the area of

UNIT 3: Methodology and Classroom Practice

curriculum design, materials development, student orientation, and teacher-training.

Question 6

> *I recently ran a two-day seminar in Germany designed to improve the negotiating skills of buyers from a well-known car manufacturer. The participants were not all German. Two participants were French and another was from Hong Kong. My aim, in brief, was to provide the group with the opportunity to learn by doing. After an initial period of theory, most of the course was given over to role-play. During the seminar I made several observations concerning learner behaviour.*
> - *Some learners seemed more concerned with grammatical accuracy. Even during the role-plays, they constantly asked me questions about correct grammar and correct pronunciation. Furthermore, although I was not an active participant in any of the role-plays, these learners made constant eye contact with me during the role-plays in a way that suggested they wanted me to correct them.*
> - *Some learners seemed more concerned with getting the message across than with accuracy. Sometimes, their speed of delivery was so fast and the inaccuracies so many, that it was difficult to understand what their message was.*
> - *Some learners were reluctant to take part in the role-plays. They seemed more concerned with their dictionaries and grammar summaries. They made very little contribution to the activities and yet, I felt they were learning something. The problem was, they did not seem to be learning what I intended to teach them.*
>
> *What range of learning styles seems to be represented here?*

For several decades now, researchers have been developing models of learning styles. Learning styles can be defined as the characteristic manner and habitual ways we approach learning tasks. Research into the concept of learning styles has generally investigated four areas. These areas are:

- cognitive
- affective and social

UNIT 3: Methodology and Classroom Practice

- perceptual (sensory)
- environmental.

The cognitive view of learning sees the learner as someone who takes an active part in the learning process, as someone who is an active processor of information. Cognitive learning styles have been investigated by several researchers. They include: Kolb (1984), Kolb et al (1995), Honey and Mumford (1982), and Willing (1988). We mentioned Kolb's (1984) model, and Honey and Mumford's (1982) model in section 9.3 of this chapter.

In a comprehensive study undertaken in Australia in 1988, Willing (1988) also investigated the cognitive styles of ESL learners. Essentially, Willing suggests that learning styles develop from a number of variables.

- Psychological and cognitive make-up.
- Upbringing.
- Socio-cultural background, schooling and previous educational experiences in a particular subject, such as English language learning.
- Perceptions of their own strengths and weaknesses.

Willing makes a distinction between what he calls field-independent and field-dependent learners. He cross-types these with community and authority-oriented learners. Field-independent learners (also called analytic learners) tend to concentrate on the details of language, such as grammar rules, and enjoy analysing words and sentences. They are sometimes unable to see the big picture because of their attention to detail.

Field-dependent learners (also known as global learners) tend to focus on the whole picture without paying too much attention to the details. For example, they are more concerned with conveying an idea than whether or not the way in which they communicate the idea is grammatically correct.

Question 7

Imagine you have been asked to teach a two-day seminar, in-company, in presentation skills. The aim of your course is to enable learners to make effective presentations for the company.

UNIT 3: Methodology and Classroom Practice

> *You soon realise that your learners are mainly analytic learners. How will you deal with this situation?*

Some researchers, for example Arnold (1999) and Horwitz and Young (1991), have focused attention on affective strategies. Learning is an emotional experience, and the feelings that the learning process evoke will have a direct and crucial influence on the success or failure of that learning. We can see the importance of the affective factor if we consider its relationship with the cognitive aspects.

Cognitive theories tell us that learners will learn when they are able to make and strengthen associations between new and already-known information and to restructure this information. Examples of cognitive strategies are: guessing from context, analysing, and taking systematic notes.

However, cognitive theories assume that the affective factor of motivation actually exists. In other words, in order to actively think about something, learners must have the desire to think about it.

Question 8

> *Imagine you have been asked to teach a two-day course in English for Marketing in a global company. Management decided that they needed to upgrade the language skills of their people in the Marketing Department. When you arrive on Monday morning, you discover that motivation is not only low, but the learners are almost hostile in their attitude towards you. As the morning progresses, you find out that the learners do not want to participate. They feel that their language skills are already excellent and that management did not ask them to attend classes. Your learners feel that they were ordered to attend and consequently, they feel insulted. What should you do?*

9.6: Conclusions

There is a growing body of research in the area of the learner, learning and learning strategies (Oxford, 2001). Teachers could conduct action research within their own classrooms so that they can get to know their students better and provide the strategy instruction that many students could benefit from. Although such research would be difficult in many

UNIT 3: Methodology and Classroom Practice

EIB situations (in-company seminars for example) teachers can, nevertheless, be sensitive to the factors that may influence their learners. Such factors are: motivation, age, gender, cultural background, learning environment, and previous language learning experience.

Researchers have developed several assessment tools to classify and identify learning styles. For those of you who are interested, we suggest that you look at two assessment tools that were specifically designed to identify the learning styles of second language learners. The first tool identifies perceptual learning style preferences. The second tool was designed to identify groupwork style preferences. These assessment tools are:

- Reid's (1987) Perceptual Learning-Style Preference Questionnaire (PLSPQ)
- Kinsella's (1996) Work Style Survey.

Reid's study is groundbreaking because before it, there was no published research which described the perceptual learning style preferences of non-native speakers. You might want to download Reid's PLSPQ from http://lookingahead.heinle.com/filing/l-styles.htm and fill it in for yourself. In this way, you might be able to find out something about your own learning style.

9.7: Answers to Questions

Question 1
Depending on the group and their level, you could "drill" the important phrases so that they become automatic. For example, phrases concerning the functions of agreeing, disagreeing, suggesting, giving opinions etc. However, we would suggest that these "drills" are short and sharp. Having said that, my preferred method is to have students use the language in context. This means setting up role-plays and/or simulations. Another way would be to give students a couple of minutes to decide on which of the phrases they might want to use in the role-play and to internalise them. My experience of most in-company courses suggests that this is perhaps the most appropriate method. Many business people associate drilling with school. In the training room, they want to be treated like adults and not as school children. Further, learning tends to occur best when learners feel comfortable and unthreatened. The constant correction of the behaviourists could discourage and demotivate.

UNIT 3: Methodology and Classroom Practice

Question 2
A wide variety of learning methods have evolved, which have come to be known as experiential learning methods. All of these focus on the learner being offered an experience, followed by reflection and making sense of that experience. Of particular relevance for EIB training are structured group activities and role-plays. The idea behind these activities is that the group undertakes an experience, after which they discuss their thoughts and feelings about the experience and apply the new learning to the real situation. Feedback from other participants and from the teacher is necessary in order for the new learning to occur.

Question 3
Cultures which are used to traditional methods from traditional guru-style teachers, for example: China, Spain, and Arab countries.

Question 4
By allowing for variety in teaching. This means variety in, for example:
- content
- the language skills
- pacing
- correction
- teaching focus - grammar, pronunciation, communication
- activities, e.g. whole-class teaching, groupwork and pairwork.

Question 5
Sinclair (1997) suggests that if we take a broad, rather than a narrow "Western" view of the concept of autonomy, we must respect the fact that different cultures will interpret autonomy in different ways. If we use a concept which recognises the relativity of autonomy, then there need be no cultural barriers to its promotion. It may indeed be regarded as a universal educational goal.

Question 6
At first glance, there seem to be three types of learning style represented here. First, learners who feel a need to focus on the details of language. Second, those learners who see only the big picture and who feel the need to deal only with communicating. Third, those learners who feel the need to study alone and from books. The idea of learning as a social or co-operative activity can lack appeal for these people.

Question 7
You have a difficult balancing act here. You have to satisfy your paymaster, who wants results, and at the same time you have the immediate problem of satisfying and motivating your group of learners. My own solution would be to:
- focus more on the linguistic structure (set phrases) of a presentation and, perhaps, give the learners practice in memorising the phrases.
- give feedback on both the effectiveness of their practice presentations and focus more than usual on grammatical accuracy. You could also make a note of the most common grammatical errors and give a feedback session to the whole class. You could also make a comprehensive note of the most common mistakes,

UNIT 3: Methodology and Classroom Practice

photocopy them and give them out so the learners have something concrete on which they can reflect.

Question 8

You have two choices. You can attempt to come to some kind of compromise with the learners themselves as to the content of the course and then get on with it. This would need sensitive handling. If it does not work, I would stop the class and see management immediately - even if this means losing two days pay! You have to protect yourself and your reputation.

UNIT 3: Methodology and Classroom Practice

Chapter 10

Evaluation and Assessment

10.1: Introduction
10.2: Objectives
10.3: Terminology and Key Concepts
10.4: Purpose of Tests
10.5: Desirable Characteristics of Tests
10.6: Classroom Assessment and Classroom Tests
10.7: Public Examinations
10.8: Reporting Test Results
10.9: In-house Tests
10.10: Assessing the Four Skills
10.11: Conclusions
10.12: Answers to Questions.

10.1: Introduction

This chapter deals with assessment and testing procedures. We shall cover a range of procedures, from formal testing, through continuous assessment to self- and peer assessment. Our main aim in the chapter is to give you ideas which may assist you when or if you have to design your own assessment methods or tests. For this reason, we have spent much of the chapter describing one public examination in Business

UNIT 3: Methodology and Classroom Practice

English. We hope it will give you some useful ideas. We have also set out guidelines for setting and marking tests. We hope these guidelines will be of practical use to you at some stage in your career.

10.2: Objectives

At the end of this chapter you will better understand:

- the purposes and types of assessment
- the characteristics of good assessment procedure
- classroom assessment and classroom testing
- how to design your own assessment methods.

Pre-reading tasks

At the end of the chapter we hope you will be able to answer the questions in the shaded box below. Perhaps you can answer some of these questions already even if you are a little uncertain. Try as many of the questions as you can and make a note of your ideas and opinions. When you have finished the text, come back and approach these questions again. How have your original answers changed?

> - Can you think of any courses in EIB where testing might be inappropriate?
> - Without using tests, how could you formally assess your learners? What would you assess? What methods would you use?
> - Is there a difference between testing pre-experience learners studying business-related subjects at educational institutions, and professionals with several years experience behind them? If there are differences, what are they?
> - How many other ways of grading results can you think of other than as a percentage figure or a letter grade? What are the advantages and disadvantages of these different methods?

UNIT 3: Methodology and Classroom Practice

10.3: Terminology and Key Concepts

Pause for thought

> *What is the difference (if any) between the terms assessment, testing and evaluation?*

There are a number of ways of collecting information on a learner's language ability or achievement. The terms testing and assessment are often used interchangeably. However, assessment is best understood as an umbrella term which includes one-off measurement instruments such as tests.

Assessment is also different from evaluation, which is concerned with the language programme as a whole and not only with the achievements of individual students. Proficiency assessment deals with the acquisition of language ability independent of a course of study. This kind of assessment is often done through commercial language-proficiency tests. Assessment of achievement establishes what students have learned in relation to a particular course of study.

Sometimes, assessment is carried out during the learning process for the purpose of collecting information in order to improve instruction. This is known as formative assessment. Assessment of a course carried out at the end of a course of study, and which often provides aggregated information on programme outcomes to educational authorities, is referred to as summative assessment.

Interpretation of results may be norm-referenced or criterion-referenced. Norm-referenced results rank learners in relation to each other, while criterion–referenced results describe learners' performance in terms of "can-do" statements, which detail the types of task that can be done in the target language.

The two key requirements for any assessment are that it should be both valid and reliable. Validity means that it assesses only the abilities it claims to assess. Reliability refers to consistency and is concerned with ascertaining to what degree scores are affected by measurement error. Variations in scores may be caused by factors unrelated to the ability being tested, for example: conditions of administration, test instructions, and fatigue. Such factors may result in inconsistent performance by test-takers. Consistency of test results over time can be estimated in terms of test-retest reliability whereby the same test or a similar test is given to a group of learners at different points in time.

UNIT 3: Methodology and Classroom Practice

10.4: Purpose of Tests

The reasons for assessment can be grouped under two main headings. The first heading would be assessment for feedback to aid learning. The second heading would be assessment to obtain a comparable measure of competence. Comparable measures are the reason for public examinations and for regular testing within educational institutions. Assessment as an aid to learning can reinforce learner confidence, involve learners in the learning process, and help them build on their strengths.

Self- and peer assessment can also be used to help teacher assessments. However, self- and peer assessment will only be valid if they are consistent. This will not be an easy task as even trained examiners need regular standardising meetings in order to achieve consistency. However, self- and peer assessment can help develop the independence that learners may need for their future progress and development as autonomous learners.

Brindley (2001) suggests that assessment may be carried out to collect information on learners' language proficiency or achievement and that this information can be used by stakeholders in the language learning programme. Stakeholders may have a variety of purposes.

- Selection: e.g. to determine whether learners have the language proficiency to undertake further study or to do certain jobs.
- Certification: e.g. to provide other people with a statement of language ability for employment purposes.
- Accountability: e.g. to provide educational funding authorities or relevant company departments with evidence that intended learning outcomes have been achieved.
- Diagnosis: e.g. to identify learners' strengths and weaknesses.
- Instructional decision-making: e.g. to decide what to present next or what to revise.
- Motivation: e.g. to encourage learners to study harder.

Within EIB, a distinction should be made between pre-experience learners and professionals with work experience. For example, students on a university programme will need assessment for certification purposes. Students wishing to follow an MBA programme in English will need an assessment for selection purposes.

However, for many EIB situations, tests may be inappropriate. On short intensive courses the time is, perhaps, better spent on input and practice. Furthermore, the real effect of, for example, a course in presentation skills or negotiating skills is likely to show itself some time after the course. However, clients do need some evidence of course outcomes, and they need to know that time and money have been effectively allocated. One company I worked for recognised the limitations of assessing short-term intensive courses and had their own assessment procedures in place. This involved agreeing course content with the individual participant's manager, teacher-assessment immediately after the course, and on-going self-assessment. If appropriate and feasible, feedback was also obtained from colleagues and clients. For example, if a participant followed a course in presentation skills so that s/he could regularly present to his/her multi-national team, the team was also asked for feedback.

10.5: Desirable Characteristics of Tests

All good tests have some common characteristics. Carroll (1980) refers to C.A.R.E. which stands for comparability, acceptability, relevance and economy. Bachman and Palmer (1996) talk of F.A.I.R. V.P. which stands for fairness, authenticity, impact, reliability, validity and practicality.

Within educational institutions, high reliability is crucial. Reliability is concerned with measuring consistently. To maximise reliability, tests may use objective testing formats such as multiple-choice with a large number of items. However, such formats provide little or no information on learners' ability to use language for communicative purposes.

With the widespread adoption of communicative language teaching principles, many language tests and assessments now include tasks which resemble the kinds of language-use situations that test-takers will encounter while using language for communicative purposes in everyday life. The kinds of tasks used in communicative assessment of proficiency or achievement typically include activities such as oral interviews, listening to and reading extracts from authentic texts and various kinds of authentic writing tasks which reflect real-life demands.

To establish the degree to which test results are stable and consistent various approaches can be used. For example:

UNIT 3: Methodology and Classroom Practice

- test/retest of the same candidates where the same test is given to a group at two different points in time
- alternate or parallel forms of the same test whereby a similar test is administered to a group of candidates
- split-half in which a test is divided into two halves and administered once. The two scores that are obtained can then be correlated.

With regard to test validity, the following questions should be addressed.

- What exactly does the test measure?
- What skills and/or language are being measured and why?
- How well does the test measure?
- Does the test correlate with outside criteria? For example: other exam marks, teachers' rating, TOEFL score and so on.
- What does the test look like to test-takers, test administrators and educators and so on?

As far as practicality is concerned, ease of administration should be considered along with ease of scoring, and ease of interpretation. For example, a user handbook could be issued to scorers. The handbook would deal with issues such as reliability, validity and the meaning of the scores.

Finally, the important question of the impact of assessment and testing on teaching and learning (known as washback) needs to be considered. All tests have a washback effect in the sense that the test will influence what is taught and how it is taught. Washback may be negative. For example, a test that uses mainly cloze may result in teachers spending too much time practising this type of question. A good test will prompt teachers to teach what learners need and in ways that enhance the learning process.

10.6: Classroom Assessment and Classroom Tests

Pause for thought

> *Is there a difference between formal tests and continuous classroom assessment? If your answer is, "Yes," how do they differ?*

UNIT 3: Methodology and Classroom Practice

Classroom assessment

Both formal testing and continuous classroom assessment are ways of assessing learners. However, the circumstances under which they are carried out can be very different. Most formal tests are done in silence and under strict supervision. Candidates are usually obliged to do the test in a certain time limit. Furthermore, they are not permitted to refer to books or to talk to other candidates. Learners are not involved in setting or marking the test.

In contrast, continuous assessment may be based on tasks carried out over a long period of time. In addition, learners may have some considerable influence over what the assessed task contains, and how it is graded. Learners may also use additional resources and discuss tasks with the teacher or their colleagues. So how and what can the teacher assess without using tests?

The grading of written assignments, done either in the classroom or as homework, is one of the most common formal ways of teacher assessment. Other activities can also be assessed. For example, reading and listening tasks where everyone can be assessed at the same time. Pair and group interactions can also be assessed. These interactions may be assessed over a period of time and, if it is available, a video camera can be used. On short courses, I have found the video-camera an invaluable resource when used carefully. However, because of time limitations, I have found it necessary to make quick judgements about what needs to be commented on, and to make a note of the counter number so that I can quickly find the right place on the tape for feedback sessions.

Self- and peer assessment may also have value as aids to learning. Self-assessment can assist learners to become good judges of their own strengths and weaknesses and to set realistic goals for themselves. Brindley (2001) claims that computer-adaptive assessment, which enables test-takers to receive immediate feedback on performance, could be effectively used for self-assessment. Furthermore, computerised versions of many proficiency tests are increasingly available (Educational Testing Service 1998). However, there are problems with self-assessment that need to be addressed.

First, self-assessment may seem threatening to many learners as it alters the traditional teacher-learner relationships. In some cultures, self-assessment may be resisted.

Second, research into self-assessment (e.g. Bachman and Palmer

UNIT 3: Methodology and Classroom Practice

1989) suggests that learners find it easier to say what they can not do rather than what they can do and that, therefore, such assessment may often be inaccurate. This has been my own experience when, for example, teaching presentation skills. Learners are often over-critical of their presentations while colleagues in the room are often very positive in their feedback.

Peer assessment in presentation skills classes can be extremely effective. Anonymous questionnaires, with peers filling in appropriate boxes to signal their responses to particular aspects of a presentation, can be very productive. There is no reason why this technique could not be extended to writing skills. There are good practical reasons for peer assessment in large classes where it is either undesirable or not possible for the teacher to assess all the tasks.

Peer and self-assessment can therefore be used to encourage learners to become self-directed. However, with learners unable to accurately estimate their own abilities, there are serious problems with the reliability of self-assessment.

Classroom tests

EIB tests may be administered as part of present situation analysis (PSA), to place, to check progress or to measure achievement or proficiency. As part of a PSA, companies may wish to test employees in order to determine which skill areas need attention. Teachers and management may then decide on the desirable target level of achievement, the time needed for this achievement and the cost.

A placement test may be used in order to group learners or to advise them which language classes to attend. Such tests may be used as part of an English for General Business Purposes (EGBP) programme and they usually have a test of reading, and perhaps a cloze passage so that scripts can be marked quickly and reliably.

Progress tests aim to measure mastery of part of a course of study while achievement tests measure mastery of a syllabus and may be used by educational institutions or by companies wishing to know whether targets have been achieved and the money has been well spent. Alternative or complementary procedures to testing achievement or progress are: structured observations of class work, progress grids, learning journals and project work. All these procedures could be developed as alternative means of measurement.

Proficiency tests attempt to measure how well students will perform in target language tasks. Most business-related tests offered by UK examining boards are task-based proficiency tests and it is to these that we shall now turn.

10.7: Public Examinations

Several UK examining bodies offer examinations in Business English: the London Chamber of Commerce and Industry (LCCI), Oxford and University of Cambridge Local Examinations Syndicate (UCLES). The design and format of these exams are similar, with all four skills tested separately. Written tasks include completing forms, writing memos, letters and reports while understanding is tested using objective exercise types such as multiple-choice, matching and gap-filling. In order to get a better understanding of these tests, we shall look in detail at one test suite - the UCLES Business English Certificates (BEC).

BEC are certificated examinations which can be taken on six fixed dates per year at approved centres authorised for BEC. They are aimed at individual learners who want to obtain a business-related English language qualification.

BEC was originally developed in the Asia-Pacific region for tests of English language in a business context. Recognition of the qualification is increasing rapidly as a number of companies are using the examination as a focus for in-company training courses. Many universities in the UK also recognise BEC Higher as a suitable entry requirement for international students wishing to follow business-related courses of study. In 2001 there were about 58000 candidates for BEC in over 50 countries.

BEC is divided into three levels: BEC Preliminary, BEC Vantage and BEC Higher. These levels correspond to the five ALTE/Cambridge levels for language assessment, and to the Council of Europe's framework for modern languages. It is also linked to the UK Qualification and Curriculum Authority's National Standards for Literacy, within the National Qualifications Network (NQF). At all three levels, the business aspect of the examination can be seen in the vocabulary, the types of text and the situations presented in the tasks.

There is a major ALTE project currently underway, which aims to establish a series of "can-do" statements describing what language users are able to do in a particular language at particular levels. For example, the BEC can-do statement for listening and speaking at

UNIT 3: Methodology and Classroom Practice

Preliminary levels is given below.

- Can take and pass on most messages that are likely to require attention during a normal working day.
- Can take part in routine meetings or seminars on familiar topics, exchanging factual information through question and answer or through receiving instructions.
- Can express his/her opinions, and present arguments to a limited extent.

The BEC can-do statement for reading at Preliminary level is also given here.

- Can understand standard types of letters such as orders, complaints, appointments, enquiries, etc and pass these on to the appropriate person for action.
- Can understand the general meaning of reports dealing with, for example, conditions and advice.
- Can understand instructions, procedures etc within own job area.

The can-do statement for writing at Preliminary level is as follows.

- Can write a non-routine letter where this is restricted to matters of fact.
- Can write a report of a factual nature, but if the report is for external consumption her/his work will require checking and correcting.
- Can draft straightforward instructions, regulations etc.

The BEC examinations cover the four language skills: reading, writing, listening and speaking. In BEC Preliminary, the tests of reading and writing are combined on one question paper. In BEC Vantage and Higher, there are separate reading and writing papers. Apart from this, the format of the examination at the different levels remains the same. We shall now look in more detail at the content of BEC Preliminary and at how it is assessed.

Reading and writing

The reading examination consists of seven parts. Each part has different input, for example: notices, graphics, or articles. There is a main skill

UNIT 3: Methodology and Classroom Practice

focus for each part, for example: reading for detailed factual information, reading and understanding of real world notices, or reading for gist and specific information. There are a variety of responses, for example: multiple-choice, matching, note completion and cloze.

All 45 answers for these components are assessed simply as right or wrong, with one mark available for each. Minor spelling mistakes at Preliminary and Vantage level are tolerated, and both British and American spellings are accepted.

The test of writing consists of two tasks. Each task has different input. The input for task one may be rubric only with the layout of the output task, for example, a memo or letter. The input for task two may be business correspondence, for example: fax, letter or e-mail. Test-takers may be required to write a message, a memo, a letter, a fax or an e-mail in order to apologise, to ask permission, to give instructions and so on.

An impression mark is awarded to each piece of writing. For each task, a General Impression Mark Scheme is used in conjunction with a Task-Specific Mark Scheme, which focuses on criteria specific to each particular task.

For Part 1, examiners use the mark schemes to assess task achievement only. For Part 2, examiners use the mark schemes to assess both language and task achievement.

Both mark schemes are divided in to five bands. So the General Impression Mark Scheme for Part 1 has the following band descriptors.

Band 5: Very good attempt at task, achieving all content points. Minimal effort required by reader.
Band 4: Good attempt at task, achieving all content points. Some effort may be required by reader.
Band 3: Satisfactory attempt at task, achieving 2 content points.
Band 2: Poor attempt at task; no content points achieved, has little relevance; task possibly misunderstood.
Band 1: No relevant response or too little language to assess.

The General Impression Mark Scheme for Part 2 has the following descriptor for Band 3 and clearly reveals the focus on both achievement and language.

UNIT 3: Methodology and Classroom Practice

Band 3
- ➢ Reasonable achievement of the task set.
- ➢ Three or four content points achieved.
- ➢ A number of errors present, but are mainly non-impeding.
- ➢ Adequate range of structure and vocabulary.
- ➢ Organisation and cohesion satisfactory.
- ➢ Register and format reasonable.
- ➢ Satisfactory effect on reader.

Acceptable performance at BEC Preliminary is represented by Band 3. Each writing task is marked by a trained examiner. Examiners mark in teams, monitored by team leaders. Each marking session is led by a principal examiner.

Listening

The listening part of the examination consists of four parts. Each part has input, for example: short conversations, short telephone conversations, monologues or interviews. Each part has a main skill focus, for example: listening for specific information or listening for gist. There are a variety of responses, for example: multiple-choice, gap-filling or note-taking.

All answers for these 30 items are assessed simply as right or wrong. As for BEC Preliminary reading, minor errors in spelling are tolerated and both British and American spelling are accepted.

Speaking

The standard test format is two candidates and two examiners: an assessor and an interlocutor. Part 1 of the examination is a conversation between the interlocutor and each candidate. There is general interaction and social language. Part 2 is a mini-presentation by each candidate on a business theme. The focus of Part 2 is the organisation of a larger unit of discourse, giving information and expressing opinions. Part 3 of the examination is a two-way conversation between candidates followed by further prompting from the interlocutor.

Each examiner marks a candidate's performance independently. The interlocutor, who speaks to the candidates, gives a single mark based on a global achievement scale. The assessor gives four separate marks based on separate scales for grammar and vocabulary, discourse management and interactive communication.

Grammar and vocabulary refers to range and accuracy as well as the appropriate use of grammatical and lexical forms. At BEC Preliminary, a range of grammar and vocabulary is needed to deal with the tasks. Minor errors and use of inappropriate vocabulary should not obscure meaning.

Discourse management refers to the coherence, extent and relevance of each candidate's performance. All contributions should be good enough for the task. Some inappropriate utterances are tolerated.

Pronunciation refers to the candidate's ability to make comprehensible utterances. At Preliminary level, use of stress, rhythm, intonation and clarity of sound are examined although some strain on the part of the listener is tolerated.

Interactive communication refers to the candidate's ability to take an active part in the development of the discourse. At Preliminary level, candidates should be able to take turns and to sustain the interaction by initiating and responding appropriately. Some hesitations are tolerated.

Grading and results

Each skill represents 25% of the total marks. A candidate's overall grade is based on the total score gained in all papers. It is not necessary to achieve a satisfactory level in each paper in order to pass the examination.

For all levels of BEC, candidates receive statements of results which, in addition to their grades, show a graphical profile of their performance in each skill. These are shown against the scale Exceptional, Good, Borderline and Weak.

10.8: Reporting Test Results

We have already seen above that the practice of reporting results as a percentage, a letter grade or just a pass/fail has largely been replaced (or is in the process of being replaced) by band descriptors. These are useful because in order to understand test results, users need to know what specific criteria they refer to.

Descriptors can be specific to a particular skill or they can give an overall assessment. For maximum information, skills-based descriptors are appropriate. For ease of reporting, a final overall descriptor may be used. Most scales operate with five, seven or nine bands. The English

UNIT 3: Methodology and Classroom Practice

Speaking Union (ESU) produced a nine-scale level. The middle five are presented here and may be useful for those wishing to develop their own descriptors for in-house tests.

Level 7: Uses the language effectively in most situations with few problems. Communication is effective and consistent, with few hesitations and uncertainties.

Level 6: Uses the language competently in a variety of situations but with noticeable problems. Communication is usually effective. When difficulties arise, communication is recovered with ease.

Level 5: Uses the language adequately in familiar situations. Rather frequent problems but usually succeeds in communicating general message.

Level 4: Uses a basic range of language sufficient for familiar and non-pressurising situations. Frequent problems restrict prolonged communication but message communicated with repetition or assistance.

Level 3: Uses a limited range of language adequate for short communication and practical needs. Problems cause frequent breakdown of communication but message usually recovered with repetition and assistance.

For most in-house testing purposes, four or five bands are usually enough. Developing suitable descriptors takes time, and it is a good idea to look at what is already available and adapt it. Band descriptors should be carefully and positively worded with a clear progression through the bands. They may also be linked to percentages or grades for those authorities that expect percentages or grades.

The benefits of band descriptors are that they give real information to learners, greater fairness and standardisation, and that they can save time.

Pause for thought

> *Consider some of the courses that you are teaching now or that you have taught in the past. Which of the ESU levels do or did they correspond to?*

10.9: In-House Tests

For many intensive short courses designed for experienced learners, formal assessment may be inappropriate because of lack of time. However, those managers responsible for sending their employees on courses usually need some kind of feedback. This may take the form of a short report from the trainer/teacher on each of the participants. These reports are often based on continuous assessment of the particular participant's performance and attendance. Sometimes, more complex and on-going processes are already in place. For example, while working in-company at ENEL - the Italian state electricity company - course objectives and the time needed to reach those objectives were specified after diagnostic testing. Achievement tests were then taken after the specified time limit, which was, in this particular case, about three months.

Some pre-experience learners at educational institutions may work towards one of the public examinations described above. However, many educational institutions will prepare their own tests. If this is the case, it is vitally important for setters of tests to apply the principles laid out in section 10.5. It is important because significant decisions are taken on the basis of test results. Learners pass or fail, are successful or unsuccessful in job applications and have their morale boosted or undermined.

Tests do not have to be written from scratch. The design of tests should be based on existing models, but adapted and modified until they are suitable for the particular situation.

Dudley-Evans and St John (1998) describe in some detail the process required to develop and mark tests so that they are both reliable and valid. The setting procedure is summarised below.

- Look at course objectives, materials and test specifications.
- Select what will be tested.
- Collect ideas for input and ideas for model questions.
- Draft questions and answer key and mark scheme.
- Circulate questions for feedback.
- Re-draft questions if necessary and change answer key and mark scheme.
- Type the question paper.
- Have the papers proof-read.
- Check the details again.

UNIT 3: Methodology and Classroom Practice

- Print the papers.

If you need a more detailed description of test setting, then read Weir (1993: pp19-29).

Test setting should involve several people. All the objectives selected for testing should be course objectives, and they should have been covered in the teaching. For those who make comments on the draft questions, it might be a good idea for them to state what they think it is that is being tested. This is important for validity. The comment-redraft process should continue until there is consistency.

As far as reliability is concerned, Dudley-Evans and St John (1998) suggest the following mark scheme.

- Select a range of sample scripts and make them anonymous.
- Hold standardisation meetings for all markers.
- Mark sample scripts according to initial key and scheme.
- Compare marks awarded, adjust and agree final key and mark scheme.
- Mark scripts applying agreed scheme.
- Meet to check borderline cases and problem scripts.

What is important here is that the group of markers agrees exactly what will be accepted and then sticks to that for all scripts. One suggestion is to agree on benchmark scripts which are examples of each band. All borderline cases should be reviewed and discussed.

10.10: Assessing the Four Skills

Writing

When testing writing, a number of issues need to be considered. The first is the categories of writing to be tested. Among the categories that can be chosen are: essays, personal or academic writing, letters, CVs, summaries and so on. Another issue that needs to be addressed is whether or not writing tests in EIB should reflect the real-life nature of purpose and audience. In many real-life business situations there has to be an immediate written response (such as sending an e-mail) to the reading of a document. One of the features of the BEC examinations is this integration of reading and writing tasks.

UNIT 3: Methodology and Classroom Practice

Decisions must also be taken on what is to be assessed. We have already seen that the BEC examinations look at both language and content of written tests. Whatever the criteria chosen, they have to be made clear to the scorers.

Design of writing tests can be improved as follows.

- Giving more than one piece of writing to increase reliability.
- Setting tasks within reach of all. The purpose of the test is to elicit samples of student writing.
- Making tasks clear and specific with full instruction.
- Pre-testing - if only on yourself or colleagues.

Question 1

Look at the following question (written in smaller font), which has been taken from part 2 of a BEC writing examination. Consider the text and then answer the questions below it.

Read this part of a letter from Peter Lam, the owner of a clothes shop.

I have recently returned to Hong Kong after a short holiday in England. While I was there, I bought one of your shirts in London and I was so impressed with the quality that I asked the shop for your name and address.

I am interested in selling the shirts in my own shop and would probably make an initial purchase of about 100 shirts. I assume that there is a discount for large orders and would be grateful if you would send me a price list with details of discounts.

I look forward to hearing from you.

Write a letter to Mr Lam:

- *thanking him for his letter*
- *saying that you are enclosing a price list*
- *informing him what discount you can give*
- *telling him the colours in which the shirts are available.*

Questions
1. *Consider the advantages and disadvantages of the input material.*
2. *For what BEC level is the question suitable?*
3. *Identify the audience and purpose given in the task.*
4. *What will you assess?*

UNIT 3: Methodology and Classroom Practice

Reading

Unless the examination is an integrated one, the question types selected should require the minimum amount of writing. Marking is therefore much more objective and quicker.

EIB reading tests will usually have several short texts and answering the questions should not be possible without the texts, for example, because of background knowledge.

Decisions have to be taken with regard to exactly what is being tested, for example: understanding lexical items and deriving meaning from context, understanding and responding to graphic symbols, identifying the central idea of a passage or its tone and style.

Speaking

Spoken tests are usually interactive (see the description of BEC examination in section 10.8). The interaction may be between candidate and examiner or between several candidates acting out a role-play or simulation. Unless the interaction is taped, the onus is on the examiners to assess each person rapidly and effectively.

A standard and effective procedure is to use band descriptors (see section 10.8 and 10.9). Once again, it is necessary to clarify exactly what it is that is being tested, for example: range and accuracy of grammar and vocabulary and/or discourse management and/or pronunciation and/or the ability to communicate meaning.

For in-house tests, it may be enough to have two parts to the spoken test. The first part may be a moment or two of small talk in order to set the student at ease. The second part may require some kind of stimulus, for example: a photograph or other non-verbal devices.

On short intensive courses in meeting skills, negotiating skills or presentation skills, we would suggest that formal testing is inappropriate. Continuous assessment may be better here, along with peer assessment and video recordings of the interactions.

Listening

The issues surrounding the testing of listening are the same as those that surround the testing of reading. For example, should the process be tested separately or integrated with speaking and/or writing as in real life? For EIB, we suggest that the listening test is integrated and includes activities such as form-filling, message-taking and memo-writing.

10.11: Conclusions

We hope that you will be better able to develop your own tests in whatever situations you find yourself. We have discussed how self- and peer assessment may be used, and we have suggested outlines for setting and marking more formal tests in such a way that the tests will be both valid and reliable.

We have also looked at the use of band descriptors for marking written and spoken production and we hope that you will be able to produce your own band descriptors in your situation.

Finally, you are recommended to follow up the chapter by looking at some of the recommended books. In particular, Weir (1993), and Bachman and Palmer (1996) are good on test construction.

10.12: Answers to questions

Question 1
- Although this is a test of writing skills, candidates are required to use reading skills before they begin writing. However, this task is designed to simulate a real-life situation in which reading and writing are integrated.
- BEC Preliminary.
- The audience is a potential buyer. The purpose is to thank, to inform and persuade.
- Language and task achievement.

UNIT 3: Methodology and Classroom Practice

Unit Bibliography

Alptekin, C. (2002) "Towards intercultural communicative competence in ELT," in ELT Journal, Vol. 56, No. 1.

Arnold, J. (ed) (1999) Affect in Language Learning. Cambridge, Cambridge University Press.

Arva, V. and Medgyes, P. (2000) "Native and non-native teachers in the classroom," in System, Vol. 28.

Ausubel, D., Novak, J. and Hanesian, H. (1978) Educational Psychology: a Cognitive View. Holt, Rinehart and Winston.

Bachman, L, and Palmer, A. (1996) Language Testing in Practice. Oxford, Oxford University Press.

BBC for Business Videos 1999 It's a Deal. London BBC.

Bickel, B. and Truscello, D. (1996) "New opportunities for learning: styles and strategies with computers," in TESOL Journal, Vol. 6, No.1.

Bonny, C. (1994) The Business Writing Pocketbook. London. Melrose.

Bernstein, B. (1971) "On the classification and framing of educational knowledge," from Young, M. (ed.), Knowledge and Control. London, Collier Macmillan.

UNIT 3: Methodology and Classroom Practice

Boyatzis, R. and Kolb, D. (1995) "From learning styles to learning skills: the executive skills profile," in *Journal of Management Psychology*, Vol. 10, No. 5.

Brindley, G. (2001) "Assessment," from Carter, R. and Nunan, D. (eds.), *The Cambridge Guide to Teaching English to Speakers of Other Languages*. Cambridge, Cambridge University Press.

Brown. D. (1994) *Principles of Language Learning and Teaching*. New Jersey, Prentice Hall.

Brown, D (2001) *Teaching by Principles: An Interactive Approach to Language Pedagogy*. New York, Pearson Education.

Brumby, S. and Wada, M. (1990) *Team Teaching*. London, Longman.

Brumfit, C. and Roberts, J. (1983) *A Short Introduction to Language and Language Teaching*. London, Batsford.

Burnard, P. (1989) Teaching *Interpersonal Skills – A Handbook of Experiential Learning for Health Professionals*. London, Chapman and Hall.

Bygate, M. (1987) *Speaking*. Oxford, Oxford University Press.

Bygate, M.; Tonkyn, A. and Williams, E. (eds.), (1994) *Grammar and the Language Teacher*. Hemel Hempstead, Prentice Hall International.

Bygate, M. (2001) "Speaking," from Carter, R. and Nunan, D. (eds.), *Teaching English to Speakers of Other Languages*. Cambridge, Cambridge University Press.

Byrne, D. (1986) *Teaching Oral English*. Harlow, Pearson Education.

Canale, M. (1983) "From communicative competence to communicative language pedagogy," from Richards, J. and Schmidt, R. (eds.), *Language and Communication*. London, Longman.

Carrel, P; Devine, J, and Eskey D. (Eds) (1988) *Interactive Approaches to Second Language Reading*. Cambridge, Cambridge University Press.

UNIT 3: Methodology and Classroom Practice

Carroll, B. (1980) <u>Testing Communicative Performance: an Interim Study</u>. Oxford, Pergamon.

Carter, R. and McCarthy, M. (1997) <u>Exploring Spoken English</u>. Cambridge, Cambridge University Press.

Casler, K; Palmer, D; Raimond, P, and Woodbridge, T. (1989) <u>Business Assignments</u>. Oxford, Oxford University Press.

Chomsky, N. (1964) "Review of B.F. Skinner, 'Verbal Behaviour'," in <u>Language</u>, Vol. 35.

Cinneide, B. (1997) "The role and effectiveness of case studies: student performance in case study vs "theory" examinations," in <u>Journal of European Industrial Training</u>, Vol. 21, No. 1.

Comfort, J. (1984) <u>Business Reports in English</u>. Cambridge, Cambridge University Press.

Cook, G. (1989) <u>Discourse</u>. Oxford, Oxford University Press.

Cotton, G. (1996) "Role-play set to boom," in <u>Management Development Review</u>, Vol. 9, No.3.

Courtney, M. (1996) "Talking to learn: selecting and using peer group oral tasks," in <u>ELT Journal</u>, Vol. 50, No. 4.

Crookes, G. and Chaudron, C. (1991) "Guidelines for classroom language teaching," in Celce-Murcia, M. (ed.), <u>Teaching English as a Second or Foreign Language</u>. New York, Newbury House.

Donna, S. (2000) <u>Teach Business English</u>. Cambridge, Cambridge University Press.

Dudley-Evans, T. and St John, M. (1998) <u>Developments in English for Specific Purposes.</u> Cambridge, Cambridge University Press.

Easton, G. (1992) <u>Learning from Case Studies</u>. Hemel Hempstead, Prentice-Hall.

Edge, J. and Richards, K. (eds.), (1993) Teachers Develop Teachers Research. London, Heinemann.

Educational Testing Service, (1998) TOEFL 1998-99. Information bulletin for computer-based testing. Princeton, NJ, Educational Testing Service.

Feinstein, A.; Mann, S. and Corsun, D. (2002) "Charting the experiential territory. Clarifiying definitions and uses of computer simulations, games, and role-play," in The Journal of Management Development, Vol. 21, No. 10.

Fisher, R. and Ury, W. (1991) Getting to Yes. London. Business Books Ltd.

Flowerdew, L. (1998) "A cultural perspective on groupwork," in ELT Journal, Vol. 52, No. 4.

Guirdham, M. (1990) Interpersonal Skills at Work. Hemel Hempsted, Prentice Hall International.

Haines, S. (1995) "For and Against Pairwork," in Modern English Teacher, Vol. 4, No. 1.

Harmer, J. (1991) The Practice of English Language Teaching. Harlow, Longman Group UK Ltd.

Harmer, J. (2001) The Practice of English Language Teaching. Harlow, Pearson Education.

Hawley, D. and Richardson, B. (1995) "The case study session as a control system," in Industrial and Commercial Training, Vol. 27, No. 6.

Hindle, T. (1998) Making Presentations. London, Dorling Kindersly.

Hofstede, G. (1991) Cultures and Organisations. London, McGraw-Hill.

Hollett, V. (1994) Business Opportunities. Oxford, Oxford University Press.

UNIT 3: Methodology and Classroom Practice

Holliday, A. (1994a) "Student Culture and English Language Education: an international perspective," in Language Curriculum and Culture, Vol. 7, No. 2.

Holliday, A. (1994b) Appropriate Methodology and Social Context. Cambridge, Cambridge University Press.

Honey, P. and Mumford, A. 1982. Manual of learning styles. Maidenhead, Berkshire.

Honey, P. and Mumford, A. (1983) Using Your Learning Styles. Maidenhead, Berkshire.

Honey, P. (2001) "E-learning: a performance appraisal and some suggestions for improvement," in The Learning Organisation, Vol. 8, No. 5.

Horwitz, E. and Young, D. (eds.), (1991) Language Anxiety: From Theory and Research to Classroom Implications. Englewood Cliffs, Prentice Hall.

Hsu, E. (1989) "Role-event gaming simulation in management education: a conceptual framework and review," in Simulation and Gaming, Vol. 20, No. 4.

Hutchinson, T. and Waters, A. (1987) English for Specific Purposes. Cambridge, Cambridge University Press.

Jackson, K. (1984) "Art of solving problems," Bulmershe-Comino Problem-solving Project. Bulmershe College of Higher Education.

Jennings, D. (1996) "Strategic management and the case method," in Journal of Management Development, Vol. 15, No. 9.

Johnson, K. (2001) An Introduction to Foreign Language Teaching and Learning. Harlow, Pearson Education Limited.

Jolles, R. (2005) How to Run Seminars and Workshops: Presentation Skills for Consultants, Trainers and Teachers. John Wiley and Sons Inc.

UNIT 3: Methodology and Classroom Practice

Kerridge, D. (1996) <u>International Business Role-plays</u>. Addlestone, Delta Publishing.

Kinsella, K. (1996) "Designing group work that supports and enhances diverse classroom work styles," in <u>TESOL Journal</u>, Vol. 6, No. 1.

Klippel, F. (1984) <u>Keep Talking</u>. Cambridge, Cambridge University Press.

Knowles, M. (1980) <u>The Modern Practice of Adult Education</u>. Adult Education Company.

Kolb, D. (1984) <u>Experiential Learning: Experience as the Source of Learning and Development</u>. Englewood Cliffs, Prentice Hall.

Kolb, D.; Rubin, I. and McIntyre, J. (1974) <u>Organisational Psychology – An Experiential Approach</u>. Englewood Cliffs, Prentice-Hall.

Kolb, D., Osland, J. & Rubin, I. (1995) <u>Organisational Behaviour: an Experiential Approach</u>. Englewood Cliffs, N.J.: Prentice Hall.

Krashen, S. (1981) <u>Second Language Acquisition and Second Language Learning</u>. Pergamon.

Kumaravadivelu, B. (2001) "Towards a Postmethod Pedagogy," in <u>TESOL Quarterly</u>, Vol. 35, No. 4.

Kumaravadivelu. B. (2005) <u>Understanding Language Teaching: From Method to Postmethod.</u> Lawrence Erlbaum Associates Inc.

Kumaravadivelu, B. (2007) <u>Cultural Globalisation and Language Education</u>. Yale University Press.

Lewis, M. (1996) "Implications of a lexical view of language," from Willis, J. and Willis, D. (eds.), <u>Challenge and Change in Language Teaching</u>. Oxford, Heinemann.

Lewis, M. (1997) <u>Implementing the Lexical Approach</u>. Language Teaching Publications.

UNIT 3: Methodology and Classroom Practice

Lightbown, P. and Spada, N. (2006) How Languages are Learned. Oxford, Oxford University Press.

Littlewood, W. (2000) "Do Asian students really want to listen and obey?" in ELT Journal, Vol. 54, No. 1.

Luk, J. and Lin, A. (2006) Classroom Interactions as Cross-cultural encounters: Native Speakers in EFL Lessons. Lawrence Erlbaum Associates Inc, US.

McCarthy, M. (1991) Discourse Analysis for Language Teachers. Cambridge, Cambridge University Press.

McKenna, S. (1999) "Organisational learning: "live" case studies and the consulting process," in Team Management Performance, Vol. 5, No. 4.

Medyges, P. (1994) The Non-Native Teacher. London, Macmillan.

Mole, J. (1995) Mind your Manners. London, Nicholas Brealey.

Nelson, G. (1995) "Cultural differences in learning styles," in Reid, J. (ed.), Learning Styles in the ESL/EFL Classroom. Boston, Heinle & Heinle.

Nelson-Jones, R. (2006) Human Relationship Skills. Routledge.

Nunan, D. (1989) "Hidden agendas: the role of the learner in programme implementation," in Johnson, R. (ed.), The second language curriculum. Cambridge, Cambridge University Press.

Nunan, D. (1995) Language Teaching Methodology. Hemel Hempstead, Prentice Hall Europe.

Nunan, D. (2000) "Seven Hypotheses About Language Teaching and Learning," in TESOL Matters, Vol.10, No. 2. Available from http://www.tesol.org/pubs/articles/2000/tm0006-01.html [Accessed 9 Oct 2002]

Oxford, R. (1990) <u>Language learning strategies: What every teacher should know</u>. Boston, Heinle & Heinle.

Oxford, R. and Burry-Stock, J. (1995) "Assessing the use of language learning strategies worldwide with ESL/EFL version of the strategy inventory for language learning (SILL)," in <u>System</u>, Vol. 23, No. 2.

Oxford, R. and Green, J. (1996) "Language learning histories: learners and teachers helping each other understand learning styles and strategies," in <u>TESOL Journal</u>, Vol. 6, No. 1.

Oxford, R., Hollaway, M. and Murillo, D. (1992) "Language learning styles: research and practical considerations for teaching in the multicultural tertiary ESL/EFL classroom," in <u>System</u>, Vol. 20, No. 4.

Oxford, R. (2001) "Language learning strategies," from Carter, R. and Nunan, D. (eds.), <u>Teaching English to Speakers of Other languages</u>. Cambridge, Cambridge University Press.

Pellone, G. (1991) "Learning theories and computers in TAFE education," in <u>Australian Journal of Educational Technology</u>, Vol. 7, No. 1 Available at: <u>http://www.ascilite.org.au/ajet/ajet7/pellone.html</u> [Accessed 7 Nov 2002]

Porter Ladousse, G. (1987) <u>Role-play</u>. Oxford, Oxford University Press.

Prabhu, N. (1987) <u>Second Language Pedagogy</u>. Oxford, Oxford University Press.

Prabhu, N. (1990) "There is No Best Method – Why?" in <u>TESOL Quarterly</u>, Vol. 24, No. 2.

Prashnig, B. (2006) <u>Learning Styles in Action</u>. Network Education Press Ltd.

Rao, Z. (2001) "Matching teaching styles with learning styles in East Asian contexts," in <u>International TESL Journal</u>, Vol. 2, No. 7.

Rees, W. and Porter, C. (2001) *Skills of Management*. Thompson Learning.

Rees, W. and Porter, C. (2002) "The use of case studies in management training and development. Part 1," in *Industrial and Commercial Training*, Vol. 34, No. 1.

Rees, W. and Porter, C. (2002) "The use of case studies in management training and development. Part 2," in *Industrial and Commercial Training*, Vol. 34, No. 3.

Reid, J. (1987) "The learning style preferences of ESL students," in *TESOL Quarterly*, Vol. 21, No. 1.

Reid, J. (ed.), (1995) *Learning styles in the ESL/EFL classroom*. Boston, Heinle & Heinle.

Reid, J. (1996) "A learning styles unit for the intermediate ESL/ EFL writing classroom," in *TESOL Journal*, Vol. 6, No. 1.

Reid, J. (ed.), (1998) *Understanding Learning Styles in the Second Language Classroom*. Prentice-Hall.

Richards, J. and Rodgers, T. (2001) *Approaches and Methods in Language Teaching – 2nd ed*. Cambridge, Cambridge University Press.

Richardson, B. (1994) "Towards a Comprehensive View of the Case Method in Management Development," in *Industrial and Commercial Training*, Vol. 26, No. 9.

Risager, K. (2007) *Language and Culture Pedagogy: From a National to a Transnational Paradigm.* Multilingual Matters.

Rogers, C. (1969) *Freedom to learn*. Columbus, Merrill.

Rosenberg, M. (2005) *In Business: Activities to Bring Business English to Life*. Cambridge, Cambridge University Press.

Ross, J. and Wright, L. (2000) "Participant-created case studies in professional training," in *Journal of Workplace Learning: Employee Counselling Today*, Vol. 12, No. 1.

Rubin, J. (1975) "What the 'good language learner' can teach us," in *TESOL Quarterly*, Vol. 9.

Scrivener, J. (1996) "ARC: A descriptive model for classroom work on language," from Willis, J. and Willis, D. (eds.), *Challenge and Change in Language Teaching*. Oxford, Heinemann.

Sinclair, B. (1997) "Learner autonomy: the cross cultural question," in *IATEFL Issues Newsletter*, No. 139 Available from: http://www.iatefl.org/frameset/frame.asp?../newsletters.asp~mainFrame [Accessed 7 Nov 2002]

Skehan, P. (1989) *Individual Differences in Second Language Learning*. London, Edward Arnold.

Skehan, P. (1998) *A Cognitive Approach to Language Learning*. Oxford, Oxford University Press.

Skinner, B. (1957) *Verbal Behaviour*. Appleton.

Stern, H. (1983) *Fundamental Concepts of Language Teaching*. Oxford, Oxford University Press.

Stern, H. (1992) *Issues and Options in Language Teaching*. Oxford, Oxford University Press.

Stuart, R. and Binstead, D. (1981) "The transfer of learning: Designing reality into management learning events," in Nixon, B. (ed.), *New Approaches to Management Development*. Gower Publications.

Sturman, P. (1992) "Team teaching: a case study from Japan," in Nunan, D. (ed.), *Collaborative Language Learning and Teaching*. Cambridge, Cambridge University Press.

Sweeney, S 1997 *English for Business Communication*. Cambridge, Cambridge University Press.

UNIT 3: Methodology and Classroom Practice

Thomas, D. and Inkson, K. (2004) <u>Cultural Intelligence: People Skills for Global Business</u>. Berrett-Koehler.

Ur, P. (1988) <u>Grammar Practice Activities</u>. Cambridge, Cambridge University Press.

Ur, P. (1996) <u>A Course in Language Teaching</u>. Cambridge, Cambridge University Press.

Watkins, M. (2003) <u>Business Communication</u>. Harvard Business School Press.

Weir, C. (1990) <u>Communicative Language Testing</u>. Hemel Hempstead, Prentice Hall International.

Weir, C. (1993) <u>Understanding and Developing Language Tests</u>. Hemel Hempstead, Prentice Hall International.

Wilberg, P. (1987) <u>One to One: A Teacher's Handbook</u>. Language Teaching Publications.

Williams, M. (1988) "Language Taught for Meetings and Language used for Meetings: Is there Anything in Common" in <u>Applied Linguistics</u> Vol. 9, No 1.

Williams, M. and Burden, R. (1997) <u>Psychology for Language Teachers</u>. Cambridge, Cambridge University Press.

Willing, K. (1988) <u>Learning styles in adult migrant education</u>. Adelaide: National Curriculum Resource Centre.

Willis, D. (1996) "Accuracy, fluency and conformity," from Willis, J. and Willis, D. (eds.), <u>Challenge and Change in Language Teaching</u>. Oxford, Heinemann.

Willis, J. (1996) "A flexible framework for task-based learning," from Willis, J. and Willis, D. (eds.), <u>Challenge and Change in Language Teaching</u>. Oxford, Heinemann.

Willis, J. and Willis, D. (eds.), (1996) <u>Challenge and Change in Language Teaching</u>. London, Heinemann.

Wolfe, J. (1998) "New developments in the use of simulations and games for learning," in <u>Journal of Workplace Learning</u>, Vol. 10, No. 6/7.

Wood, D. (1995) "Theory, training and technology: part 2," in Education and Training, Vol. 37, No. 2.

Wright, T. (1987) <u>Roles of Teachers and Learners</u>. Oxford, Oxford University Press.

Wringe, C. (1988) <u>Understanding Educational Aims</u>. London, Unwin Hyman Ltd.

York Associates (Comfort, J. and Utley, D. (1995) <u>Effective Negotiation</u>. Oxford, Oxford University Press.

York Associates (Comfort, J. and Utley, D. (1995) <u>Effective Meetings</u>. Oxford, Oxford University Press.

York Associates (Comfort, J. and Utley, D. (1995) <u>Effective Presentations.</u> Oxford, Oxford University Press.

York Associates (Comfort J. and Utley D.) 1995 <u>Effective Reports.</u> Oxford, Oxford University Press.

UNIT 4
Language, Communication and Culture

UNIT 4: Language, Communication and Culture

Chapter 1

Language Analysis - Introduction

1.1: Introduction
1.2: Objectives
1.3: Clarification of Terms
1.4: Answers to Questions.

1.1: Introduction

This chapter outlines the principal areas of language analysis. The following chapters will then look at these areas in more detail. Chapter 2 considers discourse analysis; chapter 3 examines conversational analysis, and chapter 4 looks at genre. In each of these chapters, we suggest how the findings of research into these areas may be applied to the teaching of English for International Business.

Discourse analysis has made a significant contribution to language teaching in general and to EIB in particular because it goes beyond the idea of language as an abstract system and examines language in social context. This means that it focuses on the producers and receivers of language as much as on the language forms themselves.

Research is also being carried out into spoken and written texts in Business English in order to establish which discourse types or genres exist. The work of Bhatia (1993) is particularly interesting, and we will

UNIT 4: Language, Communication and Culture

examine his ideas in some detail in chapter 4. Awareness of genre in EIB is crucial if teachers are to help learners adapt their communication skills to the social and cultural contexts in which they are operating.

The findings of research into conversation analysis are also very useful for teachers of EIB because these findings may help us better understand how, for example, participants close conversations, take turns and agree and disagree. Conversation analysis is also useful because it gives us important information with regard to how, for example, talk in meetings is different from talk on the telephone or informal and social talk.

We would stress that we are not attempting an exhaustive description of these three areas, and you are encouraged to make use of the many references in order to read further. In particular, we recommend Unger (2006) on genre analysis, Schegloff (2007) on conversational analysis and Fairclough (2003) for discourse analysis.

The essential decision teachers of EIB need to make concerns the degree to which the findings of discourse analysis, genre analysis and conversation analysis need to be taught to learners of EIB. These chapters will attempt to offer some guidance to teachers who try to make that decision.

1.2: Objectives

The aims of this chapter are to:

> ➢ clarify the terms discourse analysis, conversational analysis and genre analysis.

Pre-reading tasks

Before you start the chapter, we would like you to consider the tasks and questions below. These attempt to focus your mind on some of the main ideas in this and the next three chapters.

> ➢ *Write down the characteristics of spoken and written language.*
> ➢ *Consider this text: Parts arrive 6.00 tomorrow. sorry mate. PS Hows life after the merger Interesting? C U RG. How*

UNIT 4: Language, Communication and Culture

> *would you characterise this text? Is it spoken or written text? Where might you find a text of this kind?*
> ➢ *Consider presentations and the social chat in which people might engage at the airport. Both are examples of spoken language in Business English, but they are clearly not the same. How are they different?*
> ➢ *Much of what you hear around you might be incomprehensible to you. And yet the speakers themselves probably understand each other. How do they manage to do this?*
> ➢ *How is the term genre used in the world of the arts? What types of genre can you identify? What criteria are you using to differentiate different types of genre?*

1.3: Clarification of Terms

Cook (1989) writes that the purpose of discourse analysis is to examine, "...how stretches of language, considered in their full textual, social, and psychological context, become meaningful and unified for their users." Cook (1989) goes on to suggest that traditional approaches to language teaching have focused on pronunciation, vocabulary and grammar. Although knowledge of these remains the basis for language learning, the findings of discourse analysis can help learners develop the skills necessary to put this knowledge into action in order to achieve effective communication.

Question 1

> *The author has met many non-native speakers who have superb English from the grammatical point of view and from the perspective of vocabulary range and control. And yet, there has often been something forced or awkward about their English. Can you think of any reasons for this? When you have considered your response you might like to look again at unit 1, chapter 10 – Language, Communication and Culture.*

Discourse analysts study both written and spoken texts. McCarthy (2001) claims that there is no single defining difference between spoken and written texts, and that it is more useful to see them as a continuum and not as rigid opposites. For example, electronic mail does not fall neatly into one particular category. They are written texts but they sometimes tend to display the characteristics of speech. Consider also some spoken business presentations, which can often display characteristics of written language.

The results of discourse analysis say something about how texts work. However, when the focus of a text analysis is on the regularities that can distinguish one type of text from another type of text, then we are looking at genre analysis (Dudley-Evans and St John, 1998). The results of genre analysis will focus on the differences between discourse types. Therefore, genre analysis can best be viewed as a part of discourse analysis. Genre analysis is useful because it tells us something about the distinguishing features of different types of text.

Pause for thought

> *Think about presentations, promotional letters and company brochures. Are these examples of one genre? Once again, consider the criteria you are using to answer the question.*

Conversation is a term which is often used to describe informal talk. Discourse analysts often appear to use the term to describe any form of oral interaction. However, Cook (1989) suggests that conversation takes place when:

- it is not focused on a practical task
- any unequal power among participants is partly suspended
- the number of participants is small
- turns are short
- talk is mainly for the participants and not for an outside audience.

These characteristics are imprecise, but they are useful. However, the dividing line between conversation and other spoken discourse types is unclear. Perhaps it is better to view spoken interaction as a continuum with, at one end, formal spoken discourse and, at the other end, casual conversation. Thus, a presentation might come somewhere between these two extremes.

Stenström (1994) defines spoken interaction as a joint here-and-now social activity governed by two main principles: speakers take turns and speakers co-operate.

UNIT 4: Language, Communication and Culture

Question 2

> *Look again at Cook's characteristics of conversation and consider the questions below. When you have finished, check with our answers in the Answers to Questions section.*
> - *Can the talk heard at a formal business meeting be termed "conversation"? Why? Why not?*
> - *What about a negotiation?*
> - *And a telephone "conversation"?*

Despite this lack of clarity, the findings of conversation analysis are very significant and useful for teachers and learners of EIB. For example, any description of how people take turns, and under what circumstances they overlap or pause will be of interest to those of us who are asked to teach meeting skills or negotiating skills. Furthermore, turn-taking mechanisms and pausing can vary between cultures and languages (see also Ting-Toomey and Korzenny, 2002). Cultural awareness is vital because these mechanisms can not simply be lifted from one culture and used in another. The relative status of speakers is also important. In high power distance cultures, for example, when the teacher speaks, the class falls silent.

1.4: Answers to Questions

Question 1
There may be many reasons why this grammatically perfect English is somehow inappropriate. Style of communication will differ across cultures, for example, a preference for direct or indirect style. Language will also reflect differences in perceived relationship and status. Additionally, the rules governing turn-taking and the length of appropriate pausing might differ as a result of diverse values. Further, consider again the differences in high- and low-context communication.

Question 2
- No. Meetings are almost always (or should be) focused on a practical task, for example: problem-solving or decision-making. In fact, the distinguishing feature of a meeting is that its talk has a clear purpose.
- The same is true of negotiations.
- It depends! Telephone talk may display the characteristics mentioned in the question. Consider, however, a telephone conference or a telephone presentation or a telephone interview. Although the telephone itself is the common tool, the type of talk may be very different.

UNIT 4: Language, Communication and Culture

Chapter 2

Language Analysis - Discourse

2.1: Introduction
2.2: Objectives
2.3: Discourse Analysis
2.4: Cohesion and Coherence
2.5: Conversational Principles
2.6: Coherence and Knowledge Structures
2.7: Conclusions
2.8: Answers to Questions.

2.1: Introduction

This chapter gives you an overview of discourse analysis and suggests how the findings of research into discourse analysis may be applied to the teaching of English for International Business. For those of you who want to know more about this fascinating area of study, we suggest that you take up the references and read further. Cook (1989) is a good starting point, and Georgakopoulou and Goutsos (1997) and Fairclough (2003) are excellent and approachable introductions to the main areas of interest.

UNIT 4: Language, Communication and Culture

2.2: Objectives

The aims of this chapter are to:

- give an overview of discourse analysis
- show how discourse analysis relates to EIB
- stimulate ideas for classroom practice.

Pre-reading questions

Before you start the chapter, we would like you to consider the questions below.

> *Imagine you have been asked to write materials for an important course that will be held in your school. One morning the boss walks in and says to you, "How are you getting on with that material?" Write down what you understand by this question. Then compare your understanding with the understanding of your colleagues at work. Can you explain any different interpretations of this one remark?*
> *Talk is all around us! Listen to it. How much of what you hear is information-carrying? What is the purpose of the rest of this talk?*
> *"Students need to master the grammatical structure of a language so that they can put words together meaningfully. Only then can they communicate effectively." What do you think?*

2.3: Discourse Analysis

The vast majority of learners of EIB I have dealt with express the wish to be able to communicate effectively in a global environment. The question we consider in this chapter is what can we, as teachers of EIB, learn from the findings of discourse analysis in order to help them in their task?

Cook (1989) suggests that in order to communicate effectively, learners and teachers need to take the following levels of discoursal features into account:

UNIT 4: Language, Communication and Culture

- social relationship
- shared knowledge
- discourse type (genre)
- discourse structure
- discourse function
- conversational mechanisms
- cohesion
- grammar and lexis
- sounds and letters.

A great deal of language teaching follows a bottom-up approach and often considers only the formal language system (the lower levels above, i.e.: sounds and letters first, then grammar and lexis, and so on) without taking into account how that system operates in context (the higher levels).

A bottom-up approach may well bring good results. It may help learners understand what language is and how it works. However, this does not mean that it is the best way to teach EIB. Back at work, our learners may have to socialise, send e-mails, give a presentation, listen sympathetically to employees and/or discipline them, and all in one morning.

Clearly, some teaching does take account of the upper levels of language mentioned above, but it often deals with these levels separately. However, communication is a complex interaction of mind, language and the physical world. Although dealing with communication in discrete chunks might be easier, at some point the chunks will have to be reintegrated. After all, successful language learners must be able to handle everything at once and at high speed.

2.4: Cohesion and Coherence

Pause for thought

> *Imagine the following situation. A man and his wife are sitting in their car at the traffic lights. The wife is at the wheel. The man sends the following message, "The light's green." What does the man mean? How many ways can the utterance be interpreted?*

UNIT 4: Language, Communication and Culture

There are, perhaps, four ways in which this utterance can be interpreted. The factual component seems obvious enough, but there may also be a self-revelation component, which reveals what the man says about himself, for example: "I'm in a hurry." There may also be an appeal component, which reveals what the husband would like his wife to do, for example: "Go!" That is not all. The relational component reveals what the husband thinks of his wife and his relationship to her, "You need my help," or, "Are you blind?"

The receiver also has, in principle, the choice of which component s/he wants to react to. We might refer to these choices as "ears". The self-revelation ear asks, "What kind of person is that? What is his/her problem?" The factual ear asks, "What should I make of this factual information?" The appeal ear asks, "What should I do, think or feel based on the message?" The relationship ear asks, "Why is s/he speaking to me like this? What am I doing wrong?"

The model shows how one utterance can contain many messages at the same time. Often, only one message is openly expressed in the process and the others may be hidden. This does not mean that the other messages are less important. The clarity of communication therefore has four aspects. When your boss walks into the office on Monday morning and asks how you are getting on with that report, the factual content seems obvious. Less clear to the receiver is what your boss is saying about him/herself and what she/he is saying about you. In other words, in this one statement, many messages may be contained and there are many possibilities for misunderstandings.

An utterance can therefore have more than one meaning. A distinction should be made between the literal meaning (word-by-word meaning) and the pragmatic meaning (function acquired by context). Furthermore, even if a person says what he or she means, there is no certainty that it will be interpreted in the same way.

The exercise above shows that in order to make sense of a text, we need to understand its function in context. But, if function or meaning do not reside in the words themselves, how can we understand what is being said to us? Theories from pragmatics give us essential insights both into the nature of coherence and into the problems of communicating in a foreign language.

UNIT 4: Language, Communication and Culture

Question 1

> *How could you incorporate these ideas into your classroom teaching? Think of an activity you could use to sensitise your learners to literal and pragmatic meaning. How could your activity be used in a company in order to improve communication skills? Who could benefit?*

The idea of language functions in context goes a long way towards explaining how some stretches of language have coherence and others do not. If we can ascertain the function of an utterance, we can observe what creates meaningful discourse. The features outlined above can be described as contextual features; in other words, they exist outside the language forms themselves. Formal devices, which exist in the text itself, refer to facts that exist inside the language. These formal links between sentences and clauses are cohesive devices.

How do formal links help us appreciate coherence and how are they used in Business English? There are a number of answers to these questions. For example, the form of a verb in one sentence can limit the choice of verb in the next. If the verb form does not fit, then we know that something is wrong. There has to be some form of connection between forms otherwise a text will lose coherence.

Another link within discourse is called parallelism. Consider the following extract from a presentation given by the CEO of a well-known company. The presentation was attended by the current writer, but I have changed the name of the company to ABC.

> *So why is ABC a great company to work for? ABC is a great company to work for because of its innovations. ABC is a great company to work for because of its products. But above all, ABC is a great company to work for because of its people.*

This repetition of "ABC is a great company" is simply a device which connects because the form of one sentence repeats the form of another. It can be particularly effective in speeches, prayers and presentations.

The CEO of ABC could easily have given this presentation using other formal links. Consider the following.

UNIT 4: Language, Communication and Culture

So, to sum up. Why is ABC a great company to work for? Firstly, ABC is a great company to work for because of its innovations. On top of this, ABC is a great company to work for because of its products. And finally, ABC is a great company to work for because of its people.

The type of connectors used above (to sum up, first, on top of that, and finally) are formal links which draw attention to the type of relationship which exists between sentences or clauses.

Pause for thought

> *Apart from the use of cohesive devices, how (if at all) are the two extracts above different?*

Another cohesive device is the referring expression, or words whose meanings can only be discovered by referring to other words or parts of a context which are clear to both sender and receiver. For example, "Put it in the shredder," would have no meaning to us unless we knew what "it" referred to.

Repetition and lexical chains often avoid referring expressions by simply using the same words and expressions over and over again. This not only creates text unity but can also be used to great effect by salespeople, presenters and politicians. Think of the advertising catch phrase, used again and again until it becomes almost unforgettable, for example, "It's the real thing," or, "Just do it."

Another type of formal link is the substitution of words like "do" or "would" for a group of words which have already appeared. Finally, we must mention ellipsis, which allows us to omit a word and know that the missing part will be reconstructed, for example: "Would you like a cup of tea?" can be answered by "Yes" and not "Yes I would like a cup of tea."

The formal links above are neither necessary nor sufficient to account for coherence in a text. Their presence does not automatically lend coherence and nor does their absence render a text meaningless. We must also consider the range of possible functions of language and try to understand and/or interpret the intention of the speaker. In the absence of formal links, it is the function of a language that can bind utterances together.

But the question remains - if the meaning of an utterance is not entirely to be found in the literal meaning of words, and if people can mean and understand different things with the same words, how do we interpret what is meant and why do we not say exactly what we mean? For an accessible explanation of how discourse types can influence the listener's processes in identifying the intentions of the communicator, see Unger (2006).

2.5: Conversational Principles

Grice (1975) suggests that language is interpreted on the assumption that the sender is following four principles. We assume that s/he intends to:

- be true
- be brief
- be relevant
- be clear.

If information were the sole point of talk, these principles might make perfect sense. However, they do not explain the pragmatic aspect of language which we discussed above.

For example, the statement, "It's cold in here," flouts the principles of truth and clarity if the sender intends the statement to be interpreted as a command or request, "Please close the window." The utterance only works when there is a common understanding and appreciation of the value of indirectness. However, in the world of international business, not all cultures share this value. When a culture values directness, then the utterance above is, at best, inappropriate, and at worst, a lie.

Perhaps it is the maxims of politeness that can explain the frequency of utterances like the one above. Lakoff (1973) argues that these maxims are:

- don't impose
- give options
- make the receiver feel good.

Clearly, the politeness principle and Grice's (1975) principles of co-operation can conflict. However, this conflict might always be there.

UNIT 4: Language, Communication and Culture

After all, it may simply be a manifestation of the dual purpose of talk: to work efficiently together with others and to maintain human relationships.

Pause for thought

> *It should be obvious that the ability to work efficiently with others and to maintain relationships are very important for global businesses. How far (if at all) do Grice's (1975) conversational principles and Lakoff's (1973) maxims of politeness differ from culture to culture? Should teachers of EIB sensitise learners to any differences? If so, how?*

This dual purpose of talk is dealt with in some detail by Watzlawick's (1967) theory of communication (see unit 1, chapter 10). You will recall that Watzlawick (1967) suggests that all communication has a substantive and a relational component and that the latter determines the former. You might like to look again at the points he raises in the relevant unit and section before attempting the next question.

Question 2

> *It is clear that awareness of pragmatics is very important for international businesses. In what aspects of international business can relationships be critical?*

Cohesive links and pragmatic knowledge go a long way towards explaining how people reason their way through form to function and to construct meaningful and coherent discourse from the language they receive. If you wish to read further you are recommended to look at Tannen (1992) and McCarthy and Carter (1994).

If you are interested in the cultural implications of our discussion, you might want to look at Thomas (1983). The precise way of indicating respect for other cultures, and of relationship building, are vital in the world of international business and we should give serious consideration as to how we can help our learners develop this.

UNIT 4: Language, Communication and Culture

2.6: Coherence and Knowledge Structures

A simple model of communication is the sender-receiver model. The sender encodes a message and transmits it to the receiver. The receiver then decodes the message and gives feedback.

We can only talk of communication in the literal sense when the receiver has the chance to respond to the message of the sender (feedback). Effective and complete communication only takes place when the impression of the receiver agrees with the expression of the sender.

Pause for thought

> *What are some of the problems associated with this model of communication?*

The main challenges with the sender-receiver model are that it assumes a shared knowledge and understanding of the world. For example, if a person who is about to get married says that families are the mainstay of society, his or her utterance may be received in an entirely different way by a person who has just got divorced and who is having difficulty in seeing his/her children. Cook (1989) writes that:

> ...knowledge schemata are mental representations of typical situations, and they are used in discourse processing to predict the contents of the particular situation which the discourse describes. The idea is that the mind, stimulated by key words...or by the context, activates a knowledge schema, and uses it to make sense of the discourse.

Question 3

> *Under the box above, the writer has deliberately used the word "challenge." Would it have made a difference to the sentence if we had used the word "problem"? What is this difference?*

Schemata operate daily in the decisions we make when we omit items of information in our everyday speech. On a very basic level, if I am giving a talk about the London Underground, I must assume that listeners know what a tunnel is and what trains are.

UNIT 4: Language, Communication and Culture

However, misjudgements and mismatches of schemata are always possible and particularly likely when we try to communicate across languages and across cultures. For this reason, schemata theory is very important to us as teachers of EIB. Once, in 1989, when giving a lesson on the language of marketing to a group of Russians, I assumed (incorrectly) that they understood the concept of marketing. I also assumed that they would be able to use the Yellow Pages or the phone book (both unknown or uncommon in Russia in 1989) in order to find addresses to promote products.

Pause for thought

> Which communicative events in EIB necessitate pitching knowledge at the right level? Do assumptions of knowledge influence discourse in any other ways?

Look at the following examples of grammatically correct sentences.

1. It was the ABC Company that first invented the mobile phone. This was in 1989.
2. The mobile phone was invented by the ABC Company in 1989.

Cook (1989) suggests that the structure of a sentence can be dictated by what is happening in the mind of the sender and the assumptions s/he makes about what is going on in the mind of the receiver. The sender must make decisions about what s/he thinks the receiver already knows or does not know. These are labelled given information and new information. A typical discourse proceeds from the given to the new. Thus in sentence 1 above, the sender is focusing attention on the "given" information, that it was the ABC Company and not a competitor.

To summarise, shared knowledge, or the assumption of shared knowledge, influences every level of discourse, from the ordering of information, the quantity of information given and grammatical structure. Discourse which underestimates the degree of shared knowledge is boring, but discourse which overestimates it is probably incomprehensible.

For further reading, we suggest Tannen (1994) for those of you who are interested specifically in talk between men and women at work. Tannen (1994) deals with conversation between men and women, and

UNIT 4: Language, Communication and Culture

how they can unintentionally create communication barriers in the context of the business world. Essentially, the book provides a clear account of how we can promote more positive and productive professional relationships.

2.7: Conclusions

This chapter has focused on language as discourse rather than on language as sentences. Language as discourse is viewed as something that exists in a social context, as something which exists externally, and not solely inside the heads of individuals.

We are not suggesting that there is anything wrong with studying language as a system. Nobody would deny the fact that learners need to know how language works and how to put it together. But side by side with language as a system, learners need to be aware of the social context in which that system operates. Learners need to be aware of the features outside language, for example: the situation, the people involved, what they know and what they are doing. These features help learners construct unity and meaning.

Paying attention to discourse does not mean that teachers and learners must sacrifice the traditional emphasis on grammar, vocabulary and pronunciation. These are essential elements in communication. What we are suggesting in this chapter is that discourse and formal skills are developed together and that an appreciation of both is essential for learners of EIB.

2.8: Answers to Questions

Question 1
You could begin by incorporating the ideas into a lesson as a warmer. Give out some cards to all the students. Explain the situation to them and then tell them to write down their interpretation of, "The light is green." Next, collect the cards and pin them up on a pin board in four columns. Each column should represent one of the four "ears" - order, self-revelation, relational, factual. Discuss with the students what this may tell us about "clear" communication. If you have a very good rapport with your group you could ask them what it might mean if a person had a tendency to listen with only one ear. Then you could ask the students about their own tendencies and to give examples about how this could influence colleagues or staff in the workplace. This activity should be of interest to anyone who communicates but especially to managers who have people responsibility.

UNIT 4: Language, Communication and Culture

Question 2

We can't think of any situation in which good relationships are not critical. A negotiation that ignores relationship building will almost certainly have dire consequences at some later stage. This is particularly true in collective, high-context cultures. In China and Japan, for example, relationship creation is considered, generally, to be of paramount importance. Furthermore, a meeting that does not have harmonious relationships amongst its participants will hardly be productive.

Question 3

We feel that the word "challenge" has positive associations and the word "problem" has negative ones. The whole tone of the sentence would be changed. This is a very common device used by some people in order to persuade others of the "rightfulness" of their position. Consider another example, weapons of mass destruction (very negative) and defence capability (positive) in order to describe the same thing - atomic weapons.

UNIT 4: Language, Communication and Culture

Chapter 3

Language Analysis - Conversation

3.1: Introduction
3.2: Objectives
3.3: Turn-taking
3.4: Face-to-face and Telephone Conversations
3.5: Interviews and Discussions
3.6: Questioning Techniques
3.7: Conclusions
3.8: Answers to Questions.

3.1: Introduction

We saw in the introduction to chapter 1 that the term "conversation" is hard to define. Stenström (1994) suggests that conversation is: "a piece of discourse containing one or more topics." Cook (1989) says of conversation that any definition of it should include the fact that it is unpredictable and lacks structure. Furthermore, McCarthy (2001) writes:

> ...casual and spontaneous talk between equals...appears to be a precarious, haphazard exercise, with interruptions, diversions, competition for the floor or control of topics,

UNIT 4: Language, Communication and Culture

indeterminate in its duration, unpredictable in its outcomes. Talk, therefore, is an achievement rather than a pre-ordained text simply played out like a drama on stage.

McCarthy (2001) goes on to suggest that conversation analysis is largely associated with sociolinguistics. In this context, Schegloff and Sacks (1973) and Schegloff (2007) are interesting on the closing down of conversations, while Sacks et al (1974) deal with turn-taking in talk. Pomerantz (1983) is good on how participants agree and disagree.

3.2: Objectives

The aims of this chapter are to:

- give an overview of conversation analysis
- show how conversation analysis relates to EIB
- give suggestions for classroom practice
- encourage further reading in those areas of particular interest.

Pre-reading questions

Before you start the chapter, we would like you to consider the questions below.

> *How could you ensure that your students are aware of the differences between talking on the phone, talking in formal meetings, talking during interviews and social talking? Think about:*
> - *the opening and closing*
> - *the amount of phatic talk (warming up/winding down talk)*
> - *the degree to which the talk is predetermined*
> - *the degree to which the talk is goal directed.*
>
> *Think of ways in which you could have your students practise these different types of talk so that they can effectively develop appropriate communication skills.*

UNIT 4: Language, Communication and Culture

3.3: Turn-taking

Whatever else is unclear, we can say for sure that conversation involves turn-taking. The end of one speaker's turn and the beginning of the next speaker's turn usually latch on to one another perfectly. There may be some time where one part of what one speaker says overlaps with part of what the other says, but this occurs in only about 5% of conversation (Sacks et al 1974).

Question 1

> *Speakers usually signal to each other that one turn has come to an end and that another should begin. How do they do this? How do they do this on the telephone?*

Turn-taking mechanisms can vary between cultures and between languages. Overlap, for example, is tolerated more in some societies than in others. Furthermore, tolerance of pausing and the length of pausing can vary between cultures, and the appropriacy of interruptions can change according to the nationality of the speakers.

Question 2

> *Can you think of any situation in which overlap (interrupting before the speaker has come to the end of what s/he wants to say) would be inappropriate? Can you think of any cultures in which overlap may be considered bad manners?*

However, some turns are very closely linked; for example, when the first utterance requires a particular type of response. A greeting is likely to be followed by another greeting, and a request is likely to be followed by a refusal or an acceptance. These sequences are called adjacency pairs.

The question is: how can we, as EIB teachers, train learners in the workings of conversation? After all, face-to-face talk is vital in such areas as: conflict management, job appraisal, dealing with employee complaints and so on.

I shall now describe a task I have used successfully in the classroom (controlled dialogue) to raise awareness of some characteristics of conversation. I shall then examine this in some detail with reference to

UNIT 4: Language, Communication and Culture

some of the theory.

Controlled dialogue

The objective of the dialogue is to ensure that participants recognise ineffectiveness in their communicative behaviour. There are three participants in varying roles: A and B are the participants. C is an observer. A and B discuss a topic of their own choosing (for and against positions).

Procedure.
1. A transmits a message.
2. B repeats in his or her own words the contents of A's message.
3. A confirms or corrects the repeated message.
4. B transmits his/her own message.
5. A repeats B's message in his/her own words.

During the activity, C should make sure that the procedure is followed as accurately as possible and, when it is finished, gives feedback on the activity.

In almost all the classes with which I have done this exercise, B is unable to repeat As message entirely and accurately. The question is, why not? There are a number of reasons, and they concern both the speaker and the listener (see unit 1, chapter 3). For the sake of ease and convenience, we shall list these reasons again. Ineffectiveness on the part of speakers can include that they:

1. do not structure their thoughts
2. do not speak in a language that the listener understands
3. express themselves too loosely
4. speak too long
5. try to put as many ideas as possible into one statement
6. can not focus, lose track of the idea, digress from subject
7. do not deal with the statement of the partner
8. speak too quickly or unclearly
9. try to be pedantic.

Point 1 concerns what Stenström (1994) refers to as the basic format of face-to-face conversation and telephone calls: opening, message, close. This might consist of:

UNIT 4: Language, Communication and Culture

- I'm going to talk about two aspects of... (opening)
- The first point...and now turning to the second point... (message)
- And so in conclusion I am saying that... (close).

Question 3

> *How many other communicative events are there in Business English that have (or should have) this structure?*

Point 2 may concern schemata, or assuming that the listener has a certain level of language ability and/or knowledge of the subject. Points 4 and 6 violate Grice's principles of communication: be clear, be true, be brief and be relevant. Points 1 and 8 have, in my experience, often concerned a disregard for coherence and cohesion. Learners have been unable to use appropriate discourse markers or items that reflect organisation in a text or that act as boundary markers (Stenström 1994).

Point 4 simply ignores the fact that the receiver rarely (if ever) comprehends and senses the meaning of a message in exactly the same way as it is intended. Furthermore, the listener can store information only to a limited extent. Some information will be left out and other information will be added when the listener decodes a message. The listener will decode the message according to his/her own value systems, resentments, prejudices, education and so on. Messages which agree with the value system of the listener tend to be exaggerated. Messages which do not agree tend to be played down or repressed. Follow up questions and repetition can help limit these distorted perceptions.

Communication filter

- 100% the sender thinks
- 80% the mouth reproduces
- 60% the listener hears
- 40% s/he makes a note of
- 20% is still present the next day.

These figures are, of course, only indicative. They will change according to a number of factors. Among these are:

- how well the sender expresses him/herself

UNIT 4: Language, Communication and Culture

- the environment
- the attention of the listener
- the listener's capacity for retention
- the listener's ability to concentrate.

So far we have looked aspects of ineffective speaking. The listener also has responsibilities. Aspects of ineffective listening include that listeners:

1. are inattentive
2. think about their answer while the other person is speaking
3. only hear certain details and overlook the essential meaning
4. react to charged words
5. pay more attention to how something is said rather than what is said
6. misinterpret the message
7. interrupt the speaker because they think they know what is coming next
8. show no sign that they have understood what has been said
9. irritate the speaker with inappropriate body signals.

Point 8 concerns the non-use or inappropriate use of backchannels. Backchannels are listener acknowledgements and/or encouragements to go on. Such backchannels are usually inserted at syntactic or semantic completion points (Stenström 1994), and require a great deal of sensitivity on the part of the listener. Verbal feedback of this kind may also be replaced by silent feedback in the form of nods, gestures, eye glances and so on. Point 6 concerns schemata again.

In conclusion, I have found that the exercise above is an effective way to raise awareness of what can go wrong in conversation. Culture-specific rules and procedures for turn-taking provide many opportunities for misunderstanding. Furthermore, entering and leaving conversation, refusing entry into conversation, and interrupting are, for example, areas for which learners often have little preparation.

3.4: Face-to-Face and Telephone Conversations

The pattern of these types of talk can vary according to the situation, the place, who is talking to whom and the topic of the talk. Stenström (1994) sums up the differences between face-to-face conversation and

UNIT 4: Language, Communication and Culture

telephone conversation in the following way.

Face-to-face
- There may be no opening or closing sections.
- Openings and closings will be influenced by the degree of formality.
- Topic changes, shifts, drifts and digressions are common.
- The setting is important.
- Body language plays an important role.
- Closings and farewells tend to follow a set pattern.

Telephone Conversation
- There is almost always the following structure: opening, reason for calling and a close.
- Openings and closings require a minimal set of obligatory actions.
- Body language plays no role.

Let's look at some of these terms in more detail. Changing topic means that speakers drop one area of talk and go on to another unrelated topic. In order to do this, they often use explicit lexical markers. Shifting means that speakers move from one aspect of a topic to another related topic. Drifting means that speakers move almost without noticing from one topic to another. Digressing involves moving away from the topic being discussed. This is usually temporary.

Pause for thought

> *How do speakers mark topic changes, shifting, drifting and digressing? How important are these markers for learners of Business English? When would business people use them? Should we teach these markers? If the answer is yes, how should we do it?*

3.5: Interviews and Discussions

Interviews differ from face-to-face conversations and telephone conversations in the sense that they tend to be highly structured, they have a specific purpose and they have a specific setting. Stenström (1994) summarises interviews as having the following characteristics.

UNIT 4: Language, Communication and Culture

- They are directed towards some predetermined objective.
- They tend to follow a set pattern.
- The type of pattern is predetermined - i.e. question-response.
- Structure is predetermined - i.e. interviewer questions-interviewee answers.

Discussions also tend to be goal-directed in the sense that they usually revolve around one particular topic. Within the world of business, discussions can be either in the context of a formal meeting or they can be in the context of an informal meeting around, for example, the coffee machine or the photocopier. The differences between formal and informal discussions are listed below.

- Formal discussions tend to be well-planned whereas the informal discussion is not.
- Formal discussions are conducted in an established correct fashion whereas the informal discussion is not.
- In the formal discussion there is little simultaneous talk whereas in the informal discussion there is plenty.
- Formal discussions would have fewer digressions, asides, drifts and shifts than the informal discussion.

Stenström (1994) summarises her discussion on types of talk by stating that the features which characterise all of them are co-operativeness and the use of signals and markers.

Phatic talk and asides occur in casual conversation, in some interviews but not usually in discussions. Discussions have more in common with conversations than with interviews. Interviews and conversations are very different. If you want to know more about conversational strategies in general, we suggest that you look at Stenström (1994) or Fairclough (1989).

Clearly, if we believe what Stenström (1994) tells us and we want to enable our learners to engage confidently in effective talk, we need to sensitise them to the use of signals and markers and enhance their ability to co-operate.

With regard to the first, discourse analysis has paid considerable attention to the role of discourse markers such as: "well", "so", "right", and "I mean". These markers can reveal the intention of the speaker. If you want to read further about these markers, you are recommended to look at Micheau and Billmyer (1987).

UNIT 4: Language, Communication and Culture

With regard to the second point, one way of enhancing the ability of learners to co-operate is to give them plenty of practice in questioning techniques.

3.6: Questioning Techniques

Questions are important because they can:

- encourage dialogue
- give direction to the conversation
- activate a quiet partner
- give the person questioned a sense of importance and recognition
- convey trust
- build bridges
- demonstrate interest
- establish partnership
- separate facts from opinion
- eliminate misunderstanding.

Question 4

> *Look at the reasons for asking questions that are listed above. How many of these reasons concern co-operation and co-operativeness?*

Questions may also have negative consequences. Questions can motivate or defuse situations but they can provoke and hurt. Learners need to be aware of the following different question types.

Closed questions
These are questions that can be answered in a single word - yes or no. For example: "Will you be needing the car today?" or, "Do you agree with my proposal?" Closed questions may be posed in order to:

- clarify factual matters
- check the other's knowledge
- obtain quantitative information
- secure attention
- make matters more precise

UNIT 4: Language, Communication and Culture

- obtain agreement
- conduct the discussion in as precise and concentrated a manner as possible.

Closed questions may also have negative effects. They do not necessarily stimulate conversation and they sometimes create an atmosphere of cross-examination. They do little to encourage the pleasure of talking.

Open questions
These questions usually begin with a question word. For example: who, where, when, what...? These questions can not usually be answered in one or two words. For example, "What did you see?" or "How did the damage happen?" Open questions may be used to:

- obtain qualitative information
- encourage free expression of opinion
- stimulate ideas
- draw out views, judgements and wishes.

Suggestive questions
These are questions which already contain the answer. The intention may be to force the other person to accept the opinion of the questioner. The person being questioned only has the choice of agreeing or contradicting, while the questioner only expects agreement. For example, "We share the same view in this, don't we?" "Don't you think that...?" "Isn't it obvious that...?"

Alternative questions
These are questions which offer the partner a choice between two alternatives. For example, "Do you want to bring your car today or tomorrow?" "Do you prefer red or blue?"

Counter questions
These are answers that are posed as questions in order to avoid an unpleasant question or to gain time for reflection. Counter questions can begin with, for example: "If I understood you correctly, you're saying that..." or, "So what you're asking is..., is that correct?"

UNIT 4: Language, Communication and Culture

Provocative questions
These may be asked to entice the other person to come forward with their opinion, to set them thinking or to bring certain negative attitudes to their attention. For example, "Don't you think that you are really too old for that girl?"

Rhetorical questions
These are questions that do not require an answer but are answered by the questioner him/herself. They can sometimes be an effective way of reviving the attention of the listener or of introducing an important message. For example, "Why do I say this?" or, "So, what were last year's results?"

Pause for thought

> *There are seven different types of question listed above. Look at the following business situations and decide which type of questioning technique could be effectively used.*
> ➤ *a presentation*
> ➤ *a meeting*
> ➤ *a negotiation*
> ➤ *a face-to-face meeting with an employee who has problems at home*
> ➤ *an employee who has to deal with customer complaints at a help-desk.*

3.7: Conclusions

In this chapter, we have introduced ideas from conversational analysis and suggested how you may wish to incorporate these into your classroom practice. Students of EIB need constant exposure to native speakers and we need to draw attention to native-speaker use of discourse markers and signals. If you are unable to produce the "real thing," then we suggest you use videos or recordings of native speakers in meetings, on the telephone, at interviews or giving presentations.

Awareness is the first step, and we should encourage rather than penalise our students in their attempts to incorporate these aspects of language into their own repertoire. But we need to get them past the stage of overuse of some markers and signals, for example: "...and

UNIT 4: Language, Communication and Culture

something like that," or, "I mean..."

3.8: Answers to Questions

Question 1
Efficient turn-taking involves linguistic and non-linguistic devices. Eye-contact is one way of signalling. Cook (1989) observes that in British culture, speakers tend to look away during their turn and to look their interlocutor in the eye at the end. Body position and movement are also important. Intonation and volume also play a part. This is particularly true on the telephone when there are no visual clues. The status of speakers can also be significant both in face-to-face and telephone conversations.

Question 2
We think that interrupting your boss before he/she has finished would be unwise in any culture. It would be particularly unwise in a high power distance culture. It would probably be inappropriate in high uncertainty avoidance cultures. In the experience of the author, pausing in usually expected in Finland before replying. I found that estimating the appropriate length of pause was rather difficult.

Question 3
The most obvious example is the presentation, which should have clear sign-posting throughout. However, a good communicator will also use this basic structure to put across points in both meetings and negotiations. It is unlikely that casual conversation will have this structure. It would sound very strange if it did.

Question 4
All of them.

UNIT 4: Language, Communication and Culture

Chapter 4

Language Analysis - Genre

4.1: Introduction
4.2: Objectives
4.3: Characteristics of Genres
4.4: Cross-cultural Factors in Genre Analysis
4.5: Conclusions.
4.6: Answers to Questions.

4.1: Introduction

This chapter gives you an overview of genre analysis and suggests why the findings of genre analysis are important for teachers of EIB. We feel that the most important concept for you to consider is that of communicative purpose. This concept is essential in order to appreciate the differences between, for example, meetings and negotiations, and the differences between presentations and other forms of lengthy monologue.

For example, the writer has encountered many learners of Business English whose presentations are, in fact, lectures. These students are not fully aware of the essential point that presentations are usually persuasive events and that, therefore, their content, structure and delivery have characteristics that can differ considerably from lectures.

UNIT 4: Language, Communication and Culture

For those of you who wish to read further, Bhatia (1993) is a good starting point.

4.2: Objectives

The aims of this chapter are to:

- give an overview of genre analysis
- suggest how research findings in genre analysis may be applied in the EIB classroom
- encourage further reading in those areas of particular interest.

Pre-reading tasks

Before you start the chapter, we would like you to consider the questions below.

> 1. The Collins Dictionary defines genre as: "Kind, category, sort, especially of literary or acoustic work." Can we, therefore, describe the detective novel as a genre? What are the criteria you are using to describe it as a genre?
> 2. Now apply your criteria to business letters, presentations and reports. Can you describe these as genres?
> 3. Can you identify one absolutely defining characteristic of genre?
> 4. Can you think of any texts that are developed solely in order to inform or do all texts have some persuasive function?

4.3: Characteristics of Genres

Hammond and Derewianka (2001) write that the term genre has been commonly used to refer to particular kinds of literature or other media of creative expression (e.g. art or film). In chapter 1 of this unit, we suggested that genre analysis concerns the distinguishing features of different texts, both spoken and written.

In ESP, genre analysis began with the work of Swales (1981 and 1990). In this work (into the introduction to academic articles), Swales found that there is a regular pattern of moves and steps which come in a certain predictable order in most of the introductions analysed. A move is:

> ...a unit that relates both to the writer's purpose and to the content that s/he wishes to communicate. A step is a lower level text unit than the move and it provides a detailed perspective on the options open to the writer in setting out the moves in the introduction. (Dudley-Evans and St John 1998)

For the sake of clarification, Swales' (1990) model is shown below.

Move 1: Establishing a territory.
Step 1: Claiming centrality and/or
Step 2: making topic generalisations and/or
Step 3: reviewing previous research.
Move 2: Establishing a niche.
Step 1A: Counter claiming or
Step 1B: indicating a gap or
Step 1C: question raising or
Step 1D: continuing a tradition.
Move 3: Occupying the niche.
Step 1A: Outlining purpose or
Step 1B: announcing present research.
Step 2: Announcing principal findings.
Step 3: Indicating article structure.

In the area of Business English, Bhatia (1993) demonstrates that the techniques applied to the academic article can also be applied to business letters. Bhatia (1993, pp 22-24) claims that in order to undertake an investigation into any genre we should make a sequence of seven steps.

1. Placing the given genre-text in a situational context.
2. Surveying the existing literature.
3. Refining the situational/contextual analysis.
4. Selecting a corpus.
5. Studying the institutional context.
6. Deciding on levels of linguistic analysis.
7. Checking against specialist information in genre analysis.

UNIT 4: Language, Communication and Culture

Bhatia (1993) stresses that although linguistic analysis is useful, it tells us little about the communicative purpose of the text. He suggests that linguistic analysis alone constrains the findings to surface features and provides little information about how communicative purpose is achieved in a particular genre.

Question 1

> *Teaching business letters can often be part of the EIB teacher's job. Consider the sales letter, the letter of complaint, the letter of request, the letter of apology and so on. Are these separate genres or simply examples of the same genre?*

For Bhatia (1993) communicative purpose is crucial for identifying genre. He looks at two types of business letter – the sales promotion letter and the job application letter. He finds that they use an almost identical pattern of moves. These are shown below.

Sales Letter
Move 1: Establish credentials.
Move 2: Introduce the offer.
Move 3: Offer incentives.
Move 4: Enclose documents.
Move 5: Solicit response.
Move 6: End politely.

Job Application Letter
Move 1: Establish credentials.
Move 2: Introduce the candidate.
Move 3: Offer incentives.
Move 4: Enclose documents.
Move 5: Use pressure tactics.
Move 6: End politely.

Bhatia (1993) states that the two instances of promotional genre have rarely been treated as instances of the same genre. However, he points out that not only do they use the same medium but that:

> ...their participants have a similar role relationship. And above all, they share the same communicative purposes,

UNIT 4: Language, Communication and Culture

which are adequately reflected in the structural interpretations that can be assigned to some typical instances of these two text types. In this respect, the sales promotion letter and the job application letter should be regarded as instances of what we can call promotional genres. (Bhatia, 1993 p.74)

How can the characteristics of genre help the teacher of EIB? We suggest that you choose any company brochure or website you can find and a tourist brochure or web site. Look at the structure of the texts and see if you can find any shared characteristics with regard to moves or any other linguistic resource. Consider also communicative purpose. Do the two websites have the same communicative purpose?

It is very important that analysis of Business English continues in order to find out which genres exist, so that we can understand both the significant differences and the communicative purpose.

Question 2

> 1) *Lectures and presentations often have a similar structure and require similar skills on the part of the speaker. Can they be regarded as one genre?*
> 2) *If communicative purpose is crucial for identifying genre, can presentations be considered as one genre? If yes, why? If not, why not?*
> 3) *Consider communicative purpose in meetings and negotiations. How do meetings and negotiations differ?*

Meetings within a company may serve a variety of purposes, for example: decision-making, problem-solving, exchanging information, updating a team, and team-building. When, however, meetings occur between representatives of different companies, the meeting will probably resemble a negotiation even though little or no bargaining takes place. The purpose of such a meeting will probably be sounding out the position of the other side and checking up on developments in the business relationship. Most negotiations will also involve this level of co-operation and exchange of information (Charles, 1996).

We suggest that negotiations do have a clear purpose - reaching some kind of compromise agreement or understanding - and can therefore be considered a genre.

UNIT 4: Language, Communication and Culture

4.4: Cross-cultural Factors in Genre Analysis

Bhatia (1993) points out that an understanding of the cross-cultural factors in genre analysis is crucial for both teachers and learners. Various cultures will organise and structure ideas differently when producing texts. It is inevitable that these differences persist when non-native speakers of English produce text in English.

Bhatia (1993) cites a study by Hinds (1990) in which the author discovered that Japanese writers display a style characterised by what is referred to as a "delayed introduction of purpose." Hinds (1990) claims that this delayed introduction of purpose has the undesirable effect of making a text appear incoherent to the English-speaking reader. The experience of the writer suggests that a good number of students from high-context cultures reveal the same style, that is, their essays and reports contain a considerable amount of background detail. Further, these texts often appear to lack focus to the low-context eye. Additionally, the writer has found frequently that the explicit purpose of the text is expressed near the end or even in the conclusion.

Question 3

> *In the US and the UK it is sometimes said that a good presenter should do three things. These are: say what you are going to say, say it, say what you have just said. How far is this advice culture bound?*

Bhatia (1993) goes on to say that with most genres, local cultural constraints are likely to have implications both for the realisation of certain moves and in the way certain strategies are used to achieve specific objectives. Bhatia (1993) claims that these constraints are particularly important for genres employed in business transactions. The claims made by, for example, Hofstede (1991) are applicable to business genres because:

> Genre, after all, is a socio-culturally dependent communicative event and is judged effective to the extent that it can ensure pragmatic success in the business or other professional context in which it is used. (Bhatia 1993)

UNIT 4: Language, Communication and Culture

Dudley-Evans and St John (1998) also point to the importance of the sociological considerations of the context in which texts are used. They suggest that local discourse communities can either develop or adapt genres to meet the needs and expectations of the readership and that there will always be a dynamic tension between models for a genre and the changes in the business context that require changes to the genre. In this sense, "the teacher of EIB can be both a teacher of genre and a genre doctor" (Dudley-Evans and St John, 1998).

One of the main advantages of genre analysis is, therefore, its ability to relate its findings to the discourse community in which the genre is produced. Swales (1990) lists six defining characteristics of a discourse community.

1) A discourse community has a broadly agreed set of common public goals.
2) A discourse community has mechanisms of intercommunication among its members.
3) A discourse community uses its participatory mechanisms primarily to provide information and feedback.
4) A discourse community utilises and hence possesses one or more genres in the communicative furtherance of its aims.
5) In addition to owning genres, a discourse community has acquired some specific lexis.
6) A discourse community has a threshold level of members with a suitable degree of relevant content and discoursal expertise.

Dudley-Evans and St John (1998) admit that it is difficult in practice to produce real and concrete examples of a discourse community. Nevertheless, the concept is a useful one. A writer of novels, for example, will usually have in mind a stereotypical picture of the readership for whom s/he is writing.

In the same way, writers of reports or e-mails will prepare messages by imagining the needs of an unseen and unknown readership. Similarly, a presenter should constantly ask him/herself what his/her audience (imagined or otherwise) is expecting in terms of content, style, organisation, and structure.

In this way, the concept of discourse community is important in the sense that writers, readers and speakers will see themselves as social actors within a community and not as communicators in a vacuum.

UNIT 4: Language, Communication and Culture

Question 4

> *If the academic essay or the business report are examples of genres, how can we sensitise our learners to the concept of discourse community and the demands of that community?*

4.5: Conclusions

This chapter has focused on genres, their characteristics and how the findings of genre analysis can be applied in the EIB classroom. The concept of communicative purpose is vital. In addition, the notion of discourse community is crucial if learners are to adapt their communication style to a particular audience.

4.6: Answers to Questions

Question 1
If we take communicative purpose as the absolute defining characteristic of genre, then the answer is no. The purposes of the letters mentioned are to sell, to complain and to apologise. They are, therefore, separate genres.

Question 2
1. Although the structure of lectures and presentations can be similar, their communicative purpose may well be different. The purpose of a lecture is to transmit information. The purpose of a presentation is to convince or persuade. However, it might be argued that no text (either spoken or written) exists simply to transmit information and that the very act of deciding what to communicate suggests that there is an element of persuasion. Doesn't a lecturer want to convince students of his or her point of view?
2. If all presentations are designed to convince, then they may be considered as a genre.
3. It could be argued that meetings have (or should have) specific purposes. These are decision-making and/or problem-solving. Similarly, the purpose of a negotiation is to reach a compromise deal. In these cases, therefore, they are not instances of the same genre. However, it is not as simple as that.

Question 3
We suggest that this advice is culture-bound. How far is the advice appropriate in collective cultures in which relationship-building is paramount? How far is it appropriate in high uncertainty avoidance Germany in which background details and facts are considered to be most important and which need to be presented before getting down to the main idea?

UNIT 4: Language, Communication and Culture

Question 4

By analysing reports and essays, analysing them and pointing out the differences. Then, learners could restructure and rewrite the essay or report according to the needs of a particular community.

UNIT 4: Language, Communication and Culture

Chapter 5

Culture and Business Communication - 1

5.1: Introduction
5.2: Objectives
5.3: Working in Groups
5.4: What is a Meeting?
5.5: Meetings in Conflict
5.6: Purpose and Expectations in Collision
5.7: Culture Clash or Culture Harmony?
5.8: Success in Multicultural Meetings
5.9: Conclusions
5.10: Answers to Questions.

5.1: Introduction

Chapters 5 to 7 focus on the three business events that you are most likely to have your learners practise in the classroom. These events are: business meetings, negotiations and presentations. We have touched on these most important aspects of Business English communication in other units (notably unit 3, chapter 7). Here, however, they receive further treatment as we deal extensively with their international and intercultural scope.

This chapter examines the need to work collaboratively in

UNIT 4: Language, Communication and Culture

multicultural meetings. At the heart of these meetings lies respect for different approaches, respect for different values, and respect for different attitudes towards life and work.

If respect and understanding are a prerequisite (Berger1998), people still need to find ways of working together which are based on mutual strengths. This chapter identifies some of the challenges that people who hold meetings are likely to encounter. We also attempt to identify some solutions so that intercultural meetings may be efficient and productive. The most important message we want to communicate in this and the following two chapters is that focusing on the language of meetings, negotiations and presentations is simply not enough any more. If our learners are working within a global context, then we need to help them to adapt their skills to the cultural context in which they work. For more on the intercultural scope, see Lewis (2006) and Thomas (2004). Thomas (2004) is not confined to multicultural teams. Leadership, decision-making and negotiating across cultures are also examined.

5.2: Objectives

At the end of this chapter, you will have a better understanding of:

- the nature of groups
- the elements and purpose of meetings
- overcoming the barriers to effective intercultural meetings and promoting better teamwork.

Pre-reading task

Before you begin, consider the tasks in the box below. The tasks are designed to focus your thinking on the topic.

> - *"Preparation for meetings is a waste of time. The chair controls everything and has made the important decisions before the meeting has even started." What is your opinion?*
> - *"The main purpose of meetings is to build relationships." What do you think?*
> - *How could managers use cross cultural diversity as a strength to create synergy in meetings?*

UNIT 4: Language, Communication and Culture

5.3: Working in Groups

Brieger and Comfort (1992) define meetings as, "The gathering together of a group of people for a controlled discussion with a specific purpose."

Spinks and Wells (1995) suggest that organisational groups normally consist of about fifteen people, and that these groups may be formal or informal. Formal groups are usually designated by the organisation, for example, the marketing and finance departments. These groups are often simply a part of the organisational chart. In theory, they must also work in harmony with other organisational groups.

Informal groups tend to form by themselves, or for some specific purpose. For example, they may be composed of people who come together from various departments for recruitment purposes. Spinks and Wells (1995) suggest that informal groups usually have the following characteristics.

- Similar values and attitudes. This means that participants' feelings about right and wrong, good and bad, acceptable and unacceptable, important and less important, will be similar.
- Clarity of group norms and sanctions. This means that each member of the group should conform to certain values, expectations, attitudes and norms. Failure to conform might result in powerful group sanctions.
- Group cohesiveness.
- Group defensiveness.
- Clarity of group roles. The term "roles" here means assuming and performing tasks and assuming the authority associated with those tasks.

Question 1

How could cultural differences negatively impact on the features above, and thus render the group less efficient? How could cultural differences be utilised to give added value to a group? Consider your answers and then check with our suggestions in the Answers to Questions section.

UNIT 4: Language, Communication and Culture

Question 2

> *What are the advantages and disadvantages of working in formal or informal groups? Make a note of your answers and then check with our suggested answer in the Answers to Questions section.*

5.4: What is a Meeting?

Pause for thought

> - What is the purpose of a meeting?
> - What is a good agenda?
> - What does the chairperson do?
> - What do participants do?
> - What is an effective meeting?
>
> Now answer the questions again from the following points of view (assuming typical behaviour).
>
> - A high power distance Italian
> - A strong uncertainty avoidance German
> - A high-context Chinese
> - A low-context English person
> - A monochronic Dane
> - A polychronic Egyptian.

Little is known about what makes meetings effective (Myrsiades, 2000). Furthermore, the move towards team-based organisational cultures has created a need for meeting facilitation skills (Niederman and Volkema, 1999). These skills include managing the interaction of the meeting participants, guiding the problem-solving or decision-making process and evaluating the effectiveness of the meeting.

Myrsiades (2000) suggests that the most important issues that need to be addressed are:

1. meeting leadership (chairing)
2. group member participation
3. the problem-solving process.

The kind of leadership adopted in a meeting should, in theory, match the group that is to be led. Myrsiades (2000) suggests that there are two dominant forms of leadership: directive and reserved. Reserved leadership might be the best choice when:

- participants have sufficient knowledge of the topic to be discussed
- participants tolerate ambiguity
- participants have sufficient experience of working in groups
- the group is highly motivated
- the group is small
- there is sufficient time.

Directive style might be the best option when:

- participants need some kind of structure
- participants lack knowledge of the topic to be discussed
- participants do not have enough experience in teamwork
- participants are not motivated
- the group is large
- there is little time.

Myrsiades (2000) records that one of the primary goals of her own training sessions was to get the chairperson to act less as a boss and more as a facilitator. In other words, the chair was to avoid dominating the group. As a facilitator the chair's role should be to:

- function as a neutral guide, not as an opinion leader
- discuss and develop an agenda to guide the meeting
- open the meeting with a brisk statement of objectives
- encourage a definition of the problem
- respect individual views and involve all members
- summarise periodically and clarify any agreement
- keep the group on track
- handle problem people to control the negative effect they may be having on the others
- watch time carefully
- summarise conclusions reached and assign tasks.

UNIT 4: Language, Communication and Culture

Question 3

> 1. In your opinion, how many of the roles above can be described as useful in any meeting, regardless of whether it is monocultural or intercultural?
> 2. Using Hofstede's (1991) four dimensions of culture, which cultures might have a preference for the facilitative chairing role? Check your answers with ours in the Answer to Questions section.

According to Myrsiades (2000), the role of participants is to:

- take notes and prepare for discussion
- find common goals and establish links
- assess their own aims
- develop a strategy for more effective interpersonal interaction
- change their behaviour and objectives to conform to changed circumstances
- tackle difficult topics - not to fear conflict
- ask for and give feedback
- provide evidence to support opinions
- summarise the opinions of others.

Question 4

> *Imagine the following scenario.*
> *Harry Carter is on his way from Birmingham to Shanghai. He is going to meet his Chinese counterparts for a meeting. While on the plane, he reads the guidelines above and feels that he is well prepared for the meeting. When he eventually sits down to talk to his Chinese colleagues, he does not hesitate to bring up sensitive issues and he does so directly. He is prepared to face conflicting opinions come what may. He says what he thinks and feels and when he does not understand, he presses his fellow participants for clarification. He summarises the opinions of others without hesitation. He even points out areas that have not been explained very well.*
>
> *Harry is surprised to find that some of his behaviour meets with a certain disapproval from the Chinese participants. Why is this? Think about the situation, make a note of your answers and*

UNIT 4: Language, Communication and Culture

then check with ours in the Answers to Questions section.

With regard to problem-solving Myrsiades (2000) suggests that a good problem-solving or decision-making procedure should involve all group members. If the chairperson is a facilitator, s/he will elicit problem-solving techniques from the group rather than express the problem in his/her own terms. Myrsiades (2000) claims that groups tend to solve problems more effectively when they are framed as the group understands them.

Question 5

The points above may be true in some cultures but not in others. In which cultures might a group-framed problem-solving process work? In which cultures might it not be so effective? Check with our answer in the Answers to Questions section.

5.5: Meetings in Conflict

Most formal meetings will have: an agenda, a purpose, a chairperson, participants and a result. The result may well be expressed in a series of action points. Further, most managers in most international companies have been well trained in the skills of presenting and running effective meetings. However, in many cases, these skills are often relevant only within the managers' own country and culture. As Berger (1998) points out, "People's natural tendency is to try to transplant the skills that work in their home culture into a new culture."

Question 6

The following case study has been adapted from Elashmawi (1998). As you work through it consider the following questions.
1. *What are the expectations of the chairperson?*
2. *What are the expectations of the participants?*
3. *How far are the expectations of both chair and participants governed by cultural values?*

A sample answer is provided in the Answers to Questions section.

UNIT 4: Language, Communication and Culture

Harry Carter has been promoted to a senior position and is now in charge of a multicultural team in Indonesia. He wants to hold staff meetings every Friday morning at 8.00. On the day of the first meeting, three of the Indonesian participants arrive five minutes late. Worse still, the other three do not arrive until 8.20. Harry is already slightly annoyed that the meeting will be late starting, but he is even more annoyed when he sees that the last three Indonesians to arrive brought some uninvited members of their own staff.

Harry brings in more chairs, and when he is ready to start, he sees that the four Japanese team members have reorganised the seating arrangements so that they can sit together in a sub-group. Everyone is still waiting for the senior Indonesian member who is expected to deliver some opening comments. He arrives late and he spends more than the five minutes allotted to him. The meeting finally begins at 8.40.

Harry then goes through the agenda and objectives of the meeting and invites questions from the other participants. Nobody speaks. Then, Harry invites the senior Indonesian member to say something, and after this, the rest of the Indonesians join in the conversation.

At first, Harry thinks he is managing the meeting quite well, although he becomes irritated by the side conversations carried on by some of the Indonesians. Harry likes his meetings to maintain focus on final results and objectives.

Half way through the meeting, Harry has a discussion with one of his UK colleagues. Their discussion is open and heated and it clearly upsets both the Japanese and the Indonesians, and they suggest a break for tea and biscuits. The Indonesians are irritated that Harry has ordered tea but no snacks.

When the meeting restarts, Harry urgently wants to push towards a conclusion. He wants a democratic vote on an item they have been discussing. Furthermore, he wants Mr Hasegawa, the Japanese team leader to agree to vote on his side. Unfortunately, Mr Hasegawa asks for some days so that he can consult his boss in Tokyo. Harry is becoming frustrated and angry. Mr Hasegawa decides to take out his own frustrations on Harry at this point by asking him why, given that they sit only a few metres apart, he communicates by e-mail with him instead of walking over and speaking face-to-face.

UNIT 4: Language, Communication and Culture

It is clear that the roles and purposes of the elements of a meeting can vary according to cultural preferences. We stress the word "can," because not all people act according to their cultural stereotype. As Mole (1995) points out, behaviour in meetings will depend as much upon personality as on cultural conditioning.

Question 7

> *Most meetings will have an agenda, but attitudes towards it may differ. Assuming typical behaviour, how do you think the following would view the importance of an agenda?*
> - *A monochronic, high uncertainty avoidance German.*
> - *A polychronic Italian.*
> - *A monochronic, low uncertainty avoidance American.*
>
> *Once again, check with our answer in the Answers to Questions section.*

Pause for thought

> *The role of the chairperson may differ according to cultural preference. Assuming typical behaviour, what would the following people expect from the chairperson in terms of style and control?*
> - *a high power distance French person*
> - *a low power distance American*
> - *a high-context Japanese.*

Question 8

> *In multicultural meetings, what do you feel should be the most important characteristic of a chairperson? Try and give your opinion in one simple sentence and then compare your answer with our opinion in the Answers to Questions section.*

Question 9

> *Below you will see six descriptions of participant behaviour in meetings. The behaviour is stereotypical of certain cultures. Read the descriptions and match them with the nationalities. When you have finished, check with our answer in the Answers to Questions*

UNIT 4: Language, Communication and Culture

section.

1. *They will be well-prepared and tend to make contributions only when they feel qualified to do so. When they do make contributions, they tend to be direct and frank. Those who make contributions outside their area of expertise are frowned upon. They tend to follow the agenda and need structure. Meetings are often places where decisions are ratified rather than discussed. Discussions may well have taken place before the meeting by the relevant "experts."*
2. *They tend not to challenge the boss and feel free to wander away from the agenda. Sometimes, they may also walk away from the meeting if they have another commitment. In other words, they are not time conscious. In debate, they tend to be adversarial, dogmatic and logical.*
3. *They tend to be innovative and creative with ideas, but they tend to digress and discuss what may appear (to some people) to be irrelevancies. They also tend to expect a strong chairperson. They may often be late for the meeting.*
4. *They tend to be pragmatic and come to a meeting unprepared but with a desire to discuss all aspects of a problem and edge towards a decision. They will expect a democratic chair and they will expect to have their views listened to and respected. Opinions are often given for discussion purposes rather than as proposals.*
5. *They tend to look for the compromise solution instead of imposing a solution on others. They are also pragmatic and look for the practical rather than the theoretical. They tend to be direct in their communication style.*
6. *They may well be late for the meeting and may also wander away from the subject under discussion. They tend to dislike losing face for any reason and will often say nothing rather than look foolish in front of the other participants.*

France
England
Spain
Holland
Italy
Germany.

UNIT 4: Language, Communication and Culture

5.6: Purpose and Expectations in Collision

Mole (1995) argues that not only may different cultures behave differently in meetings, they may also come to the meeting with different expectations.

Question 10

> *Look at the following participant-expectations of a meeting (1-3). When you have read them, decide which types of culture the expectations may apply to. Then check with our answer in the Answers to Questions section.*
>
> *1. We come to meetings expecting to be briefed. We expect to be given information by the chairperson/boss and if the meeting has to finish in a decision, we expect the boss to come with a detailed plan which he will impose on us with as few changes as possible.*
> *2. We come to meetings expecting to discuss problems and pool ideas for the purpose of making a decision based on compromise and common sense. Usually we do not prepare very well but we expect our opinions to be heard. Usually, our opinions are not positions to be defended but ideas which should be used as a springboard for discussion.*
> *3. We come to meetings in the hope that mutual understanding and the will to co-operate will develop. We expect a reaffirmation of direction rather than decisions on specific steps. We also expect that most of the really important decisions will be made at the bar or over dinner. The most constructive part of the whole process is definitely the social side.*

Pause for thought

> *Imagine you have been called in to develop the meeting skills of employees whose company has just merged with a foreign company. How would you sensitise employees to possible differences with regard to expectations in meetings.*

UNIT 4: Language, Communication and Culture

My own anecdotal experience at DaimlerChrysler confirms that differences in expectations can literally paralyse a meeting. German participants on my intercultural meetings courses have described their first meetings with their new American colleagues as "horror stories," in which, after initial moves, both sides sat and stared at each other, not knowing what to say or how to carry on.

The challenges above may be further complicated by differing approaches to problem-solving. In fact, different cultures may not even be able to agree on the problem itself. Hofstede (1991) suggests the following.

- High power distance cultures have a tendency to see problems in terms of a negligent power structure (management).
- High uncertainty avoidance cultures tend to see the problem in terms of lack of clear structure or rules.
- Low uncertainty avoidance cultures/low power distance cultures tend to see pragmatic solutions to human relationship problems.
- Feminine cultures tend to see the problem as an inability to compromise.

Crookes and Thomas (1998) argue that differences in culture are responsible for differences in approaches to problem-solving between Hong Kong Chinese and British managers.

The most obvious differences between British culture and Hong Kong culture lie on Hofstede's (1991) dimensions of power distance and individuality/collectivism. Crookes and Thomas (1998) suggest that high power distance managers are more likely to accept ideas handed down to them hierarchically and less likely to propose their own ideas upwards. Conversely, low power distance managers are more likely to question a superior's opinions and claim equal value for their own views. In Hong Kong, collective and high power distance values may probably result in deference, pleasing others and maintaining harmony. Given these differences in culture, it would not be unreasonable to find differences in approaches to problem-solving.

Crookes and Thomas (1998) also point to aspects of Chinese culture which may have an influence on approaches to problem-solving. In particular, the authors suggest that the maintenance of both social and structural harmony is crucial. Social harmony is achieved through the values of Jen and Li. The former implies doing to others as you would have them do to you. Li concerns awareness of appropriate behaviour in a given situation. In particular, Li serves to structure and maintain harmony and order in hierarchies (Westwood, 1992).

Two other important aspects of Chinese culture, which concern social harmony, are face and shame. Chinese managers are likely to be motivated by a desire not to lose face or to cause others to lose face, particularly if that other person is a superior. Giving face to superiors is a prime concern, and as a consequence, agreeing with the ideas of the boss and not mentioning ones own are clear manifestations of the same mindset. Shame may be felt if a Chinese manager breaks the social norms of role behaviour.

Structural harmony is achieved through management of key relationships. In Confucianism these are identified as Wu Lun - the duties and obligations of social and hierarchical relationships. In organisational terms, this means that superiors can expect respect and obedience from subordinates, but in return, superiors must protect their subordinates. Further, role positions are clear and occupants of the role must stay in that role.

In essence, Confucian ideals place a high value on social control, harmony and a respect for those in authority. Consequently, Chinese managers would be unlikely to risk proposing radical or deviant ideas, and are, therefore, more likely to avoid risk-taking and innovative ideas with regard to the problem-solving process.

5.7: Culture Clash or Culture Harmony?

So what are the cross-cultural skills that we need to develop in order to collaborate effectively in meetings? Berger (1998) suggests that they can be broken down into three sub-skills.

1. Communication Skills. These include: making sure your language is at the right level for the other participants, recognising the different cultural meanings of verbal and non-verbal behaviour, giving and getting feedback and awareness of different attitudes towards the importance of relationships and trust.
2. Behavioural expectations. These include an awareness of how others expect to behave at meetings. This behaviour may concern, for example: punctuality, preparation and agenda management, awareness of chairing styles and use of power, awareness of decision-making style and its implications for time management.

UNIT 4: Language, Communication and Culture

3. Cultural values. These include: awareness of which cultural values are most likely to have an impact on the running of meetings, a willingness to adapt to cultures whose values are different.

Hurn and Jenkins (2000) identify the following areas in which cultural difficulties are often experienced in intercultural meetings.

- Greetings.
- Level of politeness.
- Showing agreement/disagreement.
- Small talk.
- Use of interpreters.
- Punctuality.
- Leave-taking.
- Gifts.
- Status of women.
- Body language.

Question 11

Read the following situation and then try to answer the question below. A sample answer is given in the Answers to Questions section.

Berger (1998) cites an interesting case study, which highlights the need for developing teamwork across cultures. The case concerns a merger between a French company and an English company. Although a main concern was to develop a collaborative culture, culture differences were very apparent at business meetings. Most participants (both English and French) came to see the meetings as a waste of time and tended to blame the incompetence of the "other side."

Initial training brought to light two principal learning points with regard to communication. First, the UK participants were hard to understand because of their use of slang and speed of talking. Second, the English participants were put off by the enthusiastic communication style of some of the French participants, and in particular they claimed to be intimidated by their use of gestures and other forms of body language.

Having highlighted the communication aspects of the problem,

UNIT 4: Language, Communication and Culture

> *the group was ready to face a second day of training in order to focus on how to run effective meetings.*
>
> *What would you do on the second day of training?*

5.8: Success in Multicultural Meetings

We suggest that in order to work effectively in multinational meetings, participants should develop a truly multinational approach. This approach should attempt to harmonise the differences between cultures and, at the same time, attempt to preserve national cultural strengths. Problem areas include: the need for clear, pre-agreed agendas, the need for appreciation of the differences between monochronic and polychronic attitudes towards time, and the need for a skilled chairperson who is able to understand and deal with possible cultural misunderstandings (Hurn and Jenkins, 2000).

A strategy is needed to ensure that those who think their level of English language ability is low are not excluded. Such a strategy could include carefully prepared agendas with summaries of key points discussed and agreed at certain points. The use of questions to elicit and check feedback is also important.

Hurn and Jenkins (2000) identify the factors that, in their opinion, are crucial for success in multicultural meetings. These factors are:

➢ detailed preparation
➢ agreement on gaining consensus
➢ clear objectives
➢ appropriate level of representation
➢ clear expectations
➢ appointment of a culturally-sensitive chair
➢ agenda agreed in advance
➢ socialising needs
➢ appropriate language.

In order to achieve their full potential, multinational teams must overcome barriers that uniform teams may solve relatively quickly. In other words, the advantages of cultural diversity will not be automatic.

There is a clear need to build trust. Time should be made available to develop trust when operating in different cultures because prejudices

UNIT 4: Language, Communication and Culture

and stereotypical perceptions can take a long time to die.

Relationship building is fundamental, and yet, it should not be forgotten that cultures develop and perceive relationships quite differently. For example, the Americans tend to be direct, and often take an instrumental view towards relationships. Teams may be put together mechanistically. On the other hand, the Latin and Asian view tends to emphasise building personal relationships. The initial stages of getting to know others are crucially important. Similarly, Germans may focus their trust on a person's ability to deliver on time and keep to schedules. So how can training help create synergy?

Question 12

> *Hurn and Jenkins (2000) suggest a model for creating cultural synergy. The main points of their model are shown below, but they are not in the correct order. Put them in the right order and then compare your answer with the answer in the Answers to Questions section.*
> 1. *Work out the cultural assumptions behind the situations. For example, high-context people tend to speak around the topic and assume that others are sensitive enough to know what the important points are. Low-context cultures tend to be specific.*
> 2. *Describe the situation from one's own cultural perspective. For example, there may be concern and frustration at some participants being unable or unwilling to say exactly what they mean.*
> 3. *Establish culturally synergistic alternatives based on the cultures involved in order to develop a way of working together which is acceptable to all.*
> 4. *Implement and refine the solution.*
> 5. *Having established the differences, look for areas of cultural overlap, similarities and differences and where there might be some common ground.*

With regard to the personal qualities and attributes which are necessary to produce good intercultural meetings, Hurn and Jenkins (2000) suggest:

- flexibility and adaptability
- interpersonal skills

UNIT 4: Language, Communication and Culture

- ability to think both locally and globally
- ability to work multiculturally
- linguistic skills
- listening skills
- strong identification with company culture and values
- enthusiasm
- ability to promote and achieve consensus
- patience, empathy, and a non-judgmental approach.

5.9: Conclusions

We introduced this chapter by saying that a good starting point for working effectively in intercultural meetings is to recognise that the "My-way-is-best" attitude is neither appropriate nor helpful. At the heart of effective groupwork of any kind is mutual respect. From respect and understanding ways of working together will emerge.

5.10: Answers to Questions

Question 1
Cultural differences will have an immediate impact on values. If different cultures are represented in the group, then there will be a variety of attitudes to good and bad and right and wrong. Until these are clarified, there will be no norms and expectations that participants can conform to. The result is likely to be confusion and bad feeling. Certainly there will be little or no group cohesiveness and individuals are likely to defend their own positions rather than look for a group position to defend. There will probably be confusion over group roles. For example, the role of the chair is probably perceived in one way in France and another way in the UK.

Cultural values may be utilised by looking at strengths rather than weaknesses of the nationalities involved. A good example of cultural synergy is the joint-venture between DaimlerChrysler (Germany) and McClaren (UK) in their efforts to produce a super sports car. In theory, weak uncertainty avoidance cultures are good at generating innovative ideas while strong uncertainty avoidance cultures are better at implementing. This is what happens with the super sports car. The design and creativity of the project has been largely left to the low uncertainty avoidance UK while the implementation of the project is the domain of the high uncertainty avoidance Germans. Until now, the project seems to be going very well.

Question 2
Some of the advantages are:
- a group usually has more knowledge than any one individual
- a group has more courses of action open than any one individual can have

UNIT 4: Language, Communication and Culture

- group criticism of a proposed course of action should produce a more highly refined selection of possible approaches
- various tasks can be assigned to the best individuals
- human relations value.

Some of the disadvantages are:
- formal leaders may be in conflict with informal leaders
- there may be an ongoing struggle to maintain roles
- members may lack the training or expertise to make good decisions
- conflict may destroy morale
- time taken to make and implement decisions.

Question 3
1. We suggest that regardless of culture, the chair should open the meeting with a statement of objectives, involve everyone, summarise periodically, keep the group on track, watch the time and summarise conclusions.
2. The neutral guide is probably to be found in low power distance, individualistic and weak uncertainty avoidance cultures. The same is true of the democratic development of an agenda. A high power distance leader is likely to impose his will. Low power distance leaders, on the other hand, are likely to encourage a group definition of the problem. Generally speaking then, Anglo and Scandinavian cultures will probably prefer a facilitative chairing role.

Question 4
Harmony is very important to the Chinese (collective - high-context - polychronic culture) and so Harry's insistence on focusing on "difficult" topics and facing them threatens to destroy that harmony. Harry's behaviour reflects the monochronic, individualist values of his culture. Furthermore, Harry's insistence on asking for clarification and summarising the points of others may threaten the face of his Chinese counterparts. Although Harry means well, his behaviour is culturally insensitive.

Question 5
It might work in a low power distance, individualistic, low uncertainty avoidance culture. High power distance or strong uncertainty avoidance cultures might well expect the "leader" to take control. UK business people have often been heard complaining that decisions in Germany have usually been taken before the meeting and that the group has been gathered together only to ratify that decision.

Question 6
The case study illustrates the clash between Harry's values of individualism, directness and monochronic time-consciousness, and the Japanese collective values of face-to-face discussion and polychronic consensus building.

Harry's idea of good meetings is that they should be action-oriented. He also thinks that meetings should have an agenda, and the goal of the whole process is to arrive at a decision. Harry will probably value sticking to the issues and be impatient with digressions. Harry will also believe in the value of open and heated debate (within culturally understood limits). These heated debates are not usually personal, but not all cultures put a value on this and nor can they fully appreciate the separation

UNIT 4: Language, Communication and Culture

of the issue from the individual. Most Asian cultures value the maintenance of face and harmony and such overt "aggression" is not valued (Lavaty and Kleiner, 2001). In essence, Harry has come to the meeting expecting to chair a well-informed, focused, structured meeting with open and "honest" participation. At the end of the meeting, he needs a decision and tasks should be assigned to team members.

The Japanese, on the other hand, are concerned about maintaining group harmony and consensus. Immediate decisions are rarely made. They expect to discuss problems and actions and they frequently have to wait until headquarters makes the decisions for them (Elashmawi, 1998).

High power distance Indonesians will usually expect a senior person to open and close a meeting. They may also invite other members of their department to a meeting. These uninvited members may be experts on the subject under discussion and they will readily engage in side conversations in order to clarify points (Elashmawi, 1998).

Harry threw out an open question at the beginning of the meeting. He expects all the participants to engage in open debate. Most people from individualistic cultures will feel free to do just this. However, people from collective societies will not speak up unless personally invited to do so. And when they do, they are likely to put forward the interests of their group rather than a personal opinion. Personal opinions are not logical in collective societies. Finally, high-context collective cultures tend to value face-to-face discussions rather than the impersonal memo or e-mail.

Question 7

Clearly, there is plenty of space here for misunderstandings and frustration. For example, it is likely that a German will expect an agenda to be circulated well in advance of a meeting and will expect to keep to it during the meeting itself. A polychronic Italian might not feel the need to stick so closely to the agenda and digress frequently, while an American might feel the need to negotiate changes to it at the beginning of the meeting.

Question 8

The chairperson should be culturally sensitive. Lewis (2006, pp 154-156) is particularly good on this.

Question 9
1. Germany
2. France
3. Italy
4. England
5. Holland
6. Spain.

Question 10
1. High power distance cultures and possibly high uncertainty avoidance cultures.
2. Low power distance and low uncertainty avoidance cultures.
3. High-context communication cultures.

UNIT 4: Language, Communication and Culture

Question 11

Berger (1998) suggests the following technique. First, you should simulate two meetings. One should be run by the French delegates and the other by the English delegates. You should ensure that both meetings receive feedback from all course participants. The purpose of the feedback (based on a questionnaire) is to evaluate the feelings of course members towards the simulations and to look for areas for improvement.

You might then allow the entire group to discuss the typical differences between French and English meetings. The group could draw up a list of features of a typical meeting in the UK. The main features might be that:
- the purpose of meetings is to agree actions and make decisions
- you should stick to the agenda and deviate only if new points arise
- time is important
- follow up-action points are generally agreed on
- participants should arrive on time and stay until the end.

Then, the group could draw up a second list, concerning the typical style of conducting meetings in France. The main features might be that:
- it is acceptable to wander away from the agenda
- the purpose of meetings is to give input to decisions and not necessarily to make them
- you should not argue with the boss
- the main decision-maker may not be present at the meeting
- time is relatively unimportant - people can come and go during the meeting.

Having discussed the differences, you could have the group decide which style is best suited to the company. The conclusion may surprise you. Perhaps both styles are suitable, and the style will depend on the circumstances. When quick action is needed, the UK style may be more appropriate. However, when general policy and marketing issues are to be decided, then the French style may be better.

You could then conduct further meeting simulations in which group composition is half French and half English. The purpose of these simulations is to build cross cultural teamwork. You can give the role of chair to different delegates and elicit points about how to conduct these meetings.

Lastly, you should introduce the group to the ideas of Hofstede (1991) in order to underpin the practice with a theoretical framework.

Question 12

The correct order should be: 2-1-5-3-4

UNIT 4: Language, Communication and Culture

Chapter 6

Culture and Business Communication - 2

6.1: Introduction
6.2: Objectives
6.3: Negotiation and Agreement
6.4: Influences on Intercultural Negotiations
6.5: Conclusions
6.6: Answers to Questions.

6.1: Introduction

This chapter deals with negotiations across national boundaries. We argue that although models of national culture are valuable tools, we also need to consider an individual's personality. We continue to stress that models of national culture refer only to tendencies and should not be used to stereotype.

In addition, we need to consider company culture. Lebas and Weigenstein (1986) suggest that an emphasis on employee-conformity to corporate culture is increasingly being adopted instead of rules and regulations in order to encourage productivity. As a consequence, the organisational culture in which individuals work may have a significant impact on the content and style of their negotiations.

If you have little knowledge or experience of negotiations, we

UNIT 4: Language, Communication and Culture

suggest that you look at Fisher and Ury (1981) before you begin this chapter. For those of you who are interested in the intercultural aspects of the discussion, we suggest you look at Thomas (2004).

6.2: Objectives

The objectives of this chapter are to:

- sensitise you to the main elements of negotiation
- show how culture may influence negotiation style and content
- show how the influence of culture can be tempered by company culture and individual personality
- sensitise you to the different stages of the negotiation process
- show how culture can influence these different stages.

Pre-reading task

Before you begin, try to answer the questions in the box below. The questions are designed to focus your thinking on the main ideas in the chapter.

> - *Negotiators are expected to get the best possible deal for their employers. They should focus exclusively on getting as much as possible from the other side. What do you think?*
> - *Compromise in negotiations is a sign of weakness. What is your opinion?*

6.3: Negotiation and Agreement

Harris and Moran (1987) suggest that negotiation is, "a process in which two or more entities come together to discuss common and conflicting interests in order to reach an agreement of mutual benefit."

Graham and Herberger (1983) identify four stages of business negotiations. These are:

1. non-task relationship creation
2. task-related exchange of information
3. persuasion

UNIT 4: Language, Communication and Culture

4. concession and agreement.

Fowler (1986) and McCall and Warrington (1989) suggest that all negotiations have the following characteristics.

- Two or more parties are involved.
- The parties need each other's involvement to achieve the jointly desired result.
- Each party has different interests, and these prevent the achievement of the desired objective.
- Each party should persuade the other to modify their initial position.
- A successful outcome is one that is mutually acceptable.
- Negotiation is an interaction among people.
- Each party has a degree of power over the other.

Woo and Prud'homme (1999) argue that negotiation is not a single skill or even a group of skills. Essentially, they see negotiations as:

> ...a process that takes place in a particular context. The context, in terms of subject matter, the nature of the parties involved and the degree of formality, determines the particular skills required in any specific negotiation situation. Some of these skills are common to all forms of negotiations while others are specific to a particular context. (Woo and Prud'homme, 1999)

Simintiras and Thomas (1998) argue that the negotiation process is a complex one, which is significantly influenced by the cultures in which the participants are socialised. The authors argue that each culture has its own negotiating style, and a negotiation is cross-cultural when, "the parties involved belong to different cultures and therefore do not share the same ways of thinking, feeling and behaving." (Casse, 1981)

We suggest that these cultural differences can have a significant influence on each of the four stages of the business negotiation process and any agreement reached. Ideas, expectations and behaviour can be culturally unique. Different cultures may produce different negotiation style and focus on different areas of agreement. For example, one culture might stress the implementation stage of an agreement while another might focus on relationship building. Furthermore, one culture

UNIT 4: Language, Communication and Culture

may value negotiating items one at a time while the other may value a more holistic approach and negotiate everything at once.

It is not even enough to say that all parties enter into a negotiation in order to reach an agreement. An agreement is, "an exchange of conditional promises in which each party declares that it will act in a certain way on condition that the other parties act in accordance with their promises." (Martin and Herbig, 1997)

The problem is that different cultures may interpret the word "agreement" in different ways. Martin and Herbig (1997) argue that two types of agreement exist. The first is explicit, detailed and usually written, and covers all foreseeable contingencies. Such an agreement generally requires no further co-operation. The second is implicit, broad, usually oral, and leaves room for flexibility.

Question 1

Read the situation below and answer the questions beneath it. When you have finished, check your answers with ours in the Answers to Questions section.

A major British company signed a deal with a Chinese distributor based in Shanghai. The deal concerned the distribution of the British company's products throughout parts of China. The agreement was an exclusive agreement. This meant that the Chinese distributor undertook to deal only with the UK company's products and not those of competitors.

At first, everything seemed to go as expected. After a few months, however, the CEO of the British company in London found out that their Chinese partners were actually distributing competitors' products. Initial enquiries received the response from Shanghai that practice indicated that the UK product did not completely cover the market needs and that it was better for everyone that the Chinese distributor deal with other similar products. By doing so, they could increase market coverage and thereby increase total sales - this was good for both parties.

After a while, the CEO in London decided to take action. He sent his trusted deputy to Shanghai in order to find out what was going on. The Chinese had never met this deputy. The man telephoned the Chinese office from his hotel in Shanghai and simply informed the Chinese of his presence. The Chinese

UNIT 4: Language, Communication and Culture

> *responded by delaying and finally refusing to meet his UK partner's ambassador. After a few days, the deputy went home. The British CEO reacted by taking expensive legal action.*
>
> *What has gone wrong here? Try to answer the question from both the Chinese point of view and the British point of view.*

6.4: Influences on Intercultural Negotiations

Negotiation is an area of research with numerous studies, but few have been conducted on cross-cultural negotiations (Gulbro and Herbig, 1999). Nevertheless, there are many books and articles of the "how to" variety of negotiating with companies from other cultures (e.g. Graham, 1984; Kramer, 1989; Graham et al, 1992).

Kale and Barnes (1995) suggest that cross-cultural negotiations are influenced by three distinct but interdependent constructs. These are:

➢ national culture
➢ company culture
➢ individual personality.

The authors suggest that these three constructs will, in turn, influence both the content of the negotiation and the style. Content refers to, "...suggesting, offering, or negotiating a set of product-specific utilities and their expectations," (Kale and Barnes, 1995). Style refers to, "...the rituals, format, mannerisms, and ground-rules that the buyer and seller follow in their encounter." (Kale and Barnes, 1995)

In order to achieve a satisfactory negotiation result, compatibility between buyer and seller is necessary with respect to both content and style.

The influence of culture

Gulbro and Herbig (1999) argue that any one of Hofstede's (1991) four dimensions of culture can have an impact on the following three aspects of negotiation.

1. The methods used in negotiation.
2. The expectations of each participant.

UNIT 4: Language, Communication and Culture

3. The participants' interpretation of the behaviour of others during each stage of the negotiation process.

Gulbro and Herbig (1999) go on to say that, "By using the Hofstede behavioural attributes, these behaviour differences can be somewhat predictable."

Question 2

Gulbro and Herbig (1999) carried out a survey of over 1000 US firms and 1000 multi-nationals. The survey was intended to find out if there are differences in the amount of time spent on the various stages of a negotiation, and whether or not these differences were culturally dependent.

You will see the results of this survey below (in smaller print). I have replaced the 8 terms used by Hofstede (1991) (e.g. high power distance - low power distance and so on) with the 8 letters a-b, c-d, e-f, and g-h. Each letter corresponds to an extreme tendency of one of Hofstede's dimensions of culture (so if "a" represents high power distance, then "b" represents low power distance).

Read the results and decide which letter refers to which dimension of culture. Write down your answers and compare them with ours in the Answers to Questions section. For example if you think cultures "a" represent low power distance, you write: LPD culture – "a".

Cultures "a" will spend more time in the non-task negotiating activities. Interaction and togetherness are important to "a" cultures.
Cultures "a" will spend more time in positioning during the negotiating activity.
Cultures "c" spend less time compromising. Perhaps people from these cultures see compromising as a weakness.
Cultures "e" tend to spend less time in persuasion
Cultures "g" will spend more time on the agreement stage of the process. This can be seen as an effort to reduce risk. For people from "g" cultures, contracts are firm guidelines and should be followed exactly.
Cultures "a" will spend more time planning before and debriefing after a negotiation or a negotiation session than cultures "b". Sometimes three or four days are spent debriefing in "a" cultures.

UNIT 4: Language, Communication and Culture

Gulbro and Herbig (1999) suggest their survey confirms that culture does have an impact on both negotiation behaviour and on the time spent on each stage of the negotiation process. The authors point out that preparation for any negotiation is vital, and that a large part of the preparation for a cross-cultural negotiation is to get as much information as possible about the other side and its culture. "Foreign negotiators will be different, in perceptions, expectations, motivation, beliefs and outlook." (Gulbro and Herbig, 1999)

Organisational culture

The concept of corporate culture is elusive and rather unclear. There are many definitions. For the purposes of this chapter, corporate culture is defined as something which, "...encompasses the pattern of shared values and beliefs which enable people within the organisation to understand its functioning, and furnishes them with behavioural norms." (Kale and Barnes, 1995)

Kale and Barnes (1995) suggest that five dimensions of corporate culture are particularly important. These dimensions concern whether or not the company is:

1. inward-looking or outward-looking
2. task-focused or people-focused
3. conformity-driven or individuality-driven
4. safety-oriented or risk-oriented
5. reactive or proactive.

Question 3

Below you will see five descriptions (A-E) of the five dimensions above. Please match them.

A. This dimension assesses a company's level of tolerance towards diverse behaviours among its employees. One extreme encourages people to wear the same clothes, to engage in similar work habits, and may even try to regulate private lives. The other extreme fosters and encourages diversity in lifestyle and behaviour at work.
B. This dimension examines how a company tends to react to changes. Does it tend to be proactive and spend time on

> *forecasting and analysing the economy or does it react to change when and if it happens?*
> C. *One extreme of this dimension will focus almost entirely on the product and product perfection. The other extreme will focus on market needs and will be driven by customer requirements.*
> D. *This dimension assesses how far an organisation considers its workers as people with needs, desires and wants, and how far the organisation will try to accommodate them. The other extreme of this dimension will focus entirely on work and efficiency.*
> E. *This dimension focuses on the organisation's reaction to new methods and practices, and its response to new challenges and opportunities. Is the company a leader in the market place or a follower?*

Pause for thought

> *Look again at the five descriptions in question 3. Is there a link between the type of organisational culture and Hofstede's (1991) dimensions of culture? In other words, do you think that some national cultures would have a tendency to produce certain organisational cultures? For example, how far would a company that stresses individuality be suited to a strong uncertainty avoidance culture?*

Individual personality

Individuals will, then, be partly conditioned by national culture and by the organisational culture in which they work. However, people will always exert their individual personalities. Personality is defined by Kale and Barnes (1995) as, "...an individual's consistency in behaviours and reaction to events."

Further, Kale and Barnes (1995) cite research in social psychology which suggests that the personality dimension has a significant effect on the outcome of a negotiation (e.g. Padget and Welosin, 1980; Runkel, 1956). Individual personality will, therefore, exert a powerful influence on both negotiation content and negotiation style.

We suggest that given the face-to-face nature of most negotiations, personality and personality tests can be both useful and applicable in

UNIT 4: Language, Communication and Culture

helping us understand such interactions.

The Myers Briggs Type Indicator (MBTI) is being increasingly used by companies in order to assess people's likely behaviour in a variety of situations. The Myers Briggs model of personality is based on 4 preferences.

1. Where do you focus your energy (introvert/extrovert)?
2. How do you prefer to process information (sensing/intuition)?
3. How do you make decisions (thinking/feeling)?
4. How do you organise your life (perceiving/judging)?

Based on these four dimensions, the MBTI then identifies sixteen different patterns of preferences and actions. We would like you to look at the article on the following web-page and decide your Myers Briggs type for yourself.
http://www.teamtechnology.co.uk/tt/t-articl/mb-simpl.htm

As with all personality questionnaires, the results of can be over-generalised or inaccurate. However, the questionnaire can provide valuable information, and you can do it yourself.

Question 4

Now you have looked at the four dimensions on the web-page, consider the following questions.

➢ *Look at the following terms and expressions. Would you tend to apply them to an extrovert or an introvert? Sociability, interaction, territorial, internal focus, external focus, concentration, people-oriented, ideas-oriented.*

➢ *Look at these terms and expressions. Would you tend to apply them to an intuitive type or a sensing type? Facts-oriented, focus on detail, focus on the big picture, practical, down-to-earth, imaginative, innovative.*

➢ *What about the following terms. Would you apply them to the "thinker" or the "feeler"? Logic, objective, subjective, principle, analysis, values, sympathetic.*

➢ *Finally, would you apply the following terms or expressions to "perceivers" or "judgers"? Closed options, open options, flexible, information-seeking, decisions, data gathering, flexible.*

UNIT 4: Language, Communication and Culture

Interrelationship between constructs

We have already suggested that the three constructs of national culture, company culture and individual personality, will together influence the content and style of a negotiation. We can also say that the impact of any one construct will be influenced in turn by the other two constructs. For example, a person brought up in a highly individualistic culture may be obliged to suppress this individualism when working in a company that encourages conformity of, for example: attitudes, behaviour, dress and appearance.

There is evidence (Deal and Kennedy, 1982) that there are attempts at matching personality type to organisational culture. My own experience while working as a trainer with the Human Resources department of Hewlett-Packard GmbH, suggests that recruiters look for personality types as much as for people with the "right" qualifications.

There may also be a strong relationship between national cultural characteristics and individual personality. For example, a culture characterised by high uncertainty avoidance may well have more judging types in its population. Similarly, a culture characterised by femininity may well have more feeling types in its population. Again, we stress the word, "may."

Effects of the constructs on the negotiation

A successful negotiation depends on harmony between the buyer and seller with respect to both the content and the style of communication. The content of a negotiation may revolve around a number of product features. Kale and Barnes (1995) identify five product features.

- Functionality. This feature concerns the product's performance. The value of the product is determined only by how far it does what it is supposed to do.
- Social. This feature concerns the identification of a product with a certain social or economic groups. The product may produce social image.
- Emotional. This feature concerns the identification of a product with certain emotions and feelings, for example: respect, love or hate.
- Novelty. This feature concerns the need some people have for novelty, curiosity and the exploration of new product offerings.

UNIT 4: Language, Communication and Culture

➤ Security. This feature concerns reducing the risk which is often associated with the purchase of new products.

Most products would probably contain a range of these features. However, it clearly makes good sense for the seller in a negotiation to focus on the feature which is attractive to the buyer. What is attractive to the buyer may well depend on the buyer's culture, personality and the organisational culture to which he belongs.

Question 5

> *Imagine you are selling your product around Europe and negotiating with buyers. Which aspects of the product (if possible) would you emphasise in the following countries?*
> *Germany*
> *Sweden*
> *England*
> *Italy.*

Hofstede's (1991) four dimensions of culture may also determine the preferred style of communication.

Question 6

> *1. Which types of culture might prefer a soft-sell approach and non-aggressive sales technique?*
> *2. Which types of culture might prefer a more aggressive, hard-sell approach?*
> *3. Which cultures might prefer to build strong relationships?*
> *4. In which cultures would the seller take on a subservient and respectful role?*
> *5. Which cultures are likely to be more/less trusting?*

Communication style, as we noted earlier, concerns the rituals, ground-rules, mannerisms, and format followed in communication (Kale and Barnes, (1995). The authors suggest four different types of communication style.

1. Self-oriented style. This refers to those who are more interested in their own needs and desires than those of others. It may also apply

UNIT 4: Language, Communication and Culture

to people who are more interested in extrinsic rather than intrinsic rewards and who are relatively open about their own status and self-esteem.
2. Task-oriented style. This refers to a style which focuses on the completion of the task at hand with the minimum of time, money and effort.
3. Interaction-oriented style. This means establishing a strong rapport with your negotiation partner, sharing and fostering the security of belonging.
4. Tradition-oriented style. This implies a preference for following the rituals that have been established by others and reinforced over many years.

Kale and Barnes (1995) argue that national culture, organisational culture and personality will have a significant impact on interaction style. Question 7 attempts to focus your attention on some ways in which culture may influence communication style.

Question 7

> 1. Which type of communication style would you tend to use during a negotiation with collective cultures?
> 2. Which style would you tend to use with negotiation partners from strong uncertainty avoidance cultures?

Now let's look at how organisational cultures might influence communication style.

Question 8

> What type of communication style would you adopt with the following company cultures?
> 1. An outward-looking company.
> 2. A task-focused company.
> 3. A people-focused company.
> 4. A conformity-driven company.
> 5. A proactive company culture.
> 6. A reactive company culture.

UNIT 4: Language, Communication and Culture

Finally, let's look at how personality can influence content and style in a negotiation. A salesperson is likely to interact with a number of buyers who, in total, probably manifest the whole range of personality types. However, as Kale and Barnes (1995) argue, "...a salesperson's understanding of the buyer's personality should facilitate a selling approach that has a greater likelihood of success."

Question 9

> *How will the following personality types influence the negotiation? There are certainly many way. Think of as many as you can and then check with ours in the Answers to Questions section.*
> 1. *Extroverts and introverts.*
> 2. *Intuitive types and sensing types.*
> 3. *Thinkers and feelers.*
> 4. *Judgers and perceivers.*

6.5: Conclusions

Essentially, if you negotiate across cultures you should recognise that the foreign negotiator will be different from you in many ways. You should identify and accept your counterpart's culture and be prepared to communicate on a different cultural wavelength.

Being different does not necessarily mean being better or worse, and consequently, judging and being judged may well be inappropriate. Sensitivity to new cultural norms is required along with sensitivity to how your own behaviour may be perceived.

All this means hard work, preparation and a better understanding of other people and their cultures. After all, the negotiation itself may be the beginning of a long-term, healthy relationship between both the people themselves and their companies.

6.6: Answers to Questions

Question 1
The main problem here lies in the perceived nature of the agreement. In the UK, the action of signing a contract usually represents intentions to abide by the stated terms. Such an explicit contract sets out to cover all foreseeable contingencies, and the

UNIT 4: Language, Communication and Culture

parties are bound together by an external enforcement mechanism. The explicit contract assumes no relationship exists outside the provisions of the contract. Communication and obligations are limited to those that are provided for in the contract. It may be that circumstances change, but obligations do not, and the parties involved are legally-bound to fulfil their commitments. In essence, the negotiation process stopped for the British when the contract was signed. The Chinese have broken the contract and are therefore untrustworthy.

For the Chinese, the contract represents a starting point. Implicit agreements focus on the importance of relationship, and obligations have no limits. From the Chinese point of view, the future is unknown and unpredictable. Problems are expected and room is left for flexibility. Therefore, when the Chinese do business, they focus on friendship, and specific terms are left to be determined by future events. If they find themselves in a situation where honouring specific terms may be damaging or difficult, they may turn to their partners and expect understanding, support and help by changing the terms of the agreement.

In essence, for the British, the contract closes the deal, while for the Chinese the contract simply begins a relationship. Further, the Chinese would have been insulted by the arrival of a deputy. After all, they did not negotiate with this man and they would probably see him as the servant of the company and not at the required level with regard to status. In addition, the Chinese would expect to deal with a team and not an individual. Woo and Prud'homme (1999) suggest that when negotiating with the Chinese, westerners would do well to remember the following Chinese cultural traits.

- The Chinese attach considerable importance to status and hierarchy. Commonly, they will work only with those on the same hierarchical level.
- Face: i.e. giving and receiving proper respect is vital. The easiest way to make people lose face is to criticise them in public.
- The Chinese place a high value on trust.
- Friendship is also vital before any business relationship can begin.
- Guanxi (relationship) binds people through the exchange of favours.
- Ambiguity. This trait is a manifestation of the polite nature of the Chinese, who would shy away from rejecting a proposal outright Instead, they may provide an ambiguous response.
- Patience. Chinese negotiators tend to take their time. In contrast, European negotiators tend to go for the "quicker-the-better" solution.
- Chinese protocol. This has developed over centuries and it is expected that European negotiators are familiar with it.

The main problem above is that the British have not taken the trouble to find out about Chinese cultural characteristics. The same may also be said of the Chinese. Trouble was waiting to happen!

Question 2
"a"   collective cultures
"b"   individualistic cultures
"c"   high power distance
"d"   low power distance
"e"   masculine cultures
"f"   feminine cultures

UNIT 4: Language, Communication and Culture

"g" high uncertainty avoidance
"h" low uncertainty avoidance.

Question 3
1. C
2. D
3. A
4. B
5. E

Question 4
Extrovert: sociability, interaction, external focus, people oriented.
Introvert: territorial, internal focus, concentration, ideas-oriented.

Intuitive: focus on the big picture, imaginative, innovative.
Sensing: facts-oriented, focus on detail, practical, down-to-earth.

Thinkers: logic, objective, principle, analysis.
Feelers: subjective, values, sympathetic.

Perceivers: flexible, open options, information-seeking, data-gathering, flexible.
Judgers: closed options, decisions.

Question 5
Germany is a high uncertainty avoidance culture. It would be advisable (at least at the beginning) to emphasise the product's uncertainty-reducing features. I would focus on an established brand name, for example, or superior warranty and money-back guarantee.
    Sweden is a feminine culture so it would be advisable to focus on the environmentally beneficial features of the product.
    England is a highly individualistic culture so you should consider emphasising the novelty value of the product - keeping one step ahead of the rest.
    Italy is a high power distance culture so it would probably be a good idea to emphasise the status value of your product rather than its functionality.

Question 6
1. Low uncertainty avoidance cultures.
2. High uncertainty avoidance cultures. Hofstede (1991) observed that strong UA cultures tend to experience greater anxiety and that this anxiety can display itself as aggression in social interactions.
3. Collective/polychronic/high context cultures.
4. In high power distance societies, the seller often has a low status.
5. High power distance societies and strong uncertainty avoidance cultures can see others as a threat and therefore have little trust towards them. Weak UA cultures tend to have more trust towards others.

UNIT 4: Language, Communication and Culture

Question 7
1. An interaction-oriented style. You may even consider adopting a problem-solving approach to the negotiation which will mean both parties co-operating.
2. A tradition-oriented style of interaction might be better with strong uncertainty avoidance cultures. These tend to be conservative and resistant to change.

Question 8
1. An interactive problem-solving style. If you are selling to an outward-looking company you would be wise to show willingness to modify your product in order to satisfy the buyer.
2. A task-oriented style. You should try and conclude the negotiation with the utmost efficiency.
3. Social small talk, personal rapport should be your aims and emphasising the social features of your product.
4. Standardised sales presentations, and approaches - a tradition-oriented style.
5. You should emphasise and be absolutely clear about product benefits, warranty features, and contingency clauses. A tradition-oriented style.
6. Less task-driven, and informal, and flexible - a more interactive style.

Question 9
1. Extroverts may well prefer to socialise and to engage in small talk. They will probably prefer the interaction-oriented style of communication and a strong relationship with their negotiation counterpart. Introverts may prefer the task-orientation in negotiations and they may tend to value functional performance of a product rather than the social features preferred by extroverts.
2. Sensing types will probably show a preference for performance that can be measured. They will be impressed by factual presentations with graphs and charts etc. Intuitive types will prefer novelty value and prefer the use of metaphor and implicit meaning in communication.
3. Thinkers may well be influenced by a presentation grounded in reason and logic. Feelers will be more susceptible to the use of emotional appeals and they will be impressed by the emotional features of a product.
4. Judgers will focus on closing a sale and the use of irrevocable contracts. Perceivers will want to maximise flexibility and to display indecisiveness. Perceivers are conversationalists who may wander away from the topic. Judgers will probably value product security features more then perceivers.

UNIT 4: Language, Communication and Culture

Chapter 7

Culture and Business Communication - 3

7.1: Introduction
7.2: Objectives
7.3: The Presenter
7.4: Content
7.5: Style
7.6: Conclusions
7.7: Answers to Questions.

7.1: Introduction

This chapter focuses on the giving of presentations across cultures. In order to get the most from it, we suggest that you have another look at Hofstede's (1991) dimensions of culture (see unit 1, chapter 5) and Hall and Hall's (1990) high- and low-context communication style (see unit 1, chapters 4 and 10). We also suggest that you look again at Kale and Barnes (1995) and their product features (see unit 4, chapter 6). For those who are interested in a book of the "How to…" variety, we suggest you look at Jolles (2005).

When presenting, the presenter should consider how to best deliver the talk, the best style and with the best content. "Best" can be selected using a number of environmental criteria. These criteria are:

UNIT 4: Language, Communication and Culture

- economic and market conditions
- industry type
- organisational culture
- national culture.

National culture is, therefore, only one consideration. We stress again that although models of national culture are extremely important tools which can help us better understand people from other cultures, they are not the only tools at our disposal.

7.2: Objectives

The aims of this chapter are to:

- show how the characteristics of national culture can influence the delivery of a presentation, choice of content and style.

Pre-reading task

Before you start the chapter, we would like you to consider the situation and task in the shaded box below. The task should focus your attention on the main issues in the chapter.

> *You are the marketing manager of a chain of health clubs. This chain has been very successful in the UK and you are now ready to expand into Europe. As part of your promotional campaign, you are to give a series of presentations in France, Germany and Sweden. In the UK, your marketing campaign has focused on improving bodily performance for both men and women, and increasing life expectancy. Your target audience is men and women between the ages of 25 and 45, people who are high achievers and high earners. You offer professional one-to-one training sessions and an area which includes sauna, steam room and massage.*
>
> *How will you present your health club in France, Germany and Sweden? The audiences will include company leaders, and you are hoping to get their support by promoting your clubs in their companies. Think about the content of your presentation, the type of language you will use, and the best delivery.*

UNIT 4: Language, Communication and Culture

7.3: The Presenter

A presentation given by an inappropriate person may fail as a presentation even if everything else goes according to plan. The norms governing addressor/addressee relationships in one culture do not necessarily apply in other cultures. We illustrate this in question 1.

Question 1

> *Imagine you are sending your sales professionals to give presentations in France, Germany, China and the US. Your sales team consists of: Lucy - 30 years old and a high-flying, highly competent and ambitious MBA graduate. Mark - 50 years old and a very experienced member of your team, and Jeremy - 35 years old and an expert in the field you are entering. Finally, you, as the CEO, are also available if necessary. Which of your staff would you choose for which country - assuming you are entering these markets for the first time and have yet to build relationships?*

7.4: Content

A presentation is persuasive when the presenter selects information that the audience perceives as relevant in terms of their situation and cultural values. For example, motivation differs from one culture to another. A message designed to motivate will be useless unless cultural differences are taken into consideration.

Question 2

> *Look at the following motivators. In which types of culture would you most probably find them? When you have finished, check with our answer in the Answers to Questions section.*
> *1. Opportunities for individual promotion.*
> *2. Autonomy.*
> *3. Opportunities to belong to a supportive group.*
> *4. Job security.*
> *5. Variety.*
> *6. Opportunities to co-operate with others.*

UNIT 4: Language, Communication and Culture

> 7. Personal loyalty shown by superiors to subordinates.
> 8. Service ideal.
> 9. Short and convenient working hours.

The presenter should also consider which features of a product or service s/he should emphasise during the presentation. In the previous chapter we saw that Kale and Barnes (1995) suggest the following features.

- Functionality.
- Social.
- Emotional.
- Novelty.
- Security.

Question 3

> Can you see a link between these features and Hofstede's (1991) dimensions of culture?

If the information is readily available, presenters should also take company culture into consideration. In the previous chapter we saw that Kale and Barnes (1995) suggest the following dimensions to describe company culture.

- Inward-looking or outward-looking.
- Task-focused or people-focused.
- Conformity-driven or individuality-driven.
- Safety-oriented or risk-oriented.
- Reactive or proactive.

If you answered question 3 in the previous chapter, you might recall the characteristics of these dimensions. In case you skipped the question, here is a brief description of the dimensions again.

Inward-looking cultures tend to be product-driven while outward-looking cultures tend to be market-driven. The task-focused culture will centre its efforts on work and efficiency while people-focused cultures will consider their workers and try to accommodate them. A conformity-driven culture tends to discourage diverse behaviours among its employees while an individuality-driven culture will

UNIT 4: Language, Communication and Culture

encourage diversity in behaviour. The fourth dimension (safety-oriented or risk-oriented) focuses on the organisation's reaction to new methods and practices, and its response to new challenges and opportunities. Is the company a leader in the market place or a follower? The fifth dimension (reactive or proactive) examines how a company tends to react to changes. Does it react to change when it happens or does it try and predict change?

Question 4

> *Do you think it likely that some cultures will produce more of one type of company culture than another?*

7.5: Style

In languages which offer choice, relationships can be signalled by the use of personal pronoun, for example: tu and lei, Sie and Du. In English, such pronouns no longer exist. However, this does not mean that formal and informal styles do not exist. You might want to watch politicians. When they want to appear friendly and close to the audience, they tend to use informal language. When they want to appear presidential or authoritarian, they tend to use formal, almost written language. Mead (1994) suggests that informal styles in English tend to:

1. be grammatically simple
2. use Saxon over Latin-based vocabulary
3. use abbreviations as against the full (almost written) form
4. be slurred and words run together
5. be heavy on intensifiers (very, basically)
6. be heavy on empty modifiers (kind of, sort of)
7. be heavy on empty adjectives (super, wow).

Style can also be influenced by non-verbal signalling. For example, where do presenters position themselves? Standing too close to the audience can signal a low power distance approach, which involves the audience more. Standing too far from the audience can signal that the presentation is more like a lecture, and the audience is less directly involved. Eye-contact, gestures, voice quality and volume can also be

UNIT 4: Language, Communication and Culture

used effectively depending on the style the presenter wants to adopt.

7.6: Conclusions

Question 5

> *Look at the following situation and answer the question that follows.*
>
> *Reutlingen Telecommunications (RT) is going through a bad patch. Sales are falling rapidly and the competition is gaining market share. Paul Ruff, the managing director of RT, has had a good idea. He proposes that the company raises its profile with the buying public by sponsoring a round-the-world record attempt in a balloon.*
>
> *Unfortunately, Paul must tell his workforce that this year the company will be unable to give them a pay rise. At the same time, he must inform them that 1000,000 dollars will be spent on the record attempt. On the other hand, Paul feels that he can afford not to make any redundancies this year, despite numerous rumours that redundancies are inevitable. Paul is going to make a presentation to his middle managers on Monday. He wants to tell them of his plans but he wants to motivate them. How should he structure and deliver his presentation, what content should he include and what style should he use? Reutlingen Communications is a German company and all of the workforce are German.*

UNIT 4: Language, Communication and Culture

7.7: Answers to Questions

Question 1
France is a high power distance country and age tends to be respected more than youth. It is also a strong uncertainty avoidance culture. It therefore tends to prefer hard facts. You should send either Mark or Jeremy. Germany is also a strong uncertainty avoidance culture and you should send your expert. China is a collective and high power distance culture. You should probably go yourself and with Jeremy as back-up. Teams are the norm in China. Lucy would be suitable for the US, a low-power culture which tends to respect youth and achievement.

Question 2
1. Individualistic cultures.
2. Individualistic cultures.
3. Collective cultures.
4. Strong uncertainty avoidance cultures.
5. Weak uncertainty avoidance cultures.
6. Low power distance cultures.
7. High power distance cultures.
8. Feminine cultures.
9. Feminine cultures.

Question 3
Strong uncertainty avoidance and masculine cultures would almost certainly value the functionality feature and the security features of your product. Weak uncertainty avoidance cultures might go for the novelty feature. Feminine cultures might value the social and emotional features.

Question 4
The answer to this is a big "maybe" but you would be unwise to base the content of your presentation on such assumptions. It is more likely that industry sector will have more of an influence on company culture. Imagine a computer manufacturer that was not outward looking and proactive! Also, car manufacturers tend to be conservative in whatever country they happen to be located. Having said that, presenters should try to find out as much as possible about the company and its culture when considering the best content for their presentation.

Question 5
Paul needs to think about the following.
➢ The objectives of the presentation.
➢ The content.
➢ The audience.
➢ The structure of his presentation.
➢ Style.

The objective is to motivate the audience and get them to support his ideas. Germany is a strong uncertainty avoidance culture so job security would be a motivator. Paul needs to convince them that his ideas will increase job security in the long-term.

UNIT 4: Language, Communication and Culture

He should start the presentation by stating that no redundancies are planned. Furthermore, the new strategy would safeguard jobs in both the short and the long term. Next he should explain the new strategy and, at the same time, use numbers and solid facts to back up his ideas. Paul also needs to appear to be in control so his style should be a little distant and authoritarian.

Finally, he should tell the managers that some short-term sacrifices are necessary and so there would be no pay rise this year.

UNIT 4: Language, Communication and Culture

Chapter 8

Non-verbal Communication (NVC)

8.1: Introduction
8.2: Objectives
8.3: The Elements of Non-verbal Communication
8.4: Kinesics, Oculesics and Vocalics
8.5: Space and Communication - Proxemics
8.6: Time Orientation and Communication
8.7: Conclusions
8.8: Answers to Questions.

8.1: Introduction

It has been suggested (Fromkin and Rodman, 1983) that as much as 90% of the communicative process takes place non-verbally. Trompenaars (1993) points to research which indicates that 75% of all communication is non-verbal.

Although we suggest that such figures should be approached with a degree of care, there is little doubt that NVC can have a powerful influence on listeners. It can reinforce words and charge them with meaning. NVC can also be learned. Professional or experienced communicators are fully aware of the influence that NVC can have on audiences. Body movements, eye behaviour, gestures, and the use of

UNIT 4: Language, Communication and Culture

silence itself, for example, can be carefully rehearsed and choreographed.

The influence of NVC is all the more powerful because the meaning conveyed is often received on a subconscious level, and audiences can be influenced without their being aware of it.

Wolfgang (1984) suggests that we respond more easily to the non-verbal behaviour of those who have a similar cultural, linguistic and racial background. Some non-verbal behaviours may well be universal, but there is little doubt that others are not. The purpose of this chapter is, therefore, to raise awareness of the fact that differences in non-verbal behaviour across cultures exist, and that they can potentially and fundamentally change our perceptions of what is communicated.

8.2: Objectives

At the end of this chapter, you will:

- be able to assess the role played in communication by non-verbal factors
- be able to identify and detail the principal channels of non-verbal communication (NVC)
- be able to identify and analyse the factors that can influence NVC
- be able to critically examine orientations to time and space and how these can influence NVC.

Pre-reading task

Before you begin, look at the questions in the shaded box below. The questions are designed to focus your thinking on the topic.

> 1. *What aspects of non-verbal communication should we teach students of EIB?*
> 2. *In what situations should business people (and, therefore, our students) be aware of non-verbal communication?*
> 3. *How do you currently teach NVC?*

UNIT 4: Language, Communication and Culture

8.3: The Elements of Non-verbal Communication

Non-verbal communication occurs every time one individual interacts with another. It can be intentional and learned, but it can also be unintentional. The central issue, however, is that the interpretation of this "silent" communication can have a major influence on how the event is perceived.

NVC has been widely studied (e.g. Argyle, 1994; Delmonte, 1991), and there are a number of definitions. Gabbott and Hogg (2000) suggest that NVC is:

> ...communication that transcends the bare elements of the written or spoken word. It encompasses a number of aspects of body language including facial expression, eye-contact, posture, gesture and interpersonal distance. To these can be added a number of factors associated with the delivery of speech, for example stress, loudness and intonation. In combination, these components modify the semantic content of the exchange.

Question 1

> *How could you teach NVC in the classroom? Think of some ideas and then look at our suggested ideas in the Answers to Questions section.*

Gabbott and Hogg (2000) usefully summarise the influences of NVC by categorising them into four broad areas.

1. Proxemics - the use of personal space and distance.
2. Kinesics - body posture and gestures.
3. Oculesics - communicative aspects of eye behaviour.
4. Vocalics - para-linguistice cues such as pitch and tone of voice.

Pause for thought

> 1. *How far is touching other people acceptable in your culture? Which parts of the body are you allowed to touch? Which parts of the body are taboo? In my culture, for example, I*

UNIT 4: Language, Communication and Culture

> *could touch people on the elbow but touching their feet would probably elicit a negative reaction.*
> 2. *Do you personally use many gestures? Make a list of the most usual gestures you make.*
> 3. *How far is it acceptable/unacceptable to maintain continuous eye-contact in your culture?*
> 4. *How far is it acceptable/unacceptable in your culture to raise your voice? What does this signify?*

In essence, NVC is a series of cues. These cues are encoded by the sender and transmitted either consciously or subconsciously. The receiver will then decode the cues. The problem is that even within a specific culture, numerous possibilities for communication breakdown exist.

Pause for thought

> *Imagine you are having a face-to-face conversation with another person. This person belongs to your cultural group. How might you interpret the following aspects of his non-verbal behaviour?*
> ➢ *He shouts.*
> ➢ *His arms are folded.*
> ➢ *He does not maintain eye-contact.*
> ➢ *He speaks in a monotone.*
> ➢ *He covers his mouth.*
> ➢ *He keeps leaning forward and touching your arm.*
> *How would you interpret this behaviour if your partner were from another country - for example, Italy?*

Folded arms may be interpreted as defensive, but we have to be careful about this. It may signify nothing more than that the person is cold or perhaps they simply feel comfortable with folded arms. At a more complex level, breakdown in communication can occur when verbal and non-verbal messages are contradictory. For example, think about the presenter who claims that he is "happy to be here," but who says this in a monotone and with a miserable facial expression.

Gabbott and Hogg (2000) argue that there are three variables that impact on the nature of NVC.

UNIT 4: Language, Communication and Culture

1. Gender. The authors suggest that men and women will interpret communication cues differently. They argue that men speaking to men will use different NVC from men speaking to women. The authors also maintain that, for example, men have higher levels of touch avoidance than women, and women tend to smile more and frown less, and approach closer than men.
2. Culture. Some aspects of NVC may be universal while others are not. The challenge is to make the distinction. For example, smiling may be considered to be one universal aspect of NVC. After all, most people know what a smile looks like (and sounds like). However, the people of some cultures smile at times which people from other cultures might consider to be inappropriate. The Japanese, for example, will often smile when apologetic, confused or even angry. Similarly, in Thailand, Malaysia and Singapore, for example, smiling is often used to mask embarrassment (Axtell, 1991). In most Western cultures, smiling can indicate friendliness, or friendly intentions. The majority of English people, for example, would not expect a smile to indicate anger or confusion and would probably not interpret it as such.
3. Personal characteristics. NVC is an interpersonal behaviour, and a number of characteristics influence the coding and decoding of what is communicated. These characteristics include personal traits. Boorom et al (1998) argue that there are two dimensions which can be linked to personality traits. These are: communication competence and communication apprehension.

According to the authors, communication competence deals with the ability of individuals to make sense of a conversation, the degree to which they become involved in the conversation, and the amount of turn-taking and turn-yielding. These can have a strong influence on the effectiveness of the interaction for each participant.

Communication apprehension concerns the individual's degree of fear or uncertainty with regard to communication in general or one communicative event in particular. This apprehension can sometimes lead to inattention, ineffective perception and poor responsiveness. The implication is that those with communication apprehension may well be less able to receive both verbal and non-verbal information. As a consequence, they may experience difficulty not only in interpreting what they observe, but also in formulating their own messages.

UNIT 4: Language, Communication and Culture

Question 2

> 1. Why might communication apprehension be of vital importance to those who operate across cultures?
> 2. Which types of culture might be most influenced by communication apprehension?

The final personality trait concerns the way in which the receiver perceives the attractiveness of the sender (e.g. Marlowe et al, 1996). Gabbott and Hogg (2000) suggest that the impact of communication can be directly influenced by how the receiver decodes the attractiveness of the sender. The term "attractiveness" can include familiarity, similarity and liking.

Pause for thought

> ➢ How important is another person's physical attractiveness to you?
> ➢ Do you think that high-context cultures might place more importance on physical attractiveness than low-context cultures? Why? Why not?

Research by Joseph (1982) suggests that when a speaker is perceived as an "expert", the issue of attractiveness becomes less relevant. However, when the speaker is not perceived as an "expert", then the issue of attractiveness becomes more relevant. Thus, it seems that the perceived ability to do certain tasks can be inextricably bound up with the way a person looks.

Gabbott and Hogg (2000), who are writing about the impact of non-verbal communication on service evaluation, conclude that:

> ...non-verbal communication is clearly an important consideration for service marketers. Not only can it enhance service delivery, but it can also destroy erstwhile well-designed and well-researched delivery systems. It follows therefore that customers' response to service delivery, perceived service quality or satisfaction, are dependent on their interpretation of various non-verbal signals during the encounter and the decoding of the meaning associated with them.

UNIT 4: Language, Communication and Culture

Gabbott and Hogg (2000) also point out that the impact of NVC on service evaluation may change according to culture.

Pause for thought

> ➤ Do you think that physical attractiveness is important as a tool for providers of the EIB service? Do you make yourself attractive before entering the classroom?
> ➤ Imagine you saw an advertisement for a teacher of EIB to work in-company in, say, China. How would you feel if the advertisement stipulated that the successful person had to be physically attractive?

8.4: Kinesics, Oculesics and Vocalics

Axtell (1991) suggests that our actions and gestures can be divided into three broad categories: instinctive, coded and acquired.

Instinctive gestures are those which are done almost unconsciously. Axtell (1991) points to the "eyebrow flash" as an example. The eyebrow flash is an automatic raising of the eyebrows and a wrinkling of the forehead that all humans do when they greet one another. It is a signal of openness. Crossed arms (defensiveness) and scratching the nose (telling lies) are other examples of body movement which may be perceived as indications of what is going on inside a person's mind. However, we suggest that interpretations of this kind are approached with caution.

Pause for thought

> Crossed arms may well be a sign that a person is cold or comfortable. Would you suggest that a person obliged to put across an important point in a meeting should cross their arms? How should they do it and what sort of body language should they adopt? Why is this?

Coded gestures are established through group agreement and are understood by all interested parties. For example, the gestures of a football referee are understood by most people worldwide who are interested in football. Similarly, the gestures used by traders at the

UNIT 4: Language, Communication and Culture

London Stock Exchange are understood by insiders but often a mystery to outsiders. Sign language for the deaf is another good example of coded gestures.

Acquired gestures and body language are generated in a specific social and cultural context, and are the main focus of this section. Axtell (1991) argues that acquired gestures are, "loosely and informally collected among separate societies with no particular logic except that they are widely used and understood among a certain group of people."

This, as Axtell (1991) points out, is the crux of the matter. "Identical gestures can often mean different things among different societies. Each culture seems to adopt its own set of rules."

An examination of all aspects of kinesics, oculesics and vocalics is beyond the scope of this chapter. What is more, kinesic and oculesics have been well covered by Axtell (1985, and 1991). Axtell's (1991) book is not a scientific text. Nor does the author claim it as such. However, for those of you who would like to know about body language and eye behaviour from a practical point of view, Axtell (1991) is invaluable. Nevertheless, we shall give some examples which indicate how NVC differs across cultures.

Pause for thought

> *What is the conventional form of greeting in your culture? Consider people you meet for the first time, and people with whom you are slightly acquainted. Is this form of greeting appropriate in all cultures?*

The handshake is one form of greeting, but there are many different styles of shaking hands. Some cultures value the firm handshake with direct eye-contact. Others prefer a gentle handshake with no eye-contact. Occasionally, the handshake is accompanied by the free hand covering the grip. This is supposed to add degrees of closeness or unity and is often practised by politicians in front of the media. In some cultures, the handshake is followed by a hug. However, other cultures find that direct bodily contact is almost distasteful.

Pause for thought

> *Consider all the dimensions of cultural differences we have so far discussed in this book. Is there, perhaps, a link between*

UNIT 4: Language, Communication and Culture

> *masculine/feminine cultures and the type of handshake adopted? Or is the type of handshake governed by whether or not the culture is high- or low-context? Or perhaps there are no links. Perhaps it simply depends on the individual. What is your opinion?*

In many cultures, the handshake is not necessarily the most commonly used of greetings. Consider India, for example, where the *namaste* is the most common form of greeting. This involves placing the hands at chest height in a praying position and involves a slight bow. The same gesture is used in Thailand.

In the Arab world, some people still give the *salaam*. This means touching the heart with the right hand. The hand then travels to the forehead and up and outwards. It is often accompanied by a nod of the head and the words "Salaam Alaykum," or "Peace be with you."

Business people going to Japan often worry about the greeting. In particular, their worries may concern: who bows first, how low does one bow, when are hands shaken and when are business cards exchanged and what you do with the card once you have it. It is highly likely that a Japanese person will not expect a foreigner to know these rules. However, we should be aware that Japan, like many Asian cultures, is a collective and high-context culture, and as such, the Japanese will value harmony and relationship building. A strong and assertive handshake and the eye-stare are unlikely to be appreciated in such cultures.

Farewells are, perhaps, a little less complicated but even here, there is room for misunderstanding. For example, in Italy and Greece, people wave goodbye with the arm extended and the palm up and then curling the fingers back and forth. To most English and Americans, this gesture means, "Come here."

Eye behaviour (oculesics) is another area of NVC that can cause misunderstanding. I was brought up to believe that in England, you should look others in the eye and failure to do so might be construed as weakness or dishonesty of some kind. However, in Japan, Thailand and Korea, for example, it is considered very rude to stare. Prolonged eye-contact is considered not only impolite but also intimidating and, therefore, a threat to harmony. Conversely, in the Arab world, strong eye-contact is expected.

UNIT 4: Language, Communication and Culture

Question 3

> *Imagine one of your Japanese students is sitting in class with his eyes shut while you are explaining the use of conditionals in negotiations. How would you interpret these closed eyes?*
> ➢ *He is concentrating.*
> ➢ *He is bored.*
> ➢ *He is asleep.*

8.5: Space and Communication - Proxemics

Every living creature has its own personal space. We can compare this space to a bubble, which expands or contracts depending on the person's culture, emotional state and relationship to others. Anyone who travels around the world will soon discover that some cultural bubbles are bigger or smaller than others. For example, Axtell (1991) argues that the personal bubble surrounding Americans is about 12–15 inches. This means that when two Americans speak to each other the distance between them should measure about 24–30 inches.

Asians, according to Axtell (1991), have a bigger personal bubble. Even though Japanese, for example, may be forced to stand shoulder to shoulder on a train, they tolerate the situation by averting their eyes from the person with whom they are rubbing shoulders.

Latin peoples and people from the Middle East tend to stand much closer to each other than do Americans or Japanese people. They also tend to touch much more than, for example, English people.

Touch-oriented cultures and non-touch-oriented cultures often collide. Axtell (1991) maintains that the following are touch-oriented cultures.

➢ Middle East countries.
➢ Latin European and Latin American.
➢ Some Asian countries.
➢ Russia.

The following are examples of non-touch oriented societies.

➢ Japan.
➢ US and Canada.

UNIT 4: Language, Communication and Culture

- England.
- Scandinavian countries.
- Holland.

And the following represent what Axtell (1991) refers to as "middle-ground" cultures.

- France.
- China.
- Ireland.
- India.

Personal distance is not something we all give much thought to. However, this distance is culturally conditioned and, as a result, foreign spatial clues are difficult to interpret. Invading personal space can seem aggressive or pushy, while being too physically distant can appear rude, cold or remote. None of these adjectives need apply if we remember that our own preference for personal distance will not necessarily be shared by people from other cultures.

Pause for thought

> *The use/misuse of space is very important in, for example, presentation skills. For instance, how far away from the audience should the presenter stand? What difference can this distance make in your culture? How do you teach this to students of EIB who will go on to work in a global environment? What about negotiation skills?*

Space can also be used to indicate power. As Hall (1990) points out:

> A corner office suite in the United States is conventionally occupied by the 'brass,' and a private office in any location has more status than a desk in the open without walls. In both German and American business, the top floors are reserved for high-ranking officials and executives.

Hall's (1990) view needs to be treated with some caution. Corporate culture may discourage any form of overt hierarchy. For example, Hewlett Packard has a low power distance corporate culture, and this

UNIT 4: Language, Communication and Culture

can be clearly seen in its open-plan offices worldwide. The current writer often gives courses in HP Germany. The CEO's office space is open in the same way as the office space of all other employees, and he eats at the same tables as everyone else.

DaimlerChrysler, which is on the other side of the motorway, has a completely different and "classic" corporate culture as indicated by Hall (1990) above. There is no doubt in my mind that the 'feel' of the two cultures is completely different. In DaimlerChrysler, space is sacred. Managers are compartmentalised in offices, and usually the doors are firmly shut.

This compartmentalisation is an indication that the free flow of information tends to be limited or blocked. As Hall (1990) points out:

> Germans do not share information freely except with their own particular work group, and sometimes not even with them... This highly restricted information flow is probably the greatest handicap to German business.

Gabbott and Hogg (2000) support the view that space and territory can be effectively used to give tone to communication. Writing of service quality, the authors suggest that:

> The context in which the service takes place clearly affects the primary communication exchange. A number of environmental factors have been identified...that can facilitate effective communication, for instance the physical environment can be designed to facilitate appropriate NVC. The key word here is appropriate; depending on the type of service, different non-verbal signals may be appropriate. Professional service providers may wish to communicate authority and distance, while personal service providers may be more concerned with the development of warmth and personal closeness. The environmental props associated with this management of appropriateness may include desks to signify distance, closed versus open office designs, standing versus sitting positions, the use of service tangibles, or the ability to touch the other party.

UNIT 4: Language, Communication and Culture

Pause for thought

> *Communicative methodology encourages open-plan room layout, no desk separating teacher from students, and with the teacher sitting on the same level as the course participants. Is this simply a manifestation of the values of low power distance cultures like the UK and the US? If your answer is 'yes', is it appropriate to communicate this (using the NVC of layout) to students from high power distance cultures?*

Before leaving this section on space and communication, consider high-and low-context societies again. We have already seen that in low-context Germany there is a tendency towards compartmentalisation, and this may be reflected in offices with closed doors and restricted information flow. But what about high-context offices? Would we find the same tendencies? Hall (1990) suggests that in high-context offices:

> ...information flows freely and from all sides. Not only are people constantly coming and going, both seeking and giving information, but the entire form and function of the organisation is centred on gathering, processing, and disseminating information. Everyone stays informed about every aspect of the business and knows who is best informed on what subjects.

Frei et al (1999) suggest that such a culture will impact on office design. "This style of management requires workplace design that emphasises open areas, easy access to multiple employees, and comfort to permit long periods of contact between the managers and others."

8.6: Time Orientation and Communication

Hall (1990) suggests that although there are probably many ways in which people and cultures can organise time, two major classifications can be made. These are: monochronic time and polychronic time (see unit 1, chapter 4). You will recall that monochronic time emphasises the compartmentalisation of time, with a strict adherence to appointments and deadlines. Monochrons also tend to focus on one task at a time and do not like to be interrupted.

UNIT 4: Language, Communication and Culture

An orientation towards polychronic time means a tendency to do many things at the same time with little regard for, or concern with, time restraints. Polychrons tend to be highly distractible and can be easily interrupted. The characteristics of monochronic and polychronic peoples are listed below.

Monochronic People	**Polychronic People**
do one thing at a time	do many things at once
concentrate on the job	are highly distractible
take time commitments seriously	time commitments are secondary to relationships
are low-context	are high-context
stick to plans	change plans easily and often
do not disturb others	are more concerned with family and friends
emphasise promptness	promptness is based on the relationship
tend to short-term relationships.	tend to long-term relationships.

Question 4

> *From your own experience and from your current understanding of cultural differences, how would you describe the tendencies in the following countries: monochronic or polychronic?*
> - *Germany*
> - *England*
> - *Italy*
> - *Spain*
> - *Japan*
> - *China*
> - *Holland*
> - *Chile*
> - *France*
> - *the US.*

Morden (1999) suggests that the mixing of monochronic and polychronic cultures can give rise to constant culture clash and disagreement. However, this mixing can also, if well understood and managed, give rise to powerful synergies.

Communication of information on an organisational level can differ

UNIT 4: Language, Communication and Culture

greatly depending on whether the culture is monochronic or polychronic. In Germany, for example, information tends to be highly focused, compartmentalised and controlled. In France, on the other hand, information tends to spread widely and rapidly. Further, information overload is rare because people tend to stay in constant contact. The drive to stay in touch is very strong in polychronic cultures, and therefore, interpersonal contact takes precedence over everything else, especially time constraints.

Pause for thought

> *Information is power! How would this statement manifest itself differently in monochronic and polychronic cultures?*

Time can also be used to reveal how and what we feel about others.

Pause for thought

> ➢ *Do you take pride in being punctual?*
> ➢ *Are you always on time for meetings at work? Does your punctuality depend on the person/people who are waiting for you?*
> ➢ *Do you keep some people waiting? Why? Why not?*
> ➢ *If you keep some people waiting, what criteria are you using?*

When conducting business in other countries, it is essential to know how time is treated. For example, how much lead time is needed when requesting an appointment? How much time do you need to prepare a report? How much time is needed for planning a major project? How much time do you need to close a deal?

Hall (1990) suggests that these aspects of business will depend on the culture. For example, in high-context, polychronic cultures, lead time will often depend on the relationships involved. In monochronic, low-context Germany, for example, the amount of lead time may well depend on the importance of the business to be conducted.

UNIT 4: Language, Communication and Culture

Question 5

> *Imagine you are negotiating contracts with suppliers in various parts of the world. How important to you would the relationship between you and your supplier be? How important would it be to your supplier in China? In general, how much time would you need to close the deal in polychronic cultures? What about monochronic cultures? Why does this difference exist?*

Weinstein (1996) suggests that as we begin to drown in information, technology is not the only way to resolve the resulting stress. The author argues that we are becoming less and less able to absorb and process all the information and knowledge that surrounds us and that we should consider new ways of working. Weinstein (1996) concludes that in the future we should consider sharing, co-operating, applying action learning and open-space conferencing. In essence, the author suggests that we allow ourselves time and space to think about what we really need to know.

Pause for thought

> *Does the future according to Weinstein (1996) belong to monochrons or polychrons?*

Anecdotal evidence suggests that women tend to be polychronic, and men tend to be monochronic. Does this mean that if Weinstein's future is polychronic then the future of global business belongs to women?

8.7: Conclusions

Non-verbal communication is woven into our patterns of communication. In this chapter we have examined the elements that make up NVC. We have tried to show how gestures, eye movement, and the use of space and time can give colour and tone to what we say and sometimes override the words we use.

The recommended reading for this chapter is Axtell (1991). The book gives a comprehensive view of what gestures can mean, how they are used and when to avoid them. Part 1 of Hall (1990) is also recommended.

UNIT 4: Language, Communication and Culture

Above all, we suggest that you take note of the NVC that you see around you on a day-to-day basis. The television is a wonderful source of material. Not only can you watch the NVC of your own cultural group, you can watch that of others without even leaving your sitting-room.

8.8: Answers to Questions

Question 1
One way for learners to develop skills in NVC is to work in small groups. Learners could then be asked to carry out a problem-solving role-play while others watch. The observers may be surprised at how quickly they can tell if one of the role-players is feeling defensive or is trying to mislead. Even though a role-player may feel he is hiding his discomfort or impatience, observers can often read the signals quite clearly. You can do something similar with presentation skills, negotiation role-plays and meetings

Question 2
1. Because they will almost certainly be speaking English, and that language will be foreign to them. This alone can sometimes cause anxiety.
2. Strong uncertainty avoidance cultures.

Question 3
In Japan, closed eyes can often mean that the listener is in deep concentration.

Question 4
Germany – monochronic
England – monochronic
Italy – polychronic
Spain – polychronic
Japan – polychronic
China - polychronic
Holland – monochronic
Chile – polychronic
France - polychronic

Question 5
In polychronic cultures the relationship often takes precedence over the contract. The signed contract is not the end of the negotiation. It merely signals the beginning of a relationship. Relationships usually take time to develop so if an American is negotiating in China, for example, he had better be prepared to spend longer than he is used to in forming a relationship.

UNIT 4: Language, Communication and Culture

Chapter 9

Culture and Relationships

9.1: Introduction
9.2: Objectives
9.3: Clarifying Terms and Concepts
9.4: Culture and Relationships
9.5: Relationships and Communication Style
9.6: Relationship Breakdown
9.7: Conclusions
9.8: Answers to Questions.

9.1: Introduction

The failure of many international joint ventures and mergers suggests that cross-cultural understanding and awareness are not developing as fast as they might. Halliday and Cawley (2000) argue that cross-cultural alliances are really about people, and people negotiating relationships. This view is supported by Styles and Ambler (1994), who suggest that in the context of international business, "...relationships and experience are primary and supplemented by objective data and analysis, rather than the reverse."

This chapter looks at the nature of relationships in general and examines the elements that are needed for an effective and sustainable

UNIT 4: Language, Communication and Culture

relationship. We then look at how cultural values may influence perceptions of relationships and what this might mean for those who operate internationally.

9.2: Objectives

At the end of this chapter, you will have a better understanding of:

- the nature and elements of relationships
- cultural influences on relationship formation and development
- the place of culture in relationship breakdown
- dealing with dispute and conflict.

Pre-reading questions

Before you begin, consider the questions in the box below and keep them in mind as you read through the chapter.

> - *Relationships concern only the individuals themselves. Cultural models may lead to stereotyping and prejudice and will only damage the establishment and subsequent development of relationships. What do you think?*
> - *Eisenhardt et al (1999) suggest that conflict is an essential part of group development. Without conflict, the authors suggest that groups lose their effectiveness. The alternative to conflict is not usually agreement but rather apathy and disengagement. What is your opinion of this view?*
> - *How will you deal with the issue of relationships in your classroom teaching?*

9.3: Clarifying Terms and Concepts

Pause for thought

> *What do you understand by the term, "relationship?"*

The term "relationship" is defined in the Collins Concise Dictionary as, "...the mutual dealings, connections or feelings that exist between two countries, people, etc."

Holton (2001) suggests that good relationships and collaboration result from, "...the ability...to dialogue with sufficient depth and opportunity to establish trust and open communications."

This view of good relationships is echoed by Korac-Kakabadse et al (2001) who argue that the essence of relationship building is quality dialogue. This involves a process of inner-reflection and a sharing of experiences, both of which result in greater personal understanding.

Halliday and Cawley (2000) argue that the central elements of relationships are trust and commitment. The concept of trust is one that comes up again and again in the literature. Such a vital ingredient in the building and maintaining of good relationships should be examined in more detail.

Boon and Holmes (1991) state that, "Most scholars agree on defining trust as a state of involving confident positive expectations about another's motives with respect to oneself in situations entailing risk."

There are two dimensions to trust (Gurviez, 1997). These are:

1. credibility - perceived abilities
2. fairness - perceived attitude.

Essentially then, in order to effectively deal with others, and to effectively connect with others, we need to focus on: open communication, building trust through dialogue and building commitment. However, as Buttery and Wong (1999) point out:

> Relationships...are often built on a cultural platform which means the route to developing a good relationship can be very different in Western to Eastern cultures. Not only the routes to relationship building are different, but also the relative importance of the attributes which make up the relationship are valued differently in different parts of the world.

It is to these differences that we now turn.

UNIT 4: Language, Communication and Culture

9.4: Culture and Relationships

To some extent, the nature of any relationship will depend on the life experiences, the values and the culture of the people involved. Where cultural differences are marked, we should expect to see these differences exerting a considerable influence on the way relationships are formed and sustained.

Question 1

> *If relationships are defined as the mutual connections or feelings that exist between people, how far will Hofstede's (1991) dimensions of culture influence these "connections" between people? Think of some examples and compare your suggestions with ours in the Answers to Questions section.*

Pause for thought

> *We have examined the possible influence of culture on classroom practice in unit 1 of this book. However, give some more thought now to how far Hofstede's (1991) dimensions of culture can be applied to the teacher-student relationship in the classroom. Consider student expectations of the teacher, and the style of teaching adopted by the teacher. Is there a link between the teacher-student relationship and the manager-subordinate relationship? If your answer is yes, how are these relationships similar?*

Pause for thought

> *Unit 1, chapters 4 and 10 of this book examined Hall's (1990) concept of high- and low-context cultures. How far do the characteristics of these types of culture influence the relationship between individuals?*

You will recall that in low-context cultures, low levels of "contextualised" information are assumed in any interaction. This means that considerable amounts of explicit information must be used to specify meaning. In a high-context culture, a large amount of information is assumed to be present in the situation in order to provide

UNIT 4: Language, Communication and Culture

context. This means that more time is needed to extract meaning from the information given.

Further, Hall (1990) suggests that high-context people operate within a polychronic time framework, and low-context people function within a monochronic time mode (see also unit 1 chapter 4 and unit 4, chapter 8).

Hall (1990) goes on to argue that we all behave in ways that are an extension of the system in which we live. This, in turn, will influence how we relate to others. Hall (1990) suggests that low-context people lead fragmented and individualistic lives, in which there is little involvement with others. Conversely, high-context people tend to lead lives that are interwoven with the lives of others in stable, complex, and long-term relationships. High-context people may be slow in getting to the point because they assume that the person they are talking to will be able to infer meaning from external clues. Being direct and to-the-point may be embarrassing to high-context people because this may involve losing face. In contrast, low-context people are quick to get to the point, tend to over-inform and are much more direct in delivering the message.

We saw above that one of the key elements in building relationships is dialogue. However, imagine a situation in which an American (low-context) and a Chinese (high-context) come together for the first time. The American may value a direct communication style and consider it the norm for interactions. The Chinese may value indirect communication style and see the direct style as confrontational and highly threatening. In such a situation, meaningful dialogue is virtually impossible and mistrust will develop instead of trust.

The situation may be exacerbated by the notion that people are attracted to other people who are similar to themselves. Simintiras and Thomas (1998) suggest that the greater the cultural differences, the lower the levels of perceived impression formation accuracy. Further, the authors suggest that cultural similarity can induce trust which leads, in turn, to interpersonal attraction. Unfortunately for cross-cultural interactions, the converse is also true, "The higher the level of individual differences...the lower the level of interpersonal attraction." (Simintiras and Thomas, 1998)

Worse still, the authors go on to argue that non-verbal behaviour may also have a negative influence on cross-cultural dialogue.

UNIT 4: Language, Communication and Culture

> ...it has been found that culturally determined behaviour with respect to gaze, facial expression and the use of time and space can produce adverse effects upon cross-cultural exchange of information. (Simintiras and Thomas, 1998)

With regard to time orientation, dialogue may never take place at all between people who share different attitudes to punctuality.

We have so far suggested that dialogue, trust and commitment are fundamental to relationship building. However, we also suggest that the notion of "speaking the same language" is crucial to good dialogue and, therefore, to the development of trust and commitment. Language is more than a code system, and assumptions on which utterances are made may not be shared by others.

> Awareness of and competence in a portfolio of language-related skills enable parties to navigate possible misunderstandings, to sustain discourse and, critically, to increase involvement and develop substantively-based relationships. This provides the needed context for entrustment and commitment. (Halliday and Cawley, 2000)

Halliday and Cawley (2000) also consider high- and low-context cultures and, in particular, the importance of non-verbal communication. NVC can, in the opinion of the authors, "...reach further into the psyche that does cognitive thinking." The results of this "sub-conscious" communication are feelings of compatibility which serve to help the forging of relationships.

9.5: Relationships and Communication Style

Unit 1 chapter 10 deals with the ideas of Watzlawick (1967) and the substantive and relational component of communication. The interesting point for us is that different cultures may attach more or less importance to these components. This can lead to ineffective communication, lack of trust, and finally, in a worst-case scenario, to relationship breakdown. This view is supported by Wei et al (2001), who argue that:

UNIT 4: Language, Communication and Culture

Culturally-based differences in conversation style often result in miscommunication in intercultural transactions. Such miscommunication becomes more acute in professional contexts...when the interacting parties are using the same linguistic code but not the same cultural style.

Question 2

> 1. Which types of culture might focus more on the substantive component of communication?
> 2. Which types of culture might focus more on the relational component?
> 3. How may the different focus manifest itself in communication style?

So, how do these features manifest themselves in day-to-day business interactions and how do they influence relationships?

Question 3

> Consider e-mail and sending mails to other cultures. What factors should you take into account when writing such mails? Make a list and then compare it to our list in the Answers to Questions section.

Question 4

> You are running a class on intercultural communication. In your class you have a number of low-context Germans and high-context Japanese. How would you sensitise them to the differences in communication style?

Chapter 6 of this unit examined how the cultural values of an individual can manifest themselves in negotiations. These differing values can have a dramatic effect on the relationship-building process. Wei et al (2001) identify four stages of the negotiation process. The stages are:

1. non-task relationship creation
2. task-related exchange of information

UNIT 4: Language, Communication and Culture

3. persuasion
4. concession and agreement.

The authors suggest that business negotiation in Western cultures is part of what Scollon and Scollon (1995) describe as "corporate discourse systems." These systems are driven by four features. These features can be described as being:

1. goal-orientated
2. focused
3. anti-rhetorical
4. deductive.

Wei et al (2001) contrast this with the East Asian discourse systems. These systems are driven by:

1. Confucian ideology of face relationships
2. interpersonal politeness.

The implication is that Anglo cultures tend to rush into the persuasion stage of the negotiation process. Mead (1994) supports this by suggesting that low-context cultures tend to quickly pass over initial relationship creation. In contrast, high-context cultures place great importance on the non-task relationship building stage. Essentially, the negotiation is focused on getting to know the people involved, and to build up a relationship of trust before business can begin. Many low-context people have difficulty in dealing with this apparently undirected activity.

Simintiras and Thomas (1998) echo these observations. The authors suggest that high- and low-context values will have an influence on both the non-task related aspects of a negotiation and the task-related aspects. The authors argue that in negotiations between high- and low-context cultures, there is a significant possibility that information exchange will be adversely influenced by differences between verbal and non-verbal communication and lead to poor relationship development. Simintiras and Thomas (1998) argue that:

> An individual from a low-context culture will focus on explicit messages and display a great deal of precision in the verbal aspect of communication. Meanwhile,

UNIT 4: Language, Communication and Culture

communication between members of high-context cultures is implicit and features expressive non-verbal behaviour. This can include body language, gestures and facial expressions.

Simintiras and Thomas (1998) suggest that poor relationship development at the first stage of the negotiation process will have a detrimental effect on the persuasion stage. Essentially, there are two possible strategic approaches to the persuasion or bargaining stage. These are: a representational strategy and an instrumental strategy. When representational strategies are used, communication is focused on collaborative problem-solving. When instrumental strategies are used, communication focuses on changing the behaviour of the other party. Graham (1985) suggests that instrumental strategies tend to produce less favourable outcomes. Conversely, representational or co-operative negotiation styles increase the likelihood of a result that is beneficial to both parties. Unfortunately for the intercultural negotiator, Graham (1985) suggests that culturally dissimilar negotiators tend to use instrumental bargaining strategies and tend not to achieve the desired outcomes.

It is difficult not to conclude that good relationship development will lessen the impact of cultural dissimilarity and enable negotiators to adopt a more collaborative approach to negotiation.

Many of the points we have so far raised are exemplified in the Chinese negotiation process. Woo and Prud'homme (1999) usefully summarise the characteristics of this. In the list of characteristics below, we have added our suggested background.

Status: high power distance
Face: Confucianism
Trust: collective - high-context
Friendship: Confucian humanism (Ren)
Guanxi: collective
Ambiguity: high-context
Patience: high-context
Chinese protocol: Chinese tradition.

At the beginning of this chapter, we suggested that in order to effectively deal with others, and to effectively connect with others, we need to focus on open communication, building trust through dialogue

UNIT 4: Language, Communication and Culture

and building commitment. We have just seen how differing cultural values can influence relationship building in the negotiation process. Most of the points we raised are also relevant to relationship building in multi-national teams and meetings.

Hurn and Jenkins (2000) identify nine factors that are critical to success in multicultural meetings (see unit 4, chapter 5). The authors mention two other factors, without which, the nine others would be useless. These two factors concern the development of relationships and trust. Clearly, considerable time is needed to build trust, and the importance of relationship building can differ according to the culture in which an individual is socialised.

Berger (1998) argues that in order to overcome these difficulties, the critical success factor is an understanding that what is natural in one culture may be unnatural in another. In other words, if people transplant the skills that work in the home culture into a new cultural environment, the result may be intolerance towards others and culture shock. To make matters worse, if we see others doing things which might be considered poor practice back home, we label them as incompetent and untrustworthy. Therefore, from the beginning, misunderstandings escalate, and barriers to effective communication are erected. These barriers lead to poor relationship development. In turn, poor relationships can often grow into criticism or other expressions of conflict or dispute.

9.6: Relationship Breakdown

Mead (1994) suggests that the following issues are among those that can give rise to disagreement and relationship breakdown in the workplace.

- Organisational structure, roles and responsibilities.
- Competition for resources.
- Administrative procedures.
- Competition for rewards.
- Concealed agendas.
- Clash of loyalties.
- Personality differences.
- Communication issues.
- Cultural antagonisms.

UNIT 4: Language, Communication and Culture

With regard to cultural difficulties, Appelbaum et al (1998) suggest that, "Looking at the issue of conflict as well as group development, one can see that in almost every aspect culture can have a major impact on how conflict is perceived and responded to."

The authors maintain that mistrust and miscommunication are vital elements of relationship breakdown and conflict. Other sources of intercultural conflict concern the following.

- Different manifestations of a desire for harmony.
- Different standards for social status.
- Different attitudes towards groups and individuals.
- Different attitudes towards the future, and how far we are able to control it.

Research into the challenges faced by international joint ventures (Newman, 1995) observed cross-cultural difficulties at all stages of collaboration. Among these difficulties, Newman (1995) notes:

- differences in language
- differences in business practice
- differences in legal institutions
- differences between high- and low-context communication style
- differences in motivation
- differences in performance measurement
- differences in attitudes to conflict and conflict tolerance.

Question 5

> *Look at the last point above – differences in attitudes to conflict, and conflict tolerance. To what extent do you think attitudes to conflict can be influenced by Hofstede's (1991) dimensions of culture?*

Appelbaum et al (1998) suggest that there are specific ways of dealing with conflict and disagreement constructively. However, they do point out that most approaches have been developed in the US, and their use with culturally diverse work groups should be questioned. The following is a summary of the process suggested by Appelbaum et al (1998).

UNIT 4: Language, Communication and Culture

Pause for thought

> *As you read through the process, consider how (in)appropriate it is for universal use. For example, cultural differences may have a significant impact on the identification of the underlying problem. For instance, HUA cultures may focus on lack of structure or lack of clear rules and regulations. HPD cultures may frame the problem in terms of management incompetence - assuming typical behaviour.*

Appelbaum et al (1998) suggest the following steps in the procedure.

Diagnosis. This means identifying the source of conflict. Possible sources are:

1. different interpretation of information
2. incompatible goals
3. violation of boundaries
4. unhealed old wounds
5. symptoms confused with the underlying cause.

Planning. This means developing an action plan.

1. Choose how firm or flexible to be.
2. Choose how involved you want to be with the other party.
3. Mutually agree on a time and place to meet and explore differences.
4. Decide how to monitor progress.

Implementation. This means carrying out the plan.

1. Maintain a tone of mutual respect and goodwill.
2. Consider putting any agreement into writing.

Follow-up. After agreement has been reached.

1. Monitor results to check agreement is being honoured.
2. Take corrective action if necessary.
3. Reinforce behaviour that supports agreement.
4. Learn from each experience of conflict and disagreement.

UNIT 4: Language, Communication and Culture

Fundamental to the whole process is the development of openness and trust.

Adler (1991) suggests that managing intercultural conflict or differences is best handled by defining the issues from the point of view of the cultures concerned. The purpose is to uncover the different cultural interpretations of specific issues and to develop a cultural synergy that works for all parties. This process is shown in more detail in Hurn and Jenkins (2000) - (see unit 4, chapter 5, section 8).

Apelbaum et al (1998) offer a useful summary of dealing with intercultural conflict. Managers need to:

- be aware of cultural differences
- communicate
- show respect to all cultures
- avoid stereotyping
- be empathetic
- try to define issues from all points of view
- accommodate all cultural strengths
- get senior management commitment.

If you want to read further with regard to relationship breakdown, Mead (1994) chapter 9, chapter 11, and chapter 13 are good starting points. Appelbaum et al (1998) offer a useful discussion of conflict and group processes.

Question 6

Look at the scenarios below. In all of the situations "you" have taken some action that resulted in bad feeling, hostility and possible relationship breakdown of some sort. What mistakes have you made? Check your answers with our suggested answers in the Answers to Questions section.

1. You work for DaimlerChrysler and you visit your Chinese plant for the first time in order to discuss technical details concerning the new Super X Class. You arrive in the office of your Chinese counterpart and after a couple of minutes exchange of pleasantries, you dive into your brief case and pull out your detailed information about the exact specifications for the leather you want to use in the new model.

UNIT 4: Language, Communication and Culture

> 2. *You are still in the office one hour later when your host invites you to a Chinese banquet the following day. You refuse, claiming that you have a busy schedule and have to be in Berlin for a trade fair. Anyway, you have not come to China to socialise, you are there to work.*
> 3. *You have been asked to form a work group in order to look at pay-for-performance systems in your company. You form your team from Japanese men and Danish women, and you decide to appoint a British woman to head the team.*
> 4. *You are head of a UK-Chinese joint-venture and you are in China for six months in order to find out how they do business there. You have discovered that one of your senior managers has been spending a great deal of company time helping to solve the family problems of his brother-in-law. The brother-in-law does not even work for your joint venture. You decide to take immediate and corrective action.*

9.7: Conclusions

It is clear that managers of multinational and international companies are being obliged to take greater responsibility for managing individuals and groups from diverse cultural backgrounds. These backgrounds will influence their attitudes, behaviours and interpersonal relationships. This chapter has attempted to shed some light on the issues surrounding the development of relationships across cultures. It is vital that managers, EIB teachers and trainers understand these issues and how they can influence the work situation. By understanding the issues, we can, perhaps, adapt our approaches to management or to teaching, and develop better relationships as a result.

9.8: Answers to Questions

Question 1
There are many possible examples. Those below are simply our suggestions.
Power distance is a reflection of the willingness of workers to depend on the decisions and instructions made by superiors. In HPD cultures, relationships with others tend to be hierarchical and authoritative. The less powerful are dependent on the powerful, centralisation is the norm, and the ideal boss is the good father. Although these dependencies are expected and used to personal advantage, there tends to be latent

UNIT 4: Language, Communication and Culture

conflict and mistrust between levels in the hierarchy. LPD cultures tend to want to narrow the gap between ranks.

Individualism/collectivism describes the relationship of the individual to the group. In individualist cultures, relationships between people are often characterised by competition. The rights of the individual are stressed and his or her right to individual thoughts, opinions, behaviour (within limits) is valued highly. In collective cultures, people's identities tend to be defined by the group to which they belong. Harmony is, therefore, valued highly, and confrontations with others avoided (apart from confrontations with people from another group).

Mead (1994) characterises the uncertainty avoidance dimension as, "... how far different cultures socialise their members into accepting ambiguous situations and tolerating uncertainty." In HUA cultures, there tend to be many rules - both written and unwritten - governing behaviour and relationships with others. Individual deviance is frowned on, and expectations of others are clear. For example, teachers should have the "right" answers, and managers should be decisive and issue clear and unambiguous instructions.

In masculine cultures, individuals should be assertive, ambitious, competitive and tough. In feminine cultures, relationships should be warm and trusting, and individuals should be modest and caring. Consensus rather than competition is valued highly.

Question 2
1. Low-context, individualistic cultures. We may also add high uncertainty avoidance where needs to avoid ambiguity are strong.
2. High-context, collective cultures.
3. Low-context cultures tend to be direct and pass over the relational aspects rather quickly. If the culture also has high needs to avoid uncertainty, the communication is likely to be very brisk and to the point. High-context cultures tend to be indirect and emphasise harmony and the building up of trust. In order not to offend and cause disharmony, a high-context person may say "yes" even when they mean "no" or "uncertain".

Question 3
This is not a simple question to answer. Zahir et al (2002) argue that:

> When new technologies become available and cultures adopt them, the result can be either convergence, cultures becoming more similar as a result, or divergence, when cultures adopt technology in different ways that maintain or even further accentuate their differences.

One problem is that e-mail has not yet fully developed styles of its own. How do you begin a mail? How do you finish? Should you use abbreviations? However, we suggest that until such a style has been internationally agreed upon, you should take the following into account.
1. Who are you writing to?
2. What is their status with regard to you and how do they perceive their own status? In other words, do they come from a HPD culture or a LPD culture?
3. How well do you know them?

UNIT 4: Language, Communication and Culture

4. What is their level of English (if you are writing in English)?
5. Will they value a direct and to-the-point mail or one in which the main point is hidden away and hinted at? In other words are they low-context or high-context?
6. How will you begin the mail? How will you end it?

This list is certainly not exhaustive and you can probably think of many other factors.

Question 4

Whatever you do, you should do it in an unthreatening and possibly humorous way. Simple role-plays can be an effective way to show how different cultures communicate differently. For example, you could set up a situation in a restaurant. Two students (one German and one Japanese) could be sitting in a restaurant. You can be the waiter who brings them their soup. On both "bowls" put the information that the soup is nice but too cold. A few seconds later you can return with the question, "Is everything OK with your meal?" Hopefully, you will get a different reaction! The really important part of the situation comes with the discussion afterwards. Did the Japanese complain? Why not? Was the German too direct? How do their respective reactions relate to culture? What about personality? And so on.

Question 5

Mead (1994) suggests that in HPD cultures, latent conflict between hierarchical levels is the norm, and that HPD people assume that peers are unwilling to trust each other. LPD cultures tend to value harmony between different hierarchical levels and assume that peers are willing to trust each other.

In HUA cultures, conflict is perceived as undesirable because it produces uncertainty. However, compromise tends to be seen as weakness and there is, therefore, a low readiness to compromise with opponents. If we add to this that HUA people tend to identify closely with the topic under discussion, there is little readiness to engage in debate. In LUA cultures, conflict in organisations is perceived as being natural, and competition can be a good thing. There is also a greater readiness to debate and to compromise.

Collective cultures value harmony and avoid direct confrontation. They will therefore tend to restrict expression of open disagreement, and open challenges to authority are rare. There is a preference for resolving disputes by compromise and consensus. Offenders may be punished by banishing them from their in-group. Individualistic cultures tend to see open conflict as natural and healthy. A clash of opinions can lead to greater understanding for both parties. US managers are expected to resort to confrontational tactics when negotiating contracts.

Masculine cultures tend to fight conflict with conflict. Feminine cultures tend to look for consensus.

Question 6

1. Your low-context, direct and straight-down-to-business attitude may well be appreciated in Germany, but not in high-context China where relationship building is vital. By insisting on getting down to business immediately, you will almost certainly endanger future dealings with your partner. You need to make time for building the relationship even if this seems to you like a waste of time.

UNIT 4: Language, Communication and Culture

2. This is a big mistake. A refusal to make time to take part in the banquet will certainly offend your partner. Your relationship (and future business dealings) is on a slippery slope.
3. A very insensitive decision. Japanese men are unlikely to look favourably on a woman chair and on the fact that they must work with women. Think again.
4. Again, you are applying UK values to China and assuming that yours are right and theirs are wrong. Take time to find out about the importance of networks in China and the position of managers in society and what society expects of them. Any "corrective" action on your part will almost certainly lead to serious relationship breakdown.

UNIT 4: Language, Communication and Culture

Chapter 10

Communication in a Virtual World

10.1: Introduction
10.2: Objectives
10.3: What is Virtual Communication?
10.4: Communication in Virtual Teams
10.5: Virtual Team Development
10.6: Conclusions
10.7: Answers to Questions.

10.1: Introduction

The increasing globalisation and internationalisation of large companies and institutions has led to the development of multinational teams. Some of these teams may be working within the walls of one site while others may not. In some cases, team members are scattered across the globe, and the only real alternative to flying everyone to one meeting place is to hold the sessions virtually.

This chapter examines the characteristics and challenges of working in virtual teams. First, we attempt to clarify the term "virtual communication." Then, we examine what it means to work in virtual teams and how moderators can make virtual teamwork more effective.

UNIT 4: Language, Communication and Culture

10.2: Objectives

At the end of this chapter you will:

1. better understand what is meant by virtual communication
2. be aware of the characteristics of successful virtual teams
3. have informed ideas for the further development of virtual teams.

Pre-reading task

Before you begin, look at the question in the shaded box below. The question is designed to focus your thinking on the topic.

> *"Communicating by phone, by e-mail or video conferencing will never replace face-to-face communication as the most effective way to work in teams." What is your view?*

10.3: What is Virtual Communication?

Virtual communication occurs in almost all businesses. Texting, phoning and e-mailing, for example, happen everywhere when people communicate with one another and with clients. We define virtual communication as, "Communication in English across time zones, across cultures and in different locations."

Some of the ways we use to communicate virtually are listed below.

- Telephone conferencing.
- Net meetings - where participants share the same screen. Slides can be presented and control of the screen rotated.
- Webcasting.
- Electronic mail.

So what are the implications for communication?

- You may have to rely on voice only. This will put an emphasis on clarity, brevity and tone.
- You may have to rely on the written word only. This will put an emphasis on clarity, brevity, speed and sensitivity.
- Conventions for turn-taking will differ.

UNIT 4: Language, Communication and Culture

> You may have difficulty in reading signals that are normally visual.
> It may be difficult to get people to concentrate.

Question 1

> *What are the implications of virtual communication for the moderator of a meeting or for the virtual trainer? Consider your answer and check it with our answer in the Answers to Questions section.*

10.4: Communication in Virtual Teams

We are living in an information age where work is being redefined beyond the traditional bounds of space and time. The vision of the future as imagined by, for example, Handy (1995, 1996) and Bayliss (1998) suggests that in a couple of decades, the workplace will be a very different place from the way it is today. McGregor (2000) summarises the characteristics of the future world of work. Perhaps the most important feature mentioned by McGregor (2000) is that of the virtual team. Virtual teams are described by Johnson et al (2001) as:

> ...groups of people who collaborate closely even though they may or may not be separated by space, time and organisational barriers... This workplace is unrestrained by time and space; it is a virtual workplace where productivity, flexibility, and collaboration will reach new levels... Developing community amongst people who work at a distance from each other and who might or might not be from the same culture is a new organisational challenge.

It is highly likely that in this world, virtual team membership will cross national boundaries, and a variety of cultural backgrounds will be represented in the team. Wherever they come from, Johnson et al (2001) suggest that team members will need certain characteristics.

UNIT 4: Language, Communication and Culture

Question 2

> *So - what are the characteristics of successful virtual team members? Make a note of your answer and check it with our answer in the Answers to Questions section.*

Johnson et al (2001) suggest that teams with the highest levels of trust share three traits. First, when communicating electronically, they provide some personal background before focusing on the work at hand. The authors refer to this as electronic courtship.

Pause for thought

> *Do you think that some cultures might be more suited than others at working in virtual teams? Or does it simply depend on the individual?*

Second, teams with a high level of trust set clear roles for each team member, and thirdly, the hallmark of a trusting team is positive attitude.

Communication in virtual teams can be problematic, and the facilitation of effective virtual communication is critical if rapport is to be maintained. Team members may need training in how to be linguistically precise. They will, after all, be unable to modify speech with non-verbal communication. Further, because of the absence of non-verbal clues, it may be hard to tell when something is going awry. Furthermore, when things do go wrong, it may take a longer period of time before this is noticed. Johnson et al (2001) suggest that when things go wrong, the problem should be solved by face-to-face interaction. Failing that, the options should be, in the following order: videoconference, telephone conference, e-mail, fax, or letter.

Question 3

> *What type of corporate culture do you think would be most supportive of virtual teams?*

For those of you who are interested in knowing more about virtual teamworking, the following web sites are suggested.

- Self-Directed Work Teams – http://users.ids.net/-brim/sdwtt.html

UNIT 4: Language, Communication and Culture

- Teambuilding Incorporated – www.teambuilding.com
- The Center for the Study of Work Teams - www.workteams.unt.edu

For a useful account of how to lead and develop virtual team members we recommend Garton and Wegryn (2006).

10.5: Virtual Team Development

Holton (2001) writes that:

> With the acceleration of communications technology, we now find ourselves living and working in an increasingly global virtual environment. Organisational development professionals are beginning to consider how virtual communication technology will influence the way in which we work together.

Pauleen and Yoong (2001) define virtual teams as:

> ...temporary, culturally diverse, geographically dispersed, electronically communicating work groups. Virtual teams may communicate and work synchronously or asynchronously through such technologies as electronic mail, bulletin boards, audio/video/data conferencing, automated workflow, electronic voting and collaborative writing.

According to Grenier and Metes (1995) virtual teams will be the norm in the 21st century. If this is the case, then virtual team development is a crucial issue. Pauleen and Yoong (2001) suggest that effective communication is the key to successful virtual teams. Effective communication will, in turn, depend on how well team members are able to build and develop personal relationships. There is evidence (e.g. Walther and Burgoon, 1992) that suggests strong links between good relationships on one hand, and enhanced creativity, better decisions and fewer process losses on the other. Pauleen and Yoong (2001) suggest that the challenge for virtual team facilitators is, therefore, to:

...move the team towards its objectives by encouraging collaboration. This is done through a sustained process of relationship building, idea generating, prioritising and selection. The particular challenge for virtual team facilitators is to manage this process through electronically-mediated interactions.

Holton (2001) suggests that the keys to successful virtual teamwork are:

1. deep dialogue
2. trust.

The two factors above are interdependent. Holton (2001) argues that, "Collaboration is born in the ability of a group to dialogue with sufficient depth and opportunity to establish trust and open communication." However, Holton (2001) also points to the need for training which is specific to the needs of virtual teams. These training needs include familiarisation with: virtual interaction, anonymous environments, and collaborative empowerment. Holton (2001) argues that specific competencies for the global virtual work environment include:

- cross-cultural communication
- process facilitation
- creating and sustaining remote teamwork
- managing information technology.

And on a personal level:

- social intelligence
- adaptability to the virtual environment.

Pauleen and Yoong (2001) suggest that a face-to-face meeting at the formation stage of a virtual team is probably the most effective way to build personal relationships. The authors cite their research participants as reporting that:

> ...face-to-face meetings give facilitators the opportunity to understand individual team member communication styles and personal and professional motivations, making it easier

UNIT 4: Language, Communication and Culture

to then move into virtual working relationships... Face-to-face meetings also allow a deeper kind of rapport, or trust to develop.

Question 4

> *Consider the following communication channels that may be available to virtual teams:*
> - *the telephone*
> - *e-mail*
> - *synchronous chat and messaging boards*
> - *desktop video conferencing.*
>
> *Which of these channels could be best utilised to develop relationships? Consider your answers and then check with ours in the Answers to Questions section.*

The authors also see great promise for desktop videoconferencing as, "...an affordable alternative to face-to-face meetings." This is supported by Lau et al (2000) who suggest that videoconferencing can enhance social relationships by putting a face to a name. For many companies, however, cost may well be a barrier.

E-mail is often the basis of virtual teams because it is a universal platform, cost effective and generally accessible. Some advantages are that it is fast and has the added benefit of being able to include attachments. However, whether or not it is the best channel for developing relationships seems open to debate. Pauleen and Yoong (2001) suggest that unless e-mail protocol is established, communication problems can easily occur because of differences of style. Further, poor communication, the creation of ill will and an undermining of relationships can result from delayed responses.

Pauleen and Yoong (2001) argue that although synchronous chat meetings may not always be suitable for formal virtual meetings, they may be effectively used in order to build personal relationships because they give opportunities for informal, spontaneous communication between team members.

Pause for thought

> *You might want to access and read the article by Pauleen and Yoong (2001). They give a far more detailed description of the*

> *advantages and disadvantages of the various electronic communication channels than we can possibly give here. What is your opinion about their research findings?*

10.6: Conclusions

Working virtually requires both new and old skills and talents. Familarisation with cultural differences is as important virtually as it is in face-to-face encounters. When the written word is dominant the author has found the use of emoticons very useful. It is very easy to give offence when none is intended ☺ ☹

If you are thinking of teaching in a virtual environment, then you should look at Salmon (2000). This is a guide to working effectively in the virtual world and offers excellent advice on how to become an effective e-moderator. Furthermore, the book is accompanied by a website (www.e-moderating.com) which provides supplementary material and useful links.

10.7: Answers to Questions

Question 1
Some of the implications concern the following.
- How to motivate and excite participants.
- How to support participants who do not like virtual communication.
- Checking clarity of instructions.
- How to assess the participants' ability to adapt to virtual communication.
- When the teacher or moderator should intervene.
- How the teacher or moderator monitors tasks.

Question 2
First, teams will need people who are self-starters - working remotely needs self-discipline. Second, individual accountability is vital. Team members must deliver on time. In virtual teams, it is easy to get behind schedule before it is noticed if feedback loops are not tight, if milestones are not noticeable, or if communication is not effective. Thirdly, flexibility is essential. Virtual teams function without the benefit of time-related socialisation, but norms and role-expectations must be made explicit. Finally, trust is required amongst all virtual team members. They will need to know that everyone will fulfil their obligations and behave in a consistent manner.

Question 3
An adaptive, technologically advanced, non-hierarchical organisation is likely to be more supportive than a highly-structured, control-oriented organisation (Apgar, 1998).

UNIT 4: Language, Communication and Culture

Question 4

Pauleen and Yoong (2001) suggest that the telephone is, "...the old reliable standby for facilitators when it comes to building relationships with virtual team members."

UNIT 4: Language, Communication and Culture

Unit Bibliography

Adler, N. (1991) <u>International Dimension of Organisational Behaviour</u>. Boston, MA., PWS-Kent Publishing.

Ansoff, H. (1979) <u>Strategic Management</u>. New York, Wiley.

Apgar, M. (1998) "The alternative workplace: changing where and how people work," in <u>Harvard Business Review</u>, Vol. 76, No. 3.

Appelbaum, S. and Shapiro, B. (1998) "The management of multicultural group conflict," in <u>Team Performance Management</u>, Vol. 4, No. 5.

Argyle, M. (1994) <u>Bodily Communication</u>. London, Routledge.

Arunthanes, W.; Tansuhaj, P. and Lemak, D. (1994) "Cross-cultural Business Gift Giving," in <u>International Marketing Review</u>, Vol. 11, No. 4.

Axtell, R. (1985) <u>DO'S and TABOOS Around the World</u>. New York, Wiley.

Axtell, R. (1991<u>) Gestures: The DO'S and TABOOS of Body Language Around the World</u>. New York, Wiley.

Bayliss, V. (1998) <u>Redefining Work</u>. London, RSA.

UNIT 4: Language, Communication and Culture

Berger, M. (1998) "Going Global: implications for communication and leadership training," in <u>Industrial and Commercial Training</u>, Vol. 30, No.4.

Bhatia, V.K. (1993) <u>Analysing Genre: Language Use in Professional Settings</u>. Harlow, Longman Group UK Ltd.

Bond, M. (Ed.) (1986) <u>The Psychology of the Chinese People</u>. Harlow, Longman.

Bone, D. (1998) "Communication or back to Genesis and the House of Babel," in <u>Industrial and Commercial Training</u>, Vol. 30, No. 7.

Boon, S. and Holmes, J. (1991) "The dynamics of interpersonal trust: resolving uncertainty in the face of risk," in Hinde, R. and Groebel, J. (eds.), <u>Co-operation and Prosocial behaviour</u>. Cambridge, Cambridge University Press.

Boorom, M., Goolsby, J. and Ramsay, R. (1998) "Relational communication traits and their effect on adaptiveness and sales performance," in <u>Journal of the Academy of Marketing Science</u>, Vol. 26, No. 1.

Brieger, N. and Comfort, J. (1992) <u>Language Reference for Business English</u>. Hemel Hempstead, Prentice Hall International.

Buttery, E. and Wong, Y. (1999) "The development of a Guanxi framework," in <u>Marketing Intelligence and Planning</u>, Vol. 17, No. 3.

Casse, P. (1981) "Training for the Cross-Cultural Mind," in <u>Society for Inter-cultural Education, Training and Research</u>. Washington DC, Intercultural Press.

Charles, M. (1996) "Business negotiations: interdependence between discourse and the business relationship," in <u>English for Specific Purposes</u>, Vol. 15: 19-36.

Cook, G. (1989) <u>Discourse</u>. Oxford, Oxford University Press.

UNIT 4: Language, Communication and Culture

Cortes, A. (2000) "Business protocol: a public relations approach," in *Corporate Communications: An International Journal*, Vol 5. No. 3.

Crookes, D. and Thomas, I. (1998) "Problem solving and culture - exploring some stereotypes," in *Journal of Management Development*, Vol. 17, No. 8.

Deal, T. and Kennedy, A. (1982) *Corporate Culture*. Reading, Addison-Wesley.

Delmonte, M. (1991) "Use of non-verbal construing and metaphor in psychotherapy," in *Internal Journal of Psychosomatics*, Vol. 38. Nos. 1-4.

Dudley-Evans, T. and St John, M. (1998) *Developments in English for Specific Purposes*. Cambridge, Cambridge University Press.

Eisenhardt, K.; Kahwajy, J. and Bourgeois, L. (1999) "How Management Teams Can Have a Good Fight," in *Harvard Business Review on Effective Communication.*

Elashmawi, F. (1998) "Overcoming multicultural clashes in global joint ventures," in *European Business Review*, Vol. 98, No. 4.

Elsayed-Elkhouly, S., Lazarus, H. and Forsythe, V. (1997) "Why is a third of your time wasted in meetings?" in *Journal of Management development*, Vol. 16, No. 9.

Fairclough, N. (1989) *Language and Power*. London, Longman.

Fairclough, N. (2003) *Analysing Discourse: Textual Analysis for Social Research*. Routledge.

Fisher, R. and Ury, W. (1982) *Getting to Yes*. London, Hutchinson.

Fowler, A. (1986) *Effective Negotiation*. London, Institute of Personal Management.

UNIT 4: Language, Communication and Culture

Frei, R., Racicot, B. and Travagline, A. "The impact of monochronic and Type A behaviour patterns on research productivity and stress," in *Journal of Management Psychology*, Vol. 14, No. 5.

Fromkin, V. and Rodman, J. (1983) *An Introduction to Language*. New York, CBS College Publishing.

Gabbott, M. and Hogg, G. (2000) "An empirical investigation of the impact of non-verbal communication on service evaluation," in European *Journal of Marketing*, Vol. 34, Nos. 3-4.

Garton, C. and Wegryn, K. (2006) *Managing Without Walls: Maximise Success with Virtual, Global, and Cross-cultural Teams*. MC Press, LLC.

Gaut, D. and Perrigo, E. (1997) *Business and Professional Communication for the 21st century*. Needham Heights, Allyn and Bacon.

Georgakopoulou, A. and Goutsos, D. (1997) *Discourse Analysis. An Introduction*. Edinburgh, Edinburgh University Press.

Graham, J. and Herberger, R. (1983) "Negotiators don't shoot from the hip," in *Harvard Business Review*, Vol. 61, May-June.

Graham, J. (1984) "A comparison of Japanese and American business negotiations," in *International Journal of Research in Marketing*, p.p. 51-68.

Graham, J. (1985) "Cross-cultural marketing negotiations: a laboratory experiment," in *Marketing Science*, Vol. 4, No. 2.

Graham, J., Evenko, L. and Rajan, M. (1992) "An empirical comparison of Soviet and American business," in *Journal of International Business Studies*, Vol. 23, No. 3.

Grenier, R. and Metes, G. (1995) *Going Virtual: Moving your Organisation into the 21st Century*. Englewood Cliffs, Prentice-Hall.

UNIT 4: Language, Communication and Culture

Grice, H.P. (1975) "Logic and Conversation," from Cole, P. and Morgan, J.L. (eds.), Syntax and Semantics Vol 3: Speech Acts. New York, Academic Press.

Gulbro, R. and Herbig, P. (1999) "Cultural differences encountered by firms when negotiating internationally," in Industrial Management & Data Systems, Vol. 99, No. 2.

Gurviez, P. (1997) "Trust: a new approach to understanding the band-consumer relationship," in Proceedings of the AMA Special Conference in Relationship Marketing, Dublin.

Hall, E.T. (1960) "The Silent Language of Overseas Business," in Harvard Business review, May-June.

Hall, E and Hall, M. (1990) Understanding Cultural Differences. Maine, Intercultural Press, Inc.

Halliday, S. and Cawley, R. (2000) "Re-negotiating and re-affirming in cross-border marketing processes: a learning-based conceptual model and research propositions," in Management Decision, Vol. 38, No. 8.

Hammond, J. and Derewianka, B. (2001) "Genre," from Carter, R. and Nunan, D. (eds.), The Cambridge Guide to Teaching English to Speakers of Other Languages. Cambridge, Cambridge University Press.

Hampden-Turner, C. and Trompenaars, F. (1994) The Seven Cultures of Capitalism. London, Piatkus.

Handy, C. (1995) The Age of Unreason. London, Arrow Business Books.

Handy, C. (1996) Beyond Certainty. London, Arrow Business Books.

Harris, P. and Moran, R. (1987) Managing Cultural Differences. Houston, Gulf Publishing.

Harrison, G. (1995) "Satisfaction, tension and interpersonal relations: a cross-cultural comparison of managers in Singapore and Australia," in Journal of Managerial Psychology, Vol. 10, No. 8.

Hinds, J. (1990) "Inductive, deductive, quasi-inductive: expository writing in Japanese, Korean, Chinese, and Thai," in Connor, U. and Johns, A.M. (eds.), Coherence in Writing – Research and Pedagogical Perspectives, TESOL. 97-109, Washington, DC.

Hofstede, G. (1984) Culture's Consequences: International Differences in Work-Related Values. Beverley Hills, Sage.

Hofstede, G. (1991) Cultures and Organisation. London, McGraw-Hill International.

Hollman, W. and Kleiner, B. (1997) "Establishing rapport: the secret business tool to success," in Managing Service Quality, Vol. 7. No. 4.

Holton, J. (2001) "Building trust and collaboration in a virtual team," in Team Performance Management: An International Journal, Vol. 7. No. 3.

Hurn, B. and Jenkins, M. (2000) "International peer group development," in Industrial and Commercial Training, Vol. 32, No. 4.

Johnson, P., Heimann, V. and O'Neill, K. (2001) "The Wonderland of virtual teams," in Journal of Workplace Learning, Vol. 13, No. 1.

Jolles, R. (2005) How to Run Seminars and Workshops: Presentation Skills for Consultants, Trainers and Teachers. John Wiley & Sons.

Joseph, W. (1982) "The credibility of physically attractive communicators: a review," Journal of Advertising, Vol. 11, No. 3.

Kale, S. and Barnes, J. (1995) "International Negotiation," from Jackson, T. (ed.), Cross-Cultural Management. Oxford, Butterworth-Heinemann.

Kaufman-Scarborough, C. and Lindquist, J. (1999) "Time management and polychronicity," in Journal of Managerial Psychology, Vol. 14, No. 3-4.

UNIT 4: Language, Communication and Culture

Korac-Kakabadse, N.; Kouzmin, A.; Korac-Kakabadse, A. and Savery, L. (2001) "Low- and High-Context Communication Patterns: Towards Mapping Cross-Cultural Encounters," in <u>Cross Cultural management</u>, Vol. 8, No. 2.

Kramer, H. (1989) "Cross-cultural negotiations: the Western-Japanese interface," in <u>Singapore Marketing Review</u>, Vol. 4.

Lakoff, R. (1973) "The Logic of Politeness: minding your p's and q's." Papers from the 9th Regional Meeting, Chicago Linguistics Society: 292-305.

Lau, F., Sarker, S. and Sahay, S. (2000) "On managing virtual teams," in <u>Healthcare information Management Communications, Canada</u>, Vol. 14, No. 2.

Lavaty, S. and Kleiner, B. (2001) "Managing and understanding the French employee," in <u>Management Research News</u>, Vol. 24, No. 3-4.

Lebas, M. and Weigenstein, J. (1986) "Management control: The role of rules, markets, and culture," in <u>Journal of management Studies</u>, Vol. 23, No. 3.

Levine, R., West, L., and Reiss, H. (1980) "Perceptions of time and punctuality in the United States and Brazil," in <u>Journal of Personality and Social Psychology</u>, Vol. 38, No. 4.

Lewis, R. (2006) <u>When Cultures Collide. Leading Across Cultures – 3rd ed</u>. London, Nicholas Brealey Publishing.

Marlowe, C., Schneider, S. and Nelson, C. (1996) "Gender and attractiveness biases in hiring decisions: are more experienced managers less biased?" in <u>Journal of Applied Psychology</u>, Vol. 8, No. 1.

Marin, G. (1987) "Attributions for tardiness among Chilean and United States students," in <u>Journal of Social Psychology</u>, Vol. 125, No. 5.

Martin, D. and Herbig, P. (1997) "Contractual aspects of cross-cultural negotiations," in <u>Marketing Intelligence and Planning</u>, Vol. 15, No. 1.

McCall, J. and Warrington, M. (1989) <u>Marketing by Agreement: A Cross-cultural Approach to Business Negotiations</u>. Chichester, Avon Wiley.

McCarthy, M. and Carter R.A. (1994) <u>Language as Discourse: Perspectives for Language Teachers</u>. London, Longman.

McCarthy, M. (2001) "Discourse," from Carter, R. and Nunan, D. (eds.), <u>The Cambridge Guide to Teaching English to Speakers of Other Languages</u>. Cambridge, Cambridge University Press.

McGregor, W. (2000) "The future of workspace management," in <u>Facilities</u>, Vol. 18, No. 3-4.

Mead, R. (1994) <u>International Management</u>. Oxford, Blackwell.

Micheau, C and Billmyer, K. (1987) "Discourse strategies for foreign business students: preliminary research findings," in <u>English for Specific Purposes</u>, Vol. 6.

Mole, J. (1995) <u>Mind Your Manners: Managing Business Cultures in Europe.</u> London, Nicholas Brealey Publishing.

Morden, T. (1999) "Models of National Culture – A Management Review," in <u>Cross Cultural management</u>, Vol. 6, No. 1.

Myrsiades, L. (2000) "Meeting sabotage: met and conquered," in Journal of <u>Management Development</u>, Vol.19 no. 10.

Newman, W. (1995) "Stages in cross-cultural collaboration," in <u>Journal of Asia Business</u>, Vol. 11, No. 4.

Niederman, F. and Volkema, R. (1999) "The effects of facilitator characteristics on meeting preparation, set up, and implementation," in <u>Small Group Research</u>, Vol. 24, No. 2.

Nixon, J. and Dawson, G. (2002) "Reasons for cross-cultural communication training," in <u>Corporate Communications: An International Journal</u>, Vol. 7, No. 3.

Padget, V. and Welosin, R. (1980) "Cognitive similarity in dyadic communication," in <u>Journal of Personality and Social Psychology</u>, Vol. 39, No. 4.

Pauleen, D. and Yoong, P. (2001) "Facilitating virtual team relationships via internet and conventional communication channels," in <u>Internet Research: Electronic Networking Applications and Policy</u>, Vol. 11, No. 3.

Peters, T. and Waterman, R. (1982) <u>In Search of Excellence</u>. New York, Harper and Row.

Pomeranz, R. (1984) "Agreeing and disagreeing with assessments: Some features of preferred/dispreferred turn shapes," from Atkinson, J. Heritage, J. (eds.), <u>Structure of Social Action</u>. Cambridge, Cambridge University Press.

Pritchard, J. and Stanton, N. (1999) Testing Belbin's team role theory of effective groups," in <u>The Journal of Management Development</u>, Vol. 18, No. 8.

Runkel, P. (1956) "Cognitive similarity in facilitating communication," in <u>Sociometry</u>, Vol. 19, No. 3.

Sacks, H., Schegloff, E.A., and Jefferson, G. (1974) "A simplest Systematics for the organisation of turn-taking for conversation," in <u>Language</u>, Vol. 50, No. 4.

Salmon, G. (2000) <u>Emoderating</u>. London, RoutledgeFalmer.

Schegloff, E.A. and Sacks, H. (1973) "Opening up Closings," in <u>Semiotica</u>, Vol. 8, No. 4.

Schegloff, E. (2007) <u>Sequence Organisation in Interaction: Volume 1: A Primer in Conversation Analysis</u>. Cambridge, Cambridge University Press.

Scollon, R. and Scollon, S. (1995) <u>Intercultural Communication</u>. Oxford, Blackwell.

UNIT 4: Language, Communication and Culture

Silberman, M. and Clark, K. (1999) <u>101 Ways to Make Meetings Active</u>. San Francisco, Jossey-Bass.

Simintiras, A. and Thomas, A. (1998) "Cross-cultural sales negotiations," in <u>International Marketing Review</u>, Vol. 15, No. 1.

Spinks, N. and Wells, B. (1995) "Communicating with groups: prompt, purposeful, productive team meetings," in <u>Executive Development</u>, Vol. 8, No. 5.

Stenstrom, A. (1994) <u>Spoken Interaction</u>. Harlow, Longman Group UK Ltd.

Styles, C. and Amber, T. (1994) "Successful export practice: the UK experience," in <u>International Marketing Review</u>, Vol. 11, No. 6.

Swales, J. (1981) "Aspects of Article Introductions," <u>ESP Monograph</u>, No. 1. Language Studies Unit, Aston University.

Swales, J. (1990) <u>Genre Analysis: English in Academic and Research Settings</u>. Cambridge, Cambridge University Press.

Tannen, D. (1992) <u>That's Not What I Meant</u>. London, Virago.

Tannen, D. (1994) <u>Talking from 9 to 5. Women and men in the Workplace: Language, Sex, and Power</u>. William Morrow Inc.

Thomas, D. (2004) <u>Cultural Intelligence: People Skills for Global Business</u>. Berrett-Koehler.

Thomas, J. (1983) "Cross-cultural pragmatic failure," in <u>Applied Linguistics</u>, Vol. 4, No. 2.

Ting-Toomey, S. and Korzenny, F. (eds.), (2002) <u>Language, Communication and Culture: Current Directions</u>. Sage Publications.

Trompenaars, F. (1993) <u>Riding the Waves of Culture</u>. London, Nicholas Brealey Publishing Ltd.

Unger, C. (2006) <u>Genre, Relevance and Global Coherence: The Pragmatics of Discourse Type</u>. Palgrave Macmillan.

Walther, J. and Burgoon, J. (1992) "Relational communication in computer-mediated interaction," in <u>Human Communications Research</u>, Vol. 19.

Watzlawick, P. (1967) <u>Pragmatics of Human Communication</u>. New York, Norton and Company.

Wei, L.; Hua, Z. and Yue, L. (2001) "Conversational Management and Involvement in Chinese-English Business Talk," in <u>Language and Intercultural Communication</u>, Vol. 1, No. 2.

Weinstein, K. (1996) "Information overload: permission to not know?" in <u>Career Development</u>, Vol.1, No. 4.

Weissinger, S. (1991) <u>A guide to Successful Meeting Planning</u>. New York, Wiley.

Westwood, R. (Ed.) (1992) <u>Organisational Behaviour</u>. Longman South East Asia Perspectives.

Wolfgang, A. (1984) "The function and importance of non-verbal behaviour in intercultural counselling," in Wolfgang, A. (ed.), <u>Nonverbal Behaviour</u>. New York, Hogrefe.

Woo, H. and Prud'homme, C. (1999) "Cultural characteristics prevalent in the Chinese negotiation process," in <u>European Business Review</u>, Vol. 99, No. 5.

Zahir, S.; Dobing, B. and Gordon-Hunter, M. (2002) "Cross-cultural dimensions of internet portals," in <u>Internet Research: Electronic Networking Applications and Policy</u>, Vol. 12, No. 3.

Lightning Source UK Ltd.
Milton Keynes UK
UKOW04f0819171013

219225UK00001B/145/A